SOVEREIGNTY AFTER EMPIRE

Comparing the Middle East and Central Asia

Edited by Sally N. Cummings and Raymond Hinnebusch

EDINBURGH
University Press

First published in 2011 by
Edinburgh University Press Ltd
22 George Square, Edinburgh EH8 9LF
www.euppublishing.com

This paperback edition 2012

Typeset in 11/13 JaghbUni Regular by
Servis Filmsetting Ltd, Stockport, Cheshire, and
Printed and Bound in the United States of America

A CIP record for this book is available from the British Library

ISBN 978 0 7486 4304 2 (hardback)
ISBN 978 0 7486 6855 7 (paperback)
ISBN 978 0 7486 4754 5 (webready PDF)
ISBN 978 0 7486 7539 5 (epub)
ISBN 978 0 7486 6432 0 (Amazon ebook)

Published in association with The Honeyman Foundation.

Acknowledgments

After an initial conference and two workshops the present volume has
been completed. We have greatly enjoyed the journey and thank all
contributors for their hard work. Several anonymous reviewers and our
peers have also shared their invaluable insights. We are also very grateful to Bernardo Fazeindero, Gillian Fleming, Fiona Oviatt and Mohira
Suyarkulova for the logistical efforts in organizing the various research
events around the production of this book. A sincere thanks to Ned
Conway for his help in preparing the final typescript. Our immense gratitude also to the sponsors who have helped production at various stages:
the Foreign and Commonwealth Office; the Council for British Research
on the Levant; Glasgow's Centre for Russian, Central and East European
Studies; the Institute of Middle Eastern, Central Asian and Caucasus
Studies at the University of St Andrews; and to our biggest sponsor The
Honeyman Foundation. David Corner and Bill Pagan of the Honeyman
have been a huge support in the entire process and it is to David and Bill
that we dedicate this book.

Contents

Notes on the Contributors

Laura L. Adams' research explores globalization and the nation-state in the context of the visual and performing arts, specifically in Soviet and post-Soviet Central Asia. Her book, *The Spectacular State: Culture and National Identity in Uzbekistan*, was published by Duke University Press in 2010. Currently, she is teaching in the Sociology Department and the Writing Program of Harvard University and is an associate at the Davis Center for Russian and Eurasian Studies, where she co-chairs the Program on Central Asia and Caucasus. Laura received her BA in sociology and Russian area studies from Macalester College (USA) and her PhD in sociology from the University of California, Berkeley.

Muriel Atkin, Professor of History at the George Washington University, received her doctorate in history from Yale University. Her areas of research interest are modern Central Asia, the Muslim peoples of Russia and the USSR and Russian and Soviet relations with Iran. She is the author of *Russia and Iran, 1780–1828* (University of Minnesota Press, 1980), *The Subtlest Battle: Islam in Soviet Tajikistan* (Foreign Policy Research Institute, 1989) and numerous articles and book chapters.

Michelle Burgis is a lecturer in International Law and Middle East Studies at the University of St Andrews. She holds degrees in Law and Politics from the University of Sydney and a PhD in International Law from the Australian National University. Michelle has lived and worked in human rights organizations in the Middle East, and is particularly interested in examining how international legal norms operate on the ground across the Arab world. Her publications include *Boundaries of Discourse in the International Court of Justice: Mapping Arguments in Arab Territorial Disputes* (Brill, 2009).

Sally N. Cummings is in the School of International Relations, University of St Andrews, where she also directs the Institute of Middle Eastern, Central Asian and Caucasus Studies. Her publications include *Power and Symbolism in Central Asia: The Spectacular State* (ed.) (Routledge,

2010), *The Tulip Revolution: Motives, Mobilization and Meanings* (ed.) (Routledge, 2009) and *Kazakhstan: Power and the Elite* (Tauris, 2005).

Louise Fawcett is Lecturer in Politics and International Relations at the University of Oxford and a Fellow of St Catherine's College. Her research interests include the history, politics and international relations of developing countries. She is the author of *Iran and the Cold War* (Cambridge University Press, 1992); co-editor and contributor to *Regionalism in World Politics* (with Andrew Hurrell) (Oxford University Press, 1995); *The Third World beyond the Cold War* (with Yezid Sayigh) (Oxford University Press, 1999); and *Regionalism and Governance in the Americas*, with Monica Serrano (Palgrave Macmillan, 2005). She is also the editor of *International Relations of the Middle East* (Oxford University Press, 2005), a revised and expanded edition of which was published in 2009.

Benjamin C. Fortna teaches modern Middle Eastern history at the School of Oriental & African Studies (SOAS) at the University of London. He received his BA from Yale, an MA from Columbia and his PhD from the University of Chicago. His primary research interest lies in the history of the late Ottoman Empire and the Turkish Republic, with particular attention to the issue of education and cultural change. His publications include: *Imperial Classroom: Islam, Education and the State in the Late Ottoman Empire* (Oxford University Press, 2002) and the co-edited *The Modern Middle East: A Sourcebook for History* (Oxford University Press, 2006). His latest book, *Learning to Read in the Late Ottoman Empire and Early Turkish Republic*, will be published shortly by Palgrave Macmillan.

Raymond Hinnebusch is Professor of International Relations and Middle East Politics at the University of St Andrews. He is the author of several books and articles on the international politics of the Middle East and of studies on Syria and Egypt. His books include: *The Iraq War: Causes and Consequences*, co-edited with Rick Fawn (Lynne Rienner Press, 2006); *The International Politics of the Middle East* (Manchester University Press, 2003); *The Foreign Policies of Middle East States*, co-edited with Anoushiravan Ehteshami (Lynne Rienner Press, 2002); *Syria: Revolution from Above* (Routledge, 2001); *The Syrian–Iranian Alliance: Middle Powers in a Penetrated Regional System*, with Anoushiravan Ehteshami (Routledge, 1997), *Syria and the Middle East Peace Process*, with Alasdair Drysdale (Council on Foreign Relations Press, 1991);

Authoritarian Power and State Formation in Ba^cthist Syria: Army, Party and Peasant (Westview Press, 1990); *Peasant and Bureaucracy in Ba^cthist Syria: The Political Economy of Rural Development* (Westview Press, 1989); and *Egyptian Politics Under Sadat* (Cambridge University Press, 1985).

Fred H. Lawson is Professor of Government at Mills College. In 2009–10 he was Senior Visiting Fellow at the Georgetown University School of Foreign Service in Qatar. His publications include: *Constructing International Relations in the Arab World* (Stanford University Press, 2006); *Why Syria Goes to War* (Cornell University Press, 1996); and *The Social Origins of Egyptian Expansionism during the Muhammad ^cAli Period* (Columbia University Press, 1992).

David Lewis is Senior Research Fellow in the Department of Peace Studies, University of Bradford. He has a wide range of research interests in all aspects of political change and conflict, particularly in the former Soviet Union and South Asia, with a particular focus on the dynamics of authoritarian regimes. His recent book, *The Temptations of Tyranny in Central Asia* (Hurst/Columbia University Press, 2008), examined the impact of Western policy in Central Asia after 2001.

Dominic Lieven is a professor at the London School of Economics (since 1993) and a Fellow of the British Academy (since 2001). He did his BA at Christ's College, Cambridge and his PhD under the supervision of Hugh Seton-Watson at the School of Slavonic Studies in London. He was a Kennedy Scholar at Harvard (1973–4), a Humboldt Fellow in Munich and Gottingen (1985–6) and also held research fellowships from the British Academy (1998–9) and the Leverhulme Foundation (2006–9). His major publications are: *Russia and the Origins of the First World War* (Palgrave Macmillan, 1983); *Russia's Rulers under the Old Regime* (Yale University Press, 1989); *Aristocracy in Europe* (Macmillan, 1992); *Nicholas II* (John Murray/St. Martin's Press, 1993); *The Russian Empire and its Rivals* (John Murray/Yale University Press, 2001); and *Russia against Napoleon: The Struggle for Europe* (Penguin, 2009). The latter received the Wolfson Prize in 2010.

James McDougall is university lecturer in twentieth-century history and a Fellow of Trinity College, University of Oxford. A member of the editorial advisory board of the *Journal of African History* and a former member of the editorial committee of *Middle East Report*, he previously taught at Princeton and at SOAS, London. He is the author of *History and the Culture of Nationalism in Algeria* (Cambridge University Press, 2006).

Wojciech Ostrowski received his PhD from the University of St Andrews, and is Post-Doctoral Research Fellow in International Politics of Energy and Mineral Resources at the Centre for Energy, Petroleum and Mineral Law and Policy, University of Dundee. He is the author of *Politics and Oil in Kazakhstan* (Routledge, 2010). Recent articles include "The legacy of the 'coloured revolutions': the case of Kazakhstan" in the *Journal of Communist Studies and Transitions Politics* (2009). His research interests lie in the politics of oil, authoritarian regimes and state–business relationships.

Mohira Suyarkulova is a PhD candidate at the University of St Andrews. Her research concentrates on the issues of state, sovereignty and nationalism in Central Asia.

Morten Valbjørn is Assistant Professor at the Department of Political Science, Aarhus University, Denmark, where he also received his PhD. His research interests concern: (1) politics in a(nother) "new Middle East," including issues concerning post-democratization, "the New Arab Cold War" and islamism(s); (2) the (ir)relevance of cultural diversity to the study of international relations; and (3) the Area Studies Controversy in different cultural–institutional contexts. Recent publications include: "Examining the 'post' in Post-democratization – The future of Middle Eastern political rule through lenses of the past," *Middle East Critique*, 19(3) 2010, with André Bank; "Arab Nationalism(s) in Transformation – From Arab Interstate Societies to an Arab-Islamic World Society," in B. Buzan and A. Gonzalez-Pelaez (eds), *International Society and the Middle East – English School Theory at the Regional Level* (Palgrave, 2009); "Before, During and After the Cultural Turn. A 'Baedeker' to IR's Cultural Journey," *International Review of Sociology*, 18(1) 2008.

Frédéric Volpi is Senior Lecturer in International Relations at the University of St Andrews. He is the author of *Political Islam Observed* (Columbia University Press, 2010) and of *Islam and Democracy* (Pluto Press, 2003). He is also the editor of *Political Islam: A Critical Reader* (Routledge, 2010) and of *Democratization in the Muslim World* (Routledge, 2007). His work focuses on the interaction between Islamism, democratization and political civility.

Implications of the Arab Uprising for "Empire and Sovereignty"

Raymond Hinnebusch and Sally N. Cummings

What can the tangent from empire to sovereignty tell us about the turmoil raging in the Arab World? The Arab states are, of course, almost without exception more or less creations of empire, the outcome of the imposition of a flawed Westphalian-type state system on the Middle East, with in some cases artificial states newly constructed to suit the strategic interests of the imperial powers. Yet, after a period of instability, post-imperial state-building in the region had appeared to produce stable authoritarian regimes. The Arab Uprising demonstrates, however, that this project had masked deep vulnerabilities, at least in the Republics; it is also apparent that these vulnerabilities are intimately connected to the residues of empire in the region.

The reason for republican vulnerability is that Arab republics' regimes initially built their legitimacy and bases of social support on a combination of anti-imperialist nationalism and a populist social contract whereby they provided egalitarian re-distribution and a welfare state. However, because they could not sustain capital accumulation without reviving the private sector, in time they adopted policies privileging investors, abandoned the populist social contract and, in order to re-integrate into the world capitalist economy, jettisoned anti-imperialism, indeed becoming in cases such as Egypt, client states of the US. *Post-populist authoritarianism* refers to this *strategic* shift in the regimes' political economy and social bases. *Authoritarian upgrading* is a term that has recently been widely adopted to denote the *tactical* techniques by which post-populist regimes have tried to compensate for the risks of abandoning their mass constituencies. Among these techniques were privatization as a source of patronage to build new bases of crony capitalist support; offloading welfare responsibilities to Islamic charities, hence co-opting the ⁽ulama; and limited political pluralism that allowed divide and rule by selectively including and excluding political groups from participation and exploiting divisions between secularists and Islamists. To a degree all three of these techniques have also been used by Central Asian leaders; to date, however, only the Kyrgyz Republic has witnessed the ousting of a president and his regime.

What has now become apparent is that, for every gain these techniques afforded authoritarian regimes (in MENA at least), they also had accumulating costs. Additionally, the aggrandizement of presidential families which grabbed more than their fair share of their countries' economic assets, and elderly presidents attempting to bypass their lieutenants and pass power to their sons, the increasing use of arbitrary police repression, and demographic explosions producing youth unemployment, parallel to an expansion in access to higher education, all added to a building brew of resentment. In parallel, the spread of the Internet enabled disaffected youth to overcome the fragmentation from the repression of civil society, compare grievances and techniques of resistance and organize escalating demonstrations against regimes. The success of protestors in bringing down the president of Tunisia went far to spreading elsewhere a belief that similar protests could produce similar results in other states.

Some observers expected Central Asian states to be similarly vulnerable to uprising, given the similarity of hybrid authoritarian patrimonial regimes, aging presidents, neo-liberal privatizations enriching ruling families, and Muslim populations who might be susceptible to the "contagion" effect from the Middle East. Overthrows of presidents in Kyrgyzstan and the Andijan riots in Uzbekistan had already suggested that the second decade of independence in Central Asia might replicate similar instability experienced by MENA states in their second decade (the 1950s) after independence. One year on, however, there was no sign of the spread of the Arab Uprising beyond the Arab world.

Many analysts explained this in terms of the different conditions in Central Asia. Economic conditions were better (than for example in Egypt), a function of high prices for hydrocarbons and work opportunities in Russia. Lesser viability of opposition parties, more effective repression of Islamists, low Internet penetration, and popular fear of instability were also cited.[1] The more recent Sovietization of the area and its incumbent stifling of civil society and activism continued to be a legacy. Regimes themselves did fear the contagion effect and increased their security measures, in particular targeting the social media. International conditions were also seen as less favorable in Central Asia, where all the great powers had a stake in the region and whether competition or cooperation resulted, worked to stifle radical change in the status quo. The US needed stable regimes to guarantee its supply lines in Afghanistan, China had energy access arrangements with Central Asian regimes, and Russia was determined to counter what it saw as Western-inspired subversion in its "Near Abroad"; joint exercises of Russian and Central Asia forces in the Collective Security Organization were explicitly explained as aimed at the spread of such subversion and of Islamist terrorism. And even if Russian media reports prior to the ousting of Bakiev in Kyrgyzstan appeared to show support for the president's departure, Russian authorities, along with those from Beijing, remained committed to supporting the maintenance of authoritarianism in the region.[2]

The findings of this volume provide another deeper perspective that supplements these observations. It is at least conceivable that MENA countries were more vulnerable than Central Asian regimes because of *differences in the empires* that gave birth to them, and specifically owing to the more damaging *imperial experiences and heritages* in the former. The MENA countries have to date suffered from greater legitimacy deficits compared to Central Asia as a result of their different formation under empire: the new post-imperial Arab states frustrated powerful supra-state identities, whereas in Central Asia the new states generated new state-centric identities. In MENA, powerful oppositionist trans-national Islamic movements defied and operated across artificial state boundaries, while in Central Asia transnational Islam remained weak. Moreover, while the heritage of Western imperialism, notably the Palestine conflict, keeps anti-imperialism alive in MENA – hence de-legitimizes alignments with the ex-empire or its successor, the US – no similar de-legitimation attaches to post-Soviet links of Central Asian states to Moscow; indeed at the elite level there is a shared post-Soviet political culture and at the mass level a lived collective memory of the Soviet period, factors that make arrangements such as the Collective Security Organization less controversial than, for instance, the US military presence and security treaties in the Arab world. In all these respects, the Central Asian states at the time of writing resemble less the Arab republics than a special subset of Middle Eastern states that has also largely escaped destabilization – namely, the Arab monarchies of the Gulf (with their abundance of hydrocarbons and minimalist anti-imperialism).

This by no means implies that uprisings in Central Asia are necessarily unlikely: many of the same grievances held by the Arabs against their corrupt, authoritarian regimes are likely to be existent in Central Asia. But if and when such rebellions begin, they will be products of the specific context in which Central Asian states were created under one sort of empire, and not mere spillovers from an Arab world created under very different kinds of empire. We develop this claim further in the book itself.

Notes

1. Scott Radnitz, "Waiting for Spring," February 17, 2012, available at: http://www.foreignpolicy.com/articles/2012/02/17/waiting_for_spring; Griffin W. Huschke, "Central Asia: The New Arab Spring?," http://blog.streitcouncil.org/?p=607.
2. See: http://www.telegraph.co.uk/news/worldnews/asia/tajikistan/8777123/Central-Asian-armies-start-exercises-to-counter-potential-Arab-Spring-style-unrest.html.

Introduction

Sally N. Cummings and Raymond Hinnebusch

The end of empire marked one of the main transformations in international politics in the twentieth century. In the conventional narrative, it completed the universalization of the Westphalian state system. In the West, the most competitive form of political organization, the national state, had driven out smaller and larger forms – such as empires.[1] In parallel, Western empires exported states systems to the periphery, which, with decolonization, became sovereign.[2] In the parlance of neo-realism, hierarchy gave way to anarchy.

This narrative of a sharp break between empire and sovereignty is an increasingly criticized caricature. In the real world the distinction is blurred, with many cases combining features of both empire and state, and one able to evolve into the other.[3] For historical sociology, the post-imperial world mixes elements of hierarchy and anarchy.[4] Empires can adapt to the age of nationalism, and in the age of globalization larger empire-like entities and smaller units, for example, world cities, have become more viable, while the sovereignty of nation-states is under siege.[5] Moreover, sovereignty, Stephen Krasner argues, has several dimensions, internal and external, which can be disaggregated, with a state possibly strong on one and weak on another; hence, that sovereignty is a matter of degrees.[6] Sovereignty is especially contested or precarious in the states left behind by empires, with state-builders struggling to establish internal sovereignty and defend against encroachment on their external sovereignty by great powers. In summary, then, the post-colonial global order is less one of uniformly sovereign states than one in which post-imperial states suffer "stateness" deficits and old empires have transformed themselves into multinational states (for example, India or China) or been superseded by informal empire or hegemony, particularly that of the United States, over the post-colonial world.[7]

This book follows this critical tradition in rejecting any sharp break between empire and after (sovereignty), unpacks the dichotomous concepts of empire and sovereignty in order to expose the great variation in both, and argues that variations in empire are intimately linked to variations in their successor states systems. We do this through a comparison of the Middle East/North Africa (MENA) and Central Asia (CA).[8] That empire matters for the nature of sovereignty in post-colonial states is contested. Bernard Lewis, for example, holds that the legacy of imperialism is no longer relevant for the contemporary Middle East since 'the Anglo-French interlude was comparatively brief and ended half a century ago';[9] similarly some writers have concluded that the post-Soviet space is now post-post-Soviet. We will show that it is impossible to understand the contemporary Middle East and Central Asia without reference to their imperial legacies.

Rationale and Approach of the Volume

The much renewed contemporary interest in empire has led to a spate of books on the subject. Some are historical and comparative, others are more theoretical but use comparative cases in an illustrative way, others look at empire's contemporary relevance.[10] A few have attempted a comparative study of the effect of empire on what came after.[11] Several studies have looked at empire in the Middle East or in Central Asia or the post-Soviet space and a few have tried to link empire to post-imperial statehood in one of these regions.[12] The journal collection co-edited by Deniz Kandiyoti and Juan R. I. Cole in the *International Journal of Middle East Studies* is an excellent compilation of essays that look at both nationalism and empire.[13] There has also been an explosion of interest in the concept of sovereignty, not only in the English School but also among realists.[14]

This volume aims to bring theory on empire and on sovereignty to bear in a systematic comparison of empires and of their varying consequences for sovereignty in two regions. The book attempts to make a contribution in both the disciplines of history, notably the large field of imperial history, and in international relations. It will also be useful for area specialists in both regions in that the book assembles a distinguished group of contributors who are internationally respected in the study of the regions, and since comparative treatment of the two regions throws new light and understanding on both. The book advances comparative study, while the case studies are valuable in themselves for regional studies. Finally, we aim to throw new light on the contemporary relevance of empire and the study of it.

Our point of departure is the assumption that imperial experiences matter for post-imperial states and states systems – for sovereignty – hence, that similarities and differences in the empires that ruled the Middle East and Central Asia should help to explain similarities and differences in the post-imperial outcomes in the two regions. In the analysis we follow Mill's method,[15] systematically examining associations between similarities and differences in the independent (empire) and dependent (sovereignty) variables; we then use process analysis to identify the mechanisms (intervening variables) that make variations in empire matter for post-imperial outcomes.

In this introductory chapter and in the conclusion, we present a framework of analysis for systematically comparing the relations between empire and post-imperial sovereignty in the two regions. In the introduction, we first examine the dependent variable, sovereignty, its interpretations, and, in particular, conceptualizations of how sovereignty varies in the post-imperial world. We then examine the independent variable, that is, the concept of empire and historical variations in empire. In this we draw on comparative historical literature on empires[16] to identify their shared features and their major distinctions, most importantly that between bureaucratic territorial and maritime commercial empires.[17] We also compare actual impacts of empires by drawing additionally on the wider body of existent histories of empire in the two regions.[18]

In the conclusion we resume the framework, but with the focus on outcomes of empire in the two regions, drawing particularly on the findings of the original studies in this volume. Toward this end, we examine two intervening variables that we argue condition the effect of empire on post-imperial states and state systems. These are the two drivers propelling the transition, namely, the international system and its dominant norms at transition, and nationalist mobilization within the colonies. We then identify the imperial transmissions that matter most for sovereignty, namely, state formation inheritances, the nation-building consequences of empire and the imperial economic inheritance. We link these variables in turn to the degree of rupture with empire in the post-imperial period as regards both the domestic order and external relations, that is, acceptance or rejection of post-colonial reconstructions of informal empire. In doing so, we summarize the main differences and similarities in post-imperial outcomes.

In tracing the relation between empire and sovereignty, we will be sensitive to two methodological problems. Because differences in the aftermath of empires in 1918 and 1991 could be attributed to the changed nature of the global order rather than the features of the ex-empires,[19] we we explicitly treat the dominant norms at the time of transition as an intervening variable. Second, while empire ended in MENA more than a half century ago, the five "stans" came into being only in 1991, hence we must acknowledge that some of the developments experienced in MENA could yet be replicated in CA.[20] Our aim here is not to seek to prove the validity of hypotheses, but rather our task is to identify the main variables and then to systematically explore the relations between them by synthesizing and building on the secondary literature. Far from claiming to definitively answer the questions we explore, our aim in this book is to point the way to further comparative research on the impact of empire, especially in our two regions.

Comparing the Middle East/North African and Central Asian Regions

The MENA and CA regions are particularly suitable for gauging the impact of empire on sovereignty because they constituted a continuous civilizational area during their pre-modern history, united under Islamic empires in which nomadic tribalism and Turkic peoples played pivotal roles and Islam was the undisputed religious identity; subsequently, both regions fell under the rule of non-Islamic imperial metropoles which were very different in character, but similarly resulted in imperial-engineered states systems.

In both regions, the states that emerged after empire were largely inherited by post-colonial elites, a result of imperial, not indigenous, agency. Both regions possess huge hydrocarbon reserves, which began to be exploited under empire, resulting in the world's biggest concentration of rentier states. The combination of creation from without, rent and residues of pre-imperial political culture is associated with similar states in both regions. In both enough "stateness" was inherited from empire to constitute more than quasi-sovereignty: the persistence of the internationally recognized boundaries in both regions is the most enduring and shared product of empire, but the empire also passed on authoritarian apparatuses of governance that, with some exceptions, have allowed state elites to command their territories, reinforced by the externally recognized right to dispose of the hydrocarbon resources under their soil. But in both regions state-builders have filled imperial-created shells of statehood with neo-patrimonial practices that typically combine personalistic leadership (monarchies and presidential monarchies) and clientelism with institutional underdevelopment and unincorporated opposition. States have limited infrastructural power needed to deliver public goods and few mechanisms of public accountability, hence, insufficient legitimacy to relieve them of domestic insecurity. They are arguably modernizing states, yet suffer from similar stateness (internal sovereignty) deficits, albeit with important variations that will be noted. In sum, similar patterns of imperial sponsored state creation in a shared civilizational area have resulted in similar kinds of states "after empire."

Yet these similarities in the nature of the statehood have not resulted in similar states systems. In MENA, inter-state conflict is endemic both within the region and in its relations with the core, but much less so in CA. While the Middle East states system was "born fighting" (emerging amid the 1948 Arab–Israeli war), its CA counterpart was born peaceful. While both have some border conflicts and irredentism from imperial boundary-drawing and imperial-sponsored ethnic mixing, in MENA these have led to violence, ethnic cleansing, protracted conflicts, inter-state intervention and high levels of militarization and periodic state-to-state wars, while CA experienced much less of such large-scale violence, except for the Tajik civil war.[21]

Moreover, even though both regions are still largely primary product exporting economies locked into various economic (inter)dependencies with the ex-imperial core and still magnets for great power attention and trans-national energy companies, the reactions of the two regions to the ex-imperial core(s) diverge sharply, with anti-imperialism much stronger in MENA. The Middle East has seen repeated counter-hegemonic movements and revisionist states seeking, in the name of supra-state identities, pan-Arabism (Nasser's Egypt, Saddam's Iraq) or pan-Islam (Khomeini's Iran), to expel the residue of the ex-empires and efface their enduring consequences. In CA, supra-state identity (pan-Islamic or pan-Turkic) has no comparable power, states have no comparable ambitions and populations cherish no comparable strength of anti-imperial sentiment. Some see the Middle East as the epicenter of a clash of civilizations between Islam and the West, while despite its Islamic religion, CA has largely remained outside this contest, and its much lesser incidence of international terrorism is in part a spillover from MENA. In summary, the MENA states system is much less stable and post-colonial hegemony less legitimized than in CA. How far can these divergent tangents be attributed to differences in imperial experience?

Our working hypothesis is that the similarities in post-imperial statehood in MENA and CA – notably their shared sovereignty deficits – are an outcome of their similar imperial creation, while the differences in the stability of the regions can be traced partly to differences in the empires that shaped them.

Conceptualizing Sovereignty

Both empire and sovereignty have undergone radical transformations theoretically, practically and normatively. Their fates have depended in good part on each other. When imperialism had gained most widespread legitimacy, in the eighteenth to nineteenth centuries, absolutist monarchist sovereignty was also at its height. Absolutist sovereignty gave imperial powers leverage to colonize, not least because sovereignty was viewed as relevant only in relations between imperial powers; the rule of sovereignty did not apply to the areas being colonized. Once notions of national and sovereign rights became increasingly embedded in the international system, empire grew to have negative associations. In turn, these developments would carry implications for the nature of sovereignty itself. For Jo-Anne Pemberton the logic of sovereignty would convey internal democratization and a strengthening of external obligations by virtue of the fact, as argued by Mervyn Frost, that sovereign states are constituted, at least in part, through acts of mutual recognition. Each state is implicated in the constitution of the "other."[22]

Sovereignty has been a concern for historians, sociologists, lawyers and political scientists. Sovereignty is usually thought of as encompassing a set of attributes that include a territory, a population, an effective domestic hierarchy of control, *de jure* constitutional independence, the *de facto* absence of external authority, international recognition and the ability to regulate trans-border flows.[23] Sovereignty has several dimensions which can be disaggregated. The most basic distinction is between domestic and external sovereignty. Krasner further breaks sovereignty down into four dimensions by which the extent of sovereignty can be measured: domestic, interdependence, international legal and Westphalian:

> Domestic sovereignty, referring to the organisation of public authority within a state and to the level of effective control exercised by those holding authority; interdependence sovereignty, referring to the ability of public authorities to control transborder movements; international legal sovereignty, referring to the mutual recognition of states; and Westphalian sovereignty, referring to the exclusion of external actors, typically more powerful states or international institutions, from domestic authority configurations.[24]

Crucially for our purposes, Krasner argues that these four meanings can vary, namely, that it is possible to have one category that is strong and another that is weak.

The oldest usage of the term refers to domestic sovereignty: the organization of authority within a given state and its effectiveness. As Jo-Anne

Pemberton rightly observes, there is "a tendency to conflate sovereignty with political power."[25] For Bodin and Hobbes, sovereignty was indivisible with one single source of authority within the polity. By contrast the founding fathers of the United States wanted to divide authority between federal government and the individual states. Discussions dominating reform of the Soviet Union in its last months were also essentially about the divisibility of sovereignty (see Section IV, below).

Whether domestic sovereignty is viewed as divisible would, however, not affect international legal sovereignty, argues Krasner, because, for example, failed states retain their international legal sovereignty. Recognition refers to a state's juridicial equality in the international system (including immunity for its diplomats and extraterritorial status of embassies and consulates and the right to enter into agreements with other entities), not to how power in the state is organized or how effective it is. International legal sovereignty does not necessarily follow the construction of a state or even chronologically necessarily follow the collapse of empire. Recognition has often been used as a political tool that has been withheld from some entities that are clearly states or granted to those who are not. India was a member of the League of Nations even though it was a colony of Britain, and Belarus and the Ukraine were members of the United Nations (UN) even though they were part of the Soviet Union, while communist China was long denied membership. But recognition does not guarantee domestic sovereignty which itself is primarily linked to levels of "stateness."

There are considerable variations in how far the concept of sovereignty is thought to match reality. "For neorealism and neoliberalism, sovereign states are the basic ontological given: the actors in international politics are unitary, territorial, autonomous entities; they are sovereign states."[26] Realists not only take the sovereign state for granted, but their differentiation of hierarchical control within state boundaries and anarchy without is the basic distinction around which international politics revolves. By contrast, the English School and constructivism see sovereignty as a constructed product of interactions between state elites and an institution of international society into which subsequent elites have been socialized and not an automatic attribute of states; thus, Jackson, in his discussion of quasi-sovereignty explores the consequences of the co-existence of the norm at the international level and the absence in many new states of the features of "stateness" (internal sovereignty);[27] such states are no longer deprived by imperial powers of their external sovereignty owing to international sanctity of boundaries that goes along with the globalization of the norm of sovereignty and the de-legitimation of empires.

7

Ayoub, however, argues that state-builders on the periphery are engaged in an attempt at creating "stateness" and security within in order to protect their autonomy on the world stage;[28] without enough of the latter, they may formally survive but at the cost of their real autonomy. Mayall looks at how non-Western states struggle to create states in the Westphalian mould: "really" not "quasi"-sovereign with centralization of authority, bureaucracies, standing armies, nationalism and a market. Historical sociology tells us why. It claims that the nation-state, where sovereignty is congruent with nationalism, proved more competitive and tended to drive out the alternative smaller and larger political forms, notably city-states and empires. When there is a congruence of state and nation, sovereignty is endowed with special nationalist legitimacy, a great power asset for state-builders both within and in international contests (with a population socialized into taxpaying and volunteer or conscript armies enabling the mobilization of national power against which non-national states, suffering a legitimacy deficit, are disadvantaged). It also has an advantage in economic development; thus, with the rise of capitalism in the West, the capitalist classes needed a strong state with national legitimacy to assist in the competition for commercial empire and capital accumulation abroad and to discipline and incorporate labor within. Wallerstein points out that strong states in the core promote their capitalists, while weak ones on the periphery are unable to do so.[29] In the late developing states where the state creates the capitalist classes more than the reverse, a strong "neo-mercantilist" state is all the more seen as important to the promotion of a national economy[30] – the lesson of the East Asian tigers. Thus, the imitation of success encouraged the international spread of the nation-state in a kind of "natural selection." This is also why empires, found wanting in this competition, have felt they, too, must transform themselves into multinational states with some of the features of the nation-state ideal.

At the global level the result is said, in, for example, Bull and Watson's account, to be a deepening of the anarchy constituted by sovereign states recognizing no superior authority, at the expense of hierarchy represented by empires and quasi-empire forms such as suzerain systems (as the Chinese case). However, this narrative has been contested by those who argue that a system of formally sovereign states can co-exist with actual hierarchy, that is, with hegemony and informal empires. Informal empires, indeed, may well substitute for dismantled formal empires and it is in this context that we must evaluate the reality of sovereignty on the global "periphery."

In the MENA and CA, state-builders have embraced the Westphalian norm of sovereignty, but it is a project in the making. Indeed, the experience of both regions encourages us to think of sovereignty in dynamic terms – states can "become" sovereign or semi-sovereign or they can lose aspects of it. Indeed, imperial inheritances have generated special challenges especially as the individual existing states were largely initiated through imposition from above/without, even if subsequently they have been indigenized from within/below. We might theoretically say that the Central Asian republics just prior to the Soviet collapse had come to acquire effective statehood, but were deprived of supreme control of parts of their domestic and all of their foreign policies, that is, they were semi-sovereign. The relatively strong stateness inherited from the Soviet era provided the basic foundation of internal sovereignty, but if we accept that sovereignty needs to be willed and owned by the people, that self-determination can be achieved only by a community through its own "efforts',[31] the absence of self-determination movements in CA leads us to suspect that the states do not enjoy the legitimacy bonus from national identifications. In the Middle East, Western empires also carved out territories and established ruling elites and power apparatuses, leaving behind the shell of sovereignty that state-builders have struggled to fill with substance; nationalist independence movements did fight for self-determination (except in the Gulf), but the incongruence between territorial boundaries and identities sometimes frustrated rather than satisfied national identity.

What all this suggests is that sovereignty is not an all or nothing thing with which states are endowed after empire: it has to be fought for and if they loose the battle, there are many gradations of semi- or quasi-sovereignty into which they can fall. In short, there are different degrees of sovereignty. The hypothesis of this study is that real sovereignty is constrained in both regions owing to the imperial inheritance and the persisting residues of empire, with the real consequences including weak stateness (internal sovereignty) and dependencies constraining international autonomy (weak external sovereignty).

In sum, while we endorse Fred H. Lawson's argument that the end of empire and the rise of sovereignty have to he kept analytically distinct,[32] our task, additionally, however, is to see how the emergence and type of sovereignty was indeed linked both to the features of empires and how they ended.

Conceptualizing Empire

The most widely acknowledged features of empire include: (1) a polity, whose *raison d'être* being expansion, has no fixed boundaries until it is checked by countervailing power and is hence of very large size (by contrast, a sovereign state has recognized fixed boundaries); (2) absorbing pre-existing polities, an empire is a multi-communal polity composed of diverse groups and territorial units; (3) a dominant center rules through a combination of authoritarian coercion, co-optation of local intermediaries, to whom considerable power is often delegated, techniques of "divide and rule," and provision of collective goods such as a common law, a *lingua franca*, a common currency, and communications links; and (4) the empire combines a privileged ruling class/ethnicity with quite varying degrees of exclusion or assimilation of the diverse periphery into a universal religion or higher civilization; as such, the extent to which the empire is seen as "alien" in the periphery is likely to similarly vary and should not be part of the definition of empire.[33]

Empires vary widely, but the two most important types in modern times are the land-based bureaucratic empires and the maritime commercial empire, with the former, but not the latter, constituting a territorial unity. Eisenstadt captured the typical features of pre-modern bureaucratic empires: "traditional" in that most people were passive subjects and rule was legitimized by a universalistic religion; but pre-figuring "modern" states in that rulers pursued ambitious goals through centralized differentiated bureaucracies, recruited partly on the basis of political loyalty and merit (rather than ascription) which were able to extract resources and subordinate such powerful forces as tribal elites and landed nobilities.[34] These empires varied in the degree to which they were assimilative, with some pre-figuring modern nations, like the Han Chinese which created a culturally homogeneous space in which coercion receded, and the Roman which eventually accorded citizenship to subject peoples. These empires were pre- or non-capitalist in that, while their large size often facilitated trade and economic growth and they sought to control trade routes, the economy was subordinated to socio-political goals including the extraction of taxes to support the ruling class and imperial expansion.[35]

The maritime commercial empires through which the West incorporated most of the non-Western world were artifacts, as Wallerstein showed, of the emergence and expansion of a global market differentiated, to an extent, from political rule.[36] Their initial rationale was trade and plunder, with profit and war-making combined by chartered companies seeking trading monopolies. In its early stage, Britain's maritime empire was essential to the capital accumulation that drove industrialization in the core, while in their most mature stages of monopoly finance capitalism, rival empires incorporated the non-Western world into a global division of labor in which the latter provided lower value-added primary products and markets for the industries of the core and absorbed its excess capital accumulation. Empire often started as an informal "empire of free trade" in which the metropole was content to let indigenous governments bear the burdens of protecting investment[37] and political control was typically only assumed when it was required to establish the conditions of capitalism in the periphery (order, property rights, contract enforcement, commercialization of agriculture, creation of proletariats). In time, commercial competition morphed into rivalry over prestige and strategic advantage, aiming at the protection of previously acquired assets or expressed in the scramble for new ones, and in wartime empires often proved their strategic value. However, given their substantially commercial rationale and lack of territorial contiguity with the metropole, maritime empires lacked an assimilating impulse comparable with land empires, there being no expectation that the colonies would ever be merged with the metropole into a single polity.

To survive in the age of nationalism empires have to modernize[38] or risk breaking up or becoming the victims of those that do. Imperial rivalry is identified by Lenin and Hobson as a main driver of war in which empires are made and broken; indeed, the main victims of the two World Wars and the Cold War have been empires either destroyed or fatally weakened by the costs of war and war preparation. But if empires modernize and survive, their large size may give them the competitive advantage of greater power/security and larger resources/market. As a general principle, the more empires modernize, the greater their viability in the modern world and if, for contingent reasons, they nevertheless break up, the more the newly independent periphery will be likely to possess the practical and not just the juridical requisites of sovereignty.

An empire can modernize in one sense but fail or lag in the other: territorial empires have an advantage in political modernization and maritime ones in economic modernization. Political modernization means increased inclusion, that is, transformation into a multinational state in which a supra-national identity embraces smaller national (and sub-national) identities through a common citizenship and the periphery is accorded representation at the center and some national rights/autonomy, typically under federal arrangements. Modernization in bureaucratic empires is typically sparked by military reverses at the hands of nation-state-led empires which convince the former's elites that military competitiveness requires the accoutrements of the latter, including efficient bureaucratic and taxation capacities, mass education and nationalism, industrialization and the capitalist market, all driving their evolution toward a multinational state. The more assimilative such empires were in their pre-modern stage

11

(for example, China), the more likely it is that the regime can accord participatory rights to its citizens and devolve power from the center without risking break-up. In maritime empires, political modernization is obstructed by the lack of territorial contiguity and an assimilative impulse, and, while they may, under pressure of imperial competition and war, concede some self-government in order to retain the loyalty of the colonies, they typically do not develop inclusive institutions or common citizenship.[39]

Economic modernization means substituting accumulation and investment within for plunder through territorial expansion requiring, at a minimum, a sufficient differentiation of the economy from the polity to allow capital accumulation. A main obstacle to this in bureaucratic empires is that property ownership may be precarious, the capitalist classes stifled and accumulation diverted to political ends, such as military competition and consumption. Once territorial expansion ends, empires may therefore economically stagnate, making them vulnerable to outside conquest or internal disintegration;[40] indeed, arguably this was the case in the Soviet Union, a bureaucratic empire that actually destroyed the capitalist class. As for maritime empires, since they originate in the main global centers of finance capital and spread the market and private property, incorporation into such empires stimulates some economic modernization on the periphery, although insofar as an imposed division of labor locks the periphery into lower value production, it is a dependent, distorted form. Such empires probably cannot politically modernize, but they can informally reconstitute themselves if nominally independent states remain as economic peripheries of the ex-imperial core. Thus, formal empire is replaced by "modern" forms of hierarchy that, in conceding formal sovereignty, are more compatible with the age of nationalism and dominate largely through the economic instruments typical of the deepening age of globalization.

Imperial formations in MENA and CA

The experience of the MENA and CA is not one of simple transition from empire to sovereignty since there were several empires in each area and it is their cumulative impact and relation to each other that matters. The early modern period (1500–1800) saw the rise of the Ottoman Empire, a bureaucratic empire in the Middle East, which by 1800 was engaged in defensive modernization, threatened by the similar Russian empire that progressively wrested the Caucasus from it. In a second transformation at the turn of the twentieth century, the First World War ushered in the fall of the Ottoman Empire, allowing the completion of the British and French maritime commercial empires in the Middle East, while the fall of the Russian empire opened the door to its revolutionary modernizing Soviet successor. What follows is a brief comparison of the empires as experienced in our two regions.

MENA: FROM OTTOMAN TO WESTERN COMMERCIAL EMPIRES

Because Western empires imposed themselves at the expense of the existing Islamic empire of the Ottomans, populations would have seen the former in the light of the legitimacy or lack thereof of the latter. The Ottoman Empire was ruled by a multinational elite through a partly merit bureaucracy, with no aristocracy, hence, a protected peasantry, considerable state-owned property and, in Islam, an egalitarian religious legitimation.[41] According to Lieven, the empire neither exploited its periphery, nor privileged an imperial race (Turks), and at its height provided a high standard of governance fostering a high civilization.[42] Once the West captured the trade routes from it and opportunities for plunder through expansion were exhausted, however, patrimonialization undermined bureaucratic efficiency, disorder set in, privilege started to become hereditary and tax farming led to the exploitation of the peasantry and starving of the treasury.[43] However, under early nineteenth-century "defensive modernization," subjects became equal citizens embraced by a common Ottoman identity, a stronger more centralized state with representative bodies emerged and the empire seemed on the way to transformation into a multinational state.[44] In the First World War the empire proved remarkably robust, the vast majority of its Muslim citizens remaining loyal, with the so-called "Arab revolt" actually a British-manipulated sideshow. Many scholars agree that the empire's end was not the result of any "inexorable internal disease," but an outcome of being on the losing side in the war.[45] What is crucial for the aftermath is that the Ottomans inherited and transmitted the political culture and civilizational remnants of centuries of previous Islamic empires, including universalistic identities that retained the loyalty of people long after the empire had vanished.

Western imperialism in the Middle East was initially driven by the power vacuum following on Ottoman decline, with encroachment on the Ottoman domains in part driven by the determination of European states that their rivals should not benefit from Ottoman weakness, as well as competition for control of strategic transit routes (Suez Canal, Black Sea Straits) and for market monopolies and commercial advantage. In Egypt, North Africa and Iran imperial penetration began with treaties forcing open markets and encouraging commercialization of agriculture; this was followed by export of finance capital in the form of loans to rulers, then default on loans and a European takeover of finance, and capital drain. Finally, indigenous resistance to this climaxed in military intervention or occupation.

Imperial takeover led to the incorporation of the region into a global division of labor, a process begun through the imposition of unequal treaties on the Ottomans and completed after Western conquest by the break up of the large Ottoman market, snapping regional interdependencies and re-orienting economic links to the Western core. The colonies supplied raw materials to Western industries and served as markets for Western manufactures. The result was de-industrialization, and only to the degree that there was a wartime rupture with the core or countries acquired some authority to put up tariff protection, did industry revive. The colonies were all expected to pay their own way, taxed to support the occupying armies and to pay off debts incurred before Western conquest; as such, there was limited investment in education or development, except for the modernization of agriculture and the infrastructure that tied the region to global markets, which produced mono-crop export economies.

Western empires in MENA were established and maintained through some combination of coercion and co-optation of periphery elites.[46] In Algeria and the *mashreq*, indigenous armies were defeated and civilian insurgencies repressed using artillery and aerial bombardment of cities, villages and tribes. To give local elites a stake in the imperial order, the metropoles encouraged their private appropriation of the collective patrimony – land, oil – thus, turning tribal elites into great landlords or rich rentiers and tribesmen and peasants into an agricultural proletariat.[47] In co-opting and reinforcing established elites, the social structure was frozen at the top and while educated salaried classes employed at the lower levels of the colonial state grew up under imperialism which also fostered new mercantile elements, the peripherialization of the colonial economy, the dominance of property by imperial-aligned oligarchs and the frequent control of commerce by European or minority elements was bound to limit the economic opportunities of the new indigenous strata. These new middle strata therefore assumed the banner of nationalism and the more that property-less lower strata were mobilized during the independence struggle, the more social revolutionary nationalism became. There was little large-scale non-indigenous settlement in the region, but in the cases where it did take place, Palestine and Algeria, the indigenous population was dispossessed.[48] Simmering resistance, never definitively subdued, later revived in the form of mass independence movements and attempted revolt every time Western control seemed to falter, for example in the Second World War when France and Britain faced defeat by Germany.[49]

Britain and France, in dividing up nearly the whole of the Arabic-speaking world between them, grossly violated regional identity. Where the areas conquered had been centers of high civilizations and empires (Cairo, Damascus, Baghdad) with which the mass of the population continued to identify, resistance, reinforced by the emerging ideology of Arab nationalism, was natural. This was especially so because arbitrary imperial boundary-drawing fragmented this former civilizational area into a multitude of mini-states, a deformation rightly seen as part of a divide-and-rule strategy. The Western empires accorded some measure of self-governance to the colonies, but imperial governors or high commissioners always had, at a minimum, veto power. Europeans, believing colonial peoples to be unfit for self-governance (affirmed by the international jurisprudence of the time),[50] ruled over empires in which they refused to apply the egalitarian values increasingly applied at home. Despite the oft-noted greater preference of France than Britain for direct rule and cultural assimilation, in practice the outcome was similar. Since the colonies were not contiguous with the metropole and were acquired for the extraction of wealth, and because metropolitan populations would never accept being swamped by according citizenship to vast numbers of colonial subjects (as in Rome), no political integration took place. Rather, basic distinctions between core and periphery were institutionalized in constitutional law and an ideology of racial or civilizational superiority that obstructed elite recruitment from, and inclusion of, the periphery in central representative institutions. The first generation of moderate indigenous modernizers who had wanted inclusion in the imperial establishments was succeeded by nationalists demanding complete independence. Because co-opted elites never had a say in the running of the empire, they never embraced the identity of the empire. Thus, the break-up of Western empires does appear inevitable.[51]

CENTRAL ASIA: FROM RUSSIAN TERRITORIAL EMPIRE TO SOVIET MULTINATIONAL STATE?

The Russian empire, based on an alliance of autocrat and aristocracy, was an efficient apparatus for the mobilization of resources for territorial expansion. According to Lieven, although it enjoyed aspects of proto-nationhood, it lacked a clear distinction between an imperial core/people and the non-Russian periphery and even incorporated Tatar elites into its landed aristocracy. When Russia seized Transcaucasia from the Ottomans many Muslims were driven into Ottoman lands, but thereafter more Turkic-speaking people were still living under Russian rule than under the Ottoman Empire. Russia actually liberated small-holding peasant communities in Central Asia from tenancies in what Fieldhouse called a social revolution; it protected them from Russian settlement until encroachment on their grazing lands started under an 1891 statute, expressive of a new view that nomadism was a backward way of life, which led to a Kazakh uprising in which 200,000 were killed. The Kazakhs' herds nevertheless increased and by contrast to the contemporaneous American settler empire, they were never marginalized in their own land.[52] In the settled Muslim areas of the Khanates of Khiva and Bohkara the Tsarist empire preserved the indigenous communities and was tolerant of Islam. As a result, there were only two minor rebellions against Russian rule. Resistance by the *ʿulama* was the exception as long as the new rulers did not harm the *shariʿa* and Islam could be practiced.[53] Russian conquest arguably brought Central Asia into the "modern" world.[54]

The Soviet Union carried on Russia's tradition of centralized autocracy, but its elimination of the aristocracy, state ownership of property and egalitarian universalistic religion (communism) bore similarities to the Ottoman Empire, while differing in its powerful mobilizational party and greater modernizing thrust. While Western empires in the Middle East, ruling through traditional leaders, aimed to keep people un-mobilized, Soviet power was spread by a revolutionary overthrowing of old hierarchies in the name of the workers, peasants and women. In Central Asia, the early Bolsheviks, most of whom were not ethnic Russians, encouraged indigenous languages and cadre recruitment and allied with the emerging intelligentsia, not old aristocracies, around an egalitarian modernization project. Also, by contrast to the Tsars, the Bolsheviks sought to marginalize Islam, and early revolutionary intervention in realms of law and family were perceived as alien and resisted by Muslim movements.

The communists, conceiving of the USSR as a single country, tried to create a common identity and equal citizenship, and under the 1918 Federal Constitution the larger non-Russian nationalities were accorded union republics with considerable cultural and administrative autonomy, with a (until 1991 only theoretical) right of secession,[55] and central representative bodies incorporating all nationalities. As in the Ottoman case, the top elite was multinational, and while the majority Russians dominated, political mobility into elite positions, including the supreme politburo, even if atypical, was possible for non-Russians. Although the Russian language was prioritized as a *lingua franca* and in the Second

World War Stalin came to rely on Russian nationalism, still Lieven judged that a Russian nation was not fostered and Russians did not, as a group, dominate the empire as the British did theirs.[56]

However, in order to centralize control for industrialization and collectivization, Stalin purged the Central Asian indigenous elite and collectivization killed a third of the Kazakh population. Persecution of Islam was intensified. But under Stalin there was a perverse equality among ethnic groups, with Russians exterminated as much as non-Russians. Khrushchev's virgin lands scheme sponsored settlement by 1.5 million Slavs in Kazakhstan, requiring another purge of the local elite and making the Kazakhs a minority in their own country. But, with Central Asian birth rates four times higher than among Russians, this proved temporary. Under Brezhnev indigenous elites again dominated their regions and political leadership in the union republics and although Russians often commanded the army and secret police, many of these "went native" and regional leaders achieved autonomy by building clientele networks controlling the flow of information to Moscow and buying off figures in the central elite.[57] The economy was still centrally run, the plan and budgets controlled from Moscow and high-tech and energy sectors controlled by all-union ministries which gave little care to the local environment; the cotton mono-crop exported to Russian factories and sold back to the periphery resembled Egypt under Britain.[58] Yet there was less straightforward exploitation of the region and by some calculations, the center may have subsidized the CA periphery,[59] the reverse of normal imperial practice. Industrial investment in the region was significant and if Russians provided the majority of skilled workers, engineers and managers, natives predominated in some university departments and had priority for local government jobs, although if they wanted social mobility they had to be Russian-fluent. The result was an education gap that was far narrower than in Western empires. Resistance to cultural assimilation/colonialism formed part of the discourse of CA autonomy movements in the late Soviet era, but they never developed into mass nationalist movements.

These features of the Soviet Union have led some to dispute the label of empire altogether, calling it instead a modernizing multinational state or something between the two. Terry Martin describes the USSR as "the world's first post imperial state, a new form of empire that used the norm ... of national self-determination – as instruments of non-consensual control over culturally distinct populations, thereby blurring the line between state and empire."[60] Others who believed the USSR was an empire, still concede that it did not begin as one or was a unique kind of empire.[61] Modernized territorial empires that acquire universalistic inclusion practices such as the USSR might be expected to be less vulnerable to break-up. Without an accidental failure of imperial leadership at the center (that is, the fall of Gorbachev and rise of Yeltsin), the Union might have been preserved, at least for some time. And if the USSR was an empire, it was an empire with a difference that should make for differences in post-imperial outcomes.

Empire in MENA and CA does appear to have been experienced differently. In the Middle East, forced fragmentation frustrated identities and, coming after centuries of unity under Islamic empires was bound to be experienced as a deep mutilation of the polity. The experience of CA under the Russian and especially the Soviet empire was in many ways the opposite as the union republics constituted proto-national identities rather than frustrating some previous strong, for example, pan-Turkic, identity. The Communists tried to create a common shared identity; like the Ottoman Empire, the elite was multinational, with regional elites assimilated into the Soviet political culture and represented in central bodies that governed the empire. By contrast, the sharp metropole–colony distinction in Western empires meant such inclusion was never on the agenda of these empires; non-Russians became Soviet but the Middle East's indigenous people could never be British or French. In socio-economic terms, the Ottoman, Soviet and even Russian empires were relatively egalitarian in their impacts, with the Soviet radically demolishing old social hierarchies, compared with the fostering of class inequalities under Western capitalist empires. While settlers were part of the story in both empires, their enduring impact was very different: in CA Russian settlers left or were accorded citizenship, while settler colonialism in Algeria was only reversed with massive violence, and in Palestine it resulted in permanent displacement of the indigenous people, an enduring source of continuing anti-imperialism in the region.

Chapter Breakdown

The book's structure reflects the move from empire to post-imperial outcomes. We begin in Section I with three contributions on the history of empires in the region. Dominic Lieven (Chapter 2) focuses on Russia and the former Soviet Union; James McDougall (Chapter 3) surveys the impacts of Western European empire on the Middle East and North Africa; and Fred Lawson (Chapter 4) examines the impact of economic development in the late Ottoman empire on post-imperial sovereignty.

In Section II we examine how the imperial experience shaped the paths to independence and the early independence years. Ben Fortna (Chapter 5) examines the impact of Ottoman Turkey's defensive modernization on its post-imperial statehood. Michelle Burgis (Chapter 6) concentrates on one particular way of managing transition, the mandate and on the impact of international law on empire and sovereignty. Mohira Suyarkulova (Chapter 7) looks at the Soviet discourse on sovereignty and how its evolving meaning affected the transition from empire.

In section III, authors examine the effects of empire on three types of sovereignty: political, cultural and external. Louise Fawcett (Chapter 8) examines the impact of imperialism and post-imperial informal empires on the kinds of post-imperial state which emerged in MENA. David Lewis (Chapter 9) discusses the emergence in CA of five territorially defined states with authoritarian regimes as a legacy of the Soviet state.

The cultural domain provides important insights into notions of psychic violence and cultural hegemonies that infuse writing on colonialism in this domain. In section IV, Laura Adams (Chapter 10) employs a Foucauldian analysis of how power and culture in Central Asia interacted to affect a hybrid cultural colonialism. Morten Valbjørn (Chapter 11) looks at how ideas of the "other" in the colonial period shaped anti-imperial movements and how variations in state identity were shaped by the impact of imperialism. Frédéric Volpi (Chapter 12) looks comparatively at the two regions and assesses the importance of trans-national Islamic identities and mobilization in the aftermath of independence.

The final section (section V) on imperial traces and legacies takes on external sovereignty. Raymond Hinnebusch (Chapter 13) analyzes how imperial legacies still have explanatory power as to why Syria has resisted, while Jordan has accommodated post-imperial hegemony. Wojciech Ostrowski (Chapter 14) looks at dependency and rentierism in Central Asia and how rent has a far-reaching impact on these countries' foreign policy, their relationship with Russia and state sovereignty. Finally, Tajikistan, analyzed by Muriel Atkin (Chapter 15), is the particularly compelling case study for Central Asia, since it was at once the poorest periphery in the region but also the most colonially militarized.

In the conclusion, the editors systematically compare the similarities and differences in the transition to sovereignty in the regions, the effect of imperial transmissions in MENA and CA on the states and the states systems and the degree of rupture with the ex-empire. In the process, we incorporate also the nuances and particularities identified by the authors of the case studies. Finally, we compare the outcomes for Krasner's four dimensions of sovereignty in MENA and CA.

Notes

1. Colas, *Empire*, pp. 19–26, 62–70.
2. Bull and Watson (eds), *The Expansion of International Society.*
3. Buzan, *From International to World Society?*, pp 6–26; Colas, *Empire*, pp. 18–21.
4. Hobson, *The State and International Relations*, pp. 30–38; Hobson and Sharman, "The enduring place of hierarchy in world politics."
5. Colomer, *Great Empires, Small Nations.*
6. Krasner, *Problematic Sovereignty*, pp. 7–12.
7. Hobson and Sharman, "The enduring place of hierarchy in world politics," pp. 63–98; Colas, *Empire*, pp. 158–91.
8. We take Central Asia (CA) to mean the five post-Soviet republics of Kazakhstan, Kyrgyzstan, Tajikistan, Turkmenistan and Uzbekistan. MENA includes the Mashreq (Levant), Egypt and North Africa and the Arabian Peninsula.
9. Lewis, "The hard questions: what went wrong?"
10. Historical and comparative examples: Fieldhouse, *The Colonial Empires*; Doyle, *Empires*; Lieven, *Empire: The Russian Empire and its Rivals*. More theoretical: Colas, *Empire*; Callinicos, *Imperialism and Global Political Economy*. Looking at empire's contemporary relevance: Harvey, *The New Imperialism*; Khalidi, *Resurrecting Empire*.
11. Barkey and Mark von Hagen, *After Empire*; Brysk, Parsons and Sandholtz, *After Empire*; Barkey, *Empire of Difference*.
12. Several studies looked at empire in the Middle East (e.g., Fieldhouse, *Western Imperialism in the Middle East*), and in Central Asia or the post-Soviet space (e.g., Suny, "Ambiguous categories") and a few have tried to link empire to after in these regions (e.g., Kandiyoti, "Post-colonialism compared," Fromkin, *A Peace to End All Peace*, Tsygankov, "Defining state interests after empire").
13. Cole and Kandiyoti, "Nationalism and the colonial legacy in the Middle East and Central Asia: Introduction."
14. For the English School, see Bull and Watson, Buzan and Little; for realists see Krasner.
15. Mill, *Philosophy of Scientific Method.*
16. Fieldhouse, *The Colonial Empires*; Lieven, *Empire: The Russian Empire and its Rivals*; Doyle, *Empires*; Colas, *Empire*; Dawisha and Parrott, *The End of Empire*; Barkey and von Hagen, *After Empire.*
17. Lieven, *Empire: The Russian Empire and its Rivals*, pp. 3–26.
18. Both kinds of sources will be cited at appropriate places in the text.
19. Lieven, *Empire: The Russian Empire and its Rivals*, p. 344.
20. Recent developments in Kyrgyzstan, and the civil war in Tajikistan in the 1990s, suggest these two states are most susceptible to MENA-type instabilities.

21. Uzbekistan did intervene militarily in Tajikistan's civil war to help the side which ended up winning, and for a time later in the 1990s, gave a renegade Tajikistani military officer a safe haven from which he launched attacks on Tajikistan and later sent agents, into Kyrgyzstan to attack and kidnap some political opposition figures from Uzbekistan. These were, however, essentially defensive moves.
22. Pemberton, *Sovereignty: Interpretations*, p. 6.
23. Krasner, *Problematic Sovereignty*, p. 6; Hinsley, *Sovereignty*.
24. Krasner, *Sovereignty*, pp. 9–25 and *Problematic Sovereignty*, pp. 7–12.
25. Pemberton, *Sovereignty: Interpretations*, p. 3.
26. Krasner, *Problematic Sovereignty*, p. 6.
27. Jackson, *Quasi States*.
28. Ayoob, *The Third World Security Predicament*.
29. Wallerstein, *The Capitalist World Economy*.
30. Gerschenkron, *Economic Backwardness in Historical Perspective*.
31. Walzer (1977) in Pemberton, *Sovereignty: Interpretations*, pp. 87–90
32. Lawson, *Constructing International Relations in the Arab World*, p. 2.
33. Colomer, *Great Empires, Small Nations*; Doyle, *Empires*; Lieven, *Empire: The Russian Empire and its Rivals*, pp. 3–8; Colas, *Empire*, pp. 1–11; Motyl, *Imperial Ends*.
34. Eisenstadt, *The Political Systems of Empires*.
35. Colas, *Empire*, pp. 19–22, 71, 116–17.
36. Wallerstein, *The Capitalist World Economy*.
37. Lieven, *Empire: The Russian Empire and its Rivals*, pp. 89–127; Callinicos, *Imperialism and Global Political Economy*; Colas, *Empire*, pp. 22–6, 71–115; Amin, *The Arab Nation*; Rosenberg, *The Empire of Civil Society*, pp. 91–122, 159–73; Halliday, *Rethinking International Relations*, pp. 47–73; Brewer, *Marxist Theories of Imperialism*, pp. 1–24, 42–56, 58–72, 161–224.
38. Lieven, *Empire: The Russian Empire and its Rivals*, pp. 40–50.
39. Parrott, "Analyzing the Transformation of the Soviet Union," pp. 10–11.
40. Weber, *The Theory of Social and Economic Organization*; Lieven, *Empire: The Russian Empire and its Rivals*, pp. 27–40; Colas, *Empire*, p. 24.
41. Gerber, *The Social Origins of the Modern Middle East*; Barkey, *Empire of Difference*.
42. Lieven, *Empire: The Russian Empire and its Rivals*.
43. Lieven, *Empire: The Russian Empire and its Rivals*, pp. 128–48; Colas, *Empire*, pp. 48–53.
44. Keyder, "The Ottoman Empire," pp. 30–44.
45. Yapp, *The Making of the Modern Near East*, p. 349; Fieldhouse, *Western Imperialism in the Middle East, 1914–1958*, pp. 34–5; Barkey, *Empire of Difference*.
46. Khalidi, *Resurrecting Empire*, pp. 1–36; Clancy-Smith, "Collaboration and empire in the Middle East and North Africa."

47. On Western empires in the Middle East, see Fromkin, *A Peace to End All Peace*; Yapp, *The Making of the Modern Near East*; Khalidi, *Resurrecting Empire*; Adelson, *London and the Invention of the Middle East*.

48. Adelson, *London and the Invention of the Middle East*; Ayubi, *Over-stating the Arab State*, pp. 87, 99; Amin, *The Arab Nation*; Bromley, *Rethinking Middle East Politics*, pp. 46–85; Bridge and Bullen, *The Great Powers*, pp. 188–92; Owen, *The Middle East in the World Economy*, pp. 3–9, 92; Issawi, *An Economic History of the Middle East and North Africa*, pp. 138–55; Yapp, *The Making of the Modern Near East*, pp. 1–35; Sayf, "Free trade, competition and industrial decline."

49. Khalidi, *Resurrecting Empire*, pp. 1–36, Fromkin, *A Peace to End All Peace*, pp. 449–54.

50. Burgis, Chapter 6, this volume.

51. Colas, *Empire*, pp. 62–70, 116–37; Lieven, *Empire: The Russian Empire and its Rivals*: pp. 123, 313–14.

52. Lieven, *Empire: The Russian Empire and its Rivals*; Fieldhouse, *The Colonial Empires*, pp. 334–41.

53. Khalid, "Russia, Central Asia and the Caucasus to 1917."

54. Khalid, "Russia, Central Asia and the Caucasus to 1917," p. 35.

55. For one of the most comprehensive analyses of the development and practice of nationalities policy in socialist societies, see Connor, *The National Question in Marxist–Leninist Theory and Strategy*.

56. Lieven, *Empire: The Russian Empire and its Rivals*, pp. 318–19.

57. Lieven, *Empire: The Russian Empire and its Rivals*, p. 290.

58. Atkin, this volume.

59. The question "Kto kovo?," who benefited, continues to be debated by economic historians. Watson, e.g., argues that the Central Asian periphery was subsidized by the center (except for Turkmenistan). However, the calculations on which this is based may have undervalued the unfinished or semi-finished products that dominated CA's output.

60. Martin, *An Affirmative Action Empire*, p. 19.

61. Motyl, *Imperial Ends*; Suny, "Ambiguous categories: states, empires, and nations," pp. 185–96; Beissinger, "Soviet empire as 'family resemblance.'"

Section I

Histories of Empire and After

2

Russian Empires

Dominic Lieven

No definition of empire fits all empires which have existed in history, or even all the most important ones. Since most great empires evolve over time and differ greatly between regions, one definition of empire is often hard pressed to encompass the key elements of even a single actual empire. For example, what definition of empire adequately encapsulates London's relationship with the seventeenth-century West Indies, eighteenth-century India, nineteenth-century Ireland and Africa and the early twentieth-century White Dominions?[1]

When one moves beyond the domestic constitution of empire to empire's place in international relations, similar problems of definition occur. Empire is often seen, for example, as the antithesis of multi-polarity.[2] Post-Westphalian Europe is contrasted to the regional hegemony exercised by Rome in western Eurasia or the Chinese empire in the east. But in reality Rome had to negotiate with the massive power of imperial Persia, and Chinese dynasties conducted two millennia of diplomacy with their northern neighbors, often very consciously from a position of weakness.[3] Moreover, in nineteenth-century Europe when Westphalian principles ruled supreme, most of the key players in the European concert called themselves, and by most definitions were, empires. From this I draw the conclusion that there are no correct definitions of empire, merely more or less useful ones. A definition will depend on what aspects of empire interest a scholar and its usefulness will be disputed by other scholars in part because they may or may not share an interest in these aspects.

My own definition of empire includes enormous size, multi-ethnicity and rule without the explicit consent of the governed.[4] It seems to me, for instance, that controlling vast territories with pre-modern communications was among the greatest challenges of empire. In the nineteenth century as communications technology was transformed and doctrines of popular sovereignty and nationalism spread, managing space became somewhat less problematic and managing multi-ethnicity much more so. Popular sovereignty also challenged the legitimacy of almost all imperial regimes. That goes far to explain why no polity nowadays calls itself an empire and none fit perfectly any definition derived from historical empires. Probably the People's Republic of China (PRC) comes closest to historical empire, but any comparison with true empire under the last imperial dynasty, the Qing, reveals that even the PRC is far from being a fully-fledged traditional empire.[5] Where one is dealing with "formal empire," in other words, the imperial rulers' possession of sovereignty over peripheral territories, the issue of consent is relatively clear-cut. Consent can to a considerable extent be measured by regular elections. De-colonization entails the transfer of sovereignty and the legal equality of the former metropole and its colonies as independent states. Informal empire is a much less clear-cut phenomenon, not least because no state is entirely sovereign and independent in today's world. Defining what degree of external influence adds up to informal empire is almost impossible.

On the other hand, discussion of formal and informal empire does help to focus on what seems to me to be the key element in empire, which is power. In my opinion, though size, multi-ethnicity and rule without consent are necessary elements in empire, unless a polity is sufficiently powerful to exercise a great influence on the international politics of its era then it is not truly an empire. Power comes in many forms – military, political, economic, ideological, cultural, demographic and geopolitical – and different empires embody these elements of power to varying degrees in different eras and contexts.[6] The most interesting and important empires are those whose power is bound up with a universal religion or a great civilization of potentially global appeal. Such empires play a key role in determining the fate of humanity. Power is eternal, it is never equally distributed, and it is generally used to serve the interests of those who possess it. My fourfold definition of empire therefore leads to the conclusion that whereas formal empire in its old historical definition no longer exists, the history of empire has a very great deal to say about the nature of contemporary international politics.

My definition of empire is not the usual one. Most scholars stress some variation on the theme of political domination, economic exploitation and cultural hegemony exercised by a metropolitan polity over dependent peripheral societies.[7] This definition largely works when one is discussing the modern European transoceanic empires. In their case, metropolis and periphery were sharply divided by geography, race, wealth and power. By 1900 the metropolitan state in Britain, France and the Netherlands was responsible to the political nation. Citizenship in the metropole can be contrasted to the world of subjects in most of the periphery. As always, generalizations do not perfectly fit historical realities. Ireland and Algeria are anomalies; so to an extent were Britain's White Dominions. But the definition nevertheless fits well enough to be useful.

It is far less useful when applied to most of the land empires which existed from ancient times into the twentieth century. Many of these polities could best be described as aristocratic empires. They were defined by class much more than ethnicity. Aristocratic elites felt a greater solidarity with other aristocrats within their civilization than they did with peasants, even of their own ethnicity.[8] In many aristocratic empires the metropolitan plebs might well be more heavily exploited than peripheral peasantries because it was easier logistically and safer politically to do so. This was true, for example, of the Turkish peasantry of Anatolia in the Ottoman Empire. But the Ottomans fit best into a second category of traditional land empire, namely, empires rooted in great universal religions, of which Islam was the most successful. Religious not ethnic solidarity united the Ottoman elite and legitimized its rule. A third common type of traditional empire might be called nomadic empire. Ibn Khaldun best explained the dynamics of such empires, but they were not confined to the Islamic world.[9] Semi-nomadic polities on occasion conquered and ruled all or part of China's empire. To some extent the last imperial dynasty, the Qing, falls into this category. Rather obviously, nomadic conquerors did not exercise any element of cultural hegemony over the civilizations they ruled. On the contrary, for the Manchus the price of conquest was partial sinification and self-obliteration, thereby turning one of the most fashionable current definitions of empire on its head.[10]

It is widely assumed that only the history of the modern transoceanic empires is truly relevant to contemporary politics and international relations. Lenin stressed that imperialism was the essence of late capitalist international relations and had nothing in common with the great land empires which had existed since antiquity.[11] For those interested in one of the most burning issues of contemporary politics, namely, the relationship between First and Third World, it also seems clear that the history of European transoceanic imperialism is much more relevant than the history of the Ottoman or Chinese dynasties. For a scholar of contemporary politics to ignore the history of land empire would, however, be short-sighted. Contemporary China is not a fully-fledged empire, but it bears many of its hallmarks. Moreover, a nation whose identity is so much bound up in the history and memory of empire and which still possesses empire's power is a very different polity to the great majority of nations represented in the

UN and is certain to act in very different ways. The term nation, convenient both to political scientists and politically correct bureaucrats, hides much more than it reveals.

To an extent the same is true of the United States. At one level the United States is the heir of Dutch and British empires.[12] They created the foundations of today's liberal capitalist global economy. The United States also inherited their commitment to representative institutions, popular sovereignty and the rule of law. But the United States is a country of continental size whose coastlines wash the Atlantic and Pacific. That is the geopolitical basis of its power. More important and totally unlike the Dutch and British, the United States is an assimilationist polity whose identity is rooted in ideology not ethnicity. This is a crucial element in its contemporary global power and it places the United States in a common imperial tradition with Roman, Islamic and even to an extent Chinese empire.

Where does Russia fit in to the history of empire? Obviously, it is part of the family of great land empires. Russian monarchy, which was the key to much of its success as an empire, evolved from the leadership of a military band into a divinely sanctioned dynasty, in principle standing above all social groups and political institutions, indeed, almost above the human condition itself. It did this by taking on aspects of Qingissid and, above all, Byzantine imperial tradition.[13] There are many parallels here with other imperial monarchies. Controlling Russia's immense space and mobilizing its rich resources and scattered population was an immense challenge, not least because Russia's rulers were building their polity so far from the traditional centers of world civilization and the major intercontinental trading routes which had sustained most of history's great empires. The monarchy's brilliant success in this enterprise owed a huge amount to its alliance with the landowning nobility. Compared with the Ottomans or the Mughals, the striking point is the solidity of Russia's alliance between monarch and landowning noble and the extent to which it permitted society's mobilization to sustain imperial power.[14] Comparisons with Chinese empire are also useful, though they are most revealing in the Tang era rather than with later dynasties.[15]

Another obvious parallel with other land empires is the blurred boundary between metropolitan nation and imperial periphery. The Romanovs' polity was never responsible to a Russian political nation of citizens. Russian peasants were at least as ruthlessly exploited as the non-Russian plebs. The ethno-linguistic border between Russia, Belorussia and Ukraine was extremely unclear. No oceans separated Russian colonists in the empire's southern and eastern borderlands from their motherland. The very convoluted definitions and debates of Peter Struve[16] and others in the early twentieth century as they sought to categorize, describe and defend the Russian "nation-state-empire" tell one much both about Russia's peculiarities and also about the difficulties of fitting Eurasian imperial polities into modern European political language and concepts.

But if, on the one hand, Russia belongs in the family of great land empires, it is also very much part of the expansion of early modern Europe and its rise to global dominance, on the other. The Russians are a Christian people and in that sense sharply differentiated from Islamic, Buddhist or Confucian civilizations.[17] The expansion and contraction of Russia – in terms of territory, population and power – occurred at more or less the same time as the expansion and contraction of the rest of Europe. Russian expansion from the seventeenth century owed much to borrowing European techniques and technology, and marrying them to the Russian polity's traditions and institutions. The imperial army of the long eighteenth century, for example, was a successful union of the European artillery and infantry army with a light cavalry rooted in long experience of frontier war in the southern forest and steppe theater of military operations.[18] The "victims" of Russian expansion – Muslims and nomads – were often very similar to the peoples who stood in the way of other expanding European powers. From one perspective, Khrushchev's Virgin Lands policy of the 1950s was the last example of European territorial encroachment at Asians' expense.

It is true that Russian imperialism was never primarily commercial, as was the case with the Dutch and to a somewhat lesser extent the British. Above all for that reason, Russia was less often able than the British to control an informal empire beyond its state borders. The contrast between Russian and British imperialism in nineteenth- and early twentieth-century China is instructive. The Russians could never assert the degree of informal power that Victorian Britain possessed in much of Latin America.[19] But the British Empire like the Russian was also very much a political, military and colonizing enterprise. The same was, if anything, even truer of the French and Spanish. The automatic equation of maritime with commercial and "liberal" empire comes naturally to Anglo-Saxons, but is not in fact axiomatic, as the Japanese example (among others) makes clear.[20]

Russian expansion in Asia from the eighteenth century was partly legitimized by the claims of Europe's civilizing mission. In disguised fashion this was even truer of Soviet empire. Marxism stood four-square in the European tradition of Hegel and of British political economy. Like Macaulay, Lenin believed in unilinear progress rooted in European history and values, but spreading across the globe. Non-European societies were presumed to be stagnant until touched by Europe's transforming hand. The two men were equally Eurocentric and culturally arrogant, but racially tolerant. Soviet ideology in its early pristine optimism had many of the hallmarks of Victorian liberalism's view that the world could and should be made over in their own image. For better and worse, however, the Soviet regime penetrated its periphery far more deeply and was far more committed to its transformation than was ever the case with the men who ruled Britain's non-White colonies.[21]

To define Russian empire too dogmatically as either modern European or traditional Eurasian also ignores the great variations which existed both over time and between regions of the empire. The "fur empire" in sixteenth- and seventeenth-century Siberia has parallels with the French empire in Canada. Russian rule in late nineteenth-century Central Asia has clear parallels with the British cotton empire in Egypt, not to mention with the system of indirect rule through princely states which the Russians borrowed directly from British India. The colonization of the steppe grasslands and the development of Odessa as their export outlet was Russia's answer to the opening up of North America and Australia to European farmer-colonists. Other regions of the Romanovs' empire have fewer European parallels. Most obviously, Russia ruled in much of the western borderlands over societies and above all elites which considered themselves more advanced than the empire's core. Many members of the Russian elite agreed with this claim.[22]

The Russian polity is usually seen as imperial from the time of Ivan IV's conquest of Kazan. Ivan's polity still owed much to the traditions of steppe politics and diplomacy. His Russia was more homogeneous in its Russian and Orthodox culture than was true of the post-Petrine empire with its Westernized elites and mass of acquired non-Russian territories. The early nineteenth-century empire was to a certain extent an alliance of Russian and other landed aristocracies, united under the Romanovs' scepter. Baltic German nobles were far more obvious beneficiaries of empire than Russian serfs. But the new cosmopolitan aristocratic polity merged with, rested on, but did not replace the older Orthodox polity.

From the mid-nineteenth century, Russia's rulers faced a more or less universal dilemma of modern empire. They had inherited a polity containing vast territories and many peoples. They needed to preserve this inheritance in an imperialist age if Russia was to retain its independence and its position among the world's leading powers. But how was empire to be made legitimate in an era where popular sovereignty and nationalism were increasingly powerful ideologies? As with most other empires, the Romanovs' answer was to try to make their empire more national, by identifying with its core people and trying to turn as much as possible of the empire's population into a homogeneous political nation. This explains much of the policy of russification and, in particular, St Petersburg's determination to thwart the development of Ukrainian national consciousness. Yet even now, as the Russian empire became more national, it still retained many elements of its older aristocratic and dynastic character.

Though the Romanovs' empire contained many elements, it was largely European in its priorities and its identity. Its political and economic centers were in Europe. Even the Urals heavy industrial region was closer to Berlin than to Beijing or Tokyo. The empire borrowed ideas, technologies and professional cadres from Europe. Its elites spoke French, not Arabic or Chinese. Educated Russians agonized about their European identity. If some of them turned toward Eurasianism, then as now that often resulted from a sense of rejection by the West.

Above all, the empire's development from the reign of Peter I to the revolution of 1917 was determined by the need to compete with the richer and more modern European great powers to its west. This was primarily a question of security and power–political considerations, though the regime's legitimacy and the elites' self-esteem were also heavily engaged in this competition. Peter and his successors succeeded in making Russia competitive in the eighteenth and early nineteenth centuries by creating a formidable military–fiscal absolutist state. Victory over Napoleon crowned this achievement.[23] Subsequently, however, Russia once again fell behind, above all because the Industrial Revolution originated in Western Europe and took three generations before it began to transform Russia. In the Crimean War of 1854–6, Russia was defeated above all because it operated with pre-industrial military and communications technology against enemies who were armed with the new technology of the industrial age. This ushered in a second wave of modernization designed to make Russia able to compete with the other European great powers in the industrial age.[24] This second wave spanned the revolution of 1917. Stalin's victory over Hitler symbolized Russia's success in this new competition as surely as Alexander's defeat of Napoleon had proved its ability to compete in an earlier era.

Once again, however, developments in the global economy left Russia behind in the 1970s and 1980s. Gorbachev's *perestroika* was in one sense an attempt to make Russia competitive in the era of the micro-chip and the computer. At a high level of generalization, Stalin's policy of ruthless authoritarian modernization had some parallels with the efforts of Peter I. But the parallels between "liberal modernization" under Alexander II and Gorbachev were much closer. Both in the 1860s and in the 1980s world of Thatcher and Reagan, liberal ideologies ruled supreme. Freedom was widely seen as not just desirable in itself, but also as the key source of a society's dynamism and power. Both Alexander and Gorbachev sought to unlock society's potential by economic liberalization, the rule of law and much greater freedom of expression. Both rulers soon faced all the difficulties of introducing Western values and institutions into a multi-national empire and a Russian society traditionally held together by an authoritarian regime which had relied on fear, obedience and inertia. Within six years of launching his reforms Alexander was faced with revolution in Poland and elements of the Russian intelligentsia calling for the overthrow not just of the monarchy but also private property and marriage. Six years after Gorbachev came to power in the seemingly very stable USSR, not just the communist regime but the multi-national empire had disintegrated. Gorbachev and his fellow leaders drew on the pro-Western traditions of the Russian intelligentsia and sought to re-integrate the USSR into a world they understood through (rather idealized) Western social-democratic and liberal lenses.[25] Had the leadership understood traditional dilemmas of empire and Westernization in Russian history they might have been more cautious and less naive. To that extent they were the victims of the Soviet regime's attempt to divorce itself from pre-revolutionary Russian elites and the historical memory they had accumulated.[26]

Calling tsarist Russia an empire is unproblematic, not least because that is what it called itself. Applying the term to the Soviet Union raises more difficulties and more hackles. Clearly the USSR was an empire according to my fourfold definition. Equally clearly, it was in many ways a unique empire. The USSR was never an equal society, but the ban on ownership or inheritance of property made it in most respects much less unequal than most historical empires. Though most empires ruled over their periphery in collaboration with native elites, the Soviet policy of creating new native elites and then giving them preference over Russian colonists in their ancestral homelands differed sharply from the norms both of aristocratic land empire and of modern European transoceanic empire. On the other hand, the Soviet regime's ruthless dragooning of subject peoples to serve its ideological and geopolitical priorities was imperial to a degree. In another sense, too, the Soviet regime was more wholly imperial than tsarism. From the Napoleonic era to the revolution, the rulers and diplomats of Imperial Russia saw their empire as part of the European Concert and viewed the balance of power as the key to international order. The Soviet perspective was very different. The new regime's goal was to overthrow the international order and to replace it with a universal socialist commonwealth with Moscow at its center. As regards international relations, imperial and Soviet Russia therefore represented two very different conceptions of empire.[27]

Inevitably, the Soviet empire inherited aspects of the tsarist imperial heritage. Most obviously and importantly, it occupied almost the same territory and lived within the same, extremely threatening international system of competing great powers. The needs of security bred many common tsarist and Soviet geopolitical imperatives and obsessions. The rulers of both tsarist and Soviet Russia cared deeply about their country's great power status, which itself is a key mark of empire. For all the differences between the regimes, both rejected the principle of popular sovereignty. Neither before nor after the revolution were the rulers of empire responsible to the Russian political nation: this, in turn, reinforced traditional attitudes towards power (*vlast'*) in the Russian people. The Russians were much the largest part of the population and they and their resources were the basis of its power. Their language was the language of government and empire. That basic reality in time counteracted against initial Soviet gestures of repentance for Russian nationalism and encouraged elder-brother patronization of the USSR's smaller peoples of a sort familiar under late tsarism.

Nevertheless, one should certainly not exaggerate continuities between tsarist and Soviet empire. Save to a limited extent in the armed forces, there was virtually no continuity of personnel at senior levels. The Soviet regime put great effort into uprooting traditional core elements in Russian identity – the monarchy, Orthodox Church, peasantry and Cossacks to name but four. If the Soviet regime attempted to preserve control over as much as possible of the former tsarist empire, it tried to do so on a new basis. They would solve the dilemma of modern empire by basing their polity on a new universal secular religion which would not deny ethnicity but would surmount and trump it. Creating a successfully modern socialist society would both legitimize the regime and mold citizens with common socialist and modern values and loyalties. The Soviet imperial project was therefore much more unequivocally modernizing than its tsarist predecessor, though as already noted tsarism itself had no option but rapid modernization if it was to survive in a ruthlessly competitive international environment. The Soviet problem, however, was that socialist modernization, seemingly so promising even in the early 1960s, appeared to be a dead-end two decades later. The Soviet regime collapsed above all because its project of socialist modernization failed, at least as measured against contemporary capitalism in the 1980s. Since the regime itself had made this comparison the very core of its legitimacy, relative failure had disastrous consequences.

Whether the relative failure of socialist modernity was bound to lead to the collapse of the USSR is a moot point.[28] To some extent, calling the Soviet Union an empire even clouds this issue. In the near-universal contemporary conception, empires are out of date and doomed to disappear. Both the metropole and its former colonies must inevitably become post-imperial nations. But actually, not all empires have disintegrated in this way. China, the oldest and greatest empire of all, has evolved into something approaching a nation-state. Moreover, all Asia's major polities – Iran, Indonesia and India as well as China – are vast, multi-ethnic countries which are much more clearly heirs of empire than ethnic nations in the classic European sense. The dominant Western view that the collapse of the Soviet empire was inevitable and desirable may be yet one more example of applying Western assumptions and concepts too confidently. At the very least, the role of contingency, context and personalities in the collapse of the USSR should never be underestimated.

However one evaluates its causes, the collapse of the USSR was bound to have immense consequences. To some extent the most surprising point thus far is that the results of the Soviet Union's disintegration have been relatively limited. The decline and fall of the Habsburg and Ottoman empires was both cause and consequence of world war. The twentieth-century British Empire was on the whole built on more benign principles than the USSR and its decline and demise took place over two generations. Nevertheless, its disappearance was accompanied in some cases by war and ethnic cleansing on a grand scale and its legacy includes the Palestine issue, the India–Pakistan confrontation and a host of other conflicts. A pessimist might note that the results of empire's collapse often take a generation to reveal themselves. The disintegration of the Habsburg Empire created a geopolitical hole in central Europe which resulted in a second world war occurring twenty-one years after the Habsburgs' overthrow. Among the consequences of this war of the Habsburg succession was the extermination of one of the great diaspora peoples of the empire – the Jews – and the ethnic cleansing of the other one, in other words, the Germans. The USSR collapsed less than twenty years ago. It would be surprising if we had yet seen all the consequences of that collapse.

Life is much easier for the post-imperial metropole of a transoceanic empire. It can divorce itself far more easily from post-imperial chaos in its former colonies when this is happening at the other end of the world.[29] It is easier for the British to ignore Burma than for the Russians to forget the Caucasus, with anarchy threatening lands which are still part of the Russian Federation. Empire entails burdens as well as benefits. De-colonization means shedding many of these burdens. Harold Wilson could decide in 1969 that Britain would no longer play a defense role east of Suez. Russia, on the other hand, has retained Siberia and the Maritime province. It cannot ignore their security needs in what might become a dangerously insecure Asia–Pacific region. Above all, it is easier to shed something that one has than what one is. Britain and France had overseas empires. Russia was an empire. In the typical fashion of land empires, metropole and colony were not clearly defined. Even in the British and French cases the distinction was not perfect. Algeria and Northern Ireland were provinces of the metropolitan polity.[30] For that very reason they caused Paris and London more trouble than the rest of the empire during the era of de-colonization and empire's loss of legitimacy. In the French case, the loss of Algeria resulted in a terrible war, the revolt of part of the French army and the demise of the Fourth Republic.

To make a proper British comparison to the demise of the USSR, one would have to imagine that the British Empire had collapsed suddenly in peacetime in the 1930s, at a time when the empire had lost some of its pre-1914 aura, but was still regarded by most British people as both basically benign and also a fact of nature. The empire's collapse would have been accompanied by the secession of Scotland (Ukraine) and Wales (Belarus) and by an economic depression worse than that which actually occurred after 1929. To these one would need to add the overthrow of the monarchy and parliamentary democracy as equivalents to the demise of Soviet political institutions and the value-system that partly sustained them. Even the rather stolid British of the 1930s would have become excited if faced by this combination.

British elites were thoroughly humiliated by the end of empire and Britain's diminished status, but they had some consolations. The transfer of power to the American cousins, who shared most of their values and many of their interests, was to an extent a family arrangement. The victorious wartime alliance in a good cause smoothed the transition. So. too. did Britain's continuing global role as senior ally to the United States in the Cold War, waged against an enemy that London disliked only somewhat less than the Nazis. Moreover, declining status was at least accompanied by growing prosperity for most Britons, as Harold Macmillan emphasized. None of this applies in the Russian case. Global power meant even more to the self-esteem of Russian elites than British ones. In the 1990s, Russia was reduced to taking along a begging bowl to meetings of its former Cold War enemies and to grinding its teeth as NATO moved into the former Soviet borderlands. Even so, criticisms of Russian disregard for international law or human rights amid empire's demise might have been tempered by the rather obvious British parallels, of which the intervention at Suez in 1956 and the repression of Mau-Mau in Kenya are only the most obvious examples.

In most ways comparisons between Russia and the Turkish and Austrian heirs of land empire are more revealing than attempts to compare post-imperial Russia with the metropoles of former transoceanic empires. Turkish perceptions were greatly influenced by the fact that the last century of the Ottoman Empire had mostly been a tale of defeat, retreat and humiliation. Mustafa Kemal, on the other hand, had defeated the Greeks and their British protectors, liberated the Turkish homeland and thereby created powerful national myths on which the new republican order could be built. His propaganda juxtaposed republican modernity to Ottoman obscurantism and there was enough truth in the propaganda to make it credible. In any case, post-imperial Turkey was tightly constrained by geopolitical realities and Atatürk was quite sufficiently realistic to understand and respect these limits. Ottoman rule in the region had been replaced by Anglo-French empire. By heroic efforts he had liberated the Turkish ethnic homeland, but any attempt to push forward beyond its borders was bound to fail.[31]

The Austrian case was very different.[32] Post-imperial Austrian identity was actually much more problematic than was the case with the Russians of 1990s. Russians have lived in one state for centuries. All Russians can in principle identify with Orthodoxy, Borodino and Stalingrad. No one doubts that Pushkin was a Russian; even all elements in the endlessly fractious Russian emigration could unite to celebrate his anniversary. It is less clear that Mozart was an Austrian or indeed what being an Austrian might mean. Before 1918 it might have entailed loyalty to the Habsburg dynasty and empire. It probably meant some degree of identification with German Catholicism, many of whose members lived in other states. It could well include a sense of identification with the whole German people. Loyalty to one's province was also often very strong, as was a sense of solidarity with all German subjects of the Habsburgs in their struggle against Slavs and Italians. In the aftermath of the empire's collapse, however, the Austrians were not allowed to merge into Germany, the Sudeten Germans were forced into Czechoslovakia in defiance of the principle of self-determination proclaimed by the allies themselves, and the Tyrol was partitioned and partly handed over to the Italians. The rump Austrian republic was essentially those bits of the former empire which no one else wanted or was allowed to have. Not surprisingly it evoked limited loyalty.

The external context was also very different to the Turkish one and was, as always, extremely important. Unlike the Turkish case, the last century of empire had by no means been an unmitigated disaster for the

Austrians. To be sure, the empire had lost most of its wars, but Vienna had emerged as one of the most exciting and dynamic cultural centers in the world. The Austrian imperial economy had flourished and there was good reason to contrast it to the gloomy prospects of the small successor states deprived of a common market and with long-established imperial economic ties disrupted by political barriers. To a great extent Austrians identified with the broader Germanic world. In 1914 that world had been economically and culturally dynamic. Its variation on the modern capitalist theme had been somewhat different to the Anglo-American model but no less successful. Germans had also played the key role in defining and leading the key alternative to capitalist modernity, namely, the international socialist movement. The Germanic world had been defeated in war in 1914–18 not outdone in terms of economic or cultural success or modernity. When the Anglo-American first era of liberal globalization self-destructed in 1929, Germans and Austrians had every reason to look for their own home-grown alternative.

Unlike the Turkish case, geopolitical realities by no means constrained German and Austrian reveries. The basic point about European geopolitics between 1890 and 1945 was that only the Germans and the Russians had the resources potentially to dominate Europe. The lesson of 1917–18, 1939–45 and 1989–91 was that as one of these two powers declined the other rose. The treaty of Brest-Litovsk in 1918 spelled the seeming demise of Russia and potential German hegemony in Europe. The Brest-Litovsk settlement was then overthrown by allied victory on the Western front and the Versailles treaty, which was aimed against both Germany and Russia. The great irony of 1918 was that a war which to a considerable extent revolved around the competition between Germany and Russia ended in the defeat of both empires. No European order built on the defeat and exclusion of both of continental Europe's most powerful countries could be stable and long-lasting, however. The Versailles order was in any case based on American involvement in the war, without which Germany's defeat could not have happened. With the United States retreating into isolation after 1918 the European order had little chance of surviving, particularly since the British were not committed to the settlement in east-central Europe and were attempting to sustain an empire outside Europe against powerful potential enemies and with resources which in relative terms were shrinking. None of this made Hitler or even a second European war inevitable. But it did make it entirely realistic for Germans and Austrians to yearn for a new European order with some version of Germanic empire at its core.

Such comparisons provide interesting insights into the possible futures of post-imperial Russia. Russians, and above all Russian elites, have good reason to feel scarred and humiliated by the 1990s. The history of the Soviet Union was not a tale of unmitigated humiliation. Not just victory over Nazi Germany,[33] but also Stalin's creation of a seemingly modern economy, live in popular memory at a time when too close a scrutiny of his crimes is discouraged. Unlike the British and French, let alone the Turks and Austrians, post-imperial Russia is still potentially a great power, though not a superpower. That is partly because it has retained much of its nuclear arsenal but above all because it still holds Siberia, the jewel in the imperial crown and the source of enormous mineral and energy wealth. The post-1991 order in northern Eurasia was to a great extent created against Russia, with massive Russian minorities and some regions (above all Crimea),[34] which many Russians consider theirs by right, stranded outside the Russian Federation. Most of the former Soviet republics which border Russia are weak and unstable. No sensible Russian would wish to re-annex Central Asia with all its problems and its potential for mass emigration into Russia. Indirect influence makes much more sense. In any case, an increasingly formidable China needs to be reckoned with where relations with the Central Asian republics are concerned. The Ukraine, or at least Crimea, is possibly a more enticing target. Many Russians still barely regard Ukraine as a separate and independent country. Many more would probably welcome Crimea's return to Russia if this could be managed peacefully. On the other side of Ukraine, the European Union is a less formidable potential opponent than China. NATO has not guaranteed Ukrainian independence and would be unlikely to sustain that guarantee effectively even if it were made, not least because the main threats to Ukraine's viability come from within.

Under Putin Russia has flexed its muscles to a limited extent in its so-called "Near Abroad." In the Georgian case, it has challenged the territorial integrity of a former Soviet republic, though only under extreme and foolish provocation and with a plausible claim to be defending threatened ethnic minorities. Moscow has used "pipeline-power" to further not just economic but also security interests in the Near Abroad. The recent deal with Ukraine over the lease of Sevastopol is a case in point. It is, however, also a good example of relative moderation. The trade-off between the extension of the lease and cheap energy exports made good pragmatic sense, closed off a potentially very dangerous source of conflict and would probably have been supported by large majorities of Ukrainians and Russians. Moscow has used neither military power nor the Russian majority in Crimea to seek territorial revision, for all the emotional hold that Crimea and Sevastopol have on Russian identity. In fact, in almost all cases Moscow has been very restrained in seeking to emulate Hitler's Germany by mobilizing its post-imperial diaspora in the successor states to undermine political stability or the territorial settlement that followed empire.

For the moment, thoughts about challenging the 1991 settlement are geopolitical fantasies rather than practical politics. In the longer run, however, Russia's stance in international affairs will depend greatly on the global context. We are now in the second wave of liberal, Anglophone-dominated globalization. The first wave was severely wounded by the First World War and finished off by the Great Depression after 1929.[35] A number of basic factors make it unlikely that we will revert to the world of pre-1914 or the 1930s. Above all, the existence of nuclear weapons makes incredible the old idea that wars between great powers could result in victories whose benefits would outweigh the costs involved. It is probable that in the next generation, weapons of mass destruction will to some extent be privatized and fall into the hands of non-state actors. That will enhance the stress within states on security at the expense of liberty, but it seems unlikely to reduce the taboo on the use of nuclear weapons by states against each other. It could even have the opposite effect and strengthen inter-state nuclear cooperation. Islamic terrorists with weapons of mass destruction could after all choose to target the United States, Europe, India, Russia or China.

Also completely fundamental to contemporary international relations is the conviction that economic development requires access to the global capitalist economy. Even Russian leaders nostalgic for the Soviet Union do not believe in socialist planning or economic autarchy. For the public, foreign travel is a key benefit of the post-Soviet order. Access to the global capitalist economy is a big constraint on foreign policy adventures. But this constraint will only survive as long as liberal-capitalist globalization flourishes. The last two years have witnessed the vulnerability of its financial underpinnings without changing the basic rules of global finance or making a future crash much less likely. On the other hand, the financial resources and the credit which averted complete disaster in 2008–9 have been run down to such an extent that similar rescue efforts in the coming decade would be difficult to repeat. In the event of a second great depression, protectionist pressures will become increasingly hard to avoid. Liberal capitalism and globalization will lose their remaining appeal and legitimacy. To the extent that energy, water or other key commodities will be in increasingly short supply in the coming decades, the old logic of direct territorial control will in any case partly reassert itself even without a repetition of the 1930s depression.

Fears of environmental crisis and disputes as to who should pay the price to avoid it are already enlivening international relations. If that crisis becomes actual, international instability and conflict is bound to grow. The impact of environmental crisis is certain to differ enormously from one region of the world to another. But no country will be immune to the political and economic consequences of increased international instability and growing conflict for finite resources. We are all involved in the planet's race between shrinking resources and the new self-sustaining technologies which might safely replace them. A historian of empire has no special insights on this issue, though it is worth noting that environmental factors have on occasion in the past played a big role in undermining empires and civilizations.[36] But probably no international historian could ignore the fact that the first wave of liberal globalization was destroyed in large part by Germany's assault on an Anglophone-dominated global order of which by 1914 it was actually a major beneficiary. Currently the second wave of liberal globalization faces the challenge of preserving the global order's basic structures while adapting it to accommodate the Chinese and possibly other Asian powers too. In principle, reversing the last two hundred years of Western dominance and 'bringing in Asia' is a bigger challenge than integrating Germany into the first era of British-dominated liberal globalization was before 1914.

All of this may seem far-removed from discussion of Russian empire and its aftermath. But although the memory and legacies of empire may encourage Russia's rulers to act in certain ways, the pressures and constraints on them both within Russia and in the international context will largely depend on global forces which they will often barely be able to influence and to which they will to a considerable extent be forced to react. To some extent this is to repeat one of the key themes of this chapter, namely, the overriding importance of the international context in modern Russian history. Nevertheless, and even more than is normally the case, one should beware of too many predictions of future Russian behavior rooted in its history. It is undoubtedly true that history will influence Russian perceptions and policies in the coming decades. But much of Russian history in the last three hundred years was determined by the fact that Russia was one of the leading empires in a global order dominated by the European powers. It is by no means certain that this will be a useful guide to Russia's role in a world in which it will no longer be a first-class empire, and in which power is moving back towards Asia at a time when ecological crisis may be influencing international relations in a way unprecedented in the previous era of the Industrial Revolution.[37]

Notes

1. John Darwin refers instead to a British world-system and empire project rather than merely to the British Empire: Darwin, *The Empire Project*.
2. See, e.g., Munkler, *Empires*, pp. 1–17.
3. See, e.g., the discussion in Kuhn, *The Age of Confucian Rule*, pp. 45–8.
4. My definition remains the one first advanced in Lieven, *Empire*, p. xiv and "Empire, history and the contemporary global order," pp. 127–56. As those familiar with my earlier work will quickly realize, this present chapter differs markedly from earlier writings of mine in that it seeks to answer specific questions framed by the editors of this volume, while also reflecting my response to shifts in the literature and in the contemporary international context.
5. The Qing reveled both in their initial glory as conquerors and also in the multinational aspect of their empire. They made using one nationality to control others a key principle of their rule. See, e.g., Crossley, *A Translucent Mirror* and Hostetler, *Qing Colonial Enterprise*.
6. This list owes much to Mann, *The Sources of Social Power*.
7. The most commonly cited definition is probably that of Doyle, *Empires*, p. 30. His whole first chapter is a useful discussion of terminology.
8. Andreas Kappeler, e.g., stresses the extent to which for much of its existence the Romanov empire was in part a federation of aristocracies: Kappeler, *The Russian Empire*. For information specifically on the Russian aristocracy in a comparative context, see Lieven, "The elites," pp. 227–44.
9. There is a good, brief introduction to Ibn Khaldun's ideas in chapter 18 of Black, *The History of Islamic Political Thought*.
10. For a summary of recent debates on Manchu ethnicity and signification see Rowe, *China's Last Empire*, pp. 11–19.
11. Above all in Lenin, *Imperialism*.
12. For an interesting comparison of early Anglo-Dutch imperialism, see Ormrod, *The Rise of Commercial Empires*.
13. See, e.g., the discussion in Wortman, *Scenarios of Power*, pp. 22–4.
14. For a survey of the large and often excellent historiography of centre–periphery relations in the Ottoman Empire see Khoury, "The Ottoman centre versus provincial power-holders," pp. 135–56. On the Mughals see, e.g., Richards, *The Mughal Empire* and Gommans, *Mughal Warfare*.
15. See most recently, e.g., Lewis, *China's Cosmopolitan Empire*, pp. 48–50.
16. See Pipes, *Struve*.
17. I side with Charles Halperin on this: Halperin, *Russia and the Golden Horde*.
18. On this see, above all, Fuller, *Strategy and Power 1600–1914*. I discuss and illustrate this theme in Lieven, *Russia against Napoleon*.
19. Miller, *Britain and Latin America*.
20. See, e.g., Myers and Peattie (eds), *The Japanese Colonial Empire* and Matsusaka, *The Making of Japanese Manchuria*.

21. The bible on Soviet imperial modernization is by Martin, *The Affirmative Action Empire*.
22. For an excellent survey of the Russian empire's diversity see Miller, *The Romanov Empire and Nationalism*.
23. Janet Hartley puts the eighteenth-century Russian state in this context in Hartley, "Russia as a fiscal–military state, 1689–1825." Both her work and my *Russia against Napoleon* bear out the basic argument in Tilly, *Coercion, Capital and European States*.
24. On Alexander's reforms see Lincoln, *In the Vanguard of Reform* and Eklof, Bushnell and Zakharova (eds), *Russia's Great Reforms*.
25. On this see, in particular, Zubok, *A Failed Empire*.
26. Not a very politically correct comment and all the less so for coming from the last remnant of the old imperial ruling class still engaged in writing Russian history. Since no one else seems likely to make the point, however, I decided to do so.
27. On the mentalities and conceptions of the tsarist foreign policy elite see Lieven, *Russia and the Origins of the First World War*, pp. 83–101. On Soviet perceptions see Light, *The Soviet Theory of International Relations*.
28. For all the often excellent work written on the collapse of the USSR, in my opinion Hough, *Democratization and Revolution in the USSR 1985–1991* still stands out, not least for its combination of scholarship but also of a wonder at how events unrolled which comes most easily to someone who was closely involved at the time.
29. However, immigration from the former colonies can, as in Britain, create serious problems of internal security in the former metropole.
30. See, e.g., Lustick, *State-Building Failure*.
31. Out of an enormous literature, Carter Findley provides a balanced survey of the Ottoman-to-republican transition in chapter 5 of *The Turks in World History* and Meeker, *A Nation of Empire* provides, for a historian, an idiosyncratic anthropologist's insight.
32. See Stourzh, *Vom Reich zur Republik. Studien zur Österreichsbewusstein im 20 Jahrhundert*. On the ethnic conflicts which followed Austria's disintegration, see Dunn and Fraser (eds), *Europe and Ethnicity*.
33. On memory of the Second World War see Tumarkin, *The Living and the Dead* and Merridale, *Night of Stone*.
34. See, e.g., Sasse, *The Crimea Question*.
35. In his *The Great Interwar Crisis*, Robert Boyce correctly reminds us that although the Great War wounded liberal globalization it was the intellectual and political failures of the British and American leaders and their societies in the 1920s and 1930s that nearly destroyed it.
36. The ancestor of what is now a vast number of studies on empire and environment was Crosby, *Ecological Imperialism*. A very readable introduction to the link between ecology and one of the key turning points in global history is Rosen, *Justinian's Flea*.

37. Of the many efforts to relate Russian contemporary foreign policy to the imperial past, Legvold (ed.), *Russian Foreign Policy in the Twenty-first Century and the Shadow of the Past* is in my view among the most interesting.

3

The British and French Empires in the Arab World: Some Problems of Colonial State-formation and its Legacy

James McDougall

It has sometimes been suggested that the long-term significance of European imperialism in the Middle East and North Africa has been over-rated. The imperial "moment" in the region, compared with the almost two centuries of British dominance in South Asia, the expansion of Russian power into Central Asia from the mid-sixteenth century to the 1860s, or the long life-spans of Dutch rule in Southeast Asia or of the Portuguese in southern Africa, was apparently brief, its ambitions restricted and its impact limited. Turkey and Iran escaped colonialism, experiencing only brief periods of foreign military occupation (which in the Turkish case was ended by nationalist military victory), and, with the notable exception of Algeria, actual European rule came relatively late to the Arab world and was of relatively brief duration. Syria and Lebanon were evacuated, however unwillingly, by the French in 1946 after twenty-six years' presence, at least the last five (and arguably the last ten) of which consisted in the drawn out crisis of the mandate regime. In Iraq, "formal" empire lasted just thirteen years (1919–32). After a vicious war of conquest, "settled" Italian rule in Libya lasted only twelve years (1931–43), and the entire period from the invasion of Tripolitania to effective independence – the first in Africa – spanned only forty years (1911–51). Egypt's formal independence, declared unilaterally by Britain in 1922, ended an un-"veiled" protectorate of only eight years' duration, and although British military occupation itself long preceded and outlasted formal rule, its duration, some seventy years, was "only" the length of a single lifetime.[1]

But the limits of "formal" European empire in the Arab world should not disguise the further-reaching significance of the imperial "moment" and its less tangible as well as more obvious manifestations. To begin with, a fuller appreciation of the importance of imperialism in the region needs to take account not only of the interwar "moment," but also of

44

the longer chronologies of British intervention in the Gulf from 1809 to 1971 and of French occupation in North Africa from 1830 to 1962. And if Britain's occupation of Egypt in 1882 largely precipitated the scramble for Africa, that of Tunisia the previous year initiated a parallel period of French rule (1881–1956) in that country; the Franco-Spanish occupation of Morocco after 1912 would be the final chapter in the carve-up of the continent, so that the expansion of empire in the Arab world also bookends the larger partition of Africa. While imperialism may have served as a rhetorical scapegoat in Arab politics after formal decolonization, especially in the 1950s and 1960s, its symbolic resonance was not merely the creation of a demagogic populist nationalism. And the salience of imperialism in the region persists long after decolonization not because of an irrational and emotional propensity to "blame outsiders" for the region's persistent troubles, but because of its very real and long-term, structuring effects on political institutions and political cultures.[2] The long, slow attrition of Ottoman and other sovereignties in the region, and their sudden overwhelming in the "high tide" of European empire after 1918, had both deep-running and far-reaching effects.[3]

If the colonial period and its legacies have been important, however, specifying how they have been important, and how important they have been (and may remain), is not straightforward. On the macro-level, enumerating what colonial rule prevented – a united Arab state in historic Syria after 1919; the pursuit of autonomously directed modernizing state-building in Egypt and Tunisia after 1880; independent succession in post-Ottoman Libya, Iraq or the Gulf – is easier than evaluating the degree to which colonial rule enabled and constrained the possibilities of what did in fact follow from it. This chapter suggests that the significance of the European empires for the nature of post-colonial sovereignty in the Arab world is to be found in the patterns of colonial state formation that emerged from the local dynamics of territorially bounded polities, rather than in French and British grand strategy and their frustrating effects on Arab unity. Such patterns, however, are too diverse to allow for the identification of predictable sequences of cause and outcome measuring greater or lesser degrees of "stateness" according to typologies of imperial formation (colony, protectorate, "indirect" or "direct" rule and so on) that would produce corresponding levels of domestic or external self-determination. It is not the degree of post-imperial "stateness," calibrated against a standard of ideal–typical characteristics, that ought most to hold our attention. More fundamentally, we should consider the nature of the sovereignty that was embedded in the formation of colonial states themselves before being bequeathed to their successors. Sovereignty, however qualified, has not simply been the attribute of successor states to empires – throughout the Arab world, some form of sovereignty pre-existed European over-rule. In most cases, it persisted under colonialism, being reshaped in the interactions between imperial and local forces, interests and constraints, before emerging from decolonization. In the independent "new states," sovereignty took forms whose particular constitutional, institutional and territorial shapes varied considerably. Throughout the region, however, and more broadly, basic features of colonial state-formation durably influenced the nature of post-colonial sovereignty. Founded on the effective negation of the rule of law that it ostensibly upheld, the colonial state was an institutionalized state of exception whose particularity lay in its "sealing off" of the formal fiction of sovereignty that authorized the use of power from the effective use of power itself.[4] The "national" state that replaced it inherited this structural fact, leaving sovereignty, as effective ownership of the state by its people, as a deferred aspiration or ideological fiction, co-existing with unaccountable governance outside and beyond the rule of law.

Arab States and Nation(s)

Discussion of imperialism in the Arab world has often focused on the "artificial" division of a single Arab nation by the Versailles borders. A focus on the "illegitimate" borders of the separate Arab states emerging from the 1919 settlement has directed attention to the apparent opposition between *wataniyya* (local, territorial patriotism and the organization of politics within and between the "artificial" post-Ottoman states) and *qawmiyya* (supervening loyalty to a trans-local "Arab nation" and the organization of politics around the aspiration to its "unity"). However pre-occupying, this problem has, perhaps, proven to be something of a false trail.

First, the perception of the region as characterized by "artificial" successor states has often focused too narrowly on the post-Ottoman Mashriq, ignoring the wider Arab world of North Africa and the Gulf, and has tended, taking certain aspects of nationalist rhetoric perhaps too much at face value, to suppose that some more "natural" frontiers ought otherwise to have "naturally" existed. But even in the post-Versailles Arab east, this is far from self-evident. Both pre-colonial socio-political and economic factors and the unfolding of nationalist politics in the imperial era already tended to the "normalization" of the colonial borders rather than their overthrow in the "natural" achievement of pan-Arab unity. As Crawford Young observed for Africa, in the Middle East too "the capacity of the individual colonial territory to imprint its personality on its nationalist adversary" has been striking: "however alien the geographical grid of imperial partition, the logic of struggle compelled nationalist movements to embrace it."[5] Existing regional groups, especially urban elites in the existing provincial capitals of the Mashriq, could easily adopt a "new" geographical polity as the frame of their own political self-determination when it corresponded more or less to their already recognized *watan* (homeland, in the pre-national Arabic sense of the inhabited, known and claimed territory of a particular group). Though borders were drawn by the logic of imperial strategic and commercial interests and competition, in the Arab world (unlike in most of Africa) they often produced territories that could quickly be claimed as the political hinterlands of an already well-defined metropolis, and almost always defined areas that could relatively easily be made viable units of local political agency and identification: spaces in which rival constituencies could be created and which those constituencies would contest between themselves. This was most clear, if also ultimately most fraught, in the former *mutasarrifiyya* of Lebanon and its "greater" neighborhood, claimed as a national state by the Maronite community who actively lobbied for the French Mandate that would provide the frame for their self-determination. It was much less obvious in Libya, whose three different regions would ultimately be welded together only by an especially novel constitutional arrangement and the political economy of oil wealth redistribution. It was doubtless most problematic in Iraq.[6] But Palestine was imaginable to Palestinians from early in the Mandate as a distinct "south Syria," and long before that as a distinct territory centered administratively around the *sancak* of Jerusalem and economically around Jebel Nablus.[7] Transjordan existed before Churchill's high-handed "stroke of the pen" as an extended "frontier" zone of the late Ottoman state.[8] Egypt and the states of the Maghreb[9] were long-established territorial–political entities in the perception of their inhabitants as well as in the diplomatic recognition of other states since at least late medieval (for Morocco, Egypt) or early modern (for Algeria, Tunisia) times. Although, of course, the relation of polity to territory and population operated on very different principles in these pre-colonial states to those of the sharply defined and policed borders that they obtained only in the colonial period, the political spaces of the Arab states after empire were very largely foreshadowed in their pre-imperial or Ottoman era shape.

Second, much recent scholarship on nationalism in the Arab world has illustrated the diversity and simultaneity of constructions of nationalism as political projects carried by different social constituencies, demonstrating the existence throughout the twentieth century of a rich symbolic and practical universe of political imaginations that the older, essentialist notions of a single, "really real" Arab nation in conflict with "artificial" states cannot grasp.[10] The corollary of the older view of territorial "artificiality" for the meanings of post-imperial sovereignty in the region – that "the nation" and "the state" are incongruent, or even antithetical, and that this fact has posed an insuperable limit to the integrity of "stateness" in the region and to the stability of the state system – needs to be rethought in the light of these subtler arguments about nationalism, as well as in view of the undeniable durability and overall stability of the states concerned since their "artificial" construction now almost a century ago. "Arabism" as an expression of trans-local aspirations to solidarity and (some form of) unity has in fact, over the long term, remained important not as a utopian doctrine of hollow "ideological politics" (in Kedourie's pejorative sense), but as a meaningful component of locally situated political languages operating in a trans-regionally shared-and-contested discursive field. It is the *co-existence* and complementarity rather than the apparent antinomy between *qawm* and *watan*, between nationalist ethno-politics and the operative state-structures within which they have taken shape and found expression, that ought to hold our attention. Arabism, in this view, has actually operated as an expression of distinct states' (or state elites' and institutions') interests and aspirations to pre-eminence in normal "anarchic competition." And it provides an ideological – in the Geertzian sense of a shared symbolic system – register of legitimacy largely accepted by all social strata and usable among them, not only by official propagandists to shore up authoritarian and unaccountable regimes but by society to express its political subjectivity irrespective of the vapidity of official rhetoric.[11] The putative problem of post-imperial stateness in this regard, at least, seems to have been illusory.

Patterns of the Colonial State

Perhaps, then, such questions are not the most telling ones to ask of the significance of empire and its repercussions on post-imperial sovereignty. Perhaps it is not so much the macro-structural imperial relationship, but that of the localized colonial state, its relation to a wider imperial space and the dimensions of its reach into and relations with society that should most hold our attention. The best grounds on which to situate comparative historical analysis may be found in patterns of state formation, in the ways that institutions "from above" impinge on local social relations, the ways that local power relations, interests, resources and constraints influence the form taken by institutions and the way in which the state as a "claim to domination" emerges, or fails to emerge, from such interactions as an effective ideological project.[12]

Such questions have generated intense debate in other areas of historical research, notably in African history. Crawford Young's account of the colonial state in Africa as *bula matari* ("crusher of rocks"), a distinctively "crushing, relentless force" whose characteristics became "embedded" in Africa and remain at the root of the continent's post-colonial crisis; Achille Mbembe's analysis of the post-colonial syndrome of authoritarianism and its "aesthetics of vulgarity" born of the unaccountable and arbitrary colonial practices of *commandement*; and Mahmood Mamdani's diagnosis of late colonial indirect rule's legacy of "decentralized despotism," have all in their different ways contributed powerful arguments to assessments of the colonial state as the foundation not only of the post-colonial African state but of its contemporary crisis.[13]

Other accounts have suggested that colonial states in Africa were more limited in their dimensions and effects: that their power (adapting Foucault's metaphor) was "arterial" rather than "capillary" (concentrated in core areas with little capacity for projection across space or infiltration into the domains of everyday life); that their inheritance in the era of nation-state sovereignty lies in their role as "gatekeeper" across strategic pathways of resource distribution; and that reading the "crisis" of the state from the 1970s onwards directly back into the "high" colonial period risks positing a "leapfrogging legacy" that bounds over more complex developments in the post-Second World War era, especially the continuities of state-led developmentalism and its politics of citizenship and redistribution.[14] In addition, this argument runs, we ought not to posit too linear a transition from late colonial forms of rule to national sovereignty as if the latter were as "natural" and pre-determined as nationalists themselves suppose; nation-state independence in the form and along the lines actually achieved was not always the only imaginable outcome, and in some cases perhaps not the likeliest.[15]

The debate over the nature and extent of colonial states has also drawn on legal and administrative history to argue not only that colonialism was "interactively" constructed, but that it was often significantly constrained by reliance on its intermediaries as well as by its own legal procedures and pretensions to "reform" and "good government," whose forms were often diligently preserved even when they became grotesquely absurd façades to mask the most widespread atrocities. At the same time, other work has shown that the arbitrary and unaccountable nature of colonial coercion constructed in a domain of conscious *extra*-legality could, nonetheless, be a central and enduring "core" of the colonial state until, or almost until, its very end.[16] Some of the best work on these questions has elucidated the "enduring legacies from the colonial regime that [have] constituted structures persisting as those of the [contemporary] state."[17]

Many of these insights might productively be applied to the Middle East. An equivalent critical mass of scholarship, especially in sustained comparative colonial history, has (surprisingly) not yet really emerged for the Arab world, and a few, necessarily broad-brush, considerations of these problems will have to suffice here. The nature and extent of colonial states' power, their legal–constitutional shape and the position of intermediaries in their operation, the institutional forms in which society encountered the state and in which the state sought to govern society, indicate a variety of patterns of state-formation. Underlying these can be found a more general pattern of colonial "stateness" and its relation to sovereignty.

In the Gulf, imperial over-rule was longest but also "lightest." The merchant cities of the Trucial Coast, in their rise from modest regional trading entrepôts to global hubs of oil-and-finance capitalism, have owed their "stateness" in part, of course, to conjunctures of geology, demography and the world economy. But the shape (in both the stability and the conservatism) of the Gulf is due also to the persistence through the colonial period of a system of regional relations and local political cultures that existed before the region's incorporation into the British (or better, British Indian) imperial orbit, which the colonial state in general did little to disturb and which to a great extent enabled the colonial state to exist as it did. The pre-1853 relation of the Gulf states to one another in a regional trading system, which the British-sponsored treaty system after 1853 formalized, stabilized and policed, the system of *dakhala* (territorially-based zones of protection) as a normative code of sovereignty, local dynastic precedence and a marked local social hierarchy, fitted together in a system of state–society relations which was preserved under imperial rule. At least until the end of the nineteenth century, indeed, imperial rule only functioned because it effectively insinuated itself into, and as the apex of, this system, which was largely run by the local merchant notability who provided the British resident's indispensable "native agents."[18] After a closer relationship was instituted by the treaty of 1892, British regional pre-eminence preserved the system as far as possible against threats to it, of which the revolutionary Dhofar revolt in 1962–75, crushed by British special forces and the British-officered Omani sultan's armed forces, was the only really serious challenge. In the Gulf, it was not so much the nature of the colonial state but the absence of a properly colonial state, the crystallization of existing social order rather than its dislocation, that is most striking. "Development" and "reform," the watchwords of empire elsewhere since the mid-1940s, would not reach Oman until the crisis in Dhofar pre-cipitated Sultan Qabus' coup in 1970 which, with British backing, finally began a campaign of "modernization" to prevent the region "falling" to communism.

Egypt and Tunisia offer an almost diametrically contrasting experi-ence. In both countries, indigenous projects of modernizing state-building begun in the first half of the nineteenth century were well advanced before they were themselves colonized by the strategic and economic interests of imperial intervention. In both cases, of course, financial overstretch (under highly unequal terms of credit) by the sovereign state-builders of the Husaynid and Mehmet Ali dynasties were instrumental in the downfall of their independence, but so, too, in both cases were imperial calculations of security (for the Algerian frontier and for Suez, respec-tively). In both cases, however, the colonial state overlaid local governing structures. In part, this meant supplanting existing state structures and the local intermediaries who staffed them, especially in Tunisia, where the system of Parisian-trained *contrôleurs civils* extended the bureaucratic state throughout the country by superimposing itself over the reformed structure of the pre-protectorate provincial *qiyada*s. In part (more par-ticularly in Egypt), it meant paralleling the existing offices of the state and its ruling class.[19] In Tunisia, colonial settlement, based especially on the highly interventionist state's marketing of *habus* (*awqaf*) land, and the vocal *colons'* demands, in their press and in the representation on the elected Grand Council granted them in 1922, meant that a situation somewhat analogous to that in Algeria – an exclusive ethnic democracy for Europeans, with the Tunisian population subordinated to its interests and domination of both polity and market – emerged.[20] In Egypt, the pre-existing landowner class created by the mid-nineteenth century reforms and 1860s cotton boom was the main constituency engaged in the political system established under the monarchy by the 1923 liberal constitution, providing (in the Wafd) the main antagonist to the colonial state as well as (in the "palace politicians") its main interlocutor. For ordinary people in both countries, irrespective of the legal niceties of the purely diplo-matic and "advisory" status of Britain's "Consul General" in Cairo or France's "Resident" in Tunis, the overriding fact of the colonial state was its externality and unaccountability, its "belonging" to foreign interests and its unhesitating repression of the country's own people, as Dinshaway in 1906, then the repression of the 1919 revolution demonstrated to Egyptians, and as the punitive response to the Jellaz protests in 1911, then the shooting of demonstrators in April 1938 proved to Tunisians.

The protectorate states in Syria and Lebanon were also, of course, capable of extreme coercion, as the French shelling of Damascus in 1925, killing perhaps 1,500 people in three days,[21] amply demonstrated. Their various strategies of division, between city and countryside, region, sect and "ethnic" group, are well known, and all contributed to the ultimate crisis of the mandate state from 1936 onwards, to Syrians' resentment of it and to the frictions that would plague the Lebanese republic for decades afterward. These same colonial states, however, can be seen to have instituted, in Elizabeth Thompson's terms, a kind of "civic order" within which local politics played out. The republican constitutions of 1926 in Lebanon and 1930 in Syria "explicitly granted basic rights of citizenship to all inhabitants," enabling "engagement with the state through elected parliaments and rights to free speech and association." In everyday engagements with the state "in schools, streets, public clinics, and post offices," in this view, Syrian and Lebanese men and women shaped the terms of their "colonial citizenship" and laid the ground for the post-independence political order.[22] At the same time, of course, the "civic order" was not a perfectly equal "open space" free for all: Sunni grandees, ᶜAlawi peasants and Kurdish townspeople held markedly different positions in the "order" of things and overlapping regional, sectarian and class distinctions, the emergence of new political communities of "majority" and "minority" groups (a new language in the world after 1919),[23] as well as the patterns of recruitment into the bureaucracy, the gendarmerie, and the *Troupes Spéciales*, also contributed to the making both of the colonial state and of the contentious politics that would succeed it.

In contrast to the "civic order" emerging in the Levant, in Libya the throttling of the Tripolitanian Republic's (1918–20) experiment in autonomous political representation, and the too brief life of a liberal "colonial citizenship" envisaged by the *legge fondamentale*,[24] laid the foundation not for citizenship and statehood but for what Dirk Vandewalle diagnoses as a long-term condition of "statelessness."[25] The notables who backed the Tripolitanian Republic had too narrow a social base, limited to the minuscule late-Ottoman professional and notable elite in the west of the country, many of whom quickly went into exile after 1920. The Sanusi resistance movement in the Jebel al-Akhdar and the desert had a much firmer social footing and lasted much longer (until the execution of Omar al-Mukhtar in 1931), but it was never capable of creating a counter-state. Indeed, the Sanusi monarchy, while distrusting political parties (which existed at least in embryo or in exile before independence, but were banned immediately after it), lacked the capacity or the will to reinvent itself as the core of a state-building project even when it found itself at the head of the state after 1951. The impact of the Italian state, especially in the near-genocidal conditions of the repression of the Sanusi insurrection in Cyrenaica, was uniformly destructive.[26] The process of transition to independence under the aegis of the United Nations was governed more by consideration of the military basing rights that an independent kingdom (as opposed to a UN Trusteeship) could give the United States and Britain[27] than by the development of real state structures or active political engagement with them by society.

In Algeria, to draw another contrast, the colonial state was apparently anything but absent. It was clearly defined, dense and simultaneously coercive and exclusive. Algerians, once their legal status was regulated in 1865, were its "nationals" but not (except for an infinitesimally small number until 1919, and for a small minority thereafter) its citizens.[28] In the cities of the coast and the major interior towns, and in the heavily colonized plains and valleys of the north, Algerian society lived in daily contact and constant (highly unequal) negotiation with "European" society and the French state. At the same time, however, most Algerians lived in the large "mixed communes" of the countryside where their taxes supported colonial municipalities too small to provide for themselves. These immense territories of the country's interior and mountains were barely touched by colonial settlement, its communications networks, its infrastructure or its administration. Until 1944, interactions with the state were mostly regulated by the special repressive regulations of the *indigénat* ("native regime"), which provided for summary "justice" dispensed by local administrators. It was in these "under-administered" rural areas that the revolution first gained ground after November 1954 and there, from 1955, that the colonial state suddenly appeared in force to resettle and "pacify" the population. Against this late colonial reconquest of Algeria's people and territory, the *Front de Libération Nationale* (FLN) set up a revolutionary counter-state in exile, which by 1960, despite its embattled military position within Algeria, could claim to have established itself as the legitimate expression of a mass aspiration to Algerian sovereignty.

In contrast, again, in Morocco, the extension of the *makhzen*'s effective sovereignty begun by Mawlay Hasan in the late nineteenth century would ultimately be completed by the French. A French army largely consisting of Moroccan soldiers "pacified" the Atlas and the pre-Sahara in the consolidation of the Protectorate state up to 1934. Apparently crippled in 1912 by the instability and civil war brought about by internal conflict and imperial encroachment, Morocco's dynasty and its state nonetheless survived; the ostensible preservation and strengthening of the *makhzen* imagined by the French as an enlightened policy of "association" turned ultimately, despite their intentions, into a real "reverse" colonization of the colonial state by the dynasty and its own elite. The colonial state's refusal to sanction the representative party politics that would have carried the urban nationalist notability to pre-eminence, its creation, instead, of a rallying symbol in the exiled sultan Muhammed ben Yusuf, and the latter's adroit maneuvering and mass following, set the institutional scene and provided the symbolic capital for the autocratic monarchy that succeeded to the colonial state at independence. While prominent nationalists from the protectorate-era opposition would become merely leading political figures, either (on the right) fêted and promoted but mostly deprived of substantive decision-making power or (on the left) mercilessly repressed, the key strongmen of the "new" regime would be those like Muhammad Oufkir who had learned their trade in the colonial state.[29] Those ordinary Moroccans who had most tenaciously resisted the colonial state and, as in the Rif, objected to the manner of their incorporation in the newly assertive kingdom, were vigorously suppressed.

The pattern of the state, and the characteristics of state–society relations, thus took a variety of forms across the region. The colonial state sometimes doubled or overlaid existing state structures; it sometimes insinuated itself within existing structures, instrumentalizing them but in the process fortifying them and extending their reach as never before; elsewhere it invented wholly new structures having removed existing ones.

What of colonial settlement? If we describe a simple spectrum of colonial situations roughly from west to east across the Arab world, a broader overall pattern emerges. At one extreme sits the unparalleled (in the Arab world) duration and intensity of the colonial experience in Algeria, from the decapitation of the *beylik* in 1830 through the prolonged wars of conquest up to 1870 and the installation thereafter of a regime of "ethnic democracy" dominated by a slowly coalescing European settler community determined to preserve its (meager enough) privilege on the back of the almost complete expropriation and *clochardisation* (reduction to rags) of the Algerian population. Juridically, the annexation of Algeria's civil territory to metropolitan France in 1848 – a revolutionary and democratic demand of the French left and the settlers against the hated domination of a reactionary military regime – created an almost unique constitutional blurring of metropolitan and overseas colonial territory.[30] In no other Arab territory, except, of course, in Palestine, was an existing government entirely removed at a stroke and replaced with a colonial state for incoming settlers founded on the perpetual exclusion of the majority community from equal citizenship.

Its Maghrebi neighbors, though, combined elements of the Algerian experience with some form of perpetuation, appropriation and extension of existing state structures. The protectorate regime in Tunisia and also, to a lesser extent, that in Morocco, evolved towards a state dominated by colonial commercial and landed interests under the auspices of a preserved dynastic monarchy. In the Tunisian case, a representative assembly in which settler constituencies were preponderant provided after 1922 the framework for "reformed" colonial rule, and in both protectorates (as at certain times, around the First World War and especially after 1958, in Algeria) a principal concern of the administration was the question of managing elected settlers' demands against paternal preoccupations with the plight of the *indigènes*. The other settler colony of the Maghreb, Libya, never developed as far, and with the exception of the brief "liberal period" from 1919 to 1921, no such concern with balancing indigenous with settler representation troubled the colonial regime there. But the time span of effective colonial settlement there was very short.[31]

Aside from the rather different cosmopolitan society of Alexandria, no comparably substantial settler population emerged – or, given its quite different population density, was imaginable – further east in Egypt, where the symbols of colonial occupation (and the targets of popular anger in early 1952) were Shepheard's Hotel and the Geniza Sporting Club rather than the small farms that covered the Maghrebi countryside. The British occupation, though, did destroy an existing government even if it claimed to preserve the state, and the ostensible protection of the khedive served as a thin veil over a protectorate run by a viceroy whose administration's primary function, besides guaranteeing the repayment of debt and securing productive investments, was to maintain British global strategic primacy through control of the Suez Canal. Strategic and commercial interests also predominated elsewhere where previously existing governments were removed (as in Syria where the post-Ottoman Arab state of the Amir Faisal was swept away in 1920 to make room for the French Protectorate), relocated (as in Transjordan and Iraq, the Hashemite dynasty's "compensation prizes" for Syria awarded them by the British), or preserved (as in the emirates of "Trucial Oman" in the Gulf). The presence or absence of settler colonialism, on one level, clearly marks two distinct types of colonial state.

At the same time, however, constitutional commonalities cutting across all these distinctions perhaps mattered more. No Arab territory (not even the Western Sahara) was a *terra nullius* without established sovereignty before imperial intervention. Aside from the tiny foothold of Aden, which constantly had to negotiate or assert its co-existence with the tribes of its hinterland and the imamate in Yemen, and the exceptional cases of Algeria and Libya, where prior sovereignty was terminated by *force majeure* or by diplomatic renunciation,[32] all colonial states in the Arab world, as we have seen, acted under the ostensible aegis of a super-ordinate authority other than the source of their own (metropolitan) sovereignty – the Moroccan sultan or Tunisian bey, the king of Egypt, the *shaykhs* of the Qasimi confederation, or, after 1920, the mandating authority of the League of Nations. All such colonial states in the Middle East (unlike in sub-Saharan Africa, whose pre-colonial states rarely enjoyed such consideration[33]) therefore remained to some degree expressions of the highly unbalanced, but still formally respected, international states system in which local sovereignties might be "protected" or "assisted" but could no longer, after 1880, simply be undone by force once they had established themselves (as Faisal's kingdom notably failed to do[34]). When British administrators refused the representation of Egypt at Versailles in 1919 and exiled the leaders of the Wafd, as when in 1914 they deposed the khedive and appointed a "sultan" in his place, making it plain that "the Egyptian question" was "imperial" rather than properly international,[35] they made overt the implicit subordination of an occupied sovereignty to imperial interests. But there were no grounds on which that sovereignty could simply be liquidated, and this was more than a nicety. No British high commissioner in Cairo could himself have occupied the Abdin palace, though he could (and in 1942 did) put tanks around it; no more could the French government have annexed Tunisia as a *département* of the metropole, as they had the three *beyliks* of Algeria, though they could, and did, both threaten one bey with troops (Muhammad al-Nasir Bey, in 1922) and depose another (Munsif Bey, in 1943).[36]

While the hard facts of material interests that the state represented were always very obviously foreign ones, therefore, they were also almost everywhere "nested" either under the shell of existing *de iure* indigenous sovereignty, or (in the case of the mandates) under the internationally guaranteed promise of an indigenous sovereignty existing in principle and to be attained at "maturity." All such states thus represented in an important sense, beneath the legitimizing rhetoric of transitional "tutelage" on the way towards (however long-deferred) eventual complete independence and self-determination, expressions of a foreign but "real" governing power whose defining feature was its simultaneous denial of, and necessary co-existence with, an indigenous but "fictional" sovereignty. "Sovereignty" in the Arab world thus did not simply succeed empire; it always co-existed uneasily with it. Sovereignty, or rather its shadow, sat "spectrally" alongside, or hovered unquietly over, empire's more solid form.

Degrees of Separation

How significant did this *pays réel* of the colonial state, so distinct from but co-existent with the *pays légal* of sovereignty in which its authority supposedly lay, remain for people who had once fallen under its rule? In one respect, this uneasy relationship of sovereignty and empire contributed to the perceived illegitimacy of the "local" state which a fuller realization of Arab self-determination was expected to sweep away in the long-awaited achievement of unity and "complete independence." But as we have seen, the states embedded within the colonial borders would prove to be durable, whether those borders defined the boundaries of pre-colonial polities (as in North Africa and the peninsular emirates) or created substantially "new states" as in Iraq and *bilad al-sham*. Indeed, the politics of nationalism articulating programs of "unity" and independence themselves contributed to the "Westphalian" states' durability and to the lines of conflict (of left versus right, republics versus monarchies, United Arab Republic versus Arab Union, Algeria versus Morocco, Egypt versus Iraq, Ba^cath versus Ba^cath, and so on) that divided them in the post-imperial era. Instead of being more "really" realized in overcoming (or democratizing) these "artificial" state structures, even after the overthrow of the compromised *anciens régimes* by young Free Officers and their populist coalitions – and their construction of new authoritarianisms – sovereignty, as "ownership" of the state by its people, remained a "spectral" shadow, a formal shell or a deferred aspiration, covering an exercise of power that, even when thoroughly embedded in a state's longstanding relation to local society, could nonetheless still be perceived as "foreign."

Here, a further question arises as to the identification and significance of the "intervening variable" of "rupture": how do we evaluate the importance (and the limits) of formal transfers of sovereignty such as those to Egypt and Iraq in 1922 and 1932, respectively, relative to the revolutions of 1952 and 1958? Is the rupture that matters in the Arabian peninsula less formal British decolonization c.1970 than the shift to American primacy in regional economic and security relations that had begun thirty years earlier? Or, indeed, the disappearance of Ottoman rule, the waning of Hashemite fortunes and the emergence of Saudi Arabia earlier still? How do we assess the relationship between the political rupture represented by the Algerian war of independence (1954–62) and the socio-economic continuity of labor migration that reached its greatest volume during and after the years of the war? Did the "rupture" that mattered, even in this case, occur less with the departure of the European settler *pieds noirs* and the accession to independence in 1962 than with the nationalization of sub-soil resources and French oil interests in 1971? Such questions are probably unanswerable. What matters, perhaps, is less defining the moment and the nature of the break than assessing the ability of state institutions, and the relationships between society and such institutions, or the pattern of relations between real power and formal/fictive sovereignty, to endure across the break, whether this was drawn-out, violent and traumatic or rapid, negotiated and peaceful.

In this regard, perhaps surprising continuities as well as predictable changes emerge from even the briefest survey. Where the intermediary positions of local groups in the colonial state were entirely delegitimized by the process of decolonization, the rupture was very sharp and painful. The Algerian landowning and notable families that had survived the nineteenth century and had not made the transition away from dependence on the colonial system, or, at the opposite end of the scale, the rural *qa'ids* and *adjoints*, petty officials like rural constables or policemen, or the "self-defense" militia and contracted auxiliary soldiers (*moghaznis* and *harkis*) recruited during the war of independence, were the FLN's primary targets during the revolution and suffered often terrible retribution at independence. The property and persons of the Moroccan 'great *qa'ids*', most notoriously the Glawi family of Marrakesh who had played a prominent role in the 1953 deposition of the sultan, were set upon with delighted abandon by their erstwhile "flock" on the departure of the French.

Even in Morocco and Algeria, though, where independence followed outright armed struggle, the "break" in this respect was far from total. As already discussed, the Moroccan *makhzen* emerged, strengthened beyond recognition, from the Protectorate to be recuperated by the preserved Alawi dynasty, which lost no time in deploying its formidably enhanced policing and repressive apparatus to entrench the monarchy at the core of the independent state. The rural notables who had held onto their positions under the Protectorate, not the urban patricians who had led the politics of nationalism, became the key supports of the throne throughout the country.[37] While subaltern Algerian militiamen who remained too long in French uniform were massacred or interned in draconian labor camps in 1962, Algerian officers of the regular French army, better able to catch the drift of events at the critical juncture and "desert" in time, successfully inserted themselves into the revolutionary army. In conjunction with the military security apparatus that was already emerging as the real center of power, they were able to carve an important niche for themselves near the core of the regime.[38] At a very different level, labor flows and educational patterns in revolutionary Algeria remained to a large degree tied to France as they did in Morocco and in Tunisia, whose decolonization, despite the violence of settler terrorism in 1952–4, was achieved by agreed negotiation with a new nationalist elite whose relations on every level remained close to the former metropole. It was not the French but the Tunisian nationalist leadership, with the victory of Bourguiba over Ben Youssef in the neo-Destour, who put a stop to armed struggle in Tunisia against the resistance of those who supported a wider, pan-Maghrebi and pan-Arab struggle. In contrast, in Egypt, the establishment middle- and upper-classes' early adherence to nationalist politics in the 1920s, along-side their preservation of material and social capital, and their expression of a sophisticated Arabism that made Egypt the cultural and intellectual as well as the political center of the Arab world, did not save them from being ousted after 1952.

The nature of decolonization itself is clearly important for overt forms of national symbolism, languages of legitimacy, public ritual, political culture and even the distribution of privileges, but it is clearly not the whole story. The late colonial period in the Maghreb and the correspond-ing "liberal period" in the Mashriq – in Egypt after 1923, in Syria and Lebanon the Ottoman "second constitutional period" after 1908, then the parliamentarism of the mandates, in Iraq from 1936 to 1958, even in Algeria to a degree after 1919 and more especially after 1946 – was perhaps often more important than the "rupture" with empire itself for defining the parameters, ambitions and nature of post-imperial politics. (In this case the parallel with a late-colonial developmentalist period in Africa, and the political possibilities it entailed, is pertinent).[39] Without for a moment idealizing a time that was also marked by repression, violence and, as already noted, the sharp limits imposed by colonial states to the constitutional politics they claimed to promote, it was nonetheless in this period of class formation, mass mobilization, emerging mass media, plu-ralist politics, the open confrontation of competing agendas, worldviews and programs, that the characteristics of political life and the shapes of constituencies (exclusions from as well as inclusions in the system), took shape, bargains and practices were worked out, and the political life of Arab countries coalesced within the structures of the states imposed upon them and to which they adapted. It was in this period, more perhaps than in that of decolonization itself (which more usually, especially in the tense 1950s, closed down spaces of open political activity), that popular politics were simultaneously both incorporated into emerging public spaces and excluded from gaining a meaningful hold upon the state itself.

Through these transformations, sovereignty remained deferred and "spectral," with the rulers persistently "foreign" to the people even as popular mass politics took hold. Across the Arab world, whether the colonial state created its institutions *de novo* or worked through an existing infrastructure, and whether the "transfer of power" was a matter of ceremonially lowering flags or of fighting a protracted war, the legacy of colonial state-formation lay more basically, and more enduringly, in the commonality of a particular configuration of power and authority common across the various and changing patterns of the state itself and its relation to society. Everywhere in the Arab world, with the exception of the particular case of Libya and to some extent that of Algeria,[40] colonial power "sat atop" or "nested within" existing socio-political structures. Arab societies in the colonial period were, paradoxically, always in this sense stronger than the state, more visibly so in Egypt, Syria or Lebanon but even in Algeria, where a subjugated and impoverished society overcame the dominant society's minority rule and the state forces arrayed in defense of it, even at the cost of being materially shattered itself. The state was ultimately obliged to subvert its own ostensibly liberal principles – to preserve its monopoly of force at the expense of its legitimacy – when mass politics forced the inherent contradiction between foreign domination and indigenous sovereignty to the forefront of the scene.

The struggle to hold the line, of course, ultimately proved too much for the post-Second World War powers' straitened resources and restricted autonomy in a new international system where they no longer carried decisive weight. The centers of power established by the colonial state were then taken over, at least in part, by elites emerging from within the institutions of the state itself; they had been produced by it, had preserved themselves through it, or had been preserved by it. The limits of popular enfranchisement and the preservation of the colonial state's *dirigiste*, unaccountable practices of governance (often more widely and fully implemented than had ever been possible for the relatively limited "arterial" capacities of the colonial state), including coercion alongside "development," kept the state in hands "foreign" to popular sovereignty even as it spoke the language of popular nationalism and especially when it was captured by "sons of the country" socialized into custodially-minded military institutions. The colonial state had almost always already co-existed with "notional" sovereignty – its "constitutionally" defining feature (again with the *sui generis* exception of Libya and the partial exception of Algeria) was that real power and formal sovereignty co-existed without being co-extensive. It was a state founded on rule in negation of its own ostensible "law" (the fiction of a sovereignty which it preserved or for which it prepared), not on the rule of law – and this was the determining characteristic inherited by the post-colonial state.

Specters of Sovereignty

The "anomalies" in Arab stateness connoted by imposed borders and external dependence are perhaps not the obstacles to sovereignty that they seem. They are also perhaps less significant as direct correlations of colonialism than is a more basic feature of the pattern of internal state-formation in the region: the constitution of effective rule in the polity as fundamentally detached from formal, law-bound sovereignty, even when this is notionally its guarantor and sanction. "Empire" itself in the Arab world was less important, as a trans-regional or global, macro-structural relation (though this *was* important, especially in framing the language and symbolism of nationalist politics) than were the particular processes of colonial state-formation in framing – simultaneously enabling and constraining – local political practice and state–society relations. But the diverse patterns in which colonial states related to society were themselves, ultimately, less significant overall than was the basic fact of the colonial state as a foreign domination co-existing with a principle of sovereignty that it voided of its substance,[41] and the perpetuation of this institutionally embedded fact after the departure of foreign troops and administrators.

As the form of "sovereignty" was embedded within the fact of colonial rule, so the form of "colonialism," as unaccountable government by "others," has persisted within the structures of the post-colonial successor state. Anti-imperialism, whether on the radical left in decades past or on the Islamist right more recently, has continued to resonate in the region not only because of the longstanding consequences of empire (especially in Palestine), but because of the degree to which contemporary sovereignties themselves continue to be inhabited by it, not only in their "allegiance" to external powers but in their very constitution as states that have yet to 'belong' meaningfully to their people. A certain "foreignness" persists in the nature of the national polity, notwithstanding and indeed within the (sectional) social embeddedness and indigeneity of the state. The co-existence of a "spectral" national sovereignty with the persistent disenfranchisement of the people from "their" state is the enduring kernel of empire within the post-colonial polity. As any Algerian taxi driver can tell you, speaking of his nation's hard-won sovereignty (and the phrase is presumably the same in other idioms elsewhere in the region), '*C'est pas à nous. C'est à* eux' ('It's not ours; it belongs to *them*').

Notes

1. The undeclared ("veiled") protectorate over Egypt that began with the British occupation in 1882 was formalized in 1914.

2. The argument that imperialism (and Israel) have been merely external scape-
    goats for internal failings and foils for emotional "ideological politics" has
    been made most persistently by Kedourie, *Politics in the Middle East* and
    Lewis, *What Went Wrong?*
3. Palestine, of course, presents a special case, in which the independence of
    the Yishuv after thirty years of British occupation consolidated a new settler-
    colonial state at the expense of the Palestinians, a state whose colonial reach
    would be expanded in 1967 and especially after 1977, to survive after the
    end of the White minority regimes in southern Africa as the world's last
    established "successful" settler state.
4. For a sophisticated exploration of forms of empire as "macropolities
    whose technologies of rule thrive on the production of exceptions and
    their uneven and changing proliferation," see Stoler, "Degrees of imperial
    sovereignty."
5. Young, *The African Colonial State in Comparative Perspective*, p. 241.
6. Vandewalle, *A History of Modern Libya*; Dodge, *Inventing Iraq*; Simon,
    "The imposition of nationalism"; Zubaida, "Contested nations: Iraq and the
    Assyrians" and "The fragments imagine the nation."
7. Pappé, *A History of Modern Palestine*, pp. 25–9; Doumani, *Rediscovering
    Palestine*.
8. Rogan, *Frontiers of the State in the late Ottoman Empire*; Robins, *A History
    of Jordan*, ch. 1.
9. With the exception of Libya, whose three distinct regions were "statelets"
    unto themselves even after independence, until the 1963 constitutional
    revision abandoned federalism.
10. See, e.g., Gelvin, *Divided Loyalties*; Jankowski and Gershoni (eds),
    Rethinking Nationalism in the Arab Middle East; Bashkin, *The Other Iraq*,
    ch. 4; and articles by Wien, Provence, Bashkin, Wrytzen and McDougall in
    "Relocating Arab nationalism." For nationalism's relation to colonialism,
    see Cole and Kandiyoti, "Nationalism and the colonial legacy in the Middle
    East and Central Asia: Introduction."
11. This is not to deny that, like other nationalisms, Arabism has been turned to
    demagogy and the official *langue de bois* in which, as the Syrian poet Nizar
    Qabbani famously put it, "They thunder and do not rain / They go into wars
    and do not come out again / They chew the tough hide of rhetoric and do
    not digest it." But as well as being an empty shell, a soundbox for trumpet-
    ing hollow and self-serving platitudes, as Qabbani himself and the response
    to his work demonstrated, the idiom of Arabism has also been recuperable
    as a language of protest and resistance against the regimes of "nationalist"
    oppression that have sought to monopolize it for their own perpetuation.
    The very resonance of Qabbani's "When will they announce the death of
    the Arabs?" demonstrated the vitality, in the mid-1990s, of the idiom whose
    exhaustion and corruption he raged against.
12. Abrams, "Notes on the difficulty of studying the state."

13. Young, *The African Colonial State in Comparative Perspective*; Mbembe, *On the Postcolony*; Mamdani, *Citizen and Subject*.

14. Cooper, *Africa since 1940* and *Colonialism in Question*.

15. Cooper, "Possibility and constraint."

16. For law as constitutive of the colonial state, see notably Benton, "Colonial law and cultural difference" and Roberts, *Litigants and Households*. On intermediaries, Osborn, " 'Circle of iron' "; Lawrence, Osborn and Roberts (eds), *Intermediaries, Interpreters, and Clerks*; Spear, "Neo-traditionalism and the limits of invention in British colonial Africa." For the centrality of extra-legal coercion, Mann, "What was the *indigénat*?" For a different case, in which extreme repression labored to "maintain . . . the appearance of accountability, transparency, and justice," see Anderson, *Histories of the Hanged*, p. 6. For law as façade, see the account of legal process in Halimi and De Beauvoir, *Djamila Boupacha*, and the case of the French government's "Commission to Safeguard Human Rights" in Algeria during the war of independence (Branche, "La commission de sauvegarde pendant la guerre d'Algérie").

17. Pierce, "Looking like a State," pp. 888–9.

18. Onley, *The Arabian Frontier of the British Raj*.

19. Perkins, *A History of Modern Tunisia*, pp. 42–3; Lawson, *Constructing International Relations in the Arab World*, pp. 53–66.

20. A restricted franchise elected forty-four Grand Council delegates to represent 54,000 French citizens (in a settler population of 71,000 Europeans), while 1.9 million Muslim and Jewish Tunisians were represented by eighteen delegates in a separate "native section."

21. Rogan, *The Arabs. A History*, p. 231.

22. Thompson, *Colonial Citizens*, pp. 1–3.

23. White, "The nation-state form and the emergence of 'minorities' " and "The Kurds of Damascus in the 1930s."

24. Enacted in 1919, this statute was looked to as a model of enlightened reform by Arab commentators elsewhere in North Africa, but was redundant even before the advent of fascism in 1922.

25. Vandewalle, *A History of Modern Libya*.

26. As Anderson, *The State and Social Transformation in Tunisia and Libya*, p. 221, observes, the Italian administration "permitted the Libyan population no state and no government"; instead of constructing a state, colonial conquest "destroyed the administration around which regionwide networks of political alliance and commercial exchange had [previously] developed."

27. Anderson, *The State and Social Transformation in Tunisia and Libya*, pp. 39–40.

28. From 1946, all Algerians became citizens of the French Union, but except for the minority already enfranchised into full French citizenship (who voted alongside Europeans in a "first" electoral college), they remained second-class citizens. In the Algerian Assembly, established in 1947, the Muslim

"second college" of 1.5 million electors voted for the same number of representatives (60) as did the 510,000 European electors. At the same time,
elections were increasingly obviously manipulated and opposition parties
repressed.

29. See the brilliant if polemical account in Perrault, *Notre ami le roi*, especially
ch. 2.

30. The other examples being much smaller overseas island territories like
Réunion, Martinique, Guadeloupe and Mayotte.

31. Aside from the infrastructure of schools, banks, post offices and so on that
had been implanted in Tripolitania before 1911, settler colonialism in Libya
gained a firm foothold only in the vicinity of Tripoli and in Cyrenaica after
the defeat of the Sanusi insurrection, and had been established for barely a
decade before the Second World War forced the evacuation of Italian settlers in 1942. The country's limited cultivable land in any case precluded the
creation of the large-scale commercial agriculture that provided the base for
settler society in Algeria, Tunisia or Morocco.

32. Under the terms of the 1912 treaty of Ouchy, the Ottoman state retained
caliphal representation in its Italian-occupied *vilayet*s; these nominal sovereign rights were dismissed by allied planners in London in 1915 and given
up by the 1920 treaty of Sèvres. The claim that the FLN's Algerian state
was legally entitled to reclaim the pre-1830, internationally recognized and
internally effective sovereignty of the Regency of Algiers was a major plank
in the arguments of FLN diplomats and legal experts lobbying international
opinion in 1957–62.

33. The exceptions would be the kingdom of Kongo, from the date of its first
embassy to Portugal in 1485 until its break up in the late seventeenth century,
and the empire of Ethiopia.

34. Gelvin, *Divided Loyalties*.

35. Rogan, *The Arabs. A History*, p. 165.

36. Such maneuvers became increasingly risky as the colonial order waned; by
1953, it was too late to depose and exile the sultan of Morocco, and the ill-
advised act of doing so provoked the final crisis of decolonization across the
Maghreb.

37. Leveau, *Le fellah marocain, défenseur du trône*.

38. Controversy abounds regarding the role of the so-called "DAF" (*déserteurs
de l'armée française*) officers of the Algerian army, especially in the coup
of 1992 and subsequent war, and assessments of their significance should be
circumspect. What is undeniable is that they formed an important element of
the Algerian military in the 1970s, one increasing in rank and influence in
the later 1980s, and thus that they represent a non-negligible element in the
make-up of the regime and its internal factional politics.

39. Cooper, *Decolonisation and African Society*, especially on the importance of
organized labor protest; compare Beinin and Lockman, *Workers on the Nile*
and Kraiem, *Nationalisme et syndicalisme en Tunisie*.

40. These two cases therefore mark the extremes of a spectrum of the "relative violence" with which decolonization occurred in the region, either peacefully under international auspices in the absence of any indigenous sovereignty to which power might be transferred (Libya, granted independence by UN resolution) or by recourse to prolonged armed struggle against the denial of indigenous sovereignty which was claimed to reside entirely with the occupying power. Thus, Libyan independence was by common consent an international and not even an imperial question, whereas the future of Algeria was a matter of French "internal sovereignty" over which the UN had no recognized jurisdiction.

41. Again, the important exception is Algeria, where any sovereignty other than that of the metropole was denied within the formal political system. But the exception is partial to the extent that, from 1946 onward, the declared aims of the state, promising citizenship and representation on an equal basis for all within the French Republic, increasingly conflicted with the reality of preserved minority rule. Indeed, it was precisely as the *formal* regime in Algeria became more "liberal," with the abolition of the *indigénat*, the extension of suffrage and promises of reform, that the *real* regime became more coercive: routine repression and torture seem to have become more frequent after the spectacular massacres of 1945. Significant development projects and major legal reforms would be enacted only *at the height* of the counter-insurgency war after 1958. In this sense Algeria is a variation on the dominant theme rather than (as Libya) a true exception.

4

Ottoman Legacies and Economic Sovereignty in Post-imperial Anatolia, Syria and Iraq

Fred H. Lawson

Empires exhibit a variety of economic configurations, and legacies of the imperial era play a pivotal role in shaping the economies of post-imperial states. Yet the economic implications of the end of empire remain largely unexplored, in sharp contrast to the scholarly attention that has been lavished on the political, social and cultural transformations that accompany the dissolution of imperial structures of governance.[1]

In particular, imperial economies differ from one another in at least three ways: (1) the degree of interdependence that exists among different provinces of the empire;[2] (2) whether taxation in the provinces is carried out through direct or indirect mechanisms;[3] and (3) whether trade and manufacturing are regulated in a unitary or multidivisional fashion.[4] Such structural features of the imperial order determine the extent to which post-imperial states are born with the incentive and capacity "to regulate the flow of goods, persons, pollutants, diseases, and ideas across [their respective] territorial boundaries,"[5] that is, to exercise fundamental aspects of economic sovereignty.

Economic Legacies of Empire

High levels of interdependence among provinces of the empire increase the vulnerability of post-imperial states, and give their leaders a strong incentive to turn to government agencies to ensure the stability of the local economy. Countries that inherit established industrial plants but lose secure access to raw materials and other vital inputs, for example, can be expected to embark on state-led campaigns to develop mineral and fuel production at home rather than rely on imports from other former provinces. Similarly, states that emerge out of raw materials-producing provinces are likely to build up local manufacturing, even if it might be cheaper to import manufactured goods from former industrial provinces.[6] New mines and factories can be expected to demand protection from outside competition, thereby increasing the pressure for state intervention in the economy.

To the extent that taxes get collected through mechanisms that are administered directly from the imperial capital, elites in the provinces exercise little if any influence over revenue collection. Officials dispatched from the core use the funds they appropriate to finance additional state enterprises, whose activities expand central control over more aspects of economic affairs in the periphery.[7] Centralized tax collection thus makes it unlikely that well-articulated bourgeoisies will be present in post-imperial states, thereby diminishing the prospects for sustained growth immediately after independence.

On the other hand, if tax revenues are gathered by agents acting on behalf of the central administration, who forward a proportion of the revenues they collect to the capital, then provincial elites are likely to forge lucrative partnerships with local officials in return for moderating the rate of taxation. In this way, indirect mechanisms of revenue collection contribute to the emergence and consolidation of provincial bourgeoisies, whose members' activities provide the foundation for dynamic post-imperial economies.

Finally, empires that regulate trade and manufacturing along unitary lines usually pay a high price to supervise and maintain a centralized, hierarchically structured network of exchange and production across a variety of different provinces. Officials in the capital can be expected to adopt standardized procedures in an attempt to minimize or offset governance costs. As a result, regulatory agencies in post-imperial states will end up sharing a good many institutional features, all of which will be comparatively inefficient.

By contrast, empires that impose (or tolerate) multidivisional modes of commercial and industrial regulation – that is, adopt policies that enable each province to house a number of complementary activities and enterprises, which together comprise a self-contained economic order – keep supervisory costs to a minimum, while opening the door to a profusion of alternative governance structures in peripheral areas. Under these circumstances, post-imperial economies quickly diverge from one another, and display a range of relatively efficient institutional arrangements. Empires characterized by multidivisional modes of regulation consequently give birth to states that are better prepared to construct diversified economies, and less likely to experience sharp ruptures in regulatory activities when the empire disintegrates.

Economic Legacies of the Ottoman Empire

Middle Eastern states that took shape in the early twentieth century illustrate the impact of longstanding modes of incorporation into the Ottoman economy. Anatolia, Syria and Iraq came away from the imperial era with dissimilar economic inheritances, which reflected their peculiar relationships with the core of the empire and with one another. So, in addition to legacies of imperial rule that were common to all of the former Ottoman lands,[8] these three clusters of provinces exhibit specific inheritances that determined the extent to which each country's leadership had the incentive and capacity to exercise economic sovereignty at independence.

ANATOLIA

Up until the last quarter of the nineteenth century, Anatolia constituted an economic backwater of the Ottoman realm. Districts of Aydin province in the west experienced substantial growth in the 1860s as agricultural exports from Izmir soared.[9] Adana province in the south profited from the cotton boom as well. But the hardscrabble interior provinces of Konya, Ankara, Sivas, Erzurum and Diyarbakir played no more than a marginal part in the imperial economy. Sevket Pamuk observes that "in general, barriers posed by transportation costs isolated eastern Anatolia from the rest of the Empire and the European markets throughout the [nineteenth] century."[10]

Anatolia's importance to the core districts of Istanbul, Edirne, Bursa and Izmir increased markedly during the great depression of 1873–96. Plunging world grain prices encouraged the authorities to consider low-quality Anatolian cereals to be a viable export item.[11] To transport grain to the cities of the northwest, the central administration extended the railway network from Izmit to Ankara and Konya.[12] Wheat and barley production in the central plains almost immediately jumped.[13] Meanwhile, state officials dismantled obstacles to domestic trade that had grown up when the primary suppliers of food to Istanbul, Edirne and Bursa had been Romania, Bulgaria and Rumelia. Donald Quataert reports that "in 1893 and 1894, internal tariffs on the sea transport of most important cereal grains and their flours were abolished; before 1900 these duties were lifted from most other cereals."[14] As a result, "grain shipped from Konya and Ankara gained a slight price advantage over foreign grain in Istanbul markets" as the twentieth century opened.[15]

At the same time, the central administration "with the encouragement of the Istanbul Chamber of Commerce, also sought to promote the use of Anatolian grains in the manufacture of flour at Istanbul."[16] Measures were implemented to enhance the quality of locally produced wheat and barley, and regulations that had required bakeries in the capital to use imported flour were rescinded. Consequently, fields along the railways of central Anatolia supplanted Romania, Bulgaria and Rumelia as the main suppliers of wheat to the capital.[17] Anatolian grain played an even greater role in provisioning the northwestern cities during the war years of the early 1900s.[18]

Notable shifts also occurred in the internal trade in cotton. Cotton cultivation around Adana jumped during the civil war in the United States. After that conflict ended, however, production of Anatolian cotton plummeted. A second boom in 1901–5 revived the empire's interest in cotton cultivation,[19] but sustained demand in overseas markets failed to materialize and state officials turned to domestic industry as a way of utilizing locally grown cotton.[20] The first decade of the twentieth century witnessed a drop in cotton production around Izmir and a rise around Adana,[21] extending the supply chain deeper into the interior.

Besides agricultural goods, labor flowed more massively from Anatolia to the imperial core as the nineteenth century drew to a close. Workers from Sivas, Erzurum and Van filled key niches in the occupational hierarchies of Istanbul and Bursa.[22] The influx of laborers accelerated during the 1880s, as steamship travel between the capital and the Black Sea ports of Trabzon, Samsun and Giresun became less expensive and more reliable. Greater ease of movement made it "practicable for men to spend the autumn and winter months earning a wage in Istanbul, and the spring and summer working on a family holding located along the upper Euphrates or in the vicinity of Lake Van."[23] And when employment in the capital dried up at the turn of the century, and the amount of cultivated land in eastern Anatolia suddenly contracted,[24] inter-communal tensions flared into open conflict.[25]

Economic connections between the Anatolian governorates and other provinces of the empire were less extensive. Pamuk remarks that for most of the nineteenth century "in years of good harvest, limited amounts of cereals were shipped by camel caravans through Aleppo to the export port of Iskenderun. The markets of Mosul, Baghdad, and distant India emerged as occasional outlets for the cereals of the region . . . after the turn of the [twentieth] century."[26] Trade between Anatolia and Aleppo, Mosul and Baghdad involved a limited range of goods, and fluctuated widely from year to year.[27] Cloth-makers in Aleppo supplied central and southern Anatolia with textiles well into the twentieth century,[28] while cloth manufactured in Diyarbakir provided Kirkuk with "the long tunics of the Kurds."[29] The 1880s saw the creation of large-scale wool factories at Salonica that made use of raw materials from the Anatolian highlands; these factories complemented cotton-spinning mills that "exported yarn to Macedonia, Albania, Bulgaria, Serbia, Anatolia and the [Greek] archipelago" a decade later.[30] Conversely, increased output from the mills of Salonica province "undermine[d] and then wreck[ed] a once-prosperous putting-out network [for cotton yarn and cloth] centered on Anatolian Kayseri."[31]

Moderate levels of interdependence accompanied persistent friction between the central administration and the tax-farmers who acted as the sultan's designated agents. Throughout the eighteenth and nineteenth centuries, local notables controlled tax collection from Bursa to the eastern fringes of the empire. For instance:

> In the Midyad kaza of Mardin there had been five kaimakams in a period of two years, each of whom had extorted as much money as possible and cooperated with the Kurdish dominated [advisory council] of the town . . . These men had possessed considerable power before the [1877–8] war when the Ottoman presence in areas such as this had been much more substantial, but by 1879 with virtually no Ottoman force to restrain them, they were all-powerful.[32]

Provincial governors tried to undercut the local notables by setting up irregular military formations in collaboration with tribal chieftains.[33] Playing tribes against one another strengthened the hand of the governors and advanced their efforts to institute basic administrative reforms.[34] But by the early 1890s, the activities of Armenian militants and counter-mobilization among Kurds generated a wave of disorder across eastern Anatolia. Resistance to administrative reform gained momentum after the European powers pushed for comprehensive changes in fiscal governance.[35] Local notables took advantage of popular resentment, and the apparent complicity of officials with foreign interests, to recapture a predominant position in the provinces, which they retained until the 1908 revolution.[36] Only the most ruthless governors were able to assert control over their respective domains, and they forwarded no more revenue to the treasury than did the local notables.[37]

Nevertheless, indirect taxation was not associated with the emergence of a well-articulated bourgeoisie in late Ottoman Anatolia. Imperial officials jockeyed for control over revenues with the Public Debt Administration (PDA), which had been created in 1881 by a consortium of European creditors.[38] The expansion of the PDA prompted state officials to cultivate an alliance with merchants and commercial farmers to resist foreign interference in economic affairs.[39] Meanwhile, trade and manufacturing lay in the hands of minority communities that enjoyed close ties to countries outside the empire.[40] An autonomous Anatolian bourgeoisie therefore failed to materialize.

Ottoman officials inaugurated several large-scale economic development programs from the beginning of the late eighteenth century. The best-known of the agricultural initiatives was the 1858 land law.[41] Implementation of the statute was left in the hands of provincial officials, so different governorates exhibited notably different outcomes. Across Anatolia, the law confirmed the prerogatives of small-scale landholders, with variations from district to district.[42] Variations in agricultural regulation set the stage for significant divergences in the accumulation of landed property. In some districts of Adana, almost all households worked farms that were larger than 12 hectares by 1909; around Ankara the proportion of well-to-do households was considerably smaller; Aydin and Konya hovered between the extremes.[43]

In contrast to agriculture, the imperial administration adopted a unitary mode of regulating industry. Most manufacturing projects undertaken during the 1800s clustered around Istanbul, and many factories were supervised by the same handful of managers.[44] The cost of unitary regulation soon overwhelmed the government, however, and by the 1880s private entrepreneurs had set up metal, cloth and cigarette factories around Izmir, Salonica and Bursa, while mechanized plants to process cotton opened outside Adana.[45] Post-independence, these early industries remained within the boundaries of the new Turkish state.

SYRIA

More than Anatolia, Ottoman Syria exhibited a high level of interdependence with surrounding provinces. James Reilly points out:

> Damascus's commerce was extremely dependent on the safety and regularity of the Baghdad caravans, whether they travelled to Baghdad directly via Palmyra, or indirectly via Aleppo ... Therefore Damascenes were attuned to political developments in Ottoman Iraq and Qajar Iran which could affect their commerce.[46]

As the desert track to Iraq became increasingly dangerous, trade shifted north through Aleppo and Mosul.[47] The costs entailed by the longer route were offset by heightened demand for Syrian grain in Istanbul, Izmir and Bursa during the Crimean War. European merchants who gained a foothold in the country opened the door to a flood of imported products, most of which were re-exported to surrounding provinces.

Syria's trade with Iraq was hurt by the opening of the Suez Canal, but benefited from the introduction of steamship traffic and the lifting of customs duties on inter-provincial exchange.[48] By the 1870s, Damascus enjoyed a "considerable trade in textiles and other Damascene products with Ottoman and Egyptian markets. Textiles were exported to Istanbul, Izmir, Egypt, Baghdad, Aleppo, Armenia, and other parts of Syria and the Empire."[49] Prominent merchant families maintained branches at Istanbul, Izmir, Alexandria and Baghdad, as well as in Beirut and the larger towns of Palestine.[50]

Yet Damascus' connections to Anatolia and Iraq paled in comparison with those enjoyed by Aleppo. "Aleppo was the port of (dis)embarkation and a point of exchange for the caravans from Mosul, Diyarbakir, Urfa, and Mardin which 'frequently carried their goods' to Aleppo, and Aleppine merchants orchestrated mercantile activities in and around Cilicia."[51] As European goods poured into Beirut and Damascus, "Aleppo's merchants enjoyed a healthy balance of payments with the regional centers of its economic hinterland: [ʿAintab], Diyarbakir, and Mosul and the smaller market towns of northern Syria and southeastern Anatolia."[52] The city responded to the influx of foreign textiles by shifting to items for which local demand remained strong.[53] As late as 1915, the only large-scale cloth factories in the eastern half of the empire were located in Aleppo.[54]

Produce from the agricultural districts of Aleppo province supplied markets and manufacturers far to the north and east. Tobacco represented a key item of trade with Anatolia. A French diplomat residing in Mosul noted that whenever the harvest in northern Iraq faltered, "the place receives cotton from Aleppo."[55] North-central Syria was so productive and crucial for neighboring provinces that the sultan himself purchased large tracts of farmland outside Aleppo and Homs during the 1880s.[56]

High levels of interdependence accompanied a revenue system that was dominated by tax-farmers, who enjoyed intimate ties to the local commercial and agrarian elite. The emergence of prominent families that wrested control over local affairs from the central administration was so pronounced in the provinces of Syria that it inspired Albert Hourani to formulate the concept of "the politics of notables" to describe the phenomenon.[57]

During the 1877–8 war with Russia, the reformist governor of Damascus, Ahmad Midhat Pasha, took steps to supplant the tax-farmers by ordering that all revenues be collected on a fixed scale by government personnel.[58] These innovative procedures were undercut by policies adopted by the central administration in 1880. Further attempts to restructure tax collection were ventured in 1884 and 1897–8,[59] but none succeeded in loosening the grip of the entrenched tax-farmers. Nor did the regime that seized power in the capital in July 1908: after a flurry of prosecutions for corruption and negligence, "things [in Damascus] began slipping back to what they had been before the restoration of the [1876] constitution."[60]

Indirect taxation bolstered Syria's commercial and agrarian elites, and contributed to the emergence of a well-articulated provincial bourgeoisie. As Philip Khoury remarks, "by the turn of the twentieth century, the major status groups that provided urban leadership in Syria had crystallized into a single elite with a similar economic base in land and political access through government office."[61] The bourgeoisie of Damascus consisted of two rival factions: "The first faction was supported by merchants engaged in the long-distance trade in luxury goods while the second faction was supported by merchants and artisans involved in local handicraft production and in the grain trade."[62] Competition between the two injected dynamism into the local economy, and enabled it to adjust to the disruptions that culminated in the 1908 revolution. The bourgeoisie of Aleppo exhibited even greater adaptability: merchants who specialized in luxury goods shifted to the production of textiles for surrounding markets, then bought up agricultural properties around Bab, ᶜAzaz and Minbij.[63] Aleppo's elite included Muslims, Christians and Jews, old-established families and nouveaux riches entrepreneurs alike.[64] This heterogeneous class flourished as the 1900s opened,[65] and orchestrated a remarkable round of capital accumulation during the First World War.[66]

Efforts to impose unitary regulation on the Syrian provinces boasted little if any success. The policies introduced by Midhat Pasha were applied so as to conform to existing agricultural and manufacturing structures, and did little to rationalize production. Market forces rewarded farmers in the highlands of the Hawran for producing grain for export, and transformed the towns of ᶜAintab, Marash and ᶜUrfa into cloth-making centers at the expense of Aleppo.[67] But the rapid turnover of provincial governors precluded comprehensive economic planning, and the Committee of Union and Progress-led regime that exercised power after July 1908 abjured central planning and pursued a liberal economic program, particularly outside Rumelia and western Anatolia. On the eve of the First World War, the imperial ministry of the interior directed Syria's governors to implement whatever commercial, industrial, agricultural and infrastructural policies might be best suited to their respective domains.[68]

IRAQ

Ottoman Iraq served as the central conduit for trade from Iran and India to the core of the empire, while the province of Basra stood at the heart of an extensive regional network rooted in the exportation of grain, horses and dates.[69] The opening of the Suez Canal stimulated exports of Iraqi wool, dates and cereals, which were distributed around the eastern Mediterranean littoral.[70] Basra's trade increased threefold between the early 1880s and the 1910s, with barley exports leaping more than thirty times in value.[71] Much of this trade went to Britain and the United States, but a sizable proportion consisted of foodstuffs and wool destined for Syria and other parts of the empire.[72]

Mosul represented the economic nexus between Iraq and Anatolia. Sarah Shields observes that the city's trade "encompassed an area with a radius of roughly 450 miles, the most important cities of which were Baghdad, Diyarbakir, Aleppo, Damascus, Tabriz, Erzurum, Trabzon, Bitlis, and Siirt."[73] The expansion of grain production around Mosul at the end of the nineteenth century was targeted at markets in Van, Diyarbakir and Bitlis, along with northern Syria.[74] Tanneries and distilleries located in the city supplied leather and ᶜarak to neighboring provinces, while local soap-makers competed with their counterparts in Aleppo all over eastern Anatolia. Dyed fabrics and woolen cloaks produced in Mosul were shipped to Van, Bitlis, Siirt, Trabzon and the mountains of "Kurdistan" and "Turkestan."[75] In return, Mosul received linen and cotton textiles, vegetables, fruits and nuts, especially from the districts around Diyarbakir and Rize.[76]

Imports of European manufactures did little to undermine Mosul's connections to surrounding provinces.[77] In lean years, the city's merchants relied on the farmers of Diyarbakir for grain, and whenever the cotton harvest failed, spinners and weavers brought in raw materials from Aleppo and Dair al-Zur.[78] Manufacturers in the city proved adept at responding to foreign competition, and developed products and designs that reflected the tastes of local consumers. Consequently, economic connections between northern Iraq, northern Syria and central and eastern Anatolia remained vibrant up until the First World War.

Taxation in late Ottoman Iraq was structured much as it was in Syria. Tax-farmers supervised revenue collection in rural and urban areas alike.[79] Provincial authorities found themselves at a particular disadvantage relative to the tribal chieftains who dominated the outlying districts of Baghdad and Basra governorates. A campaign to reconfigure the tax system was undertaken in 1869, but foundered when the governor abruptly resigned his post. According to Gokhan Cetinsaya, "there followed a reaction against the decentralizing [sic] aspects of the [Governorate] Law [of 1864], with opponents arguing that it set up 'little absolute states' in which the governor-generals had the powers of proconsuls, or quasi-independent vassal princes."[80]

A succession of governors came and went after 1880, each of whom struggled in vain against the entrenched tax-farmers and local military commanders. Jockeying proved especially intense in Baghdad, where Mushir Nusret Pasha (nicknamed "the mad") assumed the title of Honorary Inspector of the Sixth Army. Nusret dispatched "lengthy reports to Istanbul, complaining about high-ranking government officials, including the [governor] and the [head of the provincial treasury]."[81] No provincial governor could avoid the infighting among Nusret, the tax-farmers and the tribes long enough to formulate a viable reform program. By 1905, British and Iranian diplomats had joined the tug-of-war.[82] Administrative affairs were even more chaotic in Mosul,[83] while the governors of Basra tended to be senior military officers who concentrated on strategic rather than fiscal matters.[84]

Baghdad stood out from the rest of Iraq, due to the direct involvement of Sultan Abdülhamid II in local agriculture.[85] The Ottoman ruler owned one-third of all arable land in the governorate, and taxes on the royal properties were collected by imperial troops.[86] Royal involvement did little to improve the financial circumstances of the central administration, however, since "the tithes collected flowed to his personal, not the imperial[,] treasury."[87]

Nevertheless, indirect taxation engendered a comparatively well-articulated bourgeoisie in the Iraqi provinces. This class was just as active in Basra as in Baghdad, despite notable sectarian differences between the two governorates.[88] Iraq's commercial and agrarian elites did, however, face three obstacles that their Syrian counterparts were spared: a rival class of tribal chieftains that exercised a substantial amount of influence in the countryside; a pronounced lack of basic infrastructure; and a paucity of capital-intensive enterprises that might have taken advantage of economies of scale.[89]

Indirect tax collection accompanied ineffective attempts to introduce multidivisional regulation. Plans for comprehensive infrastructural and agricultural governance in Baghdad province were drawn up in 1879–80, but never implemented.[90] Nusret Pasha hit on the idea of linking local development schemes to the enrichment of the Privy Purse; he recommended that Baghdad and Basra be subjected to martial law, and that a corps of "qualified experts" be assigned to carry out a census to obtain the data required for an integrated economic and social program.[91] The proposal was reviewed by the authorities in Istanbul but filed away for lack of resources.

Widespread popular unrest in Mosul and Basra on the eve of the 1908 revolution persuaded the central administration to revive plans for comprehensive economic regulation in Iraq. In the fall of 1907, an imperial commission charged with reconfiguring the three governorates made the arduous journey to Baghdad.[92] The commission immediately fell into conflict with the governor of Baghdad, which lasted until the 1908 revolution brought the effort to institute multidivisional regulation to an end.

DIVERGENT INHERITANCES

These three sets of provinces exhibit substantially different economic legacies of Ottoman rule. Anatolia experienced a relatively low level of interdependence, although reciprocal dependence between the Anatolian governorates and Istanbul, Edirne and Bursa increased during the first decade of the twentieth century. Tax revenues were collected indirectly, but tax-farming did not accompany the emergence of a well-articulated bourgeoisie; much of the bourgeoisie that emerged, moreover, would exit in the conflicts surrounding imperial collapse. Finally, regulation of agri-culture in the Anatolian provinces took a multidivisional form, whereas industry tended to be regulated in a unitary fashion.

Syria, by contrast, experienced high levels of interdependence with other Ottoman provinces. Taxes were collected indirectly, and tax-farming contributed to the consolidation of a bourgeoisie that melded commercial, industrial and agricultural interests into a coherent political–economic for-mation. The mode of governance of the local economy can best be charac-terized as a series of failed initiatives to impose unitary regulation, which eventuated in *de facto* multidivisional regulation of trade and industry in the provinces of Damascus and Aleppo.

Iraq presents yet a third mix of features: Mosul, Baghdad and Basra experienced high levels of interdependence with both Syria and Anatolia. Indirect taxation facilitated the emergence of a coherent bourgeoisie, although the palace's direct involvement around Baghdad, combined with the power of tribal chieftains and a comparatively weak infrastruc-ture, kept this class from becoming as fully-developed as its counterpart in Syria. State officials tried repeatedly to introduce multidivisional regulation into the Iraqi governorates, but failed to reconfigure the local economy. As a result, commerce and manufacturing in Mosul, Baghdad and Basra were left comparatively unregulated during the last decades of imperial rule.

Impact of the Mandate Era

Post-imperial states in the Middle East passed through a transitional phase of modernizing reform that overlapped with the disintegration of the Ottoman Empire. In April 1920, the League of Nations awarded France and Great Britain "mandates" that authorized them to take charge of Syria and Iraq, respectively, and provide these countries with the "advice and assistance" necessary to "stand alone" in the modern world.[93] The two mandatory powers adopted very different approaches to the task at hand: France highlighted its "sacred duty" to bring enlightenment to the benighted Syrians, whereas "British governments had no *particular* feeling of moral purpose in their policies towards Iraq."[94] More important, French officials dived head-first into reorganizing Syria, while "Britain regarded a degree of parsimony as necessary from the very beginning, and generally stuck to this principle."[95] The equivalent of the mandate period in Anatolia was the decade of rule by the Committee of Union and Progress (CUP), which began in July 1908. In all three cases, the transitional phase largely reinforced the legacy of Ottoman rule, and did little to alter the incentive or capacity of post-imperial states to exercise economic sovereignty.

ANATOLIA

Economic difficulties dogged the CUP regime from the moment it came to power. Tax collection across Anatolia quickly broke down, while public expenditure continued apace. Workers walked off their jobs to protest the deterioration of real wages, generating a wave of strikes that severely disrupted commerce and industry.[96] State officials therefore turned to foreign lenders to obtain the funds necessary to keep the central administration running.[97]

With public indebtedness soaring, Britain's representative on the PDA proposed an innovative mechanism to restore stability to the empire's finances. British financiers and local commercial interests would set up a National Bank of Turkey to coordinate investments in manufacturing, trade and public works. The bank received authorization to operate in early 1909,[98] but the CUP pressed for a massive loan to pay off existing debts instead of submitting plans for new projects. Competition between the National Bank and the Imperial Ottoman

Bank soon converged with ongoing rivalry between London and Paris for influence over Turkish finances to subvert the National Bank's primary mission, and in June 1913 the institution announced that it was terminating its activities.[99]

Few other steps were taken by the CUP regime during its initial years to transform the Anatolian economy. Property relations remained largely intact.[100] Invitations to European governments to take on a greater role in commerce and manufacturing elicited meager response.[101] Industrial action by trade unions and other labor organizations prompted draconian countermeasures. For the most part, government policy aimed to encourage the expansion of private enterprise and market forces, rather than augment the state's capacity to regulate the cross-border flow of goods, labor and capital or create a diversified domestic economy.[102]

Exigencies associated with the Balkan and Libyan wars prompted state officials to take steps to reduce the empire's vulnerability to external threats. In 1913, the government introduced low-interest loans to support investment in industry and agriculture;[103] the following year saw the introduction of new tariffs and a law designed to build up domestic manufacturing.[104] The authorities encouraged Muslim citizens to set up joint-stock companies that excluded foreign nationals,[105] and even organized a Society for National Consumption to convince the public to purchase locally made goods. More important, the authorities deployed the CUP Special Organization (Teskilat-i Mahsusa) to force Christian businesspeople to use the Turkish language and harass anyone suspected of "treacherous and shameless greed."[106] Large numbers of Greeks and Armenians fled the empire rather than comply.

Unitary regulation of Anatolian industry received a further boost when the First World War broke out. Feroz Ahmad reports that the shift to closer supervision of manufacturing can be tracked in the local press:

> alongside the articles on military and political affairs, there were usually articles dealing with the important issues in the country's economic life. One can read about the state of the harvest in a particular district or the measures being taken by the peasants, the authorities, or the specialists to combat vermin amongst the crops and cattle.[107]

Applications to initiate industrial projects continued to be submitted to provincial officials, but a sustained effort was undertaken to coordinate manufacturing across the country. After the Turkish victory at Gallipoli, the Ministry of Commerce and Agriculture was rechristened the Ministry of National Economy,[108] and a state-affiliated Special Trade Commission was set up to oversee the joint-stock companies.[109] By the fall of 1916, the central administration had taken control of industrial development throughout Anatolia.[110]

Unitary regulation was gradually introduced into agriculture during the war years as well. In March 1913 provincial taxation was decoupled from the fiscal affairs of the central bureaucracy.[111] Each province was ordered to draw up a budget and assume responsibility for raising revenues. The manner in which this was to be accomplished was left up to the provincial governor, working with an elected General Assembly.[112] But as trade with Romania, the Ukraine and Russia collapsed after 1914, the core of the empire became more reliant than ever on grain from Anatolia.[113] Furthermore, state officials raised vital funds by selling wheat and barley to Germany and Austria-Hungary under the auspices of the Committee for National Defense (CND). As a result, provincial units of the CND were superseded in 1916–17 by local branches of the Office of War Production, whose primary responsibility was to coordinate the cultivation and distribution of staples throughout the empire.

SYRIA

French officials recognized that Syria's high level of interdependence with other Ottoman provinces was likely to cause economic difficulties after the empire disintegrated. These fears were confirmed when the authorities in Ankara subjected trade between Anatolia and French-dominated Syria to steep tariffs shortly after French troops pulled out of Cilicia.[114] In April 1921, the mandatory authorities negotiated a commercial treaty with the British administration of Palestine to retain preferential access to that lucrative market for Damascene manufactures. Repeated attempts to conclude a similar pact with the Turkish Republic proved unsuccessful,[115] inflicting severe damage to industry in Aleppo.[116] By 1930, restrictions on trade with Iraq had reduced Syria's textile exports to its eastern neighbor by some 75 percent.

Increasing reliance on exports to Palestine put the merchants and manufacturers of Damascus at odds not only with the British mandatory authorities, but also with Zionist entrepreneurs. Escalating tensions led French officials to explore other ways to heighten demand for locally produced goods. One strategy was to promote mechanized industry, which would improve the competitiveness of Syrian products by standardizing quality and slashing labor costs.[117] Another strategy was to raise customs duties, which by 1926 reached 25 percent.[118] High tariffs turned out to be less helpful to Syrian industry than they might have been, since they were levied uniformly on all imports, raw materials and finished products alike. Not until the Great Depression did the mandatory authorities revise Syria's tariff structure so as to maximize benefit to local industry.[119]

Protective tariffs did contribute to the diversification of the Syrian economy. Cement production, food processing, textile and clothing manufacture, cigarette-making and other activities blossomed behind the barriers to trade that were erected by the French.[120] The success of the tariff regime in nurturing local enterprise convinced the chambers of commerce and industry of Damascus and Aleppo to support sustained state intervention in economic affairs, a position their members had previously opposed.[121] Groups of merchants and manufacturers formed joint-stock companies that took names like the National Company for Manufacturing Cement and Building Materials and the Syrian Spinning and Weaving Company. The trend toward "nationalist" appellations reflected a desire

> to distinguish [these enterprises] from the foreign-owned concessionary and insurance corporations [that had been] established since later Ottoman times. But also this distinction reflected a conception that in some sense they were truly 'national' enterprises whose activities were part of building the future of the Syrian nation.[122]

Industrial expansion combined with the persistence of indirect taxation to strengthen Syria's bourgeoisie. Despite the initial misgivings of French officials,[123] taxes on agricultural land continued to be collected by local notables who forwarded revenues from their respective districts to the central administration.[124] Making effective use of existing tax-farming arrangements in the countryside enabled the authorities to avoid serious fiscal difficulties until the mid-1930s.[125]

Moreover, French policy reinforced the multidivisional mode of regulation that Syria inherited from the Ottoman era. In November 1925, the Banque Agricole de l'Etat de Syrie was set up to coordinate farm-related investments across the country.[126] The bank paid special attention to matching cotton cultivation to the requirements of the domestic textile industry, as well as to the demand for Syrian cotton in metropolitan France.[127] The creation of a comprehensive political–economic order stood at the heart of an ambitious plan adopted in the mid-1930s to "reorganize the institutions through which the interests of commercial, industrial, and rural capital, as well [as] those of workers and peasants, were expressed."[128] Geoffrey Schad calls this "attempt to regiment both business and labor institutions . . . a colonial species of corporatism," which shaped Syrian politics into the 1960s.[129]

IRAQ

British commanders took steps to reorganize the economy of Basra as soon as Indian Expeditionary Force D gained control of the province in November 1914:

> Military governors were appointed in the various towns as [British-Indian troops] occupied them, with full control, under the Senior Local Military Officer, within the limits of their towns . . . Assistant Political Officers were appointed to take charge of the Political and Revenue Administration of the districts with their tribes and cultivation.[130]

But the administration operated under disadvantageous conditions:

> All the latest records had been removed by the Turks when they left. The remainder, mostly out of date, had been mixed up in vast and inextricable heaps on the floor of the offices, the only papers in any kind of order being the registers of title-deeds to land and registered documents.

British commanders therefore kept the existing tax collection system in place, albeit with minor modifications. Around ᶜAmarah, for example, annual fees were reduced:

> to a sum which allowed a considerable margin of profit to the farmer and his [laborers] and [still] enabled the Shaikh to meet the many demands on his pocket in the shape of armed retainers and private allowances and benefactions.[131]

After Baghdad fell in the spring of 1917, a Revenue Board was set up to supervise the collection of agricultural taxes and customs duties, as well as to oversee religious endowments.[132] This was followed by an Agricultural Board, which sponsored a campaign to increase wheat production in order to ensure that Iraq contributed to the "restoration of Imperial autarky."[133]

Otherwise, British officials did little to transform the structure of the Iraqi economy. The mandatory authorities relied on local notables to supervise tax collection and local administration, thereby overturning what few reforms the last Ottoman governors had managed to effect. Peter Sluglett observes that "by the mid-1920s an informal alliance had grown up between the Iraq Government and the larger landowners, whereby in return for their support, the landowners would be left as far as possible to their own devices."[134] The flow of revenue to the treasury predictably diminished,[135] even as the power of tribal chieftains in the countryside rebounded.[136]

Around Mosul, British commanders allowed Kurdish notables to take charge of the local administration.[137] Paradoxically, concern that the cost of imposing direct British control over the province would spiral out of control persuaded the cabinet in London to veto all new investments in agriculture and infrastructure in the north.[138] The British administration constantly feared that integrating the economies of Mosul and Baghdad would strengthen the Iraqi nationalist movement.[139] Consequently, elected councils ended up exercising control over economic affairs in most Kurdish districts.[140]

It became clear in the mid-1920s that Iraq could not meet its financial obligations. British officials dispatched a commission to Baghdad to determine "what steps should be taken to ensure that it shall be possible to balance the Iraqi budget during the Treaty period and afterwards." The commission's final report proved "disappointing": it suggested only that additional "economies and reductions in salaries [should be carried out] in the lower ranks of the Ministries of Health, Education, Agriculture and, incredibly, Irrigation."[141] Confronted with Iraq's precarious financial situation, the British in June 1926 announced that they would not insist on monetary compensation for assets that had been turned over to the Iraqi authorities.

British officials did, however, adopt policies that increased the state's ability to regulate the flow of goods, labor and capital across Iraq's borders. The tariff system was revamped in 1927 to stimulate imports of specific kinds of industrial equipment and restrict access to the local market.[142] Import duties on carpets, silk goods, candies and tobacco products were raised two years later, precipitating a marked increase in silk weaving and cigarette manufacturing by Iraqi entrepreneurs.

Conclusion

Legacies of the Ottoman Empire had a significant impact on the incentive and capacity of Middle Eastern states to exercise economic sovereignty. Anatolia, Syria and Iraq illustrate the effects of divergent modes of incorporation into the Ottoman order. While economic interdependence had grown throughout the empire, Syria and Iraq emerged from provinces that had been highly interdependent with other parts of the empire. Rupture was thus very costly and they had a strong incentive to reduce post-independence vulnerabilities by regulating trade and investment in order to foster national economies in the period after imperial break-up. In the Anatolian case, the lower level of interdependence between the Anatolian governorates and surrounding provinces meant rupture with the Arab provinces was less costly, hence less of an issue; moreover, after independence, eastern Anatolia was integrated with Istanbul and western Turkey into an emerging new national economic space.

Whether or not post-imperial states had the capacity to create and sustain post-imperial national economic institutions was largely determined by other features of the imperial order. Indirect taxation via tax-farming generally fostered the emergence of a well-articulated bourgeoisie; it might well have generated strong bourgeoisies in all three countries, but circumstances peculiar to Anatolia (minority dominance, hence exit of the bourgeoisie) and Iraq (powerful tribal competition) left commercial and industrial elites in those countries substantially weaker than their counterparts in Syria. Moreover, Syria's experience of multidivisional regulation provided it with a more diversified economy than either Iraq or Anatolia, although the latter would suffer less since post-imperial boundaries did not cut it off from western Turkish areas where regulation had concentrated industrialization.

Inheritances from the Ottoman era were largely reinforced by the transitional regimes that ruled each country just prior to independence. Efforts by the Committee of Union and Progress to expand manufacturing and create a "national bourgeoisie" gained little traction, partly due to the CUP's underlying liberal proclivities, but also as a consequence of Anatolia's experience with low levels of interdependence and unitary industrial regulation. It took the major wars of 1912–18 to give the CUP regime an incentive to heighten state intervention in the local economy, and a concerted effort to exercise economic sovereignty was not undertaken until the 1930s.[143] The government of Iraq had little more success exercising economic sovereignty at independence in 1932, due to the policies carried out by the British mandatory regime, which perpetuated the country's comparatively weak bourgeoisie and narrow agricultural and industrial base.

By contrast, the mandatory administration in Syria exercised considerable influence over the cross-border flow of goods, labor and investment as early as the 1920s, despite the fact that officials in Damascus had been charged by the League of Nations to inculcate free trade. Syrian nationalists of the 1940s thus found it easier to regulate foreign commerce and construct a diversified domestic economy than the governments in Ankara and Baghdad had during the 1920s and 1930s, respectively. Syria's ability to exercise greater economic sovereignty at independence than either Turkey or Iraq can be traced directly to the divergent legacies of Ottoman rule.

Notes

1. Suny, *Revenge of the Past*; Beissinger, "Demise of an Empire-State"; Brubaker, "Nationhood and the National Question"; Dawisha and Parrott,

End of Empire?; Barkey and von Hagen, *After Empire*; Rubin and Snyder, *Post-Soviet Political Order*; Motyl, *Imperial Ends*; Spruyt, *Ending Empire*; Barkey, *Changing Modalities of Empire*.

2. Abdelal, "Purpose and Privation."
3. Mann, *Sources of Social Power*.
4. Cooley, *Logics of Hierarchy*.
5. Krasner, *Sovereignty*, p. 12.
6. Berend and Ranki, "Economic Problems of the Danube Region," pp. 171–6.
7. Freudenberger, "State Intervention."
8. Black and Brown (eds), *Modernization in the Middle East*; Brown, *Imperial Legacy*.
9. Kasaba, *Ottoman Empire and the World Economy*, pp. 88–92.
10. Pamuk, "Commodity Production," p. 194.
11. Quataert, "Ottoman reform and agriculture in Anatolia," pp. 187–8.
12. Quataert, "Limited Revolution," p. 141; Schoenberg, "Evolution of Transport."
13. Quataert, "Ottoman reform and agriculture in Anatolia," pp. 189–91.
14. Quataert, "Ottoman reform and agriculture in Anatolia," p. 198.
15. Quataert, "Ottoman reform and agriculture in Anatolia," p. 197.
16. Quataert, "Ottoman reform and agriculture in Anatolia," p. 199.
17. Quataert, "Ottoman reform and agriculture in Anatolia," pp. 201–2.
18. Quataert, "Limited Revolution," p. 159.
19. Quataert, "Ottoman reform and agriculture in Anatolia," pp. 281–2.
20. Quataert, "Ottoman reform and agriculture in Anatolia," p. 291.
21. Quataert, "Ottoman reform and agriculture in Anatolia," p. 294.
22. Clay, "Labour Migration and Economic Conditions," p. 6.
23. Clay, "Labour Migration and Economic Conditions," p. 8.
24. McCarthy, "Foundations of the Turkish Republic," p. 145.
25. Clay, "Labour Migration and Economic Conditions," pp. 27–8.
26. Pamuk, "Commodity Production," p. 191.
27. Khoury, "Political economy of the province of Mosul"; Shields, "Take-Off into Self-Sustained Peripheralization"; Khoury, *State and Provincial Society*; Shields, *Mosul Before Iraq*.
28. Quataert, "Age of reforms," p. 926.
29. Soane, *Report on the Sulaimania District of Kurdistan*, p. 97.
30. Quataert, "Age of reforms," p. 902.
31. Quataert, "Age of reforms," p. 905.
32. Duguid, "Politics of Unity," pp. 142–3.
33. Duguid, "Politics of Unity," p. 145.
34. Duguid, "Politics of Unity," pp. 146–7.
35. Duguid, "Politics of Unity," p. 150.
36. Kansu, *Revolution of 1908*, pp. 40–8.
37. Kansu, *Revolution of 1908*, pp. 69–70.

38. Blaisdell, *European Financial Control*; Birdal, *Political Economy of Ottoman Public Debt.*
39. Keyder, *State and Class in Turkey*, p. 41.
40. Exertzoglou, "Development of a Greek Ottoman Bourgeoisie."
41. Quataert, "Age of reforms," pp. 856–61.
42. Owen, *Middle East in the World Economy*, p. 208.
43. Quataert, "Age of reforms," p. 865.
44. Clark, "Ottoman Industrial Revolution"; Quataert, "Age of reforms," pp. 898–901.
45. Quataert, "Age of reforms," pp. 901–3.
46. Reilly, "Damascus Merchants and Trade," pp. 6–7.
47. Reilly, "Damascus Merchants and Trade," pp. 9–10.
48. Tabak, "Local Merchants in Peripheral Areas," p. 201.
49. Reilly, "Damascus Merchants and Trade," p. 17.
50. Schilcher, *Families in Politics.*
51. Tabak, "Local Merchants in Peripheral Areas," p. 191.
52. Masters, "Aleppo: The Ottoman Empire's Caravan City," p. 73.
53. Quataert, "Age of reforms," pp. 924–6.
54. Shaw, *Ottoman Empire in World War I*, p. 235.
55. Shields, "Economic history of nineteenth-century Mosul," p. 73.
56. Owen, *Middle East in the World Economy*, p. 254
57. Hourani, "Ottoman reform and the politics of notables."
58. Saliba, "Wilayat Suriyya," p. 108.
59. Saliba, "Wilayat Suriyya," p. 225.
60. Saliba, "Wilayat Suriyya," p. 251.
61. Khoury, "Continuity and change in Syrian political life," p. 1382.
62. Khoury, "Continuity and change in Syrian political life," p. 1383.
63. Sluglett, "Aspects of economy and society in the Syrian provinces," pp. 149–50.
64. Schilcher, "Grain economy of late Ottoman Syria," p. 189.
65. Watenpaugh, *Being Modern in the Middle East.*
66. Sluglett, "Aspects of economy and society in the Syrian provinces," p. 153.
67. Quataert, "Age of reforms," pp. 926–7.
68. Shaw, *Ottoman Empire in World War I*, p. 237.
69. Fattah, *Politics of Regional Trade in Iraq, Arabia, and the Gulf.*
70. Issawi, "Notes on the trade of Basra."
71. Owen, *Middle East in the World Economy*, pp. 274–5
72. Fattah, "Politics of the grain trade in Iraq."
73. Shields, "Economic history of nineteenth-century Mosul," p. 59.
74. Owen, *Middle East in the World Economy*, p. 279.
75. Shields, "Economic history of nineteenth-century Mosul," p. 78.
76. Shields, "Economic history of nineteenth-century Mosul," p. 63.
77. Shields, "Mosul and the free trade treaties."
78. Shields, "Regional trade and 19th-century Mosul," pp. 21–4.

79. Kiyotaki, "Practice of tax farming in the province of Baghdad."
80. Cetinsaya, *Ottoman Administration of Iraq*, p. 10.
81. Cetinsaya, *Ottoman Administration of Iraq*, p. 52.
82. Cetinsaya, *Ottoman Administration of Iraq*, pp. 61–2.
83. Cetinsaya, *Ottoman Administration of Iraq*, pp. 63–6.
84. Cetinsaya, *Ottoman Administration of Iraq*, p. 71.
85. Jwaideh, "Sanniya lands of Sultan Abdul Hamid II in Iraq."
86. Owen, *Middle East in the World Economy*, p. 280.
87. Quataert, "Age of reforms," p. 868.
88. Visser, *Basra, The Failed Gulf State*.
89. Owen, *Middle East in the World Economy*, p. 285.
90. Cetinsaya, *Ottoman Administration of Iraq*, p. 28.
91. Cetinsaya, *Ottoman Administration of Iraq*, pp. 31–2.
92. Cetinsaya, *Ottoman Administration of Iraq*, p. 46.
93. Sluglett, "Les Mandates/The Mandates," p. 103.
94. Sluglett, "Les Mandates/The Mandates," p. 120.
95. Sluglett, "Les Mandates/The Mandates," p. 120.
96. Karakisla, "1908 strike wave in the Ottoman Empire."
97. Ravindranathan, "Young Turk revolution," p. 232.
98. Kent, "Agent of empire?," p. 371.
99. Kent, "Agent of empire?," pp. 386–7.
100. Ergil, "A reassessment: the Young Turks," p. 33.
101. Ergil, "A reassessment: the Young Turks," p. 54.
102. Toprak, "Nationalism and economics in the Young Turk era," pp. 259–60; Zürcher, *Young Turk Legacy*, p. 219.
103. Ergil, "A reassessment: the Young Turks," p. 57.
104. Toprak, "Nationalism and economics in the Young Turk era," p. 261; Zürcher, *Turkey: A Modern History*, p. 130.
105. Zürcher, *Young Turk Legacy*, p. 219.
106. Zürcher, *Young Turk Legacy*, p. 220.
107. Ahmad, "Vanguard of a nascent bourgeoisie," p. 43.
108. Ahmad, "Vanguard of a nascent bourgeoisie," p. 46.
109. Zürcher, *Turkey: A Modern History*, p. 130.
110. Ahmad, "Vanguard of a nascent bourgeoisie," pp. 49–50; Hanioğlu, *Brief History of the Late Ottoman Empire*, p. 189.
111. Ahmad, *Young Turks*, pp. 122–3.
112. Ahmad, "Vanguard of a nascent bourgeoisie," p. 34.
113. Zürcher, *Turkey: A Modern History*, p. 131.
114. Peter, "Dismemberment of empire," p. 419.
115. Burns, *Tariff of Syria*, pp. 54–9.
116. Peter, "Dismemberment of empire," p. 424.
117. Peter, "Dismemberment of empire," p. 428.
118. Peter, "Dismemberment of empire," p. 433.
119. Peter, "Dismemberment of empire," p. 435.

120. Peter, "Dismemberment of empire," pp. 439–40.
121. Peter, "Dismemberment of empire," p. 441.
122. Schad, "Colonialists, industrialists and politicians," p. 259.
123. Schad, "Colonialists, industrialists and politicians," p. 97.
124. El-Saleh, "Une évaluation de la gestion mandataire de l'économie syrienne," pp. 393–6.
125. El-Saleh, "Une évaluation de la gestion mandataire de l'économie syrienne," p. 403.
126. El-Saleh, "Une évaluation de la gestion mandataire de l'économie syrienne," p. 401.
127. Schad, "Colonialists, industrialists and politicians," pp. 109–12.
128. Schad, "Colonialists, industrialists and politicians," p. 186.
129. Schad, "Colonialists, industrialists and politicians," p. 189.
130. *Review of the Civil Administration of the Occupied Territories of Al ʿIraq*, p. 3.
131. *Review of the Civil Administration of the Occupied Territories of Al ʿIraq*, p. 4.
132. *Review of the Civil Administration of the Occupied Territories of Al ʿIraq*, p. 8.
133. Mejcher, "Birth of the mandate idea," p. 164.
134. Sluglett, *Britain in Iraq*, p. 232.
135. Ireland, *Iraq: A Study in Political Development*, p. 88.
136. Dodge, *Inventing Iraq*.
137. Eskander, "Britain's policy in southern Kurdistan."
138. Eskander, "Britain's policy in southern Kurdistan," pp. 159–60.
139. Eskander, "Southern Kurdistan under Britain's Mesopotamian Mandate," p. 162.
140. Eskander, "Southern Kurdistan under Britain's Mesopotamian Mandate," p. 166.
141. Sluglett, *Britain in Iraq*, p. 128.
142. Langley, *Industrialization of Iraq*, p. 35.
143. Takim and Yilmaz, "Economic policy during Ataturk's era."

Section II

Paths to Sovereignty: Views from the Core and Periphery

5

Sovereignty in the Ottoman Empire and After

Benjamin C. Fortna

As the most direct heir to the Ottoman Empire, the Turkish Republic enjoys a particular position among its fellow post-imperial states. This chapter examines the dynamic of legacy between empire and republic through the lens of sovereignty. It argues that despite its strong, sometimes extravagant desire to separate itself from the *ancien régime*, the early republic owed much to its imperial predecessor and shared much in common with its fellow post-Ottoman successor states. It goes on to explore comparisons with these states in order to highlight the extent to which the particular circumstances of its pathway to sovereignty resulted in a distinct profile that increasingly separated Turkey from the other newly created states, especially those that emerged in the formerly Arab provinces of the empire.

The Ottoman Empire conquered the Arab lands of Syria, Palestine and Egypt (and by extension the Hejaz and the Islamic holy cities of Mecca and Medina) in the early sixteenth century and lost them in the aftermath of the First World War. The intervening four centuries of imperial cohabitation have been marked in popular historical perception by a combination of amnesia and ill-feeling engendered only in the final years of this long time span. Writing many years ago, Albert Hourani remarked that in spite of these four centuries of shared imperial existence, the history of Ottoman, or "Turkish," rule was largely omitted from Arab histories of this period.[1] The wrenching final years of the empire's existence, which included over a decade of warfare from 1911 to 1922, and in particular the miseries of the First World War, and the rising tide of exclusivist nationalism combined to suppress the memory of a largely compatible Turco-Arab accommodation in favor of what Şerif Mardin has referred to as tales of back-stabbing and mutual recrimination.[2] The "Arab Revolt," although waged by the Şerif of Mecca in return for British gold and what later turned out to be compromised promises for independence after the fighting stopped, together with wartime traumas occasioned by Ottoman conscription, famine and the hangings of nationalist activists, managed in retrospect to capture the collective popular memory of the Ottoman period.

In examining the last decades of the Ottoman Empire and the first of the post-Ottoman era in Turkey and the Middle East from an historical, as opposed to a popular, perspective, one is immediately struck by both the continuities and breaks that marked the political, social and economic history of the period. Of these, it is the breaks that have attracted most attention. Let us take the case of the Ottoman-to-Turkish republican transition as an example. For a variety of reasons, including the success of the Kemalists in disseminating the foundation myths of the Turkish Republic and the selective approach of the dominant historical narrative, over-emphasis has been given to the eye-catching but largely superficial differences between empire and republic. The years immediately following the demise of the empire witnessed a rapid succession of changes. The institution of the sultanate was abolished with the formation of the republic in 1923 and the caliphate followed in 1924. New laws abolishing the Islamic system of education, from Qur'an schools to the higher *medreses*, outlawing the mystical brotherhoods of Islam and prohibiting the wearing of certain forms of "Islamic" dress soon followed. Perhaps most eye-catching was the 1928 "language revolution" (*dil devrimi*) which replaced the Arabo-Persian script with a modified Latin one.[3] Citizens of the new republic were given a year to become up-to-date with the new alphabet which was deemed to be more conducive to rendering the sounds of Turkish. A deeper objective was to detach the population of the new state from its Islamic and Ottoman cultural moorings. Taken together, this dizzying array of prohibitions and innovations signaled the radical republican intent to depart from its formidable Ottoman inheritance.

Sovereignty holds a special position in the Turkish "revolution." One of the rallying cries of the nationalists both during the "War of National Liberation" and in the early years of the republic was "sovereignty belongs unconditionally to the nation/community" (*Hakimiyet bila kayd ü şart milletindir*). On the face of it, this represented a massive shift from the Ottoman era when sovereignty belonged to the Ottoman dynasty – the Ottoman territories were referred to as the "well-protected royal domains" (*memalik-i mahruse-i şahane*) – and, unlike the situation in modern nation-states, there was no immediate connection between the dynasty and its territories. Like all empires, the Ottoman state was almost by definition multinational and its attitude to specific territories was pragmatic and more or less devoid of romantic association. In other words, while the empire was naturally interested in extending and defending its territorial sovereignty, its conception of rule was almost never invested in the territory *per se*; the empire was simply coterminous with its borders, wherever they reached. As these borders shrank over the course of the eighteenth, nineteenth and early twentieth centuries, the preoccupation with territory, or rather the loss it, naturally became stronger. The state began to adopt policies that attempted to bind its provinces – and its subjects now increasingly being treated as proto-citizens – closer to the center. But the encroachment of an array of foreign actors, including investors, diplomats, military observers and missionaries, meant that the empire's range of movement was severely restricted. It found its fate increasingly decided by the "Great Powers" in the international arena. Financially, its room for maneuver was increasingly restricted due to loans arranged with overseas financiers since the 1850s; after 1881 an international debt commission took control over approximately one-third of the empire's tax revenues. Missionaries and other foreigners were able to open and operate schools without much effective imperial oversight. All of these actors impinged on Ottoman sovereignty, as noticed by both Ottomans and foreigners alike. As Lord Derby noted as early as 1879, "The daily surveillance of which Turkey is the object in her domestic affairs has reduced her sovereign authority to practically zero."[4]

Any examination of the concept of sovereignty in the late Ottoman and early Turkish Republican period must start from this very low ebb, the recognition that the late Ottoman state was an empire without full sovereignty. This realization was made all the more difficult to endure by both the illustrious Ottoman imperial past and the ambitions of a range of the Ottoman population, from statesmen to schoolchildren, to restore a level of independence and self-respect that they felt to be commensurate with that proud history. In light of the contrast between the high expectations generated by the past and expected of the future, on the one hand, and the low level of actual Ottoman sovereignty in the late nineteenth century, on the other, we can trace the outlines of a movement to restore first Ottoman and then Turkish sovereignty across this period.

In the period of the Tanzimat reforms (1839–76) the empire's leadership accepted an unprecedented degree of foreign advice and imported Western institutions in a manner that would later appear to have been rather uncritical. The middle decades of the nineteenth century were marked by a fairly high degree of cooperation between the empire and the Western powers. The Ottomans fought alongside the British and the French against Russia in the Crimean War, and Ottoman independence and territorial integrity were guaranteed according to the terms of the Treaty of Paris (1856). These promises did not last terribly long. Just over twenty years later the empire's erstwhile allies failed to intervene in the Russo-Ottoman war of 1877–8, a conflict with profound territorial and demographic consequences for the Ottomans. To make matters worse, Britain extracted control over Cyprus for her role as broker of the post-war negotiations at Berlin, the outcome of which ameliorated the harsh terms imposed by the Russians at San Stefano. During the reign of Sultan Abdülhamid II (1876–1909) Ottoman policy responded to the altered strategic and demographic terrain by adopting a wariness of Western influence, by trying to play the Powers against each other (the rise of Germany was especially useful here), by avoiding major wars, by reasserting the Islamic dimension of Ottoman rule and in general by making the best of a weakened hand. But this cautious approach was deemed insufficient by the younger generation, many of whom had imbibed the pain of the slights to Ottoman sovereignty along with the belief in progress, social Darwinism and military solutions.

Following the "Young Turk" revolution of 1908, the Ottoman Empire entered a period in which the issue of sovereignty was increasingly at the center of political life. The men in power behind the scenes were members of the Committee of Union and Progress (CUP), an organization whose core Ottoman Muslim membership was as sensitive to the patronizing slights inflicted on the empire in the international arena as they were to the condescension and seniority of their erstwhile superiors.[5] They represented a new generation that was impatient with the old style of politics and they were convinced that a more direct, military approach would allow the empire to reassert control over its own destiny.

In the crucial years leading up to the First World War, questions of war, liberation and modernity dominated the intellectual atmosphere in the Ottoman Empire. Resentment against international double standards, foreign control in the political and financial realms and European schemes for further territorial humiliations were linked with the need to modernize in order to realize a "new society" and a "new life."[6] A crucial development was the Italian invasion of Tripolitania (Libya) in 1911. This attack on the last remaining Ottoman sovereign possession in Africa – Tunis had been taken by the French in 1881 and Egypt remained Ottoman only in name since the British occupation of 1882 – inflicted a heavy shock on the Ottoman leadership. The failure of the other states of Western Europe to act in the face of Italian aggression was a bitter blow and left no uncertainty about the value of Great Power promises of safeguarding the empire's territorial integrity. The Ottoman response, although ultimately unsuccessful in thwarting the Italian annexation of Libya, was indicative of the new Ottoman mood. Officers and volunteers (*fedais*) loyal to Enver Paşa, active in what would later become formalized as the "Special Organization" (*Teşkilat-i Mahsusa*), an intelligence and special operations branch, mustered local resistance to the Italian invasion.[7] On the home front, the CUP organized an economic boycott of Italian goods, reflecting a trend toward mass politicization, the importance of public opinion and the increasing visibility of economic nationalism. The Balkan wars that quickly followed forced Istanbul to come to an accelerated accommodation with Italy. Far more threatening to the empire's existence, these conflicts further inflamed Ottoman public opinion and strengthened the hand of the CUP. Having lost power briefly in 1912, the CUP played on the inability of the opposition to retain Edirne (Adrianople), a former Ottoman capital, as a result of the settlement after the first phase of the Balkan wars. The CUP led a popular campaign to pressure the government into recapturing the city, which duly occurred in July 1913, a significant reassertion of Ottoman sovereignty in the teeth of both its neighbors and the will of the Powers.

With the CUP now firmly in power, attention turned to another persistent problem affecting the empire's ability to exercise its sovereignty, namely, the Capitulations. First granted to European trading nations from a position of Ottoman strength in the early years of the empire, these economic privileges had become by the late Ottoman period a symbol of foreign control and as such were bitterly resented. The CUP made annulling the Capitulations one of its chief priorities along the road to a "national economy."[8] During the First World War, the Ottoman government took the opportunity to abrogate the Capitulations in spite of the disapproval of its allies. The terms of the Sèvres treaty had them reinstated, but they were finally done away with at Lausanne, reflecting the Turkish Republic's ability to assert its newfound sovereignty.

A final word on sovereignty in the Young Turk era: the Ottoman search for an alliance with a major European state needs to be understood at least in part through the lens of dignity and equality. After the Balkan wars, Istanbul was convinced that in order to survive the empire had to form an alliance with one of the European powers or the alliances they had formed. After sounding out Britain, France, Austria-Hungary and even Russia, all states that had their own territorial designs on the empire's lands, the CUP government settled finally on Germany. This determination was made in no small part on the basis that Germany was willing to negotiate with Istanbul on equal terms. The war and the eventual defeat that it brought meant that the Ottoman Empire, or whatever leadership that emerged in its aftermath to represent the Ottoman Muslim population, would have to defend its sovereignty on its own. The emergence of the nationalist movement in the interior of Anatolia would eventually provide the answer to this question, but its pursuit of a nationally-based sovereignty was largely conditioned by the late Ottoman experience.

Sovereignty itself is a good example of the importance of the late Ottoman legacy for understanding the continuity between empire and republic. The instrumental phrase that claimed sovereignty for the nation/community unsurprisingly had its origins – like much of the nationalist program in spite of its rhetoric to the contrary – in the late Ottoman period. It derived from the 1909 Ottoman Constitution, according to the terms of which the sultan had to pledge to be faithful to the nation and the religious community (*vatana ve millete sadakat*). Rephrased by the nationalists in 1921 at the Ankara Grand National Assembly, the first article of the Constitution was that "Sovereignty resides unconditionally with the nation/community" (*Hakimiyet bila kayd ü şart milletindir*).

The phrase served a very useful double purpose for the nationalist cause, allowing it to position itself against an array of both foreign and domestic threats. The anti-foreign stance was a response to the plans by irredentist neighbors, minority groups and the foreign powers to partition what was left of the Ottoman lands. The challenges to the sovereignty of the rump Ottoman state could hardly have been starker. The Muslim population looked on aghast as a combination of foreign armies (French, British and Italian) and Allied-sponsored forces (the independent Greek invasion and the Armenians who appeared alongside French troops) took possession of significant portions of Anatolia in the immediate aftermath of the fighting. After the signing of the Mudros Armistice, British forces continued their northward march in Mesopotamia, occupying the province of Mosul and its oil fields and setting off the "Mosul question," and took Maraş and Ayntab, which had until the armistice formed part of the Ottoman province of Aleppo. Meanwhile, French troops landed at Alexandretta and fanned out across the provinces of Cilicia in late 1918. The terms of Mudros envisioned Allied protection for the Armenian population in the provinces of eastern Anatolia; the presence of Armenian units among the French forces in the southeast provoked Turkish suspicions about Allied intentions to establish an Armenian state.[9] French and British forces occupied Istanbul in early 1918, led symbolically and provocatively by General Franchet d'Espèrèy's entry into the imperial capital on a white horse in an apparent attempt to emulate Mehmed II's capture of Constantinople in 1453. The Italians, not to be excluded, took possession of territory around Antalya in March 1919.

But it was the Greek invasion that was to prove the galvanizing factor in provoking a Turkish national response. Britain's imperial resolve was crumbling in the aftermath of the First World War. Financial problems, an increasingly alarming revolution in Ireland and a general sense of imperial fatigue combined to limit Britain's post-war ambitions. It was against this less than buoyant mood that David Lloyd George made the fateful decision to allow Greece, which had joined the Allied cause very late in the course of the war, to invade western Anatolia on behalf of the Allies. The Greek landings in Izmir in May and their subsequent transgression of the Milne Line, drawn by Britain to contain the proxy Greek occupation force, precipitated a major reaction on the part of the Turkish nationalists who had already begun organizing in the interior of Anatolia, away from the Ottoman government under Franco-British occupation in the capital. It was one thing to contemplate foreign occupation as a temporary, tutelary measure – an American option was supported by many Turks – but an invasion by a neighboring country with both an ideological and historical claim to Anatolian land and an immediate past history of warfare and territorial aggrandizement stemming from the Balkan wars was a much more alarming proposition.[10]

After the defeat of the Greek forces, the nationalists still had to overcome a potentially formidable military obstacle in the form of the British forces occupying the Straits zone. With the Greeks gone there was no buffer between the nationalists and the British. The nationalist forces demanded a right of passage across the water and into Europe, while the British refused to back down. The Çanak crisis of 1922, as it became known, reflected a lack of collective Allied resolve. Britain called on its allies and its overseas Dominions for help, but very little was forthcoming.[11] Lloyd George suffered a humiliating climb-down after a rift appeared between London and Paris over the crisis and between London and important members of the Commonwealth, especially Canada. Eventually the officers on the spot resolved the question. The British would control the territory pending the final settlement but the resolve of the nationalists to take on any comers was firmly recorded.

With the foreign danger largely minimized, the nationalists could turn their attention toward a number of Ottoman-era groups who were now deemed to be enemies of the nation. The anti-foreign stance was extended to include the House of Osman – and to those who refused to choose to side with the nationalists and break away from the old regime – due to their supposedly traitorous behavior under Allied occupation. Apprehensions concerning the intentions of foreign powers with respect to the territorial unity of the Turkish Republic, the so-called "Sèvres syndrome," continue to this day in wariness over US and EU policy toward the Kurdish question.

The ability of the nationalists to maintain a largely unified leadership during the fighting for Anatolia was crucial to their success. In this regard they were helped by what might be referred to as the creative ambiguity of the definition of their constituency. The vagueness of the term "millet" in the phrase "sovereignty belongs unconditionally to the nation/community" led many Muslim sub-groups in Anatolia (especially the Kurds but also some – but by no means all – of the important Circassian elements[12]) to believe they shared common cause with the nationalists.

The international community, although divided with respect to the ultimate nature of the settlement for the core Ottoman territories, nevertheless recognized the new approach to sovereignty to an important degree. It was enshrined in Woodrow Wilson's Twelfth Point which linked sovereignty with the concept of self-determination, stating, "The Turkish portion of the present Ottoman Empire should be assured a secure sovereignty, but the other nationalities which are now under Turkish rule should be assured an undoubted security of life and an absolutely unmolested opportunity of autonomous development."[13] This last stipulation, along with the subsequent condition that the Straits should be open to international navigation, represented a clear qualification of the nature of Turkish sovereignty as envisioned by the American president. This restricted sense of sovereignty was enshrined in the Treaty of Lausanne, which settled the boundaries and political status of the Turkish successor to the Ottoman state. The new republic had to accept a major share of the financial debt that the empire owed to European investors, a demilitarized status for straits of the Dardanelles and the Bosporus and internationally protected status for the non-Muslim population. Given the harsh terms that had been dictated at the Mudros Armistice in 1918 and those that would have been incorporated into the Sèvres treaty had it come into force (including, *inter alia*, the creation of foreign zones of occupation), Lausanne was a great improvement from the Turkish perspective. Nevertheless the negotiations were very difficult and tense. The Turks correctly felt that they were not being treated as equals. Lord Curzon "adopted an extremely patronising and arrogant attitude, which contributed to the bad-tempered atmosphere."[14] The Turkish delegation was led by İsmet Paşa (İnönü), who used his deafness to temporize; ill-feelings remained afterwards.

To appreciate the sense of qualified success on the part of the Turkish nationalists, it is necessary to understand the emergence of the national movement in the immediate aftermath of the war against the backdrop of territorial division and foreign occupation. After defeat in the war and the

Franco-British occupation of the capital, the Ottoman government continued to function, albeit within the constraints of allied surveillance. The palace adopted a policy of appeasing the allies in the hopes of achieving a favorable peace settlement. The harsh terms announced at Sèvres thus undermined the sultan's stance. Time worked against the palace, the allies and the liberal factions. The overall peace treaty negotiations dragged on, partly as a result of the need to reconcile the largely irreconcilable promises made by the allies during the war. All the while the nationalists were gathering strength. Mobilizing networks established prior to the war, especially among the military, they began to prepare the ground for a resistance movement, both in the capital and increasingly in the provinces of Anatolia, beyond the reach of the allied occupation. Eventually, to make a long story very short, they managed to organize an alternative government. After meetings in Erzurum and Sivas, this fledgling government, increasingly under the control of Mustafa Kemal, settled in Ankara where they formed the Great National Assembly in April 1920. It was this body that announced its constitution in the name of the nation/community the following year.

This superficially radical break – investing political sovereignty in the people[15] – was, of course, not altogether followed up in immediate practice. The nationalists had cut their political teeth in the Young Turk era and many of them – in fact, all of the important ones – had been members of the CUP, a group well known for its strident elitism and profound skepticism of, and sometimes outright disdain for, the masses. So the Kemalist regime that emerged in Turkey after independence was one that ruled in the name of people – populism (*halkçılık*) was one of the six arrows of Mustafa Kemal's Republican People's Party (CHP) that dominated the single-party period until the aftermath of the Second World War – but led by an elite that believed itself singly able to act on their behalf and jealously guarded its monopoly over the reins of power. In fact, it quickly became apparent that "the people" it had in mind when it spoke in the name of populism needed to be thoroughly reinvented, eliminating their religiosity, their "superstitions" and training them in the ways of Western materialist progress.

In spite of its radical social and cultural agendas the new republican regime, like many of the post-First World War states in the region, depended on a number of trends, institutions and personnel it had inherited from the imperial past. It was the direct beneficiary of a long tradition of bureaucratization, with a strong centralizing streak, that dated back to the late eighteenth century when the empire began in earnest to reinvent the way it ruled its sprawling territory. This process was driven first and foremost by military considerations. As a result, the militarization of late Ottoman society, which emerged gradually but was given special fillip by the warfare of the early twentieth century when it drew increasingly on national sentiment, was a direct legacy for the republic. So also were features of the political landscape such as the concept of representative government, elections, and the introduction of party politics with all of its positive and negative aspects. Rather more tangibly, the empire bequeathed to the republic a core of administrators and military officers who had considerable managerial experience, and a rapidly growing educational system that was raising literacy rates and allowing the state to communicate directly with its citizens. While the late Ottoman state had begun to use this and other vehicles for disseminating its ideational strategies, especially with respect to legitimization of the regime, the republic would vastly expand these capacities, taking advantage not only of the ground prepared by the empire but also of the reduced size of the republican territory.

As with all of the post-Ottoman states, the trick was to find a strategy for post-imperial rule that at the very least concealed and more usually denigrated the debts they owed to the imperial past. The experience of the First World War proved extremely useful in this regard as it allowed the vast majority of loyal Ottoman subjects to reinvent themselves as nationalist citizens of varying stripes once the war was over. Here they took their cue from the Ottoman-turned-national elites who quickly repositioned themselves in the post-Ottoman era, reflecting perhaps the skills developed by generations of notables to react to the changing circumstances of empire in ways that furthered their own interests.

This is, of course, not to say that nothing changed in the aftermath of empire. In many ways, an old world gave way to a new. Important changes in language, in politics and in economics reflected the altered dispensation. Yet it is nevertheless striking to observe just how many patterns continued, with obvious refinements and aberrations, in spite of the rhetoric so stridently directed against the old regime and in the name of new forms of sovereignty.

Now, let us turn to consider the Turkish experience in a comparative framework by contrasting its ability to project sovereignty with other post-Ottoman states in the Middle East. By considering what made the Turkish imperial legacy unique and what made it similar to the many other post-imperial state-building efforts, we can attempt to highlight the interaction between the pull of the common past and the push of the distinctively Turkish particularities. The states to emerge from the Ottoman Empire shared some broadly similar attributes, both in terms of their social and political structures, their many shared cultural features (such as language, dress, cuisine and so on) and history and in terms of their historiographical treatment of that common experience.[16]

In comparison with the post-Ottoman Arab states, the Turkish Republic enjoyed several major advantages with respect to its ability to act in a sovereign manner. These advantages fall into two main categories. First, the republic inherited the core of the late Ottoman state; along with ministries and procedures came personnel and the expectation of rule. This legacy had its disadvantages, to be sure, particularly in the financial and legal realms, but from the perspective of a state concerned with its image and its ability to project power, it was highly fortuitous. Moreover, and rarely noted in this connection, the young republic was in many respects now in a position to take action with respect to many of the frustrated, pre-existing agendas of the late imperial period. In other words, unlike its fellow successor states the Turkish Republic had a ready list of areas for action. For example, one of the first acts of the republic was to pass the Law on the Unification of Education (*Tevhid-i Tedrisat Kanunu*) in March 1924. By imposing a single mechanism for overseeing all of the educational institutions in the country, including those run by foreign missionaries and the indigenous religious communities, the republic was fulfilling a wish that the empire had lacked the military and diplomatic status to accomplish.

Second, the manner by which the young republic established its independence was critical. As the only portion of the empire to defy the intentions of the victorious powers to impose partition and mandatory rule, the early Turkish Republic accrued to itself a crucial degree of respect and a unique status among its fellow post-Ottoman states. While Syria, Palestine, Transjordan and Iraq were all saddled with European mandatory regimes of varying intensity and length, the young Turkish Republic was free to pursue its own agenda with respect to state- and nation-building. While it might be argued that in the headiness of this newfound freedom the Kemalist state pursued some regrettable excesses with respect to national redefinition and the suppression of sub-national identities, what is clear is that it enjoyed the unfettered ability to act on its own sovereign terms. Able to portray itself with considerable justification as having vanquished the colonial ambitions of the allied powers and defended the motherland from its enemies, both real and imagined, the republican leadership – the military in particular – were in a very enviable position. In Syria, by contrast, the French mandatory administration pursued a policy of divide and rule, apportioning the country into separate regions and favoring certain ethnic groups over others, a strategy with significant long-term implications for Syrian politics and society.

This strong stance inevitably shaped the course of republican history, as can clearly be seen by contrasting it to the post-Ottoman Arab states where the experience of colonial rule, the fragmentation of the wider Arab nation and the frequently unsatisfactory experience of consolidating real independence in the post-First World War period constituted an enduring liability. Furthermore, these varied experiences invite exploration of the relationship between the former core and periphery. Why, it might be asked, did Turkey not attempt to resurrect its former role in a post-imperial guise and to play a leading role among its fellow post-Ottoman states? Although there were certainly incentives for the young republic to incline toward this path – not least in the form of oil fields in what became Iraq, for example – Turkey's ideological orientation and abiding wish to avoid regional entanglements meant that under the leadership of both Atatürk and İnönü, Turkey's foreign policy downplayed and occasionally even obstructed regional opportunities in order to concentrate on attempting to enhance its standing as a Western and, indeed, a European state. The principle of staunch neutrality inherent in Atatürk's famous dictum, "Peace at home, peace abroad" (*Yurtta sulh, cihanda sulh*) was largely maintained throughout the twentieth century (and afterwards, as indicated by Turkey's refusal to allow access to US military forces in the lead-up to the second Gulf War). Undoubtedly, Turkey's ability to thwart Allied post-First World War partition plans afforded it the opportunity to build a largely positive and more nearly equal relationship with the West as it emerged as an important independent regional power. It has only been in recent years that solid progress has been made toward restoring more neighborly relations with the Arab world.

In historiographical terms it is notable how powerful the separation between Turkish and Arab history has become. For regions so historically intertwined, Anatolia and the Levant seem to have gone their separate ways. In large part this reflects the strong impact of the official, nationalist approach to history in all of the states created in the wake of the First World War. Linguistic divisions and the rapid growth in the emerging subfields of "Turkish" and "Arab" history have surely played their part in reinforcing this separation. It is telling that the most important history of the Arab world to appear in many years makes hardly any reference to Turkey at all, so entrenched has the disjuncture become in less than a century.[17] Despite the many common features of their imperial and post-imperial trajectories, Turkey and the Arab world have been seen to travel different routes in the nation-state era. The irony here is that it is precisely the common features of nationalist historical imagining – and forgetting – that have conspired to emphasize dissimilarity over similarity in a largely self-fulfilling trajectory of national particularity.

SOVEREIGNTY IN THE OTTOMAN EMPIRE AND AFTER

Notes

1. Hourani, "The Ottoman background to the modern Middle East," p. 1.
2. Mardin, "The Ottoman Empire," p. 115.
3. Lewis, *The Turkish Language Reform.*
4. Blaisdell, *European Financial Control in the Ottoman Empire*, p. 24, as cited in Ibrahim, "The transformation of Ottoman sovereignty, 1908–1918," p. 10.
5. On the CUP, see Hanioğlu, *The Young Turks in Opposition* and *Preparation for a Revolution.*
6. Aksakal, *The Ottoman Road to War in 1914*, p. 29.
7. Ahmed, "War and society under the Young Turks, 1908–1918," p. 131; Zürcher, *Turkey: A Modern History*, p. 109.
8. Hanioğlu, "The second constitutional period, 1908–1918," p. 97.
9. Kayalı, "The struggle for independence," p. 119.
10. Kayalı, "The struggle for independence," p. 121.
11. Zürcher, *Turkey: A Modern History*, pp. 155–6.
12. Gingeras, *Sorrowful Shores.*
13. Kayalı, "The struggle for independence," p. 118.
14. Zürcher, *Turkey: A Modern History*, p. 161.
15. Mustafa Kemal's famous phrase is often translated as, "Sovereignty belongs unconditionally to the people," "people" here standing in collectively for the "nation" or the "religious community." The religious overtones of the term "millet" were naturally dropped given the laicist spirit of the early republic.
16. For an overview of the common Ottoman inheritance in a variety of fields, see Brown (ed.), *Imperial Legacy.*
17. Rogan, *The Arabs: A History.*

6

Mandated Sovereignty? The Role of International Law in the Construction of Arab Statehood during and after Empire

Michelle Burgis

Although it is often claimed that international law remains peculiarly absent from the Middle East and North Africa (MENA) region with its persisting conflicts and conflagrations,[1] its role has in fact been seminal in the (re)configuration of statehood across the region. In particular, the inter-relationship between international law and colonialism has played a central role for MENA states now inhabiting a post-colonial space. This chapter therefore considers how international law has shaped and continues to shape MENA states by considering the inter-related factors of international legal personality (ILP), self-determination claims and the adjudication of boundary disputes. General cross-regional themes will be acknowledged, but the chapter will focus on three case studies in the colonial and post-colonial periods: (1) the mandate states; (2) the case of Western Sahara's (failed) self-determination bid; and (3) some of the small states of the Gulf. How can we draw upon international legal scholarship to understand the transition from colonialism to independence in these states? Were international legal arguments used in struggles over independence and how? Has international law been an enabling force for Arab states seeking independence or has it, instead, continued to uphold legacies of the colonial past so that in fact it is difficult to speak of an era *after* colonialism?

A growing body of literature devoted to the ways in which international law has been used as a means of colonization and the denial of non-European sovereignty will ground the chapter within wider debates about the scope and nature of a "universal" international law.[2] To what extent are "new" states still shaped by colonial legacies of boundaries, personality and definitions of selfhood? Has international law permitted a re-evaluation of sovereignty in the post-colonial era? The chapter takes issue with traditional narratives of rupture and instead points to continuities.[3] In particular, I focus on the inter-war period of the mandate system to highlight the inseparable relationship between formal and informal empire and its enduring legacies across the Arab world. It will be argued that international law has played an important role in delimiting and limiting the possibilities of post-colonial statehood in the MENA region. Thus, it is only in understanding international law in the colonial and mandatory eras that we can make sense of the present. For as Pahuja reminds us, " 'post' in postcolonial designates a state neither clearly beyond nor after the colonial"[4]; we cannot escape the reality that "first of all there was colonialism."[5]

Defining Sovereignty under International Law: International Legal Personality for non-European Entities

Sovereignty has been notoriously difficult to define both for scholars of international law and international relations (IR). This section first reviews Koskenniemi's approach to sovereignty and then introduces the concept of "international legal personality." Related to sovereignty and characterized as a spectrum of full, quasi and non-existent variations, ILP can be understood as a way of gauging rights and responsibilities at the international legal level. In particular, we can assess the degree of an entity's ILP by considering its capacity to enter into treaty relations, its participation in international organizations and litigation, as well as its ability to invoke immunities.[6] Although many IR scholars might look to international law for precision in the quest for defining ILP, it is argued here that such an endeavor is not possible. Far from being a priori, definitions of ILP are instead embedded in the given legal and political context of international society, whether in its pre- or post-colonial configurations. Thus, once we compare contemporaneous notions of sovereignty with colonial practice we will see how elastic were the definitions applied to non-European entities. Who possessed full ILP before and during colonialism? Did once fully recognized states, such as the Ottoman Empire's components "lose" their sovereignty in the heyday of empire only to then be re-admitted into "international society" through acceptance by European powers? How are we to regard protectorates in the Gulf which ceded their external sovereignty while retaining control over internal affairs? By considering non-European statehood and then testing it through the examples of ILP for the Ottoman Empire and the Gulf protectorates, this section demonstrates the indeterminate nature of sovereignty within the discipline of international law.

As a term, "sovereignty" is readily invoked by scholars and practitioners of international law at regular intervals, but what exactly are they referring to? Is there a commonly agreed definition of sovereignty within the international legal academy? Various cases and treaties can be relied upon here,[7] but on closer scrutiny, contradictions and uncertainties soon reveal the term to be a Pandora's Box of perplexity. This is not surprising, for in seeking to understand the contours of sovereignty, we confront the most enduring conflict within modern international law: that between state right and international regulation. Was it law that came first and endowed states with authority and jurisdiction, or was it states that through their consent, gradually shaped an ever-expanding international legal architecture?[8] For Kennedy, modern international law cannot escape both tendencies:

> Sovereignty becomes not only a description of ultimate political discretion, but also a legal idea – indeed, it is law which provides a language to explain, ratify, protect sovereignty. And the most important rules and principles of international law come to be deductions from the idea of sovereignty rather than consensual rules of constraint.[9]

Furthermore, how are "new" states created – by their own sovereign will or by recognition from other states?[10]

Although some international lawyers state their positivist or naturalist credentials explicitly, many seek to fall in step with a disciplinary sensibility that regards it best to deny this tension at all costs. Such a practice allows lawyers to invoke terms like "sovereignty" in a variety of ways and for a variety of (often contradictory) purposes. In his discussion of the term, however, Koskenniemi discounts such gestures:

> The expression "sovereignty" or any definition thereof cannot have fixed content as to be "automatically" applicable. It is not only that they are ambiguous or have a penumbra of uncertainty about them. There simply is no fixed meaning, no natural extent to sovereignty about them. Moreover, assuming that sovereignty had a fixed content would entail accepting that there is an antecedent material rule which determines the boundaries of State liberty regardless of the subjective will or interest of any particular State.[11]

Thus, when speaking of "sovereignty" in international law we must be ever mindful of the way it is given meaning and for what political ends.

The politics of "sovereignty"-speak was particularly palpable for European international lawyers in the nineteenth and early twentieth centuries when colonialism was at its height. Intermittent and often informal interaction between European and non-European worlds gave way to increasingly formal and hierarchical legal relations. Although early imperial encounters had required little assistance from international lawyers,[12] this was no longer the case by the late nineteenth century, as epitomized by the 1885 Treaty of Berlin and the concomitant carving up of the Congo.[13] This episode and various others in the period attest to the imposition of European oversight across the non-European world through a marriage of (positivist) international law with the sufficiently nebulous "standard of civilisation."[14] Although international lawyers at the time were generally averse to using "imperialism" and "international law" in the same sentence lest their field be sullied by the presence of "politics," they were still vital for the imperial project of domination through and by law. In particular, Koskenniemi points out that flexible interpretations of sovereignty had profound effects at this time: "It was their failure to spell out the meaning of sovereignty in social and political terms, as applied in non-European territory, that in retrospect made international lawyers such hopeless apologists of empire."[15] A whole range of legal techniques could be utilized simultaneously to draw in and then emasculate non-European peoples. ILP was applied to non-European peoples creatively and flexibly depending on the political exigencies of any particular case.[16] For example, treaties of cession endowing non-European peoples with only limited ILP were vital for the colonial project and cannot simply be regarded as "political" documents devoid of legal force. Thus, for Miéville:

> Let us be clear – these unequal treaties were not ostensibly but *really* legal, they *created* the general principles of international law: they are not fraudulent, but the truth of nineteenth-century international law. That is the law we inherited.[17]

International law and colonialism were one and the same.

Some more recent scholarship has sought to disavow this "dark" period in the annals of the discipline by downplaying this period of parochialism and particularism. Thus, in relation to the absence of ILP for most non-European entities at the time, Alexandrowicz depicts this as an exception for various entities which had possessed and would reclaim their sovereignty with the advent of decolonization.[18] Other less optimistic writers point to pathologies within European thought that had always regarded non-European peoples and powers as somehow "less" civilized than themselves.[19] Thus, international law was able to be employed whenever necessary to define and deny selfhood and, thus, statehood for much of the non-European world. The flexibility of "sovereignty" proved to be allusive for those wishing to "enter" international society, but it also proved elusive: impossibly elastic definitions were hard to satisfy and yet ever more desperate attempts at their fulfillment only solidified the image of "backward" peoples not yet ready for full participation in international society.

This chapter rejects the approach of Alexandrowicz, which regards international law as a universal body of rules that were misapplied only during colonialism. On the contrary, we must acknowledge international law's European origins and make sense of its expansion through colonialism.[20] The mainstream international lawyer of today carries with her or him a faith in the progress and promise of a contemporary international law that is radically different and better than its colonial past. No matter how "difficult the project will be, international lawyers share an orientation to a past of sovereign states and a future of international law. The discipline looks forward, confident that we will arrive in the future with history at our side."[21] Despite this disciplinary tendency to overlook unpleasant moments from its past, Anghie reminds us, however, that it was the colonial encounter between the European and non-European worlds that produced international law and its enduring dynamic of differentiated and unequal statehood.[22] Thus, any understanding of modern sovereignty cannot overlook the colonial "past."

The Ottoman Empire's "admission" into "international society" (or the European state system) in 1856 is one such example of the paradox of ILP for non-European states. Various scholars have considered both the legal and political effects of the Sublime Porte's accession to the Treaty of Paris,[23] which speaks of Ottoman admission to the Concert of Europe.[24] Whether we regard this moment as marking the beginning or simply an intensification of pre-existing European–Ottoman relations, we cannot deny that it symbolizes a period of ever-increasing interference in Ottoman "internal" affairs. Thus, the ability to invoke "external" sovereignty came at the price of emasculated "internal" sovereignty that was required to fulfill the indeterminate notion of European civilization. It is ironic that we can point to full Ottoman ILP when the regime of capitulations and general European interference were at their strongest. Thus, for the Ottomans and their subject peoples, the promise of international law was very much a double-edged sword: membership of international society and the possession of "external" sovereignty came at the cost of the erosion of "internal" sovereignty.[25]

This paradox of statehood for non-European entities during the colonial period is well-captured in the case of the Trucial States, which largely fell into British hands with the demise of Ottoman control in the Gulf. The protectorate had emerged as the main territorial entity for Berlin-style colonialism, but had also been used earlier outside the African continent. Like treaties of cession, protectorate agreements were often based on arbitrary interpretations of sovereignty and personality, perhaps providing the sufficient quotient of ILP for rulers to enter into agreements that would then erase their presence on the international stage.[26] According to Andrews, "there was an enormous variety in the styles of protectorate, some of which were scarcely dissimilar from colonial status in the extent of control assumed by the protecting power."[27] Shaw explains the proliferation of protectorates through an account of how the classical ideal of protectorates increasingly gave way to colonial exigencies. Initially, protectorates were based on bifurcated sovereignty: external sovereignty for the protecting power and internal sovereignty for the protégé.[28] Later on, and especially in Africa, there was no real difference between protection and cession.

The classical understanding of protection informed a series of treaties entered into between Britain and the Gulf sheikhdoms from 1820 onwards. Local rulers retained their domestic control, while, for example, pledging that neither the chief of Bahrain nor his heirs were to enter into agreement or communication "with any Power other than the British Government."[29] Although the Gulf fared much better than Africa in the sovereignty stakes, even here, categories of ILP remained fluid.[30] Reading the pleadings from the Qatar/Bahrain dispute, for example, highlights the extent to which British internal interference muddied the formal difference between a colony and a protectorate. Furthermore, when adjudicating their boundary dispute decades later and as discussed below, it became clear that the administrative decisions of British officials would have enduring effects on the contours of the two states' territories. Even for the relatively privileged status of protectorates then, European control over parts of the Arab world left a profound impact. Thus, we can see that uses and abuses of the boundaries of ILP have been central to the contours of colonial and post-colonial statehood.

Mandated Statehood: The League of Nations and Arab Peoples on the Path toward Self-Rule

With this backdrop of colonial experience, after the First World War victorious European powers continued to rely on international law to regulate their relations with the Arab world, especially those territories formerly under the Ottomans. International law, however, could not simply be used to continue the colonial system of the long nineteenth century. Questions generally about Europe's civilizational pedigree and specifically its positivist, formalist legal tradition in the wake of the war suggested that colonialism would have to be modified.[31] Also, a rising tide of support for self-determination meant that European powers supportive of its realization on their doorstop (Eastern Europe) would have to at least pay lip-service to the idea further afield. Thus, under the League of Nations the mandate system was devised, which would act as a new protection regime for those unable "to stand alone."[32] Traditional international legal accounts of this period tend to overlook the significance of the mandate regime for post-colonial statehood, and, if this period is discussed, it is generally quarantined both from its colonial past and the more positive future. Historical studies of the Middle East too often fail to engage with the particular characteristics of the mandate system and international legal effects. What was unique about the mandate system for the Arab world? How were the mandates both similar and different from their colonial counterparts? How important was international law in this period for defining the requirements of statehood for a time after the mandate? In this section, I consider debates about the nature of sovereignty and colonialism through the prism of League institutions. A rich array of international legal scholarly debate on the nature of the mandates develops our understanding of the indeterminate nature of ILP for non-European peoples. A consideration of one case from the Permanent Court of Justice (PCIJ) about mandates in the MENA region highlights the enduring effect of international law for Arab states in this period: mandated sovereignty.

Before considering legal controversies over the nature of mandate sovereignty, it is useful to interrogate the motivations of France and especially Britain in developing the mandate system. Although some recognition can be given to humanitarian ideals in conceiving of this system of tutelage,[33] we must not forget that much of the non-European world remained under various forms of "protection" or colonialism that neither France nor Britain were ready to relinquish. Although Britain favored an informal approach to empire in much of the Arab world, as in her condominium over Sudan with Egypt, we still need to understand the relationship between Britain and various Arab peoples under her authority as a fundamentally unequal one. Diplomatic dealings during the First World War[34] and the emergence of the mandate idea should not mask the fact that Britain often regarded its approach to mandatory, colonial or protectorate territories in a similar light.[35] According to Prime Minister Lloyd George in 1919, "there was no large difference between the principles of the Mandate System and those of the Berlin Conference" of 1885.[36] Control over much of the Arab world served British interests in India,[37] and new economic ventures proved that the "burden" of trusteeship was usually worthwhile.[38] Although it is still common to regard Britain's position in the Arab world at this time as disinterested and even a case of accidental empire, Sluglett argues that this is disingenuous.[39] Darwin echoes these sentiments for greater critical work when he argues that "neither the motives which drove British expansion nor the local factors which shaped it have been scrutinised as much as their counterparts elsewhere. Yet it was here that was played out the last, if not the highest, stage of British imperialism."[40] Whether by accident or design, Britain found itself in control of large swathes of the Arab world in a spectrum of informal empire whose effect would endure well beyond the termination of various protectorate and mandatory agreements.

Lawyers are peculiarly fearful of legal voids and this is amply demonstrated by contemporaneous as well as more recent debates about the nature of mandatory powers and their territories.[41] Where did sovereignty vest during the League period and could it be ceded to another power? Under classic colonialism, of course, the answer was simple: cession or conquest would result in the imperial power gaining title over the territory. We have seen, however, in relation to protectorates that very often the status of non-European ILP was unclear and, in fact, the mandate system must be understood within this wider context where informal empire was often the most useful form of European domination. In his study, which appeared only shortly after the mandates' inception, Lauterpacht examined League of Nations provisions and concluded that the regime was radically different from colonialism. Territories were classified along a spectrum of most advanced (A) to least advanced (C) Mandates. It was understood that only A Mandates could expect independence soon, whereas C Mandates were presumed to require many years of education and acculturation into the international system before gaining statehood. Lauterpacht expressed misgivings about C Mandates, but as for the more "advanced" A and B Mandates it was incorrect to speak of annexation.[42] Sovereignty lay with the League, and consequentially mandate territories could not be subsumed under the territory of the mandatory power.[43] Crawford's discussion of the "received view" reinforces Lauterpacht's position. Crawford shows that the dominant narrative distinguished colonial rule from the mandates; France and Britain did not possess sovereignty over these territories.[44] Instead, sovereignty was held "in trust" by the League.[45] Such accounts are seminal for a discipline grounded in narratives of international legal progress: we can look to the mandate system as a break from the colonial past and as a prelude to the exercise of self-determination in the period of decolonization. Such accounts overlook continuities not only between pre- and post-First World War realities, but also institutional similarities between the League and the United Nations.[46] By treating each episode discretely, it is then far easier for international lawyers not to see enduring imperial qualities embedded in the heart of international law.

The traditional narrative is challenged by Anghie, who, in asking whether it is best to regard the institution of the mandates as the negation or re-creation of colonialism, favors the latter response.[47] Article 22 of the League Charter is reminiscent of nineteenth-century colonialist discourses on the "Standard of Civilisation" when it speaks of a "sacred trust of civilization."[48] Under this system, peoples were to be guided along a single trajectory of eventual independence; diversity was not permitted in this schema as, instead, those "not yet able to stand by themselves" were ushered into a system of seeming sovereign similitude. This paradox of enforced "freedom" is captured by Anghie:

> In seeking to liberate the mandate peoples from the "strenuous conditions of the modern world," the system instead entraps the mandate peoples within those conditions. The peculiar cycle thus creates a situation whereby international institutions present themselves as a solution to a problem of which they are an integral part.[49]

Thus, far from being absent, we see again that international law was seminal in shaping sovereignty into the post-colonial present.

Despite their exalted status as class A Mandates, this was perhaps especially so for the Arab territories of Transjordan, Palestine, Iraq and Syria, whose expected independence could come only after the wholesale examination of their societies by the mandatory power and the Permanent Mandates Commission (PMC). Thus, "the task confronting the mandate system involved far more than the granting of a simple juridical status. Rather, international law and institutions were required to create the economic, political and social conditions under which a sovereign state could come into being."[50] Rajagopal shows us how in this period, law and science were melded together by the PMC to allow for new and more effective techniques of administrative control.[51] This can also be seen as a shift from positivism to pragmatism in the application of international law at a time witnessing a turn from formal to informal empire.[52] Faith in a single trajectory of development,[53] too, resulted in the subordination of native interests to those of the "open door" and international standards. Over time, "well-being and development" was more narrowly interpreted so that it became synonymous simply with economic well-being.[54] Such an approach continued throughout the period of decolonization with discourses of development and intensifying intervention by international institutions.[55] Thus, the mandate system was seminal in the internationalization of European domination and of the economization of native societies that would persist and deepen in the UN period.[56] The mandates continued the trend of European domination through international law, but in a radically and far more interventionist form.[57] It was:

precisely because sovereignty over the mandate territory could not be located in any one entity that the Mandate System could have complete access to the interior of that territory. It was for this reason that the League, rather than being restricted by assertions of sovereignty, could develop a unique series of technologies and techniques for entering and transforming the very recesses of the interior of the mandate territory in order to realize this pragmatist, sociological vision of the sovereign state.[58]

As in the case of flexible interpretations of ILP before the First World War, we thus see in this period new ways of shaping and speaking of sovereignty which served the interests of empire and the development of non-European statehood.

In surveying the scope for League as well as general international legal supervision of Arab territories, a small number of PCIJ cases from the period all attest to the fluidity of non-European ILP and the startling fact that Arabs themselves never figured in such proceedings.[59] In contrast to a rich case law on self-determination within Europe and general international legal principles, the PCIJ was rarely given the chance to review mandate practices. Part of this can be explained by the fact that jurisdictional requirements in contentious cases meant that mandatory territories possessed no ILP of their own and instead were represented by their mandatory overlord. Perhaps this then accounts for the rather curious fact that our only available case treating Arab mandates concerns the contractual rights of a former Ottoman, turned Greek national in Palestine: Mr Mavrommatis.[60] The Greek government, representing Mr Mavrommatis, called on the Court to affirm its national's concessions granted by the Ottomans to develop electrical and water utilities in Jaffa and Jerusalem. The Court not only had to consider the validity of these pre-War agreements, but also their nature within the legal context of Mandate Palestine. Under Article 4 of the 1922 Treaty,[61] a Jewish Agency was established to assist the mandatory power with public affairs and the Court linked this provision with Article 11 which reads:

> The Administration of Palestine shall take all necessary measures to safeguard the interests of *the community* in connection with the *development* of the country, and, subject to any international obligations accepted by the Mandatory, shall have full power to provide for *public ownership or control* of any of the natural resources of the country or of the public works, services and utilities established or to be established therein ... The Administration may arrange with the Jewish agency mentioned in Article 4 to construct or operate, upon fair and equitable terms, any public works, services and utilities, and to develop any of the natural resources of the country, in so far as these matters are not directly undertaken by the Administration.[62]

In considering these provisions vis-à-vis the plaintiff, the Court went into some detail about the nature of "public control" and the interests of the community. Ultimately, a reading of the case is far more useful for discovering what was left unsaid than the formalist arguments espoused in support of Mr Mavrommatis' concessions. In particular, the mandate provisions affirm a close relationship between the British authorities and the Jewish Agency in pursuit of extensive social and economic development. Such findings reinforce the work of Anghie and Rajagopal discussed above, which characterize this period as ushering in a massively interventionist approach to governance in the Third World. The Court overlooks the presence of the Arab populations entirely in its judgment, but, of course, we must remember that these peoples would be the recipients of these new modes of governance. The Court also fails to appreciate the dichotomy established between those interests of a "community" granted preferential rights under the mandate and another (majority) community whose interests and rights remained marginalized from international legal consideration. The classic model of settler colonialism is here perpetuated in a modified form and whose effects are still felt across the region.

Ever more creative interpretations of "sovereignty" during the League period allowed for greater and more sustained interventions in the domestic settings of mandate societies. Far from imposing only artificial boundaries and therefore limiting Arab external sovereignty, we can see that new modes of international legal governance also shaped aspects of internal sovereignty.

Bounded by Law? Territorial Delimitation and Post-colonial Possibilities

By the time self-determination could take root across the Arab world, the lingering effects of colonial and mandatory rule were too pronounced to allow their simple denial. In spite of the mandatory architecture being short-lived as well as the declared "informal" nature of many other European Arab holdings, their influence would continue well into the era of Arab nationalism. In trying to trace the particular role of international law in the shaping of post-colonial Arab statehood, this final section considers the inter-relationship between selfhood and statehood as articulated in territorial adjudication before the International Court of Justice (ICJ), the PCIJ's successor.[63] In particular, this section considers the extent to which Arab states and peoples represented in The Hague could question and redraw colonial boundaries.[64] What space has international dispute resolution allowed for historical reckonings? Has international law moved beyond its colonial past? To answer these questions, I will examine some of the arguments used in the advisory opinion on the status of Western Sahara as well as the boundary dispute between Bahrain and Qatar mentioned above.

Before turning to these cases, however, it will be instructive to review the legal architecture of territorial boundaries that emerged in the period of decolonization. When speaking of "independence" for Arab states, we must remember that such a step had to take place within extant colonial boundaries and existing legal approaches to statehood. Although the Arab world has witnessed and continues to witness supra-national challenges to the norm of bounded statehood, more importantly, we can also point to the gradual acceptance of this norm by most states. In fact, from the inception of the Arab League it is clear that strong undercurrents of support for sovereignty informed the approaches of most regimes. Barnett has shown us that Arab nationalism's force was a powerful one in the 1950s and 1960s, but that it always vied with a narrow approach to sovereignty.[65] International law could assist in this endeavor too as conservative approaches to boundary-drawing within international law have meant that the chance of re-appraising current territorial configurations is limited indeed.

Thus, despite the promise of self-determination for non-European peoples, we need to consider how international law came to define the "self" that would be "determined." Particularly in relation to the African continent it soon became clear that the European model of nation-state would lead to chaos, and so, instead,[66] former colonial territorial boundaries defined the limits of the self, thus creating the post-colonial "territorial state."[67] Such a practice was seized on by various self-interested elites anxious to preserve their own power and this was crystallized in the 1964 Cairo Declaration of African heads of state, which subordinated the ideal of self-determination to the pragmatism of *uti possidetis iuris*.[68] This Latin term refers to the basic idea of recognizing former colonial administrative boundaries as international borders and it has been employed by various Third World states to shore up their sovereignty.[69]

This contest between *uti possidetis* and self-determination or between the self and the territory after colonialism is perfectly illustrated by the Western Sahara case. Here, the United Nations General Assembly called upon the ICJ to provide it with an advisory opinion about the status of the territory at the moment of Spanish colonization and the effect this had on relations with Morocco and Mauritania.[70] Such information could then inform the Assembly's policy in the wake of Spanish withdrawal and competing indigenous, Moroccan and Mauritanian claims to the territory. Like earlier PCIJ jurisprudence relating to the Arab world, the people directly affected, the Sahrawis, possessed no standing in the courtroom because of a lack of ILP; as Spanish colonial subjects, it was left to Algeria to speak for them in the pleadings. Such a turn of events was a blow to the aspirations of the recently formed Polisario Front,[71] which expressed its disbelief over a judgment that would "convey the destiny of peoples before the Court of The Hague in our total absence."[72] In the words of a prominent activist, "the Sahrawis will not accept the whole world speaking for them as if they were cattle."[73]

For our purposes here, what is most striking is how in trying to protect a self-determination unit from the clutches of its neighbors, the Court accepted colonial definitions of the territory. This is despite Judge Dillard's well-known statement from the case which assures us that "it is for the people to determine the destiny of the territory and not the territory the destiny of the people."[74] Yet no real consideration was given to "the people" in this instance as, according to Nesiah, "the discussion of self-determination is expressive of the Court's desire to lay out its own normative commitments by pulling Western Sahara into the normative and jurisprudential framework of international law, a statist or administrative framework of territory."[75] Thus, in his classically doctrinal approach to international law, Brownlie is correct when he asserts,

> There is a complementarity between *uti possidetis* and the principle of self-determination. It is *uti possidetis* which creates the ambit of the pertinent unit of self-determination, and which in that sense has a logical priority over self-determination.[76]

In considering the creation of sovereignty through self-determination then, we can see that the inter-relationship between international law and European colonialism was an enduring one in this case. It is a pattern that has been repeated throughout Third World territorial adjudication.

For Arab peoples already safely housed within the confines of statehood, the chance to evaluate extant boundaries again presented the Court with a dilemma about the extent to which it was willing and able to interrogate the enduring effects of colonialism for Bahrain and Qatar. We saw above that these states fell under British protection until their independence in 1971. In the interests of exploiting their oil and gas reserves, these two states called on the Court to demarcate their land and sea boundaries, and after ten years of litigation a verdict was duly delivered. Part of the case concerned title of the Hawar Islands, which were claimed by both the former British protectorates of Bahrain and Qatar. Initial British investigations of the islands coincided with Britain's admission that "the ownership of the Hawar Group is of great importance because it is directly in . . . the oil 'line.' "[77] In anticipation of competing claims to this resource-rich area, the British had issued a "provisional decision" in 1936 which acknowledged that "it might . . . suit us politically to have as large an area of possible included under Bahrain" for oil concession purposes.[78] The details of this "preliminary" decision by the British were never relayed to Qatar, and, furthermore, Qatar was never given the chance to rebut claims made by Bahrain, which had become the presumptive beneficiary of the decision.

In its pleadings, Qatar had presented a significant amount of material to support its account of this "flagrant miscarriage of justice committed by the British,"[79] and it thought that the Court would agree:

> The Court will no doubt conclude that the British authorities in the Gulf had by this time become so caught up in a spider's web of their own making that they simply could not render an objective and impartial decision on the issue of title to Hawar. In effect this meant that the provisional decision of 1936 had become a final decision even before the so-called "enquiry" into the question of title had begun.[80]

Compelling evidence aside, the Court, in what the dissenting judges describe as a "surreal"[81] gesture, chose to disregard all other arguments offered by the parties (such as proximity, maps,[82] *à titre de souverain* and *effectivités*) to hold that the 1936 award was based on consent and constituted a binding "administrative" decision on the parties. Here is a clear example of the pre-eminent international judicial body favoring colonial practice over a variety of arguments relating to indigenous control and jurisdiction.

For Qatar and Bahrain, the matter before the ICJ was not the first occasion where a third party had sought to determine territorial and maritime issues of the utmost importance. Further, although it may seem tendentious to equate the earlier motives of Britain in the Gulf with those of the ICJ, the outcomes were similar: an occasion where "consent" to jurisdiction was established in the face of significant protest and lingering doubt. At least in contrast to the flawed and unsatisfying decisions of Britain over its protectorates, it was hoped that the ICJ would be able to settle the affair "once and for all."[83] To further this goal, both Bahrain and Qatar issued extensive (even if not always accurate) historical accounts of their connections with the territories in question. Indeed, the proceedings should be appreciated as much for their historical narratives as for their legal exposition.

Some of the arguments reconstructed from the annals of history, as well as their corresponding acceptance or rejection by the Court, illustrate broader themes about how to approach the relationship of international law with a less than palatable colonial past. The majority judgment is emblematic of a Court as well as the mainstream of international legal scholarship wedded to a narrative of rupture, rather than continuity, so as to divorce present international law from its colonial lineage. Judge Shahabuddeen beautifully captures this disposition in the territorial dispute between Libya and Chad:

> The case at bar recalls a world now left behind. In telling flashes, it illuminates an age when international law tended to develop as a legal construct supportive of the global projection of the power of a single region; when in important respects it was both fashioned and administered by leading members of a select community; when that community, by itself called the international community, bore little resemblance to the world as it then stood, and even less to the world as it stands today.[84]

In contrast to such sentiments, judges Bedjaoui, Ranjeva and Koroma in their minority opinion for the Qatar/Bahrain case asked, "Why . . . should anyone be surprised that the taste in the mouths of the crowd, both in Bahrain and in Qatar, is a sour one?"[85] Particularly in relation to the Court's denial of underlying British motives and ongoing concerns about natural resources, it is to be expected that this judgment will be viewed partly as an endorsement of European domination over non-Europeans in the Gulf. Moreover, the majority's "curtailed"[86] treatment of the parties' various legal grounds and historical arguments indicates unwillingness or even an inability on the part of the ICJ to embrace the legal heritage of non-European litigants.

Conclusion

This chapter has shown not only that the relationship between international law and colonialism was an intimate and vital one, but more importantly, that this relationship persists in the post-colonial present of universal "sovereign" statehood. Far from being divorced from politics, the colonial and post-colonial periods demonstrate how, in fact, law and politics rely on each other for legitimizing and obscuring differentiated treatment of European and non-European entities At times lawyers can disavow acts as being purely political, while at other times non-lawyers can use the law as a device of seeming neutrality. Like the rest of the non-European world, Arab states have not been immune from the legacies of this disguised marriage: mandated sovereignty. We saw how the indeterminacy of "sovereignty" as well as ILP furnished European powers with a variety of techniques for subordinating much of the globe, whether on an informal or formal basis. In spite of the diversity over time and place in these instruments of rule, international law remained central throughout these endeavors.

Many within the discipline of international law struggle to accept its colonial heritage and the implications this has for its very legitimacy today. In contrast to such a stance, however, this chapter has emphasized continuities over ruptures. New institutional forms for Third World states in the wake of decolonization cannot belie deeply embedded institutional patterns laid down during the colonial and mandate periods. In particular, it was the mandate period for the Arab heartland that in such a short space of time nonetheless laid the groundwork for persisting problems of legitimacy. The case of Palestine impacts upon the configuration of the entire region in its quest for stable statehood, whether in terms of boundaries or the related dilemma of nationalism. More generally, the modes of governance tested during the mandate period were then perfected in the post-colonial present allowing for more creative forms of intervention, so that in fact the most recent invasion of Iraq cannot simply be understood as "illegal" at all. Instead, it represents the dynamics between law and politics as played out in the Middle East and challenges perceptions of the progressive promise of international law. Despite all this, a consideration of Arab statehood has shown that avenues do exist for former colonial territories to question and challenge colonial practices. The space currently available though for such an endeavor is very limited indeed for Arab states and their peoples seeking to dismantle their mandated sovereignties.

Notes

1. Allain, "Orientalism and international law," p. 391. In reaction against "Middle East legal exceptionalism," see my discussion on the case of Palestine: Burgis, "A discourse of distinction?," p. 41.
2. Berman captures this quest by asking, "Can international law, written by history's victors, muster the courage to look frankly, painfully, at the horrors of its own past?," Berman, "The Grotius Lecture Series," p. 1554.
3. Especially see Kennedy, "When renewal repeats," p. 335.
4. Pahuja, "The postcoloniality of international law," p. 469.
5. Nesiah, "Placing international law," p. 21.
6. E.g., see the *Reparations* case (Advisory Opinion), p. 174.
7. Some classic cases, all from the League of Nations period, would include *The Case of the S.S. "Lotus" (France/Turkey)*; *Island of Palmas Case*; *Legal Status of Eastern Greenland (Denmark/Norway)*; and *Customs Regime*

between Germany and Austria. The classic treaty source on statehood for this period says that "a person of international law should possess the following qualifications: (a) a permanent population; (b) a defined territory; (c) government; and (d) capacity to enter into relations with the other states." Article 1, Montevideo Convention, December 26, 1933.

8. Generally, see, Koskenniemi, *From Apology to Utopia*, pp. 242–302.
9. Kennedy, 'International law and the nineteenth century," p. 413.
10. Generally see Crawford, *The Creation of States in International Law.*
11. Koskenniemi, *From Apology to Utopia*, p. 242.
12. Thus, in the early nineteenth century, "The colonial encounter took place between individual natives or native tribes on the one side and private individuals, missionaries, humanitarian associations, and trade companies on the other. Beyond appealing to humane behaviour on both sides, there was no need to envisage norms governing the formal relations between European and non-European communities, even less of jurisdictional boundaries between European States." Koskenniemi, *The Gentle Civilizer of Nations*, p. 114.
13. General Act of the Conference of the Plenipotentiaries of Austria-Hungary, Belgium, Denmark, France, Germany, Great Britain, Italy, the Netherlands, Portugal, Russia, Spain, Sweden-Norway, Turkey (and the United States) respecting the Congo, February 26, 1885, 165 CTS 485.
14. Of course, Koskenniemi argues that like "sovereignty," the "existence of a 'standard' was a myth in the sense that there was never anything to gain. Every concession was a matter of negotiation, every status dependent on agreement, *quid pro quo.* But the existence of a *language of a standard* still gave the appearance of fair treatment and regular administration to what was simply a conjectural policy" (emphasis in original), Koskenniemi, *The Gentle Civilizer of Nations*, pp. 134–5. Generally, see Gong, *The Standard of "Civilization" in International Society.*
15. Koskenniemi, *The Gentle Civilizer of Nations*, p. 169.
16. "European states adopted different views of native personality, depending on their own interests. The problem was that native personality was fluid, as it was created through the encounter with a European state which would inevitably 'recognise' the capacity of the non-European entity according to its own needs." Anghie, *Imperialism, Sovereignty and the Making of International Law*, p. 79.
17. Italics in original. Miéville, *Between Equal Rights*, pp. 246–7.
18. Alexandrowicz, *An Introduction to the History of the Law of Nations in the East Indies*; Alexandrowicz, "New and original states," p. 465. Also see Jessup, "Diversity and uniformity in the law of nations," p. 341.
19. Anghie, *Imperialism, Sovereignty and the Making of International Law*, ch. 1.
20. In his study of the history of international law, Onuma discusses a variety of separate regional legal systems that would only later give way to the

supremacy of the European states system: Onuma, "When was the law of international society born," p. 1. According to Grewe, what "happened in the nineteenth century was certainly not the narrowing of a universal law of nations to a regional, European law of nations, as Alexandrowicz asserted. On the contrary, the European law of nations gradually grew into a global legal order, the members of which were, it is true, only the 'civilised nations'. This development cannot be interpreted as a 'regionalisation' or 'Europeanisation'. Rather, the dualism of the Christian–European law of nations and the natural law-based universal law of nations dissolved into a single, universal legal system, albeit one which had been deprived of its natural law foundation by the rise of positivism. This universal legal system introduced a new differentiation through the criterion of civilisation, thus laying the foundation of a new, colonial law of nations separate from the general one." Grewe, *The Epochs of International Law*, p. 466.

21. Kennedy, 'When renewal repeats', p. 347. For a general discussion on this theme, see Skouteris, *The Notion of Progress in International Law Discourse*.

22. As argued throughout his book, *Imperialism, Sovereignty and the Making of International Law*.

23. Article 7 reads: Sa Majesté la Reine du Royaume Uni de la Grande-Bretagne et d'Irelande, Sa Majesté l'Empereur d'Autriche, Sa Majesté l'Empereur des Français, Sa Majesté le Roi de Prusse, Sa Majesté l'Empereur de toutes les Russies, et Sa Majesté le Roi de Sardaigne, déclarent *la Sublime Porte admise à participer aux avantages du droit public et du concert Européens*. Leurs Majestés s'engagent, chacune de son côté, *à respecter l'indépendence et l'integrité territoriale de l'Empire Ottoman*: garantissent en commun la stricte observation de cet engagement: et considéront, en consequence, tout acte de nature à y porter atteinte comme une question d'intérêt général (italics added). Treaty Guaranteeing the Independence and Integrity of the Ottoman Empire, April 15, 1856, 114 CTS 497.

24. In particular, see McKinnon Wood, "The Treaty of Paris and Turkey's status in international law," p. 262; Toyoda, "L'aspect univeraliste du droit international européen du 19ème siècle et le statut juridique de la Turquie avant 1856," p. 19.

25. See my discussion on this in Burgis, "Faith in the state?," p. 37.

26. Koskenniemi, "International law and imperialism," Freestone, Subedi and Davidson (eds), *Contemporary Issues in International Law*, p. 212. For a general discussion, see Baty, "Protectorates and Mandates," p. 109.

27. Andrews, "The concept of statehood and the acquisition of territory in the nineteenth century," p. 420.

28. Shaw, *Title to Territory in Africa*, p. 47.

29. Great Britain–Trucial Sheikhdoms, Exclusive Agreements, March 6/8, 1892, 176 CTS 457.

30. For the judgment, see *Case Concerning Maritime Delimitation and*

Territorial Questions between Qatar and Bahrain (Qatar/Bahrain) (Merits), p. 40. The pleadings can be accessed on the ICJ's website, available at: http://www.icj-cij.org/docket/index.php?p1=3&code=qb&case=87&k=61. Also see my detailed discussion of the case in Burgis, "(De)Limiting the past for future gain," p. 557.

31. Anghie, *Imperialism, Sovereignty and the Making of International Law*, pp. 131–2.
32. Article 22, Covenant of the League of Nations, June 28, 1919, 225 CTS 188.
33. Mills, "The Mandatory System," p. 52.
34. On this, see especially Fieldhouse, *Western Imperialism in the Middle East 1914–1958*, p. 2.
35. E.g., Darwin quotes Lord Balfour in 1918 as saying that "We will have a Protectorate [over former Ottoman lands] but not declare it." Darwin, "An undeclared empire," at fn. 1.
36. Quoted in Berman (1999), "The Grotius Lecture Series," p. 1526.
37. Darwin, "An undeclared empire," p. 163.
38. Palestine perhaps is the exception here, especially during times of civil unrest when large numbers of troops were required by Britain to try and somehow keep the peace between two communities endowed with fundamentally different status under the Mandate.
39. Sluglett, "Formal and informal empire in the Middle East," p. 424.
40. Darwin, "An undeclared empire," p. 161.
41. Under international law, this can be expressed in the idea of *non liquet* which, e.g., arose in the Advisory Opinion of the International Court of Justice on the Legality of Nuclear Weapons. The Court could not find a rule in international law definitively outlawing the use of such weapons. Thus, the Court pointed to a gap in the fabric of international rules and was criticized for not working harder at smoothing it over. *Legality of the Threat or Use of Nuclear Weapons (Advisory Opinion)*, p. 26.
42. Lauterpacht, "The Mandate under international law in the Covenant of the League of Nations," pp. 37, 65.
43. Lauterpacht, "The Mandate under international law in the Covenant of the League of Nations," p. 49.
44. Crawford, *The Creation of States in International Law*, p. 573.
45. For a fascinating exploration of a later consideration of Mandate sovereignty for South West Africa, see Berman, "Sovereignty in abeyance: self-determination and international law," p. 51.
46. In particular, see Mazower, *No Enchanted Palace*.
47. Anghie, *Imperialism, Sovereignty and the Making of International Law*, p. 146.
48. The relevant text of Article 22 reads:

> To those colonies and territories which as a consequence of the late war have ceased to be *under the sovereignty of the States which formerly governed them*

and which are inhabited by *peoples not yet able to stand by themselves under the strenuous conditions of the modern world*, there should be applied the principle that the *well-being and development* of such peoples form a *sacred trust of civilisation* and that securities for the performance of this trust should be embodied in this Covenant.

The best method of giving practical effect to this principle is that the *tutelage* of such peoples should be entrusted to *advanced nations* who by reason of their resources, their experience or their geographical position can best undertake this responsibility, and who are willing to accept it, and that this tutelage should be exercised by them as Mandatories on behalf of the League.

The character of the mandate must differ according to the stage of the development of the people, the geographical situation of the territory, its economic conditions and other similar circumstances.

Certain communities formerly belonging to the Turkish Empire have reached a stage of development where their existence as independent nations can be provisionally recognized subject to the rendering of administrative advice and assistance by a Mandatory until such time as they are able to stand alone. *The wishes of these communities must be a principal consideration in the selection of the Mandatory.* (italics added)

Covenant of the League of Nations, June 28, 1919, 225 CTS 188.

49. Anghie, *Imperialism, Sovereignty and the Making of International Law*, p. 178.

50. Anghie, *Imperialism, Sovereignty and the Making of International Law*, p. 136.

51. Rajagopal, *International Law from Below*, pp. 50–72.

52. Anghie, *Imperialism, Sovereignty and the Making of International Law*, pp. 127–8.

53. Anghie, *Imperialism, Sovereignty and the Making of International Law*, p. 145

54. Anghie, *Imperialism, Sovereignty and the Making of International Law*, p. 156.

55. Generally, see Rajagopal, *International Law from Below*.

56. Anghie, *Imperialism, Sovereignty and the Making of International Law*, p. 179.

57. "Whereas previously the internal character of the sovereign European state was immune from scrutiny, in the inter-war period it was precisely through the Mandate System that international law and institutions had complete access to the interior of a society. It was in the operations of the Mandate System, then, that it became possible for law not merely to enter the interior realm, but also to create the social and political infrastructure necessary to support a functioning sovereign state." Anghie, *Imperialism, Sovereignty and the Making of International Law*, pp. 135–6.

58. Anghie, *Imperialism, Sovereignty and the Making of International Law*, pp. 148–9.

59. A lack of space precludes discussion of two cases concerned with French rule in the Protectorate of Morocco: *Nationalities Decreed Issued in Tunis and Morocco (French Zones) on November 8th, 1921*; and *Phosphates in Morocco*. For a consideration of the powers of the Council of the League to determine the boundaries between Iraq and Turkey, see Article 3, Paragraph 2, of the Treaty of Lausanne (Frontier between Turkey and Iraq).

60. *The Mavrommatis Palestine Concessions Case*; *The Mavrommatis Jerusalem Concessions Case*; and *Case of the Readaptation of the Mavrommatis Jerusalem Concessions (Jurisdiction)*.

61. "An appropriate Jewish agency shall be recognised as a public body for the purpose of advising and co-operating with the Administration of Palestine in such economic, social and other matters as may affect the establishment of the Jewish national home and the interests of the Jewish population in Palestine, and, subject always to the control of the Administration to assist and take part in the development of the country. The Zionist organization, so long as its organization and constitution are in the opinion of the Mandatory appropriate, shall be recognised as such agency. It shall take steps in consultation with His Britannic Majesty's Government to secure the co-operation of all Jews who are willing to assist in the establishment of the Jewish national home."

62. Italics added. July 24, 1922.

63. Since its founding in 1946, the ICJ has heard only a small number of cases dealing specifically with territorial disputes in the Arab world either through its contentious or advisory jurisdiction, including *Qatar/Bahrain* and *Western Sahara* discussed below as well as Case Concerning the Territorial Dispute (Libyan Arab Jamahiriya/Chad); Legal Consequences of the Construction of a Wall in the Occupied Palestinian Territory (Advisory Opinion). It has also heard the following maritime delimitation cases: Case Concerning the Continental Shelf (Libyan Arab Jamahiriya/Malta); Application for Revision and Interpretation of the Judgment of 24 February 1982 in the Case Concerning the Continental Shelf (Tunisia/Libyan Arab Jamahiriya).

64. Generally see Burgis, *Boundaries of Discourse in the International Court of Justice*.

65. Barnett, *Dialogues in Arab Politics*.

66. As captured by Koskenniemi in his discussion of the Libya/Chad case: "Le droit international doit-il servir à effacer les consequences négatives de colonialisme sur l'ensemble des structures sociales et politiques de l'Afrique? Ou bien doit-il être considéré comme un instrument destiné à renforcer la stabilité des structures existantes, de façon à prévenir, ou à tout le moins à retarder, 'des luttes fratricides.'" Koskenniemi is quoting the Chamber in the *Frontier Dispute (Burkina Faso/Mali)*. "L'affaire du différend territorial (Jamahiriya Arabe Libyenne c. Tchad) Arrêt de la Cour Internationale de Justice du 3 février 1994," p. 453.

67. Shaw, *Title to Territory in Africa*, p. 186.
68. Resolution AHG/Res.16(1), on Border Disputes Among African States, adopted by the First Ordinary Session of the Assembly of Heads of State and Government in Cairo, July 21, 1964. See Shaw, "Peoples, territories and boundaries," p. 494. The principle of *uti possidetis* also appears in Article III(3) of the AOU Charter and paragraph 7 of the preamble. Maluwa, "International law-making in post-colonial Africa: the role of the Organization of African Unity," pp. 94–5. All African states supported the *uti possidetis* doctrine except Somalia and Morocco. Somalia called for Greater Somalia at the OAU's opening session in May 1963 and Morocco "reserved its position with regard to Article 3(3) of the OAU Charter." Klabbers and Lefeber, "Africa: lost between self-determination and *uti possidetis*," p. 58.
69. The full term is: *uti possidetis, ita possideatis* (as you possess, so may you possess). Generally, see Shaw, "The heritage of states: the principle of *uti possidetis juris* today" and Ratner, "Drawing a better line: *uti possidetis* and the borders of new states."
70. The relevant part of the UNGA request reads: "Was Western Sahara (Río de Oro and Sakiet El Hamra) at the time of colonization by Spain a territory belonging to no one (*terra nullius*)?". If the answer to the first question is in the negative, what were the legal ties between this territory and the Kingdom of Morocco and the Mauritanian entity? UNGA Resolution 3292. The full text of the resolution is reproduced in the Opinion: Western Sahara (Advisory Opinion) (1975) *ICJ Rep.* 12, at 13–14.
71. POLISARIO, or Frente Popular de Liberación de Saguía el Hamra y Río de Oro (Popular Front for the Liberation of Saguia el-Hamra and Río de Oro) was officially established on May 10, 1973 in pursuit of independence from Spain. Once Spain left the territory, it was replaced by Morocco and Mauritania until 1979, and now only Morocco as the occupier. POLISARIO continues to struggle against the occupation. For general information on the origins of nationalism and POLISARIO, see Hodges, *Western Sahara*, at chs 14 and 15.
72. Hodges, *Western Sahara*, p. 186.
73. Hodges, *Western Sahara*.
74. *Western Sahara (Advisory Opinion)*, p. 122.
75. Nesiah, "Placing international law," p. 15.
76. Brownlie, "Boundary problems and the formation of new states," p. 191.
77. Letter from Captain T. Hickinbotham, British Political Agent (officiating), to the British Political Resident, May 9, 1936, Bahrain, Counter-Memorial, Vol. 2, Annex 73, p. 236. This was also the opinion of Loch: "[Hawar] may have considerable value now that oil has been found in Bahrain and is hoped for in Qatar," Letter from Lt. Col. Loch, British Political Agent, to Lt. Col. Fowle, British Political Resident, May 6, 1936.
78. Quoted in *Qatar/Bahrain (Merits)*, at para. 311.

79. *Qatar/Bahrain (Merits)*, at para. 15.
80. *Qatar/Bahrain (Merits)*, at para. 9.
81. *Qatar/Bahrain (Merits)*, at para. 42.
82. Qatar in particular discussed map evidence at length, e.g., see *Qatar/Bahrain (Merits)*, at paras 1–78.
83. *Qatar/Bahrain (Merits)*, at para. 2.
84. *Libya/Chad* (separate opinion, Shahabuddeen), p. 44.
85. *Qatar/Bahrain (Merits)*, at para. 7.
86. *Qatar/Bahrain (Merits)*, at para. 4.

7

Reluctant Sovereigns? Central Asian States' Path to Independence

Mohira Suyarkulova

We do not have enough energy for the peripheries, neither economical, nor spiritual energy. We do not have enough energy for the Empire! – and there is no need, and let it fall from our shoulders: it is exhausting, it is draining us, and accelerates our demise . . . So, we need to announce the definite right to full secession of those twelve republics – urgently and firmly. And should some of them hesitate whether they ought to secede, we must with the same resolve announce OUR secession from them.

Aleksandr Solzhenitsin[1]

We were in opposition but we were constructive. I myself view the collapse of the Soviet Union as a tragedy for Kazakhstan . . . Gorbachev wanted to draft a more equal Union Treaty. But then Yeltsin wanted to remove Gorbachev. In order to achieve that, he exploded the whole Union. We say that it is not worth burning the whole fur coat to kill one flea. But that is exactly what Yeltsin did.

Olzhas Suleymanov[2]

Sovereignty was a useful word for everybody . . . It could make the most cautious politicians sound radical, which was useful for the Communists, in order to please the people; and it made the radical politicians sound moderate, which was useful for the implicitly pro-independence movements, who did not yet want to be out in the open. Nobody, after all, could seriously quarrel with the idea of sovereignty.

Steve Crawshaw[3]

Central Asian states are often described as having been "forced to become independent nations" by the decision of the leaders of the three Slavic republics who met in Belovezhskaia Pushcha on December 8, 1991.[4] This is despite the predictions of some Sovietologists in the late 1980s that the demise of the USSR would be brought about by the revolt of the Soviet "Moslem" peoples.[5] According to such analyses, the Central Asian republics were a "ticking time bomb" with their explosive population growth, colonial economy in deep crisis, plethora of ecological disasters, lowest living and health standards and looming rise of Islamic fundamentalism.[6] This chapter discusses whether the republics of Soviet Central Asia (or, rather, in Soviet parlance, "Middle Asia and Kazakhstan") were indeed reluctant sovereigns. Apart from being a rather unique experience of decolonization, Central Asian republics' path to independence teaches us a fascinating lesson in the various meanings of the concept of "sovereignty" that different political organizations, institutions and groups negotiated over the course of Soviet history. This history of the changing conceptions of sovereignty influenced the types of states and regimes that resulted from the peculiar process of peaceful decolonization of the USSR.

I argue that despite their unswerving resolve to try and rescue the Union, despite the fact that overwhelming majorities of their populations voted for the preservation of the USSR in March 1991, despite their exclusion from the decision-making process on the dissolution of the USSR, and, even despite their tardiness in declaring independence, Central Asian states were not willing to settle for less sovereignty than would have been allocated to, or demanded by, other union republics. The independence of the Central Asian republics was the result of the process of "outbidding" over the concept of sovereignty between the Union republics and the "Center." Central Asian republics were "follow-up" bidders, as they were negotiating their status from a position of relative political, economic and institutional weakness.

The constitutional federative structure of the USSR institutionalized the concept of formal sovereignty of all Union republics, thus granting them formal sovereign equality, while in practice some were "more equal than others."[7] Nonetheless, this very principle allowed the Central Asian republics to claim just as much sovereignty as the more radical counterparts wanted. The Soviet Union disintegrated along the Union republic boundary lines because of the federal structure, entitling each "nation" to their own territorial statehood. In sum, far from being passive followers and imitators of the Union-wide trends, Central Asian elites engaged actively in the process of negotiating wider and deeper spheres of autonomy. The difference between their vision of sovereignty and that of the more radical republics was that the republics' elites saw their sovereign futures within a new and improved union, while for their counterparts in the Baltic states, the idea of genuine sovereignty within a renewed union was an oxymoron.

Through a reading of debate transcripts, speeches, legal documents and newspaper articles from the period between 1989 and 1991, this chapter looks at four different areas of articulation of the meaning of "sovereignty" as seen by the republics' elites at the time:

(1) the civil and "opposition" movements in Central Asia, which formed during the *perestroika* period around the issues of native languages, environment and economy;

(2) the process of negotiations around the new Union treaty;

(3) the all-union referendum of March 17, 1991 on the preservation of the USSR and its alternative interpretations (including additional questions and interpretations of exactly what "sovereign" in the referendum meant); and

(4) the "parades" of sovereignty and independence during 1989–91, and the differences between understandings of "sovereignty as greater autonomy" and "sovereignty as independence within a confederation."

For analytical reasons, these four areas of articulation are presented as separate; however, all four were closely intertwined.

A Brief History of Soviet Conceptions of Sovereignty

The genealogical study of the Soviet conception of sovereignty undertaken by Robert Jones traces the development of Soviet discourses and policies regarding sovereignty, "national self-determination," and "revolutionary intervention" from the early days of the Bolshevik state to Gorbachev's *perestroika*.[8] Soviet concepts of sovereignty incorporated elements of Marxist doctrine, which were adapted to the realities of post-Second World War international relations. They balanced vertical (class struggle) and horizontal (inter-state) definitions of sovereignty in their external (recognition and independence in the international arena) and internal (legitimate supremacy within their own territory) aspects. Respect for sovereignty was declared to be intrinsically connected to the very nature of the Soviet system based on popular sovereignty.[9] Lenin envisaged a classless system – whereby there would no longer be divisions into petty states – achieved through the gradual processes of "drawing together" (*sblizheniie*) and fusion (*sliianie*) of peoples; however, in the meantime, a distinction was made between the bourgeois and the Soviet varieties of sovereignty. Whereas in capitalist states sovereignty was just a guise for the class inequality and supremacy of the bourgeoisie, the sovereignty of the Soviet state stemmed from the genuine sovereignty of peoples.[10]

Soviet theoreticians linked the internal and the external dimensions of sovereignty through the Marxist understanding of "popular sovereignty" as class rule. "People" were inscribed as proletariat, led by a professional vanguard of revolution (the Communist Party). This allowed the Soviet government to employ the "legal-positivist" approach against Western interventions into Soviet internal affairs, while applying the principles of "proletarian internationalism" in justification of Soviet interventions.[11] This distinction between genuine "peoples' sovereignty" and capitalist pretence sovereignty became the basis of the so-called "Brezhnev doctrine" of "limited sovereignty" within the socialist bloc.

The Soviet Union was portrayed as the biggest champion of the principle of sovereignty in both its external and internal aspects. The Union republics were proclaimed "sovereign Soviet socialist" states, their very emergence or continued existence the result of the Soviet government's effort to promote national self-determination. The right to secession of the union republics was enshrined in the constitution of the USSR. This "affirmative action empire" thus was seen as the only way to end inter-ethnic conflict and achieve genuine "friendship of the peoples" (*druzhba narodov*) by allowing each nationality to practice cultural and linguistic autonomy.[12]

The Soviet vision of "popular" sovereignty as a necessarily proletarian sovereignty allowed the Bolsheviks to fight the "bourgeois-nationalists" in Central Asia in the 1920s. In 1924 the USSR was founded as an ethnicity-based federative state comprised of a hierarchy of ethno-territorial units (the *matrioshka* model of sovereignty). At the top of the pecking order were the Union republics (SSRs) which were proclaimed "sovereign" by virtue of their right to secession. Contained with the SSRs were the autonomous republics (ASSRs), oblasts (AOs) and so on, representing peoples considered either too small in number or lacking in national consciousness to justify granting them a separate statehood. The criteria for becoming a Union republic were the size of population, degree of economic and cultural development as well as geopolitical location (that is, bordering a foreign state). These criteria were rather loosely observed in practice, and within the first two decades of the establishment of the Union some ASSRs were promoted to SSRs, while some ASSRs were demolished altogether.

The National Territorial Delimitation of 1924–9 reorganized the political boundaries and introduced a radically new principle of social and political identity in the Central Asian region. The process of delimitation has been covered at length elsewhere[13] and we will not delve into this fascinating, yet highly complex question here. Suffice it to say, the federal structure formed in the 1920s to 1930s and the institutionalization of the sovereign status of the Union republics were ultimately what determined the disintegration of the USSR along the boundary lines of those republics.[14]

The *perestroika* years (1980s) saw adjustment of the Soviet understanding of "sovereignty" from a vertical (class struggle) to horizontal (inter-state) plane. In both its internal and external aspects, popular sovereignty stopped being equated with the will of the omniscient Communist Party and the emphasis thus shifted from class struggle to inter-state cooperation (international) and inter-ethnic relations (domestic). Ideological understandings of sovereignty were downplayed and "normalized" to meet the common global interpretations of the concept.[15]

Liberated Against their Will?

There are a number of facts that are habitually cited as proof of the Central Asian republics' reluctance to embrace sovereignty understood as independent statehood:

(1) they were the staunchest supporters of Gorbachev's plans for a renewed Union treaty;
(2) their populations voted overwhelmingly in support of the preservation of the USSR in the March 17, 1991 all-Union referendum;
(3) they lacked strong, pro-independence movements like the Popular Fronts of the Baltic republics;
(4) most of the Central Asian leaders tacitly supported the *coup* in August 1991; and
(5) they were excluded from the decision-making process surrounding the dissolution of the Union on December 8, 1991.

This section attempts to engage with these facts and their interpretations and argue that:

(1) Despite supporting the idea of remaining in some form of federative state, the Central Asian republics were not prepared to sign a new Union treaty that afforded them less autonomy than their counterparts in the Western parts of the USSR.
(2) The results of the March 17, 1991 referendum were not as unambiguous as Gorbachev wanted them to appear. Despite obvious popular support for the idea of preservation of the Union in Central Asian republics, the vague phrasing of the referendum question, as well as the inclusion of an additional question and absence of reference to a concrete draft treaty, all made it impossible for the positive outcomes of the plebiscite to be translated into effective policy action.
(3) The nascent pro-democracy/pro-independence "informal" political and civic movements of Central Asia were successfully sidelined and their agendas highjacked by the Communist Party elites.

(4) Two of the Central Asian republics – Kazakhstan and Kyrgyzstan – actually voiced decisive condemnation of the *coup* attempt on August 19–21, 1991. The failure to react to the putsch in Tajikistan led to the eventual resignation of the republic's President Mahkamov.

(5) The Central Asian states were indeed "divorced" by the Slavic republics as an unwanted burden on their economies and legacy of empire. The outcome of this, however, was the emergence of a unified region of "Central Asia," which replaced the Soviet concept of "Middle Asia and Kazakhstan." For a short period, there was a project of "regional sovereignty" based on the European Economic Community model.

"We Want What the Baltics Want": Civil Movements and Demands for Sovereignty in Central Asia, 1989–91

In the Central Asian republics, especially Uzbekistan, *perestroika* was received cautiously as it was seen as the continuation of Andropov's anti-corruption campaign, which collectively branded the Uzbeks and Central Asians as a whole as corrupt and incompetent. Indeed, the investigations into the so-called "Cotton" or "Uzbek Affair," led by notorious prosecutors Gdlyan and Ivanov, continued into the first years of the *perestroika* period. Such reforms were threatening to the Central Asian elites and were seen as unfairly singling out the southern republics for the crimes brought about by unrealistic quotas on cotton production imposed by the Center.[16]

At the same time, the authority of the Communist Party in the Central Asian republics remained strong and allowed the ruling elites to maintain a monopoly over the "sovereignty" discourse. The flourishing of opposition movements in Central Asia occurred rather late and could not reach its full potential with the abrupt end of the Union, although one could argue that the first mass protest of a nationalistic nature did occur in Kazakhstan in December 1986.[17] This initial protest, however, failed to gain momentum and was successfully framed by the authorities as hooliganism and vandalism of a mob organized by mercenary motives, rather than people with legitimate grievances.

Immediately before the dissolution of the USSR, the meaning of "sovereignty" was negotiated between Moscow and the Union republics, as well as within the Russian Federation itself. The many different uses of the word in the political discourse during that period included, among others:

(1) sovereignty as decentralization and greater autonomy;
(2) as a right to positive affirmation of federal legislation;
(3) as a right to pre-emptive legislation;
(4) as fiscal autonomy;
(5) as a "single channel" tax system;
(6) as property claims;
(7) as other forms of "economic sovereignty";
(8) as a right to negotiate bilateral power-sharing treaties with the federal government;
(9) as a right to determine collective powers delegated to the federal government;
(10) as a unilateral right to determine powers delegated to the federal government;
(11) as a right to secession in accordance with federal law;
(12) as a unilateral right of secession;
(13) as recognition of being "a subject of international law";
(14) as full independence under "international law"; and
(15) as freedom of action for the independent state.[18]

The distinguishing feature of the *perestroika* civic movements was that they were initially cultivated within the Communist Party structures (such as *Komsomol*) in an attempt by the authorities to create "pocket" opposition/informal groups. Beginning in 1988, the common tendency was for such informal groups, mostly taking the form of discussion clubs, to be organized within such establishments as the Academies of Sciences, Writers', and Cinematographers' Union.[19] The pro-reform movements in Central Asia were led by urban intelligentsia, who increasingly became involved in politics. Many famous artists, writers, scientists and actors were elected as deputies, thus becoming public figures and influential politicians (for example, film director Davlat Khudonazarov in Tajikistan, poet Muhammad Solih and physicist Abdurakhim Pulat in Uzbekistan, poet Olzhas Suleymanov in Kazakhstan, and writer Chingiz Aitmatov and physicist Askar Akayev in Kyrgyzstan).

Inspired and feeding off (but not entirely derivative of) other Popular Fronts and civic movements elsewhere in the Soviet Union, the cultural intelligentsia in the Central Asian republics mostly concerned themselves with the issues pertaining to culture (native languages status, worth of national culture, re-evaluation of history and rehabilitation of repressed writers), and issues related to the economy and environment (cotton monoculture, relationship with the Center, environmental pollution, the desiccation of the Aral Sea, public health and infant mortality).[20] These movements were contained mainly within the capitals and regional centers, whereas the majority of Central Asian populations were still rural people. However, more radical calls for the revision of national histories and borders were voiced. For instance, a revisionist Tajik dissident in Samarkand was quoted as saying, "Lithuania for us is like a textbook, which we are reading carefully."[21] The programs of the *Birlik* (Uzbekistan) and *Agzybirlik* (Turkmenistan) movements called for "shed[ing] the light of truth on historical events." Thus, *Agzybirlik* were "opposed to the idea that Turkmenistan voluntarily entered into the Russian empire,"[22] while *Birlik*'s charter listed the "unbiased and truthful interpretation of history of Uzbekistan," including the history of *basmachi* movement, as one of the main tasks of the movement.[23]

At times, it was difficult to differentiate between "opposition" and Party elites' agendas as they both appealed to greater sovereignty. In his interview to the *Komsomol'skaya Pravda* newspaper, Abdurahim Pulatov (at the time one of the *Birlik* leaders) tried to distinguish the movement's sovereignty agenda from that of the Communist Party:

> To declare sovereignty does not mean to achieve it. It can be simply a transfer of power. A broken-down administrative-command system is now being recreated on a republic scale, and this is no secret ... We believe that immediate sovereignisation would lead to a rigid, khan-like, totalitarian regime being established in Uzbekistan. For us, however, it is important now to obtain freedom and democracy, and this is possible only from within the union. Our slogan is – to independence via democracy.[24]

However weak the civic movements in the Central Asian republics were, they stimulated public debate on controversial issues and therefore acted as agenda-setters. However, their demands were often far from radical and so it was easy for the governments to take them onboard while making the opposition groups irrelevant. Thus, for example, founded in November 1988, the *Birlik*[25] (Unity) movement's draft program included a demand for the republic to become "sovereign" (*mustaqil*),[26] however, it did not envisage complete independence as the sovereign status was to be affirmed within the Soviet Union in accordance with the original principles of the "Leninist nationalities policy."[27] A later statement dated October 1989 called for a hybrid model of sovereignty for Uzbekistan, arguing that its relationship with the Center should be formed "on the basis of a federation in the social–political field, on the basis of a confederation in the economic field, and on the basis of full sovereignty in the national-cultural field."[28] The removal from power of Rafiq Nishanov in June 1989 and the ascent to power of Islam Karimov, a party functionary willing to adopt key elements of the *Birlik/Erk* agenda, meant that the opposition was left with no room for radicalization. The declaration of sovereignty adopted by the Supreme Soviet of the Uzbek SSR on June 20, 1990 was also based on the draft submitted by *Erk* (moderate splinter group of *Birlik*, led by Abdurahim Pulat). The text of the declaration asserted various aspects of the republic's sovereignty, including the precedence of republican laws over Union legislation, but in the published edition Article 12 read: "The present declaration constitutes the basis for the elaboration of the new Constitution of the Uzbek SSR and the new Treaty of the Union."[29] As Muhammad Solih later recalled:

> The democratic party *Erk* was created around the idea of national independence. That idea motivated us to rise above mercantile interests and to strive to find an understanding with the government. On June 20, 1990 our party proposed to include a draft of the "Declaration of Independence" on the agenda of the parliament. The motion was supported by majority of communists and adopted by the parliament. But the leadership of the republic replaced the word "independence" with "sovereignty" when publishing it. This was a signal to Moscow that Uzbekistan has not left the Soviet Union.[30]

Similarly, on July 16 (two months before the Kazakh sovereignty declaration) the *Azat* coordinating council submitted a draft sovereignty declaration to the republican Supreme Soviet. The draft declaration was never officially acknowledged, but several of its points were nonetheless included in the final text.[31]

In most of the Central Asian republics, except Tajikistan, the Communist Party succeeded in highjacking the agendas of the opposition movements, and after dissolution reinvented themselves as the various democratic parties, changing their ideology from Marxist–Leninist to nationalist, thus ensuring continuity of personnel and power. One can see such maneuvers to delegitimize and even ridicule the opposition in the speeches of Islam Karimov and Saparmurat Niyazov. Karimov tried to portray his political competition as redundant and irrelevant.[32] Similarly, Niyazov belittled Turkmen democrats in his April 1989 speech to the representatives of mass media:

> Recently a small group of people made an attempt to set up a so-called people's movement in Mary. The group is made up of a number of teachers, artists, and one lawyer. At first glance, it appears that these people are expressing concern at the situation in the economy, in interethnic relations, and the ecology. It must be noted that all their aspirations coincide with the aims of the republic's Communist Party organisations and the work of the Soviets, trade unions, and the *Komsomol*. So why create a new socio-political structure? It is no more than

pandering to fashion; it is blind and absurd imitation. After all, their program is a carbon copy of the program of a movement established in one of the Baltic republics, where the socio-political situation is totally different.[33]

That the situation in Central Asia was somewhat different from that in the Baltics was also felt by some Tajik intellectuals. For instance, F. Kadyrov, a Tajik historian interviewed by Michel Hammer, reacted to the decision of the Supreme Soviet to confer economic sovereignty on Estonia and Lithuania in July 1989, saying that this measure was insufficient, but when asked about his homeland, responded: "As for Tajikistan, it belongs in a renewed federation, with autonomous status. Its position is not comparable with that of the Baltic countries."[34]

The most successful democratic movement of all the Central Asian republics as measured by its ability to integrate into power structures was the Democratic Movement of Kyrgyzstan (DMK). It was an alliance of twenty-two groups, including most importantly, *Ashar* (the youth organization demanding land for housing projects), *Asaba* (a Frunze youth organization) and the Association of Young Historians, which together managed to mobilize a majority of 114 deputies in the republic's Supreme Soviet and elect Askar Akayev as the new president of Kirghizia in October 1990. The program of the DMK adopted in May 1990 called for "a struggle against party rule and the command economy, for complete economic and political sovereignty within a confederation, and for restoration of national language, history and culture."[35]

Unlike in the Baltic republics, independence did not automatically translate into democratization in the Central Asian republics, and many of the opposition leaders of the *perestroika* years foresaw that. As Muhammad Solih put it:

> We were standing on the threshold of the collapse of the Soviet Empire, our minds were dreaming of independence. However, at the same time, we realized that independence does not equal democracy. We guessed that after throwing off Moscow's yoke we would have to confront the internal yoke and fight it. Nonetheless, we valued independence above democracy.[36]

In the same vein, Olzhas Suleymenov in his 1995 interview said that although he was not nostalgic about the USSR, he thought that the current independence was illusory and bogus.[37]

New Union Negotiations and the "Parade of Sovereignties"

The decision to initiate the new Union treaty was announced on June 11, 1990, one day before the Russian Federation's declaration of sovereignty.

This triggered the so-called "parade of sovereignties." All of the republics who had not done so yet were now motivated to declare sovereignty in order to be able to negotiate from a position of equality. Gorbachev's attempts to negotiate a new Union treaty proved futile with each subsequent draft leaving the Center with fewer powers, thus raising the bargaining stakes for everyone and frustrating the more hard-line core of the Party.

After the first draft treaty was published on November 24, 1990 and opened to negotiations, those republics that chose not to take part in the process were still considered by the Center to be bound by the 1922 Union treaty. This fact, combined with the virtual impossibility of secession under the Law on Secession, stopped a downgraded version of the Union from emerging, despite calls by Nazarbayev to make membership voluntary, to have a "core" of committed republics (Byelorussia, Russia, the Ukraine and the Central Asian republics) and see if the rest would want to join. In his address to the session of Kazakhstan's Supreme Soviet on February 11, 1991, Nazarbayev stressed that "the central bodies of power have been losing initiative" and thus along with it the last hopes of "preserving the country's integrity." The appeal underscored the idea that a "renovation of the Union" could be achieved only on the basis of "a Union treaty concluded by sovereign and equal republics." Special emphasis was placed on the declarations of sovereignty adopted by the republics, which were believed to be of particular importance because it was at a time when central agencies had "clearly displayed a trend towards ignoring the republics' sovereign rights."[38]

Already in April 1989, during a discussion on republican self-management (*khozraschet*), Buri Karimov of Tajikistan said that the republic's subsidy from the USSR budget had been growing since the prohibition of alcohol and drop in wine production. This was augmented by the fact that 90 percent of cotton produced in the republic was processed elsewhere, while the republican budget received nothing from the processing industries: "We simply do not have a mechanism for drawing up a budget."[39] Central Asian republics complained about economic exploitation of the region as "raw materials bases" for the industrialized European republics and that the "overall economic importance of the region" was underestimated. Shortly before declaring sovereignty, Uzbekistan and Tajikistan refused to export food to other republics at the low prices decreed by the state.[40] "Economic wars" broke out within the Union with regions withholding goods from each other. At the same time, all Central Asian republics agreed that the Soviet economy was so interconnected and interdependent that it would be in everyone's best interest to preserve some form of federative union.

The discussions on the draft of the Union treaty in Uzbekistan's Supreme Soviet were centered around the two competing versions advanced by the central government, on the one hand, and the "working group" of republican representatives, on the other. The central government's draft was based on the idea of preservation of a unitary state, while the "working group" pushed for "sovereignty" of the republics, which meant independence in the structuring of the management of the economy, price-formation mechanisms, systems of fiscal and budgetary control and agricultural, housing and welfare policies.[41] The Central Asian republics insisted that reforms aimed at a transition to a market economy should take into consideration existing inequalities in the republics' levels of development. Such a leveling of the playing field, the parliamentarians stressed, should not come in the form of hand-outs but as targeted investments on a mutually beneficial basis.[42]

On December 7, 1990, in his interview to a television program, Islam Karimov said that the latest published version of the treaty did not meet the expectations of the republic. Therefore, he said, "we shall not sign the treaty in this form." Although the republic linked "its future to a union federation," there were certain conditions that had to be met for Karimov. He further elaborated on what the demands of Uzbekistan were:

> These matters include bringing up to standard the levels of Uzbekistan's development and the standard of living of the population and tackling ecological problems, especially those concerning the Aral Sea, and matters connected with the fact that we must in practice and not just in words be a sovereign state – and, what is most important, we must have an outlet to foreign links. In other words, we must have all the rights that accord the notion of a sovereign state. That is to say, we must in our own territory and in external economic relations be self-reliant and tackle all issues solely in the interests of our people, first and foremost within the composition of a unified federation.[43]

Tajik president Kakhar Mahkamov was adamant that the new Union treaty would need to have mechanisms to ensure actual sovereign equality of Union republics, not just proclaim it. He also spoke in favor of a clear delineation of spheres of authority of the central government and the peripheries, guaranteeing greater autonomy to the republics. Mahkamov denied the claims that Central Asian republics supported the renewed Union only because they would not be able to survive on their own:

> . . . a subsidy is a perverted form of redistribution of their [Central Asian republics'] own products to which they have a legitimate claim. The main motive behind our republic's sincere support of the Union Treaty is that the new Treaty meets the basic interests of all the republics and of the whole country.[44]

Moreover, the consequences of the disintegration of the USSR would be disastrous, equivalent to "cutting living flesh."[45] However, in his interview with *Pravda*, Mahkamov admitted:

Everybody realizes that they will not be able to live without an economic union. Isolation leads to self-destruction. This is why it is most important to see the realities today and not to harbor ambitious illusions, typical of some leaders. The Union of our republics must be preserved and consolidated on a new foundation.[46]

The "sovereignization" of the Union republics led to the conclusion of a number of inter-republican bi- and multi-lateral treaties, most notably the treaty of cooperation among the Middle Asian republics (*sredneazi-atskiie respubliki*), which Kazakhstan signed in June 1990 thus creating a concept of a new united region called "Tsentral'naia Aziia" (Central Asia).[47] Not only did such treaties assert the republics' "sovereignty" through mutual recognition while establishing inter-republic relations circumventing the Center, they also gave the Central Asian bloc greater leverage in the negotiations over the conditions of their entrance into the renewed federation. At the same time, there were other combinations of states, such as the "big four" – the three Slavic republics (Belorus, Russia and Ukraine) and Kazakhstan – which was to become the "core" of the new Union treaty, leaving it open for other states to join at their will. Uzbekistan's Karimov expressed the "Middle Asian" republics' dismay at Kazakhstan's position:

No matter how this treaty of the four is disguised it is nothing other than an attempt of the stronger . . . republics to dictate their conditions to others. The signing of such a treaty means ignoring our interests . . . Will Kazakhstan . . . think about the interests of Uzbekistan? It seems not . . . the possibility of the other republics joining this treaty . . . is simply the gesture of good will on the part of the strong republics . . . I am not even talking about whether there will be any kind of body for supervising this union of four. It is known to me that the other Central Asian republics are of the same opinion as Uzbekistan. I think that on this question my friend Nursultan Nazarbayev was hasty. Firstly, today, when the sovereignty of the republics is not yet a real fact, it seems premature to talk about a treaty on the basis of the norms of international law. The subjects of the federation have not yet received the status of an independent sovereign state.[48]

Thus, Kazakhstan had a unique role in the new Union treaty negotiation. On the one hand, Kazakhstan acted as an unofficial representative of the "Middle Asian" republics, on the other, its intermediary role was resented by regional brethren. Kazakhstan was ultimately snubbed by the three Slavic republics when it came to disintegration. During the negotiations regarding the new Union treaty, Nazarbayev spoke of the "inevitability" of the USSR's collapse. To him, the system could not be preserved in its imperial shape, but could be saved if it were remolded according to the "Leninist plan":

> A building with a bad foundation will not stand for long ... The basically sound Leninist plan for our common home had not been properly implemented. After all, the republics did not unite around the central government, but the central government attached the republics to itself. So now we are seeing the inevitable process of collapse. At the same time a new Union is arising ... I am referring to the signing of treaties between republics in which each other's sovereignty is recognised, current borders are confirmed, and direct economic ties and coordinated interests are established. I am certain that these documents form the basis for a new Union treaty, and foundation and structures of our renewed federation that Kazakhstan supports.[49]

It is unsurprising that the Central Asian republics' leaders would use the Soviet idiom of Lenin as the master-signifier after the Communist Party had been discredited as the ultimate depository of popular sovereignty. Leninist postulates of the right of nations to self-determination now functioned as the only legitimate way to represent republican interests, with Union republics being the rightful containers and transmitters of popular sovereignty.

March 17 Referendum and its Results

The decision to conduct a referendum on preservation of the Soviet Union, which asked, "Do you consider it necessary to preserve the Union of the Soviet Socialist Republics as a renewed federation of equal sovereign republics, in which the rights and freedoms of people of all nationalities will be guaranteed in full measure?" was adopted in December 1990 at the Fourth all-Union Convention of the People's Deputies (*s'ezd narodnykh deputatov*). It was preceded by the so-called "parade of sovereignties" (see Appendix, below, p. 149), the turning point of which was the Russian Federation's declaration of sovereignty. After that, all "loyalist" republics felt compelled to declare themselves "sovereign." The political intrigue behind the referendum concerned the fact that in the Russian Federation an additional question was included on the ballot papers, in effect sabotaging and subverting the point of this symbolic non-binding vote designed to legitimate Gorbachev's power. The additional question asked the voters whether they wanted to introduce an institution of presidency in the Russian Federation, elected by direct popular vote and endowed with significant powers, thus distancing the administration of Russia from the Soviet central command.[50]

The referendum took place on March 17, 1991 and was supposed to preserve the Union. What is somewhat paradoxical is that the referendum called for the preservation of something that had never existed. The renewed federation of equal sovereign states was a vision of a return to the purity of Leninist principles of nationality policies, an attempt to disassociate the USSR from the epithet of an "empire." The main referendum question did not mention the draft of the new Union treaty, and therefore the results are hard to interpret. Besides, in many republics the main question was accompanied by additional questions, often contradicting the main one.[51] Six out of fifteen Union republics – Lithuania, Latvia, Estonia, Armenia, Moldavia and Georgia – refused to take part in the referendum.

The results of the referendum were seemingly impressive. Out of 186.6 million people eligible to cast their votes, 148.6 million showed up at the ballot boxes – an 80 percent turnout. Overall, the general results for all of the republics that participated were as follows: 113.5 million people (76.4 percent) voted in favor and 32.3 million voters (21.7 percent) against. These results were significantly higher for Central Asian republics (see Table 7.1).

Table 7.1

USSR republic (country)	Voter turnout (%)	Those who voted "in favor" (%)
Russian Federation (Russia)	75.4	71.3
Ukrainian SSR (the Ukraine)	83.5	70.2
Belorussian SSR (Belorus)	83.3	82.7
Uzbek SSR (Uzbekistan)	95.4	93.7
Kazakh SSR (Kazakhstan)	88.2	94.1
Azerbaijan SSR (Azerbaijan)	75.1	93.3
Kyrgyz SSR (Kyrgyzstan)	92.9	96.4
Tajik SSR (Tajikistan)	94.4	96.2
Turkmen SSR (Turkmenistan)	97.7	97.9

The Novo-Ogarevo process that started on April 23, 1991 with the "9 + 1" agreement (Gorbachev and the leaders of the nine republics that participated in the referendum) stated that "the primary task is to ratify a new treaty among the sovereign states taking into account the outcomes of the all-union referendum." However, the process was never concluded

141

by the signing of a new Union treaty. One day before the planned signing of the draft, the hardliners from within the Communist Party of the Soviet Union (CPSU) staged a coup d'état, which defeated its self-proclaimed purpose of stopping "the dismembering of the Soviet Union," and thus "trampling upon" the results of the nationwide referendum. The coup resulted in the "parade of independences."[52]

However, one should not interpret the referendum results literally. We should remember the nature of Soviet polls, which could be easily manipulated. Besides, the unclear wording of the referendum question as well as the fact that many republics chose to include additional questions on the ballot papers, which were often contradictory to the main one, meant that the referendum results were not as unambiguous as they seem. In fact, Uzbekistan's official historiography after independence insists on a radically different interpretation of the March 17 referendum results.

The official narrative interprets the results of the referendum as the manifestation of the will of Uzbek people for sovereignty. By emphasizing the part of the wording in the ballot question that defined the role of the member states in the renewed Union as "sovereign" or "enjoying equal rights," they thus equate the affirmative answer with the desire for political independence. A high school history textbook thus narrates Uzbekistan's path to independence as the following:

> The evidence to the gradual movement towards the republic's independence by the leadership and the Uzbek people are the results of the referendum that took place on March 17th 1991. Besides the questions approved by the Higher Council of the USSR, a new question was added to the main list on the ballot papers. It asked from people the following: "Do you agree that Uzbekistan will enter the renewed union (Federation) as a (*ravnopravnaia*) republic enjoying equal rights [with others]?" 93.9% of the voters expressed their opinion as being in favour. Thus, the referendum demonstrated that the overwhelming majority of the voters gave their voice in favour of independence and therefore expressed their full support to the policies conducted by the leadership of the republic.[53]

Alimova and Golovanov, two leading historians of Uzbekistan, report the results of the same referendum in a similar fashion:

> We can judge about the political mood among the population of Uzbekistan, their real will at that time by the outcomes of the referendum regarding the future of the republic that was conducted in the beginning of 1991. To the question on the ballot paper: "Do you agree that Uzbekistan remains within the renewed Union (Federation) as a sovereign republic?," 93.9 % of all those who cast their votes expressed support to independence and to equality (*ravnopravnii*) of Uzbekistan.

This clearly expressed support of the idea of sovereignty on the part of the multiethnic population of Uzbekistan gave the leadership of the republic a firm confidence in the rightfulness of the chosen political course, of the difficult struggle with imperial forces of the Centre.[54]

Both of these historical analyses of the event can be traced to the speech by Uzbekistan's president Islam Karimov, given in 1996, five years after independence of the Central Asian republics:

Then it was the Soviet period – the period of the totalitarian regime. And the referendum of the 17th of March was conducted in the conditions of pressure. At that time in Uzbekistan, a second ballot paper was included. For the citizens of Uzbekistan on the territory of our country we offered the second ballot paper. In other words, along with the question offered by the all-union referendum, offered by the Centre, we put forward our own as well. In its essence, our question was in contradiction with the question asked by the Centre, and they mutually cancelled one another, they were mutually exclusive. We asked that question from people. That is why, we can say with the full evidence, that the attitude of the people of Uzbekistan to the question asked by the referendum of the 17th of March 1991 was expressed at that time clearly and firmly.[55]

Karimov's speech was a response to the argument by the Russian parliamentarians that the dissolution was illegal as it ignored the will of the people as expressed in the results of the referendum. Karimov maintained that the independence of Uzbekistan was legitimized by the results of the March 17 referendum rather than being questioned by those results. Independence, according to the authoritative narrative in Uzbekistan, was a result of the prolonged and bitter struggle of Uzbeks for sovereign statehood, an outcome of the natural course of history. Therefore, the acquisition of independence in 1991 as a result of the collapse of the USSR is still interpreted as a "rebirth" of national sovereign statehood rather than its accidental "birth," despite the absence of an independence movement and the results of the referendum of March 17.

The referendum results could mean that the Union could be preserved in its downsized version and with the devolution of significant powers to the remaining republics. Thus, it is possible to question the results of the March referendum, but, most importantly, the above discussion demonstrates that while sovereignty may have been accidental, it has nonetheless been jealously guarded since it was acquired.

August Coup and the Dissolution of the USSR

This chapter does not go into the details of the events of August 19–21, 1991, which have been discussed at length elsewhere. Suffice it to say that it was the turning point for the possibility of preservation of the Soviet Union in the shape that Gorbachev and Central Asian leaders hoped to see it.

By the end of October that year all Union republics apart from Russia and Kazakhstan had declared independence, including even the most loyal supporters of the renewed Union (Belorus and the Central Asian republics). Kyrgyzstan and Uzbekistan declared independence almost simultaneously on August 31 and September 1, respectively. On September 9, 1991 Tajikistan declared its independence, "hopping on the independence bandwagon." Parliamentary spokesman Aliyev put it succinctly saying, "We can't lag behind other republics. Everybody is declaring independence so we are as well."[56] Turkmenistan followed the rest rather tardily on October 27.

As with the "parade of sovereignties" that preceded it, not all "independences" were equivalent. While some republics held referenda before declaring independence, others did not. Moreover, while some flatly refused to take part in any negotiations to renew their membership in the Union, for the Central Asian republics declarations of independence did not amount to full secession. They were simply a means by which to gain a position of equality when negotiating a new union treaty. As Karimov said, "We have not discarded the idea of signing the union treaty, but its draft might be radically redrawn."[57]

Apart from Kyrgyzstan's Askar Akayev and Kazakhstan's Nursultan Nazarbayev, who expressly condemned the August coup and refused to follow its decrees, all other Central Asian republics' leaders' reactions were either delayed or rather cautious, failing to take a categorical stance on the situation and thus tacitly supporting the coup. In Tajikistan on August 19, Kakhar Mahkamov told a local journalist that the coup leaders promised to uphold "the principles of democratisation and republican sovereignty" and also said that he supported the decree of the Emergency Committee "in principle." After the failure of the junta, the president appeared on Tajik television but did not condemn the conspirators.[58] Uzbekistan's Islam Karimov was visiting India during the coup, but upon his return he declared that *perestroika* had reached a dead-end. Local newspapers did not comment on Gorbachev's return to Moscow, only publishing the relevant TASS reports. Meanwhile, the Turkmen president also remained silent on the issue of the attempted coup until August 22, when all decrees issued by the Emergency Committee were declared to be null and void.[59] In Kazakhstan, Nursultan Nazarbayev called an extraordinary meeting of the Cabinet of Ministers, after which an address to the people of Kazakhstan was issued appealing to citizens to "maintain calm and show restraint," and calling on the armed forces, police and KGB units to "adhere to constitutional norms, to respect the right of the individual and the local authorities," stressing in particular that "a state of emergency is not being introduced in Kazakhstan, and that in accord with adopted Declaration on State Sovereignty and the Constitution of the Kazakh SSR, all authority lies with the Soviets."[60] On August 20, Nazarbayev read out a statement on Kazakh radio and television condemning the coup:

> If we continue along the crooked path of lawlessness, the people will not forgive us. Above all, in these difficult days, we wish to hear the opinion of Mikhail Gorbachev himself. He must personally confirm his incapacity to perform the duties laid upon him.[61]

According to Nazarbayev's memoirs, "Kazakhstan was the second republic after Russia to express sharp condemnation of the putsch."[62] Kyrgyzstan followed on August 21.

The strongest reaction to the silence of local leaders was witnessed in Tajikistan, where President Mahkamov eventually had to resign under pressure from opposition groups (*Rastokhez*, the Democratic Party of Tajikistan, the Islamic Renaissance Party and *La'li Badakhshon*). On August 27, Davlat Khudonazarov, a famous film director and then a people's deputy of the USSR's Supreme Council, accused the leadership of Tajikistan of involvement in the putsch, reading out several coded telegrams which were received by the Tajik Communist Party apparatus from the State Committee of Emergency Situations.[63] Otahon Latifi, a journalist and future significant leader of the United Tajik Opposition (UTO), accused Mahkamov personally of involvement in the events of August 19–21, saying that there was an audio recording to prove it.[64] Having thus been completely discredited, Mahkamov announced his resignation on August 30.

An appeal of the Extraordinary Session of the Supreme Soviet of the republic of Tajikistan to the Congress of People's Deputies of the USSR and to the Supreme Soviet of the RSFSR issued on September 3, 1991 condemned the coup (rather belatedly) and called for the resignation of Kahhor Mahkamov, who failed to react promptly and seemed to have supported the putsch. The democratic forces in Tajikistan gained the moral high ground over the conservative Communist Party after the August coup failed in Moscow, but the appeal nonetheless did not indicate any intention of seceding from the Union. In its rather emotional wording, one can clearly see that even the opposition forces were determined to preserve the Union:

We cannot look with equanimity upon the process of collapse of the Soviet Union which is now before our eyes. We are convinced that, acting alone, outside of our longstanding collaborative relationship with the republics, it will be impossible to overcome the current crisis. We call for the preservation of the new, genuine, and non-artificial union of sovereign states. Taking into account the lessons of the August events, we call upon you to make it possible to resume the process of negotiation for the completion and signing of the Union Treaty.

We cannot imagine our future outside of the Union and without the long-standing and unbreakable ties that bind us to Russia and to the other fraternal republics.[65]

In the wake of the August putsch, an extraordinary session of the Supreme Soviet, which was called by the State Emergency Committee, convened to determine the future of the state. On August 27, Nursultan Nazarbayev gave a speech in which he called on the government to recognize the independence of the Baltic republics, Moldova and Georgia unconditionally. He also added that the new Union Treaty would have to be reconsidered in light of the coup attempt. His proposal favored a loose confederative structure with close economic ties, rather than a federation as was envisaged in the draft treaty.[66] Therefore, after the coup attempt failed there was no going back to the definition of sovereignty agreed upon before and the stakes were raised to radicalize the definition. This period was characterized by "multiple sovereignties." After August 1991 the Central Asian republics began to insist on a looser version of the USSR, debating the differences between a "union state" and a "union of states," between a federation and a confederation – all these subtle differences obscuring the meaning of "sovereignty" within the Union even further. For example, Akayev advocated that the future union should be a "synthesis of all the principles of both federalism and confederalism," which should be possible to adopt "on the principle of community" like that found in Europe, possibly styled after the British Commonwealth.[67]

Apart from being a part of a general "bandwagon" effect, the declarations of independence by the Central Asian republics were also motivated by neo-imperialist tendencies in Russia, such as the statement made by Yeltsin on August 27 about a possible revision of borders should some republics refuse to participate in the new Union treaty negotiations. In response to such bullying, Nazarbayev expressed his concern that "on the wave of a democratic upsurge there may appear the foam of chauvinism," which might lead to inter-ethnic conflict or even "inter-republican war" and impede integration because of the "past experience of life in a totalitarian state" and "the basic fear of finding oneself yet again in a subordinate position."[68] This same remark, however, suggests that Yeltsin remained committed to the preservation of the Union until November 1991. The turning point was the referendum on independence in the Ukraine and the subsequent interpretation of its results by President Kravchuk as meaning complete secession from the Soviet Union. He flatly refused to consider any discussion of a draft treaty, saying, "You can persuade Kravchuk, but you cannon persuade the Ukrainian people. The old Soviet Union is doomed."[69] Another decisive factor for Yeltsin was his impatience to start a radical reform of the economy, which would be impeded by the conservative Central Asian republics. As a result of all these events, and arguably the continuing political rivalry between Gorbachev and Yeltsin, the Belovezhskaya Agreement was concluded at an all-Slav summit near Minsk on December 8. Entitled "Agreement on the Creation of a Commonwealth of Independent States," the document effectively put an end to the seventy-four-year history of the USSR.

Reaction to the Dissolution of the Union

The three Slavic republics later tried to justify their right to unilaterally dissolve the USSR by the fact that they were the three surviving representatives of the four founding signatories of the 1922 Union treaty. Both Yeltsin and Nazarbayev (perhaps to save face) wrote in their memoirs that Nazarbayev was invited to the Belovezhskaya Forest, but refused to come. In any case, the exclusion of the Central Asian republics from the process of dissolution was perceived as a split between the Slavs and the Asians. Nazarbayev later made clear his irritation with the turn of events saying that basing the new union on "national–ethnic [i.e., Slavic] principles is a vestige of the Middle Ages."[70] One can hear the obvious disappointment in the words of Kazakhstan's Nursultan Nazarbayev after the signing of the Belovezhskaia Pushcha agreement by the three Slavic republics in December 1991: "To our great sorrow, leaders of a number of former Soviet republics equated sovereignty with autarchy."[71] This perception of a Slav–Central Asian split is reflected in the reaction of the *Birlik* movement. As Abdurahim Pulat recalled, on December 15 the joint session of the *Birlik* Peoples' Movement and Party took place where the members decided on whether to participate in the upcoming presidential elections. The second item on the agenda was the reaction to the Belovezhskaia Agreement. *Vremya* (the main news program of Soviet TV) reported that day on the decision adopted at that meeting to call on the states of the region to create a Commonwealth that would include the Central Asian states and Azerbaijan.[72]

However, despite his bitterness, fears of inter-ethnic strife and separatist tensions in the northern part of the country, combined with economic considerations, compelled Nazarbayev to initiate a meeting of five Central Asian leaders in Ashkhabad, Turkmenistan, on December 17. One day before that summit, Kazakhstan finally declared independence in order to put itself on equal footing with its former peers. It was the last republic to do so.

The Ashkhabad summit resulted in all five of the Central Asian states joining the CIS under the condition that they would be granted equal status to the founding Slavic states. This was the beginning of the road for the Central Asian states to become independent states.

Conclusion

Although the republics of the Soviet Middle Asia and Kazakhstan were among the most loyal supporters of the preservation of the Soviet Union, their path to sovereign statehood can hardly be described as the trajectory of inanimate objects "catapulted into independence."[73] Their road to independence also challenges the common-sense assumption that decolonization is brought about by the will of the colonized people through a revolt on the periphery of the empire. Central Asian republics were excluded from the ultimate decision-making process during the dissolution of the USSR. In the Belovezhskaia Forest, paradoxically, it was the core that declared its independence from the periphery. Despite this, there was a considerable push for greater "sovereignty" from within the Central Asian republics through the activities of "informal" political groups of the fledging opposition movements leading up to the dissolution.

Thus, the independence of Central Asian states was a result of both centrifugal and centripetal forces, whereby the less developed Asian republics were in the "slow lane" of sovereignization, while the more radically-minded republics followed by the Russian core led the process of decolonization.

The "reluctance" to match the highest bidders in the "sovereignty" game – the Baltic republics, Georgia and Armenia – could be explained by two main factors: history and economy. First, unlike the more radically-minded republics, Central Asian states had no history of nation-statehood within their present borders, so the political imaginations of the leaders could not refer to past examples of sovereignty outside the Soviet framework. Second, despite the injustice and inefficiency of economic management from the Center, the Central Asian elites realized the degree of interdependence of the republics' economies and saw the possibility of disintegration of the Union as a catastrophe.

However, there were many in Russia who saw the Central Asian republics as dangerous ballast holding the already weak economy back. Some were also uncomfortable with the image of an empire as being incompatible with entering the international arena as a "civilized" state. Following the advice of Aleksandr Solzhenitsin, Russia was shaking off the burden of its "Middle Asian underbelly,"[74] while conveniently transferring power from the weakened Gorbachev to the young and ambitious Yeltsin.

Thus, while the Central Asian states took part in the Union-wide process of negotiating greater "sovereignty" from the Center, they were a solid block backing Gorbachev's attempts to preserve the Union, albeit in a new, reinvented form, arguably finally fulfilling the original Leninist vision of a free union of truly sovereign states. Instead, Central Asian states found themselves on a path toward more conventional sovereignty as independent states, which they have since embraced and have been rather successful in asserting and guarding.

Appendices

Table 7.2 Declarations of sovereignty by Union republics

Union republic	Date
Estonian SSR	November 16, 1988
Lithuanian SSR	May 16, 1989
Latvian SSR	July 28, 1989
Azerbaijan SSR	July 23, 1989
Georgian SSR	November 18, 1989
Russian SFSR	June 12, 1990
Uzbek SSR	June 20, 1990
Moldovan SSR	June 23, 1990
Ukrainian SSR	July 16, 1990
Belorussian SSR	July 27, 1990
Turkmen SSR	August 22, 1990
Tajik SSR	August 24, 1990
Kirghiz SSR	October 24, 1990
Kazakh SSR	October 25, 1990
Armenian SSR	none

Table 7.3 Declarations of independence

The USSR republic (country)	Date
Georgian SSR (Georgia)	April 9, 1991
Chechnya	June 8, 1991
Estonian SSR (Estonia)	August 20, 1991
Latvian SSR (Latvia)	August 21, 1991
Ukrainian SSR (the Ukraine)	August 24, 1991
Belorussian SSR (Belorus)	August 25, 1991
Moldovan SSR (Moldova)	August 27, 1991
Azerbaijan SSR (Azerbaijan)	August 30, 1991
Kyrgyz SRR (Kyrgyzstan)	August 31, 1991
Uzbek SSR (Uzbekistan)	September 1, 1991
Tajik SSR (Tajikistan)	September 9, 1991
Armenian SSR (Armenia)	September 23, 1991
Turkmen SSR (Turkmenistan)	October 27, 1991
Kazakh SSR (Kazakhstan)	December 16, 1991

Notes

1. Solzhenitsyn, "Kak nam obustroit' Rossiyu."
2. Suleymenov ,"The collapse of the Soviet Union is tragedy to us," interview, *Dagens Nyheter*, April 28, 1995.
3. Crawshaw, *Goodbye to the USSR*.
4. Olcott, "Central Asia's catapult to independence."
5. E.g., Rywkin, *Moscow's Muslim Challenge*; D'Encausse, *Decline of an Empire*; Bennigsen and Broxup, *The Islamic Threat to the Soviet State*; D'Encausse, *The End of the Soviet Empire*.
6. Aron, "Gorbachev's Central Asian time bomb is ticking."
7 Orwell, *Animal Farm*.
8. Jones, *The Soviet Concept of "Limited Sovereignty."*
9. Jones, *The Soviet Concept of "Limited Sovereignty,"* p. 10.
10. Jones, *The Soviet Concept of "Limited Sovereignty,"* p. 10.
11. Jones, *The Soviet Concept of "Limited Sovereignty,"* p. 17.
12. Walker, *Dissolution*.
13. See, e.g., Haugen, *The Establishment of National Republics in Soviet Central Asia*.
14. Walker, *Dissolution*.
15. Jones, *The Soviet Concept of "Limited Sovereignty,"* p. 244.
16. Text of broadcast of a speech by the president of Uzbekistan Islam Karimov, December 18, 1990.
17. "The events in Kazakhstan – an eyewitness report', *Central Asian Survey*, pp. 73–5; Kuzio, "Nationalist Riots in Kazakhstan," pp. 79–100.

18. Walker, *Dissolution*.
19. Guboglo and Chicherina (eds), *Grazhdanskie dvizheniia v Tadzhikistane*.
20. Fierman, "'Glasnost' in practice," pp. 4–5 and Carley, "The price of the plan," pp. 1–38.
21. Rosenblum, "AP Newsfeature: Samarkand."
22. Draft Platform of the "Agzybirlik" Society, June 1991.
23. Charter of the Birlik People's Movement to Protect the Natural, Spiritual, and Material Wealth of Uzbekistan, September 1989, *CACC*.
24. Mursaliyev and Sorokin, "Interview with A. Pulatov and P. Akhunov."
25. The full name was "Birlik Movement for the Preservation of Uzbekistan's Natural, Material and Spiritual Riches."
26. "Mustaqil" could be translated from Uzbek as both "sovereign" and/or "independent."
27. "Charter of the Birlik People's Movement to Protect the Natural, Material and Spiritual Wealth of Uzbekistan," in Furtado, Jr and Chandler (eds), *Perestroika in the Soviet Republics*.
28. Quoted in Fierman, "The Communist Party."
29. "Declaration of Sovereignty Adopted by the Supreme Soviet of the Uzbek SSR on June 20, 1990," *Pravda Vostoka*, No. 141, June 22, 1990.
30. Salih, "Shortly about our movement."
31. Excerpt from an article by *Azat* co-chairman Isinaliyev, "An anxious time."
32. Quoted in Fierman, "The Communist Party."
33. "Speech by Niyazov, First Secretary of the CPTu, to the Republican Conference on the Tasks of the Mass Media in Perestroika," April 28, 1989 in Furtado, Jr and Chandler (eds), *Perestroika in the Soviet Republics*.
34. Hammer, "Perestroika as seen by some Tajik historians," p 48.
35. Sneider, "Change comes slowly to Kirghizia," p. 4.
36. Salih, "Shortly about our movement."
37. Interview with Suleymenov, president of the Peoples' Congress of Kazakhstan, "The collapse of the Soviet Union is tragedy to us."
38. Dildyaiev, "A Union treaty must be signed immediately."
39. "Discussion of 'general principles' for republican self-management," Editorial report of phone-in program, "Restructuring problems and solutions," Soviet television 1500 GMT, March 29.
40. Rosenblum, "Islam, economics, ecology."
41. "In the Supreme Soviet of Uzbek SSR: in the interests of the Republic and the Whole Federation," *Pravda Vostoka*.
42. "In the Supreme Soviet of Uzbek SSR: in the interests of the Republic and the Whole Federation," *Pravda Vostoka*. September 1, 1990, No. 199, pp. 1–2
43. "Congress of Communist Party of Uzbekistan," Soviet television report, 1600 GMT, December 7, 1990. *BBC Summary of World Broadcasts*.
44. Mahkamov, President of the Tajik SSR, speech to the 4th Congress of

People's Deputies of the USSR, December 20, 1990, Official Kremlin International News Broadcast.
45. Mahkamov, speech to the 4th Congress of People's Deputies of the USSR.
46. "Tajik president: the Union must be preserved," *TASS*, December 21, 1990.
47. Agreement on Economic, Scientific-Technical, and Cultural Cooperation of the Uzbek, Kazakh, Kirgiz, Tajik and Turkmen SSRs, *Kazakhstanskaya Pravda*, June 23, 1990. Other agreements include: A bilateral treaty between Kazakhstan and Ukraine, February 21, 1991; a treaty between Kirgizia and Kazakhstan, February 20, 1991; Turkmen–Tajik treaty, August 12, 1991 and so on.
48. Niyazmatov, Interview with Islam Karimov, President of Uzbekistan, *Sovet Uzbekistoni* (in Uzbek), March 12, 1991.
49. Nazarbayev, "To be or not to be."
50. Nadler, "Gorbachev's gamble: what is Soviet referendum all about?"
51. Brumley, "Two duelling Soviet leaders able to claim victory in referendum."
52. "Message to the Soviet people from the State Committee for the State of Emergency," *TASS*, August 18, 1991.
53. Juraev and Fayzullayev, *Istoriia Uzbekistana*, p. 18
54. Alimova and Golovanov, *Uzbekistan v 1917–1980*, p. 78
55. Karimov, Speech at the session of the Khorazm regional Council of People's Deputies, March 16, 1996, available at: http://2004.press-service.uz/rus/knigi/9tom/4tom_21_3.htm.
56. "Tajikistan hops on independence bandwagon," *Seattle News*, September 10, 1991.
57. Gray, "Gorbachev upbeat on union."
58. Latifi, "Heard about the coup?"; Zainutdinov, "What the president was silent on."
59. Latifi, "Heard about the coup?"
60. Nazarbayev, *Without Right and Left*.
61. Nazarbayev, *Without Right and Left*, p. 151.
62. Nazarbayev, *Without Right and Left*, p. 151.
63. Nazriev and Sattarov, *Respublika Tadzhikistan*, p. 17.
64. Nazriev and Sattarov, *Respublika Tadzhikistan*, p. 21.
65. Appeal of the Extraordinary Session of the Supreme Soviet of the republic of Tajikistan to the Congress of People's Deputies of the USSR and to the Supreme Soviet of the RSFSR, *Kommunist Tadzhikistana*, September 3, 1991.
66. Nazarbayev, *Without Right and Left*, pp. 158–9.
67. Zherebenkov, "Kyrgyz President on Status of Union Treaty," report from USSR Supreme Soviet Session, Russian radio, August 26, 1991, *BBC Summary of World Broadcasts*.
68. Nazarbayev, *Without Right and Left*.
69. Quoted in Walker, *Dissolution*, p. 158.
70. *New York Times*, December 10, 1991.

71. Quoted in "Kazakhstan president confident," Reuters News Agency, December 11, 1991.
72. Pulat, "Turkestan – on the road to integration," pp. 11–15.
73. Olcott, 'Central Asia's catapult into independence," *Foreign Affairs*, Summer 1992.
74. Solzhenitsyn, "How to rebuild Russia."

Section III

Empire and Domestic Sovereignty

8

The Middle East after Empire: Sovereignty and Institutions

Louise Fawcett

What has "empire" meant in a Middle Eastern context? And what is the link between the meaning and experience of empire and the post-imperial outcome of the sovereign state? From formal structures to more informal practices and understandings, the impact of imperialism has been extraordinarily pervasive across the region and remains so today, as evidenced by events in Iraq, Iran, neighboring Afghanistan and Israel–Palestine, and also by what might more loosely be called the mood on the "Arab street." It has closely informed and conditioned the different aspects of state sovereignty as these have evolved and developed over the past century. This chapter explores the different, often contradictory, meanings of empire and sovereignty in the history of the modern Middle East and considers how they have interacted, positively and negatively, with the development of states and institutions. It is argued that the experience of Western imperialism and state-building interacted, often negatively, with pre-existing notions of sovereignty, leadership and modes of territorial, political and social organization, contributing – alongside other factors – to contested states and institutions. The introduction and maintenance of Western sovereignty models, but above all their qualified or bounded nature, have been a source of resistance and instability facilitating stubborn authoritarianism and continuing acts of external intervention.

Introduction

The concern of this chapter is to explore how an imperial past affects sovereignty outcomes, perceptions and choices, and the consequences for sovereignty of different imperial styles. It draws upon the different effects of formal and informal empire in the Middle East under both Ottoman and European colonial rule.[1] It examines in turn the Ottoman and European legacies of imperialism and colonialism and their different, at times parallel, at times competing, consequences for subsequent state-building and sovereignty. The chapter focuses on the different meanings of sovereignty after empire, in particular, the complex inter-relationship between international legal sovereignty, on the one hand, and Westphalian or "external" and domestic or "internal" sovereignty, on the other. It shows how even where the former is obtained the latter remains conditional. The grant of formal sovereignty with independence, thus, did not resolve the wider sovereignty issue resulting in contested states and institutions, impeding democratization and contributing to what is regarded as a longstanding and region-wide (with few exceptions) legitimacy crisis and a continuing cycle of state weakness and external intervention.

In considering these questions this chapter does not attempt to provide any detailed analysis of the state of sovereignty in the region known today as the Middle East, past and present. Rather it offers a *tour d'horizon*, addressing some broad themes pertinent to the development of sovereignty in the Ottoman Empire and its successor states[2] with the aim of highlighting those variables that appear most significant in determining its content and trajectory. This then provides a basis for comparison with other regions.

Empire and its Meanings

Understanding the impact of empire requires some precision as to the imperial experience of different regions, notably its content and timing, and, as the editors' introduction highlights, to the very definition of empire itself.[3] This is far from straightforward: as Gallagher and Robinson write, "the imperial historian . . . is very much at the mercy of his own particular concept of empire."[4]

Viewed from the perspective of the twenty-first century it is clear that both fixed and floating meanings may be attributed to empire. We may refer loosely to differences in terms of formal and informal structures, to mechanisms of control and influence, but also to differences in terms of perceptions and understanding – the latter may persist long after the former has ended. Clearly, in reference to the cases considered in this volume, the imperial experiences were often quite different in their timing, content and reception and legacy. Indeed, scholars may question the appropriateness of the term "empire" when applied to the USSR, a question unlikely to be raised in relation to the Russian empire, the Ottoman Empire or European imperialism in the Middle East, though in themselves they were very different. However, the central elements of control and influence were present in all these cases and in this respect Ronald Robinson's definition is both illuminating and accommodating. He describes imperialism as "a process whereby agents of an expanding society gain inordinate influence or control over the vitals of weaker societies . . . The object is to shape or reshape them in its own interest and more or less in its own image."[5]

Despite differences in its nature and intention, control was a common variable in these different arenas. There were other similarities; for example, in the political geography, multinational and predominantly Muslim character of the Ottoman and Russian/Soviet empires in the Middle East and Central Asia, and in the double exposure to empire that both regions experienced in the space of less than a century, allowing us to isolate common features to compare. What were the consequences for sovereignty of imperial control and its formal ending? Did states accept the sovereignty outcomes offered by imperial powers or resist them? And to what extent did "informal" or neo-imperialism continue beyond empire?

In respect of the Middle East there are two distinct, though ultimately linked, imperial experiences to draw upon, one – the Ottoman – long in duration, the other – the European – rather short in contrast, yet with both impacting heavily on sovereignty outcomes. Though the Ottomans enjoyed the formal structures, trappings and longevity of empire in a way that the European powers mostly did not (the Middle East mandates were short, embodied a commitment to independence and were regulated by international law), there was also much that was "informal," or at least decentralized, and, for its citizens, attractive in Ottoman rule, notably in the level of autonomy permitted to certain national and religious groups. Conversely, though the experience of European colonialism in much of the Middle East lacked many of the characteristics of formal empire (in contrast to the imperial experience in India, for example), its very nature and *modus operandi*, its relative lack of resources, together with its short time frame (both characteristics of "late" European empire), cast a long shadow making it a source of continuing contention and state weakness. Above all, elites apart, many citizens of the new states neither adjusted to nor accepted the new boundaries of colonial rule. Whatever their intentions, and these clearly differed where France and Britain were concerned, the ruling powers did not create a sense of permanence – and here one early distinction may be drawn between the Middle East and Central Asia.

If independence and its accompaniment, the award of legal sovereignty and with it membership of a wider international society, became a common and realizable goal, the actual drawing of borders and the formalities of state-building itself, mostly reflecting contemporary European interests, were critically received and the latter often subverted as the pre- and post-independence rebellions and revolutions in core Arab states showed. State institutions and the ideologies they embodied thus had shallow roots and often ran counter to existing local arrangements, cultures and expectations which had flourished under Ottoman rule, but also had pre-Ottoman origins. Hence, it is not enough merely to consider "formal" versus "informal," or even more ostensibly "liberal" imperial structures in relation to the development and adoption of sovereignty, but rather how the different structures and understandings of empire were regarded and how they fitted or became molded to local reality and practice; here timing – both in the sense of the length of the imperial experience and its wider geopolitical context – is also crucial. While the Ottoman experience was firmly embedded long before Europe's "Age of Empire," the British and French experience took place against a backdrop of imperial decline, or at least retrenchment, when the stirrings of nationalism were fanned by a Wilsonian discourse of self-determination that was particular to the early twentieth century.

This implied contrast between the two imperial styles is too absolute. First, European imperialism, formal and informal, in what is now known as the Middle East was already prevalent during the late Ottoman period – it did not begin where Ottoman imperialism left off. Consider the case of Egypt. Already virtually independent from Ottoman rule, its occupation by Britain in 1882 marked merely the culmination of a series of moves by European powers to transform the Egyptian economy.[6] Outside Egypt, European powers widely used the modality of the "friendship" or "free trade" treaty to establish preferential arrangements with weaker states like Persia and the Ottoman state itself. Further, there were many meeting points between the Ottoman and European styles of rule – particularly in the later period when the Europeans were expanding at the Ottomans' expense. Indeed, European imperialism itself closely informed the Ottoman reform movement and the changing relationship between rulers and ruled.[7] In this sense, the late Ottomans, rather than providing an alternative sovereignty script, may be seen as having begun to adopt parts of the European sovereignty one, and, indeed, this script was played out in the rump Ottoman state: Turkey.

How far these Ottoman reforms had penetrated beyond an imperial urban core remains a subject for speculation, however,[8] and helps explain the bumpy start to many of the new states. This chapter tries to uncover which were the particular features of the two imperial experiences – as opposed to other possible factors – that may help to account for the sovereignty outcomes that emerged and which have, arguably, contributed to a

160

protracted and continuing sovereignty crisis for the region. Here a sovereignty crisis is understood to mean both the failure of states of the region to enjoy full external (Westphalian) sovereignty, and the parallel and linked failure to achieve a state of domestic sovereignty that lies beyond the power of the ruling elite and locates ultimate sovereignty in the people.

While focusing on the political development of the Near Eastern domains of the Ottoman Empire, later to become European mandates, points of contrast are provided by considering the distinctive case of Egypt, as well as that of modern Turkey, itself an Ottoman product, but one whose future was less directly influenced by the European imperial powers, and whose sovereignty developed on very different lines. Another comparative case considered is that of the Ottoman's neighbor, Iran, again not a formal product of European empire, but one that was nonetheless deeply penetrated by imperial influence.

Sovereignty In and Beyond Empire

As with empire, definitions of sovereignty differ. In this respect, while acknowledging the position of scholars that the concept has multiple meanings and suffers from lack of clarity,[9] the analysis in this chapter draws on the four-way usage of sovereignty suggested by Stephen Krasner.[10] Krasner's distinction between international legal sovereignty, external or Westphalian sovereignty, domestic sovereignty and interdependence sovereignty is useful as it helps to unbundle sovereignty and separate the formalities of sovereignty as international legal personality from the practical day-to-day effects of sovereignty. There are parallels here with Robert Jackson's concept of "quasi states" in which a distinction is drawn between negative and positive sovereignty.[11]

This chapter is mostly concerned with two of the aspects of sovereignty described above: Westphalian sovereignty defined as "political organization based on the exclusion of external actors from authority structures within a given territory"; and domestic sovereignty, or "the formal organization of political authority within the state and the ability of public authorities to exercise effective control within the borders of their own polity."[12] These two aspects demonstrate not only the impact of empire upon sovereignty at the time of "rupture," but also the elements of continuity in the imperial project "beyond empire." It is in the meaning and (mis)application of Westphalian and domestic sovereignty that we find the persistence of hierarchies in international relations.[13]

Following Krasner, it can be argued that the evolution of states, and the adoption of Western notions of sovereignty, was not a "random event," but reflected the functional advantages enjoyed by states over other structures.[14] However, it is also true, as Roger Owen observes that ideas about the state, or nation-state, have come directly from Western political experience.[15] As such, in a region like the Middle East, with little previous direct exposure to Western political systems, their import was likely to be contested. The award of international legal sovereignty – as independence – was important and highly valued in the Middle East as in the rest of the colonial world, but the link between the new entities created and imperial influence was strong, generating resistance to both their territorial and institutional arrangements. This, in turn, invited further acts of intervention, while distorting or slowing down the demand for popular sovereignty. Hence, the formal award of independence, when it came, had a built-in sovereignty deficit.

From the above it should not be inferred that the experiment of statehood was doomed to fail in such non-Western settings, but it did mean that its trajectory was very different. Uncontroversially, it can be agreed that "the implantation of Western models of the modern nation state in the Middle East, as well as in many other parts of the world, have led to very different patterns of formation."[16]

One particular source of difficulty in the modern Middle East, unlike other regions where independent states progressed more naturally from previously existing colonial boundaries, was the fact that the borders, size and composition of the state were, at least to some extent, externally determined, and in some cases were quite new and consequently deemed "artificial" with resultant problems for the evolution of domestic sovereignty. Consider here Hinsley's general observation about the relationship between the evolution of domestic sovereignty and the creation of states:

> The concept of sovereignty will not be found in societies in which there is no state. Far from arising at once with the emergence in a community of the forms of the state, the concept will not have appeared until a subsequent process of integration or reconciliation has taken place between a state and its community.[17]

There is considerable variation across cases. The above argument is less compelling for the more homogeneous and previously autonomous entities like Egypt or Tunisia. Ilya Harik and others have also pointed out the over-simplification in the use of the word "artificial" as applied to modern states of the region whose deep historical and unifying roots have been overlooked.[18] Nonetheless, the process of community integration and reconciliation, where it existed, was at best overlaid or interrupted; at worst, quite distorted by the colonial experience.

The modern Iraqi state was a case in point. Notwithstanding the rediscovery of Iraq's rich history of "regionness" in the Ottoman period,[19] the state that emerged was neither physically nor culturally homogeneous. As Malcolm Yapp points out, "very few citizens of the new state thought of themselves as Iraqis."[20]

In another sense, while states of the region certainly appeared "stronger" over time,[21] their strength and authority derived not from popular legitimation, but from the power of the leaders and their supporting elites; from a strengthening executive–bureaucratic alliance. In this way, without the development of a broadly based social contract, most states – old and new – have failed to meet the essential criteria for modern (popular) sovereignty and its embodiment: constitutional government.[22] And here again the link between the effects of imperialism and regime type, if less straightforward, is unmistakable.

The following sections of this chapter consider how the evolution of states has played out in three different historical settings, providing three linked "sovereignty beyond empire" stories. First, and briefly, in the late Ottoman imperial setting, which provides an important backdrop and prelude to the emergence of the modern system; second, in the Middle East after the First World War during the era of the European mandates and what has been called "partial sovereignty"; and third, in the period after the Second World War as most states moved to consolidate their formal independence. In each case I explore the particular setting, features and understandings of empire and pathways to sovereignty, and how these interacted with existing structures and expectations. Finally, I consider how sovereignty has evolved "beyond empire" into the contemporary era and how far it is still conditioned – in its internal and external dimensions – by the actions and influence, whether direct or indirect, of former imperial and post-imperial powers.[23]

The Ottoman Setting

The Ottoman setting provides essential background to understanding the subsequent trajectory of sovereignty in what became the modern Middle East. Long-established patterns of governance and statehood, while subject to external and internal pressures for change, became enduring landmarks for many of the citizens of the new states. In this respect the arguments of historical institutionalists[24] are useful in highlighting how the ideas and practices of the Ottoman period endured even where institutional forms changed.

While a detailed characterization of Ottoman sovereignty and Ottoman subjects is beyond the scope of this chapter, some features of the empire may be briefly referred to here providing a contrast to what was to follow. First, unlike the European experience, this was one of geographically contiguous empire. Imperial rule under the Ottoman Sultan, as caliph, provided unity and legitimacy – most of his subjects were Muslims. Yet the broader administrative framework was highly decentralized, providing for significant regional autonomy and incorporating diverse practices of patrimonialism, clientalism and tribalism. Importantly, it provided a means of accommodating difference: a feature that was mostly lacking in European imperialism. As Michael Walzer has noted, "imperial autonomy tends to lock individuals into their communities and therefore into a single ethnic or religious identity. It tolerates groups and their authority structures and customary practices."[25]

By the nineteenth century, the pressure of new ideas from within and without were intruding on these settled patterns of existence, and revealed alternative pathways to sovereignty, or at least shifted understanding of the concepts of sovereignty and empire. At once challenged and influenced by Europe, the empire in its Tanzimat phase adopted some modernizing and Westernizing reforms which started to shift the locus of political authority and were reflected in the introduction of the first Ottoman Constitution in 1876.[26]

The Ottoman was but one of a number of experiments with the idea of constitutional government in and around the Ottoman territories, including those already autonomous units, whether in the Balkans, Tunisia and Egypt, or in the Ottoman's rival neighbor, Iran.[27] For some commentators, these (like other later attempts at modernization and constitutionalism), were merely "a parody of what happened in Europe,"[28] and as such were destined to fail. Elie Kedourie has dismissed the possibility of popular sovereignty or constitutional government emerging within "oriental despotism" where "the state is always stronger than society . . . no interests in society can resist the demands of the ruling class or withstand its powers."[29] For others, in contrast, such efforts were seen as the birth of representative government within the empire.[30] For its citizens, whether at the center or on the periphery, this was a time of turbulence and change. Some were relatively untouched by the reforms, suggesting a town–country divide; others resisted them. The effect was to produce a "tense dualism"[31] between old and new ideas, arguably revealing many of the tensions that would later be present in more acute form in the short period of Western state-making.

It was above all this "tense dualism," both in its internal and external relations that characterized the late Ottoman Empire. Albert Hourani has captured these tensions in describing the experience of the Arab region with modernization in the nineteenth century, writing how

> It would be better . . . to see this history of this period as that of a complex inter-action: of the will of ancient and stable societies to reconstitute themselves, preserving what they have of their own while making the necessary changes in order to survive in a modern world increasingly organised on other principles and where the centres of power have lain for long, and still lie, outside the Middle East.[32]

If changes in and around the empire pointed toward the development of independent states and the beginning of attempts at constitutional government, in another sense, the Ottoman Empire itself, by the nineteenth century, already displayed many of the trappings of evolving Western statehood and practice: not just in its membership of an international system which was a reality, but an international society of sovereign states, as demonstrated by its longstanding participation in the global economy; and in strategic alliances, diplomatic relationships and multilateral conferences.[33]

At its demise therefore the empire had already revealed the diverse pathways and possibilities of sovereignty which would come to inform later state-making. Some of these pathways had scarcely been tried beyond the imperial core; others were cut short. The Ottoman regime at home and abroad was destined to fail: the onset of war, the growth of competing nationalisms, the clash of new and old ideologies and the competition of ruling elites – aided and abetted by external powers – sealed the fate of the once successful multi-communal enterprise. Both the moment and speed of rupture were important. Different successor states responded to the Ottoman legacy in different ways. In some, modern ideas of statehood came to be more readily accepted, particularly where some groundwork had been laid, in others this process was delayed. Yet it remained, for many of its subjects, particularly the early post-Ottoman generation and those less touched by the late Ottoman reforms, a vital and enduring point of reference, an example of a path not taken, raising the tantalizing question of what would have happened had the war not been lost. Appeals to the past, or the construction of an alternative vision of the present through Islamism, Arabism, or the constant pull of sub-state groups and identities, against the growth of states and their respective nationalisms, resonate through the modern history of the region which may be understood alternatively as revering or rejecting the Ottoman legacy.

The Inter-war Setting

The subsequent European colonial legacy would ultimately be subject to a very different interpretation than that of the Ottomans. Against a backdrop of widespread confusion, contestation and mistrust fed by the uncertainties of war and peace-making, a new Middle East system emerged in which the hand of Europe was predominant. In 1914, Britain ended the formality of Ottoman sovereignty of Egypt and by 1918 the Arab provinces of the Ottoman Empire were occupied by Britain and France, to become League of Nations mandates. Elizabeth Monroe writes how "the compromises evolved for Egypt and these mandated territories were different in letter, but alike in spirit . . . a cross between liberalism and adherence to war aims."[34] They were not "old-style" colonialism, because the charter implied a limit and accountability to the League and this principle was important. Nor were these infant states colonized by European settlers. Yet neither the fact of non-settlement nor "new-look" colonialism made for a successful recipe for state-building. In constructing a new "Westphalian" system, the core principle of Westphalian (external) sovereignty was not observed. Nor was the new (internal) sovereignty script written to reflect or accommodate the kind of tensions revealed above; rather, it was mostly written by the imperial powers to reflect their imperial interests and choices at that time. In the case of Palestine, most tellingly, there was no sovereignty script at all beyond that provided by the Mandate itself.

In all states sovereignty was conditional. And the path taken with respect to state-building, like the 1920 San Remo Convention itself, was one in which little direct reference was made to the wishes of the local populations, whether in determining the territorial units that would comprise the new state system – the sovereign entities created – or the manner in which the states would be governed. As David Fromkin writes:

> It was an era in which Middle Eastern countries and frontiers were fabricated in Europe. Iraq and what we now call Jordan, for example, were British inventions, lines drawn on an empty map by British politicians after the First World War; while the boundaries of Saudi Arabia, Kuwait and Iraq were established by a British civil servant in 1922, and the frontier between Moslems and Christians were drawn by France in Syria–Lebanon and by Russia on the borders of Armenia and Soviet Azerbaijan.[35]

Whether or not this now familiar account of colonial state-making may have been overstated, it can scarcely be denied that in the area that became the Middle East, the post-war settlement was largely imposed, involving major territorial, political, demographic and social adjustment. Though providing a ready formula for legal sovereignty and independence, the door was left ajar to continuing intervention and interference, which would have profound consequences for the internal development of states and the evolution of domestic sovereignty.

If the definitions of, and pathways to, sovereignty were thus initially set by colonial powers, some only to be later rejected, it would be wrong to regard all the effects of state-making as negative: institution-building and constitution-writing were important in providing an ordering framework and in defining the nature of the state and arena of political authority.[36] Nor could resistance to Europe and aspects of European influence and control disguise the real and growing attractiveness of the principle of legal sovereignty that was bestowed on newly independent states. Rulers in particular were quick to recognize that attempts to foster national identity and political authority were linked to international recognition and resources: "recognition is a signal about the viability of a political regime and its leaders."[37]

Genuine attempts at statecraft were not lacking. In Iraq, a state created from three Ottoman provinces, a hereditary constitutional monarchy was installed under the Organic Law of 1925. Its Ottoman-based constitution, though subject to the constraints of the Mandate, included the principle of popular sovereignty, and looked on paper "as powerful as any that existed."[38] The arrangement in Transjordan provided for an initially more fragile, yet ultimately durable construction in which royal (Hashemite) authority was paramount. The Egyptian case, in contrast, revealed a more comprehensive experiment in parliamentary government: Britain ended the Protectorate in 1922 and the following year a new constitution established a delicate balance between the king and politicians.[39] Crucially, however, Britain preserved significant rights and influence; the ensuing period was one of instability and a growing nationalism which ultimately led to the ousting of British influence and its chosen instruments of governance.

Of the new regimes established many came under challenge from the start: the year 1920 saw revolts in both Iraq and Palestine. One particular problem, with important consequences for state-building during the mandate period and after, was that the kind of accommodation of subject groups, or the state–society contract, that had been an important feature of Ottoman arrangements was eroded in the new states. This was partly by design: in Iraq and Syria, for example, the colonial powers developed alliances and links with favored groups and individuals so disrupting existing patterns of authority. The new institutional arrangements provided less room for difference. To quote Walzer again: "Toleration in nation-states is commonly focused not on groups but on individual participants, who are generally conceived stereotypically, first as citizens, then as members of this or that minority."[40] In the mandates and successor states new regimes of toleration did not easily emerge.

In other, at times unpredictable ways, the colonial powers found themselves confronted by nationalist forces that they could not readily harness and control, including the persistence of broader Arab nationalist sentiments which aspired to reunify the Ottoman provinces. This idea had different expressions: one was King Faisal's attempt to defy Europe and create an independent Arab state with Damascus as its capital. Though such efforts were frustrated, the peoples of the newly constituted Syrian state continued to thwart the efforts of France to impose its administrative structures and order in the Mandate. In none of these cases were the bases for legitimate and durable structures put in place. Of the mandates, only Lebanon's constitutional formula, based on the consociational principles established under the earlier Ottoman regime, survived into the modern period, only to be later torn apart by civil war.

Turkey, in contrast, emerged as fully independent, with a new state built on more modern and secular lines around older Ottoman structures. War against the Greeks helped to foster a sense of unity and pride, and Turkey aligned with rather than against the West. Yet Atatürk's efforts to forge a common national identity also had serious consequences for subject minorities like the Kurds, and, hence, for the development of domestic sovereignty. The Hijaz and Yemen also achieved independence in this period, with the first absorbed into Saudi Arabia under the leadership of Ibn Saud, a successful if traditional state-builder who eschewed the use of modern institutions, but was also dependent on Britain and later the United States for his regime's stability.

Even those states not formerly part of the Ottoman Empire and therefore subject neither to territorial adjustment nor direct political control – Iran, for example – were profoundly affected by the effects of European imperialism. Britain's attempt to impose a bilateral treaty on Iran (the Anglo-Persian Agreement of 1919) was rejected, but Britain retained considerable influence in Iran's affairs: in its relationship with the first Pahlavi monarch, Reza Shah, its monopoly share in the exploitation of Iran's oil resources; and its role in the forced abdication of the Shah in 1941 and the installation, then re-installation in 1953 of his son, Mohammed Reza Shah, against a tide of nationalist sentiment, an event with ultimately profound consequences for the development of Iranian sovereignty.[41]

In sum, the shortness of the inter-war colonial moment belied its lasting consequences. Unlike other post-colonial regions, neither the parameters of states nor their internal arrangements went uncontested for long. Above all, the new states and their leaders lacked legitimacy; their constitutional experiments were incomplete and associated with external agency. This, basically, was an era of limited and conditional sovereignty. Though some benefited from the new arrangements, particularly where local elites had aligned themselves with colonial interests, for many these were an unwelcome and unsettling intrusion into previously established modes of existence. Elizabeth Monroe writes of the frustration of a younger generation of Arabs who wanted the freedom to experiment with their own styles of democratic governance, but "were obliged to try it in leading strings held by foreign mentors."[42] As the short period of mandates drew to a close, often through reluctant, at times bloody compromise, the wider processes of state- and nation-building were quite unfinished. The kind of path dependencies created by Ottoman institutions had been disrupted, but no durable substitutes had been found.

The Post-1945 Setting

The third phase to consider is that of the post-independence period, stretching from the Second World War to the present. It was marked, initially, by the end of European empires and the gradual and at times violent consequences of the withdrawal of Britain and France from most of the former Ottoman territories, though pockets of Western influence remained. It ends at a time of continuing change and uncertainty in the region, one in which sovereignty, internal and external, remains above all contested and fragile. While the contemporary state system itself, in part thanks to continuing external influence and oil and security rents, has remained relatively stable in a territorial sense, there are longstanding areas of "problematic sovereignty" in Krasner's terms, notably as regards to the situation of Israel and the Palestinians,[43] where the full sovereignty of two peoples seems irreconcilable. And apart from the reconstitution of the Iraqi state, there is a continuation of the wider sovereignty crisis already alluded to: the persistence of domestic sovereignty defined as authority and control, but the absence of popular legitimacy. Put differently, the region may be characterized today as having sovereign states and constitutions like any other, but not popular sovereignty and its vital accompaniment, constitutionalism. It is a striking paradox that, while the region's European mentors in the European Union have moved "beyond sovereignty" in their own domestic and external arrangements, much of the Middle East is yet to arrive at a sovereignty settlement for its individual states, let alone proceed to any higher stage of regional integration.[44]

There is not space to relate in detail the contested endings of European imperialism or the process surrounding the emergence of independent states, a process that in the case of the smaller Gulf states extended, though less controversially, until the late 1960s. Of interest here is the effect on sovereignty of the European experience and exit and the subsequent roles assumed by other actors in sovereignty outcomes, most notably the United States, though to some extent the Soviet Union also, in an era of Cold War and growing oil rents which continued to link inextricably the political future of the region to great power interests. A few general observations and examples must suffice.

The formal ending or "rupture" of European imperialism came rather quickly, accelerated by local resistance and then by the effects of the Second World War. In the Middle East, as elsewhere, the newly independent countries were seen as stages in the apprenticeship of statehood, democracy and membership of international society.[45] Such ideas had been promoted in the age of the mandate with the intention that partial sovereigns would become full sovereigns in the image of the Western powers. This was always a dangerous assumption: the construction of states and their insertion into the international system was risky, bringing with it the possibility of resistance.[46]

Resistance, manifest already under the mandate, remained a common feature of the post-independence period. There was some early continuity: many states of the region started their independent life with some form of constitutional government embodying at least the principle of popular sovereignty, the direct legacy of the colonial power. In most cases, though the timescales and circumstances were different, this proved ephemeral and its shallow institutional roots were quickly disrupted. Above all, the formalities of independence did not free the field for autonomous state development. In many respects, as Krasner puts it, this new sovereignty was no more than "organized hypocrisy."[47] On the one hand, interference and outright Western intervention was still evident in many parts of the region and continued to condition political and economic outcomes in the independent states, and the different examples of the oil nationalization crisis in Iran, the Suez War and Baghdad Pact are exemplary. Economic dependency, and the persistence of "informal" empire, remained a familiar feature of this, as well as other Third World regions. Even where the traces of colonial power and influence mostly disappeared, they were often replaced in some form by that of a superpower proxy that, in different ways, conditioned the sovereignty experience. On the other hand, the partial, incomplete and unsatisfactory attempts at guided constitutionalism and state-building – in large part the result of European influence – left a longer legacy that gave way to "anti-constitutionalism" and eventually to stubborn authoritarianism.[48] To be sure, the forms of authoritarian rule, often linked to military regimes, presented themselves in many forms as different cases from North Africa, the Gulf and Fertile Crescent demonstrate. However, authoritarianism came to provide a ready formula for ending colonial influence, securing the prize of Westphalian sovereignty and achieving economic development and security against enemies at home and abroad. It combined a state-building, regional security, Cold War and an oil rent rationale, but it was also an outcome of a weak and contested state–society contract established under the brief period of colonial influence.

The above developments were reflected in different ways as modern states developed. Turkey and Sudan saw an alternation between some form of constitutional and military rule, with the former becoming more firmly embedded in the Turkish case – in many respects the exception to our limited sovereignty story. Elsewhere, many monarchies adopted constitutional texts, but in none were durable, constitutional regimes established. In core Arab states a succession of military coups led instead to the installation of populist–nationalist regimes which cut short the earlier "liberal" Western-guided experiments: "The new social contracts that were forged saw the marginalisation or postponement of liberal politics."[49] Hence, in Egypt the monarch and constitution were overthrown in 1952; a succession of coups followed in Iraq and Syria; and revolution in Yemen in 1962 also ended a period of monarchical rule. In the surviving monarchies, traditional forms of rule continued. Jordan, despite its fragile beginnings, enjoyed a period of limited constitutional government from 1952 to 1957, though a combination of internal and external crises led to the strengthening of the monarchy and security apparatus and a corresponding reduction of freedoms thereafter.

In these processes the idea of the imported state and above all its rejection prevailed. Even as the Middle East drew away from its colonial past and developed as a more independent system, the concept of import was never far away. While for some states, notably Turkey, this import was less problematic – indeed, the development of modern Turkey became closely linked to a modernizing and Westernizing story – for others it was profoundly so. With the birth of Israel in 1948 as a constant reminder and point of reference, the progress of external and internal sovereignty became woven into a post-colonial and Cold War story in which concepts like "dependent development," "rentierism" and non-alignment acquired particular significance.

Egypt may be singled out as an example to demonstrate how the construction of a modern state was increasingly identified with anti-imperialism in its economic, political and security dimensions. This, in many ways, also implied a rejection of Western sovereignty formulations whether at home or abroad. Despite Egypt's need for Western aid and development assistance, the Nasserite project ultimately saw the rejection of such opportunities, partly through the popular appeal of such a move, the conditionalities attached to it and the availability of alternative (Soviet–Eastern bloc) assistance. Even in its regional policy, the nation-building project self-evidently rejected, and went "beyond Westphalia," appealing to and drawing in a wider Arab public.[50] In this respect it may be likened to the later pan-Islamic appeal of Iran's Islamic revolution and subsequent fundamentalism which also implied rejection of the Westphalian state model and appeal to a broader Islamic ^{c}*umma*.[51]

Elsewhere in the region, at the risk of over-generalization, it is difficult to escape the conclusion that as regards the Ottoman Empire's Afro-Asian successors, while states are indeed formally "sovereign" and regimes vigorously defend this sovereignty against external encroachment, the Westphalia hypocrisy continues,[52] and a study of domestic arrangements quickly reveals a popular sovereignty or democracy "deficit." This has given rise to the claim of Middle Eastern or Arab exceptionalism.

Until the 1980s the Middle East might not have been regarded as exceptional in its "sovereignty as legitimacy" deficit. If democracy was lacking this was a feature of many developing countries. Roger Owen has noted how the difficulties experienced in the post-independence decades are quite similar to other areas where "ambivalent commitments to pluralism and parliamentarianism also tended to give way to military or one party rule."[53] And, like much of the rest of the world, the Middle East was caught up in democratization's "Third Wave." However, the achievements of this period – whether in the Gulf, Yemen or Morocco, with evidence of growing parliamentary activity and multi-party elections, or in Lebanon with the revival of consociational democracy – were still modest in comparison with other areas.[54] And at the turn of the century the term "deliberalization" had crept into references to the political development of a state like Egypt. Beyond the Arab states, only Turkey has further consolidated its democracy and institutions, though there limits to constitutionalism are also evident as the protracted negotiations for European Union membership show. And in Iran, the post-revolutionary pluralism, expressed in President Khatemi's "Dialogue of Civilisations," revealed a tantalizing yet brief vista of the possibilities of Islam's co-existence with Western democracy.

It has been argued here that the imperfect application and observance of the principle of Westphalian sovereignty has an interdependent relationship with domestic sovereignty in that it has encouraged, broadly speaking, persistent "non-constitutional" forms of authority and control.[55] While Middle Eastern constitutions, in themselves, embed and reinforce the formal principles of sovereignty, they have not provided the basis of legitimate political authority. Not only has the short experience with European imperialism failed to consolidate European notions of sovereignty and statehood, it has led to their very rejection: even as regimes embraced such notions, the very boundaries and definitions of states were still being contested, whether with regard to the formation of a United Arab Republic, Iraq's longstanding pretensions to Kuwait or the Palestine–Israel conflict. States have been further buffeted from "above" by pan-movements and ideologies and from "below" by sub-state groups rejecting these sovereignty scripts and demanding their remaking.

Even today as the age of empire recedes further into the distance, the notion that the Middle East region has evolved autonomously or has achieved a degree of freedom from external influences is challenged by the powerful post-Cold War notion of a world of regions embedded in the "American imperium," where sovereignty choices, external and internal, remain constrained.[56] In this way, the legacy and reinterpretation of empire continues to leave its mark on sovereignty.

This sovereignty problematic extends from states to a wider arena: that of regional cooperation and institutions. At first sight puzzling perhaps, and the subject for further consideration, is the fact that the opportunity to revise or consolidate a new regional sovereignty script – through the promotion and development of regional institutions – has been hitherto little tried. The reasons for this failure, as different scholars of regionalism have pointed out, are partly internal to the region,[57] but also reflect external interference.

Conclusion: Sovereignty and its Pathways "Beyond Empire" in the Middle East

The experience of empire and pathways to sovereignty in the modern Middle East are unquestionably varied – contrast a century of history in Turkey, Tunisia, Egypt and Iraq. However, there are certain common characteristics. Notably the adoption of Westphalian-type states and sovereignty structures – as the by-product of European imperialism – and the territorial and political arrangements they embodied, have been a common variable in domestic sovereignty and the development of political institutions. Since the path to sovereignty was set and mostly managed by Western powers, whether by default or design, it has been the subject of contestation, revolt and remaking. Most notably, it has contributed to a continuing crisis of legitimacy, as described by Michael Hudson and others in which states remain subjected to intense pressures from above and below.[58]

The end-point then, like the starting point of this chapter, is that sovereignty and its accoutrements have become identified as part of "the legacy of the Western encounter with the Middle East."[59] As such they have been deeply problematic. Westernization attempted to fill the "empty" post-Ottoman space, following the deconstruction of the Ottoman order,[60] but never completely – its hold on states and institutions remains fragile. The collective memory still retains and reconstructs elements of the Ottoman and pre-Ottoman experience – alternative pathways not taken. Even as the modern system developed and as imperial influence waned, the tension between old and new ideas remained, sustained in an era where conflict, Cold War and the effects of oil and security rents intervened.

In this sense the case of the modern Middle East shows how the term "after empire," implying that empire is a finite process and that "sovereignty" once gained is total, is deeply problematic. Indeed, the pathways to sovereignty, its adoption and development in the modern region show that sovereignty is incomplete and remains subject to multiple interpretations and challenges as revealed in the distinctive cases of contemporary Israel and Iraq.

Modern states and constitutions embed and endorse the sovereignty principle, in the Middle East and elsewhere. The sovereignty script was largely provided by Western powers, and parts of that script were enthusiastically adopted by most states – or at least by incumbent regimes. Yet the "unbundling" of sovereignty in the modern state shows how it has been porous and violated. It also explains how modern constitutions have failed as instruments for the establishment of legitimate authority.

The imposition and violation of the Westphalian principle has compromised and continues to compromise domestic sovereignty, with the consequence that the very concepts underpinning the Westphalian state have been repeatedly rejected and undermined. As Western powers sought to embed the Westphalian ideal, the context, timing and manner of its introduction meant that the model was downgraded, its application skewed and its legitimacy contested. The effect of this has been that while public authorities in many states may enjoy effective control, they lack popular legitimacy. This has been repeatedly revealed in the contemporary waves of Islamic revival and protest.

This story of incomplete sovereignty, as suggested above, has become inescapably linked to the modern democracy story. It is difficult to argue with the broad observations of Larry Diamond and others that "there are no Arab democracies."[61] In explaining the democracy gap, scholars point to cultural and religious factors, economic structures, authoritarian statecraft or the "coils of geopolitics."[62] These coils of geopolitics highlight the disproportionate agency attached to external powers, which reinforce economic and security structures and contribute to authoritarian statecraft. The result is a continuing popular antipathy to external or "imperial influence" and its association with incumbents and the reification of other alternative pathways to sovereignty. Attempts to reject Western concepts of sovereignty based on "nation-states" by appealing to the broader Arab or Islamic nation have complicated and arrested the state-building process by offering competing narratives.

This is not to say that sovereignty's failures are to be attributed merely to Western agency. However, the nature and timing of European imperialism against the backdrop of the late Ottoman period – its rejection of multi-communalism and pan-ideologies in favor of the promotion of dominant national groups and its finite resources in a period of waning imperial power – provided fragile foundations for the task of state-building.

Nowhere is this more evident than in the contemporary Iraqi case. There the prize of sovereignty, defined and awarded by the Western powers, was indeed the mainstay of successive post-independence regimes. But it was never complete, and the domestic abuse of power and reckless foreign policy ultimately saw the violating of Iraq's external sovereignty and the rewriting of its internal sovereignty script. And, today, as in the past, such rewriting is not interests free. Charles Tripp, contrasting US policy in Iraq to that of Britain in the 1920s, has shown how in claiming to bring the benefits of democratic governance to the country, the United States has been reluctant to give over control of the process.[63] And Rashid Khalidi, writing in 2004, commented darkly: "American troops increasingly risk being received as are most occupation armies, and as were the British in Iraq after World War I: with hostility and ultimately with widespread armed resistance."[64] Alternative perceptions of sovereignty for Iraq today, or Palestine, or Iran, even the "modernizing" monarchies of the Gulf, remain indelibly linked to the imperial legacy and a longstanding and ongoing tension between its rejection and its renewal.

Notes

1. For a description of the formal–informal divide see Cain and Hopkins, *British Imperialism.*

2. For a definition see Black and Brown, *Modernization in the Middle East*, pp. 1–9.
3. E.g., Doyle, *Empires*; Tilly, "How empires End"; Motyl, "Thinking about empire."
4. Gallagher and Robinson, "The imperialism of free trade," p. 1.
5. Robinson, "Non-European foundations of European imperialism," pp. 118–19.
6. Owen, "Egypt and Europe," pp. 195–209.
7. Davidson, "The advent of the principle of representation," p. 193.
8. Hanioğlu, *A Brief History of the Late Ottoman Empire*, p. 105; Keyder, "The Ottoman Empire," p. 32.
9. Laski, *Studies in the Problem of Sovereignty*; James, "The practice of statehood in contemporary international society"; Hinsley, *Sovereignty*.
10. Krasner, *Sovereignty*; Krasner, *Problematic Sovereignty*.
11. Jackson, *Quasi States*.
12. Krasner, *Sovereignty*, pp. 3–4.
13. Lake, *Hierarchy in International Relations*.
14. Krasner, *Sovereignty*, p. 68.
15. Owen, *State, Power and Politics*, p. 3.
16. Zubaida, *Islam the People and the State*, pp. 145–6.
17. Hinsley, *Sovereignty*.
18. Harik, "The origins of the Arab state system," pp. 1–28.
19. Visser and Stansfield, *An Iraq of its Regions*, pp. 1–9.
20. Yapp, *The Near East Since the First World War*, p. 69.
21. See Migdal, *Strong Societies and Weak States*.
22. Hinsley explains this with reference to the contrast between Hobbes' Leviathan and Rousseau's *contrat social*. Hinsley, *Sovereignty*, p. 153.
23. Khalidi, *Resurrecting Empire*.
24. Peters, *Institutional Theory in Political Science*, pp. 71–4.
25. Walzer, *On Toleration*, pp. 15–16.
26. Faroqhi, *The Ottoman Empire*, pp. 1–38.
27. This section draws on Fawcett, "Neither traditional nor modern," pp. 123–4.
28. Kedourie, *Arabic Political Memoirs*.
29. Kedourie, *Politics in the Middle East*, pp. 12, 14.
30. Davidson, "The advent of the principle of representation," pp. 193–208.
31. Hanioğlu, *A Brief History of the Late Ottoman Empire*, p. 104.
32. Hourani and Wilson (eds), *The Modern Middle East*, p. 4.
33. Bull, "The emergence of a universal international society"; Naff and Owen, *Studies in 18th Century Islamic History*.
34. Monroe, *Britain's Moment in the Middle East 1914–1956*, p. 71.
35. Fromkin, *A Peace to End all Peace*, p. 17.
36. Yapp, *Near East since the First World War*, p. 36; Owen, *State, Power and Politics*, pp. 19–23.
37. Krasner, *Sovereignty*, pp. 17–18.

38. Brown, *Constitutions in a Nonconstitutional World*, pp. 45–50.
39. Vatikiotis, *The History of Modern Egypt*, pp. 273–9.
40. Walzer, *On Toleration*, pp. 23–7.
41. Fawcett, *Iran and the Cold War*, pp. 141–4.
42. Monroe, *Britain's Moment in the Middle East 1914–1956*, p. 119.
43. Krasner, *Problematic Sovereignty*, p. 3.
44. See further, Fawcett, "Alliances, cooperation and regionalism in the Middle East," pp. 188–207.
45. Badie, *The Imported State*, p. 1.
46. Badie, *The Imported State*, p. 100.
47. Krasner, *Sovereignty*.
48. Schlumberger, *Debating Arab Authoritarianism*, pp. 1–6.
49. Ibrahim, "Liberalism and democratization," p. 36.
50. El-Fadl, "Divergent pasts, diverging choices: foreign policy and national building in Turkey and Egypt during the 1950s."
51. Abrahamian, *Khomeinism*, pp. 13–15.
52. Jackson, *Quasi States*; Khalidi, *Resurrecting Empire*.
53. Owen, *State, Power and Politics*, p. 26.
54. Ibrahim, "Liberalism and democratization."
55. Brown, *Constitutions in a Nonconstitutional World*; Fawcett, "Neither traditional nor modern," pp. 123–4.
56. Katzenstein, *A World of Regions*.
57. Barnett and Solingen, "Designed to fail or failure of design?"; Harders and Legrenzi (eds), *Beyond Regionalism?*.
58. Hudson, *Arab Politics*.
59. Khalidi, *Resurrecting Empire*, pp. 1–36.
60. Badie, *The Imported State*, p. 100.
61. Diamond, "Why are there no Arab democracies?," p. 93.
62. Diamond, 'Why are there no Arab democracies?," p. 101.
63. Tripp, *Iraq*, p. 283.
64. Khalidi, *Resurrecting Empire*, p. 171.

9

Sovereignty after Empire: The Colonial Roots of Central Asian Authoritarianism

David Lewis

Central Asian states achieved independence during a period when there was widespread support for liberal-democratic norms throughout the international system, but all five states in the region nevertheless developed primarily authoritarian forms of government. In two cases – Uzbekistan and Turkmenistan – extreme authoritarian regimes emerged, which have faced international censure for their abuses of civil liberties and human rights. Some initial political pluralism in Kyrgyzstan in the 1990s contracted significantly in the first decade of the twenty-first century. Kazakhstan mixed central authoritarian control and neo-patrimonial dynamics with economic progress and relatively liberal social norms. In Tajikistan power became increasingly centralized in the hands of the president after the end of the civil war in the late 1990s.

Popular explanations for the dominance of authoritarian political systems in Central Asia after independence have tended to rely on the actions or beliefs of particular political leaders, the various cultural attributes ascribed to particular peoples or ethnic groups, the contingency of particular historical events or the policies of external powers and international organizations active in the region. These explanations all echo wider theoretical positions in the literature on democratization, but the scholarly debate on democratization and authoritarianism in Central Asia has perhaps underplayed some factors that have been seen as critical in other regions which have faced similarly persistent authoritarian regimes. In the African context, for example, a complex debate continues about the legacy of colonialism and the dominance of non-democratic regimes in the continent.[1] This chapter will discuss whether Central Asian authoritarianism can be viewed in some way as a legacy of empire, while accepting that many other factors have contributed to the emergence of the present political systems that dominate the region.

The resilience of authoritarianism in Central Asia provokes immediate comparisons with the post-colonial history of the Middle East, where consolidated democracies have also not developed. Although authoritarianism in the Middle East in the 1960s and 1970s was frequently based on one-party or military regimes, in the twenty-first century both Central Asia and the Middle East have experienced regimes that in many cases can be described as "neo-patrimonial authoritarian." While maintaining a rational–legal bureaucratic system and all the external paraphernalia of a modern state, officials with formal positions in the state often exercise their powers in a way that reflects the patrimonial dynamics of political domination and economic advantage. Opposition is dealt with both by excluding groups or individuals from the patron–client network and also through repressive means, using politically controlled courts and security services.

In both regions, these regimes, with occasional exceptions, have proved to be exceptionally durable, despite claims by their critics that they face formidable structural difficulties and are incapable of dealing with complex economic and political challenges. This durability is only one aspect of such regimes that is not well understood. Authoritarian regimes are often studied as if they were "regimes of omission": they exist only because democratic political systems have failed to consolidate, and are seen as transitional phenomena between the colonial state and the eventual emergence of liberal democracy. As a result, the internal dynamics of authoritarianism are far less well understood than the internal workings of democratic systems, particularly in post-colonial Africa and Asia. This is beginning to change, with a new interest being demonstrated among scholars in the everyday politics of authoritarianism and more theoretical approaches to non-democratic regimes.

However, the debate about the sources of authoritarianism remains a highly contested field, which has significant implications for the internal politics of such states and for external engagement with such regimes. Central Asian governments often point to cultural factors as making such forms of rule inevitable and, indeed, more suitable and appropriate for their particular populations; their critics, on the other hand, often point to individual actions and political choices, or instrumental uses of repression to protect elite self-enrichment as the primary explanations for the durability of such regimes. In this chapter, it is assumed that all these factors play some role, but that historical–structural factors are also of significance in the emergence of political systems. The historical legacy of empire, particularly that form of empire seen in the Soviet period in Central Asia, has contributed to the emergence of authoritarian political systems in two important ways. First, the nature of sovereignty that emerged in the post-Soviet period in Central Asia owes much to the attitudes of Soviet-era national elites towards the borders of the Soviet republics in Central Asia, which emerged partly as a result of deep involvement in the bureaucratic politics of resources in the Soviet period. This, in turn, contributed to the emergence of a type of authoritarian regime that reflected this particular understanding of sovereignty. Second, the nature of authoritarianism in Central Asia – its neo-patrimonialism in particular – stems in part from the informal structures of social organizations and resource distribution that developed in Soviet Central Asia in the 1970s and 1980s. To a certain extent these mirrored political and social developments in other parts of the Soviet Union, but in Central Asia they were framed within a particular discourse about ethnicity and a state system which, despite its anti-imperial rhetoric, was often characterized by colonial principles and discourses. In this sense, authoritarianism in Central Asia becomes more comprehensible when viewed through a post-colonial lens.

Legacies of Empire

The turn to colonialism and post-colonialism as a framework for understanding post-Soviet Central Asia is still disputed, not least by many Central Asian intellectuals themselves. The debates over the colonial nature of the USSR are well known, and are not covered in detail here.[2] In this chapter, I argue that reassessing Soviet policies in Central Asia through a colonial framework and using some of the concepts of post-coloniality in the Central Asian context offers theoretical insights that other approaches do not offer.

Like Adams,[3] I find useful the Beissinger approach to empire that views it not as an ideal type, but as "a Wittgensteinian 'family resemblance' whose meanings and referents have altered significantly over time."[4] This allows us to move away from technical comparisons of defining attributes of empire toward a more rewarding discussion of comparative methods of governance, modes of dominance and colonial discourses. For example, instructive parallels exist between the Soviet regime and what Osterhammel terms the "late colonial interventionist state"[5] in the post-1945 French and British colonies, particularly with the French *mission civilisatrice*. The formal rhetoric of progress and equality, a focus on social change, on the position of women, on education and on the development of "native elites," were all present in both contexts, although with wide differences in implementation and consequences. Importantly, all these political environments shared the kind of commitment to modernization that Hirsch sees as fundamental to a Soviet understanding of nation-building,[6] and shared a similar discourse on backwardness that legitimated radical policies of social change and assimilation.[7] The shifts in policy between indirect and direct rule, reminiscent of Western European empires on their peripheries, is a significant dynamic in the Soviet period also.[8] Two great waves of "nativization of cadres" occurred, first in the 1920s and 1930s, and later in the 1960s and 1970s,[9] producing particular types of national elites in Central Asia that had a significant impact on post-Soviet developments.

By using a framework of empire and colonialism, two aspects of the post-Soviet legacy can be better understood. The first is the nation- and state-building process that was engendered by the USSR, and the contested idea of sovereignty that emerged. The second is the formation of national elites, able and willing to manage a transition to independence and to preserve post-Soviet sovereignty, albeit in a particular form that encouraged the emergence of authoritarian political systems.

Post-colonial Sovereignty

The first important post-colonial legacy is in the form and content of post-Soviet sovereignty, which has its most important roots in the Soviet period. There have been repeated tensions over border regimes and demarcation among Central Asian states, but for the most part territorial integrity has not been seriously challenged. The acceptance of these borders as the new frontiers of post-1991 independence was partly a reflection of the norms and rules of the external environment, but was also a consequence of important historical and administrative developments. Although these borders had no real significance for ordinary people in the Soviet period, they did have importance in the minds and plans of Soviet bureaucrats and party apparatchiks. Thus, officials from the Uzbek Communist Party were used to operating primarily within the borders of the Uzbek SSR, and their powers of patronage, for the most part, were constrained by these bureaucratic borders that had little physical shape on the ground. The Soviet-era elites who occupied positions of influence in republican party and state structures were mostly comfortable with these frontiers; their shapes were familiar, comforting even, and had taken on a cartographical reality familiar to three generations of Soviet schoolchildren.

Recent scholarship has challenged or nuanced the notion that Central Asian borders were imposed by Moscow with no reference to local elites or sensibilities.[10] In many cases, border delimitation was contested by local elites, demonstrating that it had both instrumental and emotional aspects for Central Asia's new, emerging Soviet-era leaders. The border delimitation that was finalized in 1936 was the result of a profoundly political process, in which national elites were deeply involved. It could have resulted in several alternative outcomes ranging from some form of federated Central Asian republic to a division into more or fewer than five republics. However, the republics that did emerge quickly became of significant bureaucratic importance, as each republic gained its own Communist Party structures, alongside extensive state and representative structures, such as a republican Supreme Soviet and the symbolism of national symbols and celebrations. Although none of these structures had genuine political autonomy, they offered huge opportunities for patronage for those in charge of party structures at every level, and, importantly, covered the full range of social groups, including political appointees, economic officials and cultural figures in institutions such as republican writers' and artists' unions. This ensured the emergence of elites within the Soviet system at a republican level with a strong bureaucratic consciousness of sovereignty and autonomy in everyday affairs (personnel appointments, resource distribution, representation and so on), defined for the most part by a named ethnic identity (Uzbek, Kyrgyz, Tajik and so on), and linked to institutionalized modes of cultural production at the same level as bureaucratic sovereignty.

This was a shift in understandings of sovereignty from that expressed by an earlier generation of Central Asian leaders. In the early 1920s some Uzbek leaders had campaigned for a Central Asian delimitation that suited ideas of a "greater Uzbekistan."[11] These ideas of federal republics that fitted much more closely with the boundaries of habitation of the titular nationality were largely ended by the final delimitation of 1936 (and the physical destruction of many nationalist leaders in the purges of the 1930s). Thereafter, where there is a sense of sovereignty, it becomes associated primarily with the symbolism and bureaucratic machinery of republican structures. While "bourgeois nationalism" was strongly suppressed in this period, there was also a continued opposition on the part of Central Asian elites to any restriction of the limited forms of autonomy provided by the Soviet federal system. Central Asian leaders opposed successive plans for some kind of Central Asian regionalism during the Soviet period, from the 1920s ideas of a Soviet Central Asian Federation through to plans in the 1960s for a Central Asian Economic Region.[12] While resisting plans that would undermine informal and formal autonomies, republican elites consistently maximized their power and patronage within existing borders and within existing state and party institutions at the republican level. As a result of this process of normalization of the Central Asian border delimitation, and the essential continuities in elites in the post-Soviet period, these Soviet-era sovereignties and borders retained broad legitimacy among key decision-making power elites in each republic after independence.

Ilkhamov notes the two types of elite that operated in the Central Asian Soviet republics: those who held official office in either party or state structures; and those who had influence in society, in informal networks of power, based partly on kinship and regional affiliation, but fuelled primarily by patronage, nepotism and informal distribution of resources. For most of Soviet history, these two elites largely coincided, with leading party and state figures also developing power within informal networks in society. Ilkhamov also points to Beissinger's notion of a "mediating elite,"[13] which in other colonial contexts might be termed a "collaborating elite," in which a national elite acts as a conduit between the demands of the metropolitan center and the realities of power and control on the periphery. Such elites are engaged in a constant process of fluid hybridity, at times resisting the center for the sake of local power dynamics, at other moments using the center to maintain control of resources on the periphery and to act against potential rivals. This role of mediating elite was vital in Central Asia, but it worked only when official office-holders and leaders of informal power networks were one and the same people, who could respond both to the demands of Moscow and also to tensions and threats from within society itself. When the demands from the center became too great, this process was put under considerable stress; official and informal elites became distinct categories, and this role of mediation between center and periphery broke down.

The result of this form of colonial elite formation is a very particular understanding of sovereignty, which emerges primarily from the workings of party and state bureaucracy within republican boundaries over many years. As a result, post-Soviet Central Asian concepts of sovereignty do not emerge from an intellectual project, or as a result of a popular, nationalist struggle rooted in an ethnic version of history. Such projects were in evidence in the late 1980s and early 1990s, when many Central Asian intellectuals were motivated by alternative visions of sovereignty informed by language issues, ethnic nationalism and irredentism. Tajik nationalists, for example, suggested that a sovereign Tajikistan could include the old centers of Persian-language culture, Samarkand and Bukhara, while some Uzbek nationalists saw the potential for a potentially greater Uzbekistan to emerge, including within its borders majority-Uzbek areas in neighboring states, such as Osh (Kyrgyzstan) and Khodjand (Tajikistan). Groups that tended to combine ethnic nationalism with broadly democratic ideals, such as Rastokhez in Tajikistan, or the Azat Party in Kazakhstan, had a completely different intellectual tradition and concept of sovereignty and the state from that of Soviet-era leaders. Kazakh intellectuals in this strand of political thought talked openly about both "real democratization" and "the complete decolonization of Kazakhstan."[14] However, their Western-inspired nationalism failed to mobilize mass support to compete with informal networks of power and their leaders. Instead, such nationalist visions – almost all of which were based on rather mythical views of ethnicity and history – were swiftly defeated by Soviet-era elites in the early 1990s in Uzbekistan, Kazakhstan and Turkmenistan, and eventually in Tajikistan later in the decade.

While post-Soviet leaders in Central Asia used nationalist symbolism and pursued various policies on language, education and cultural issues that could be termed "nation-building," none of this first generation of leaders openly espoused any overtly nationalist political program (with the partial exception of Turkmenistan). However, the sovereignty of these new republics was an important part of the political narrative, and was repeatedly proclaimed as both a great achievement and as being under threat from both inside and outside the state. Importantly, however, although this narrative was closely linked in language and symbolism with the titular nationality in each state, this proclaimed sovereignty continued to be concerned primarily with state-level institutions and the mechanisms for the distribution of resources rather than mythical notions of a particular ethnos. As a result, this type of sovereignty did not derive from some implicit or explicit form of social contract or any kind of campaign of popular mobilization. Post-Soviet sovereignty had no need for a democratic mandate; it did not rely on the populist impulses of ethnic nationalism and was wary of appealing too strongly to mass nationalist sentiment. Instead, it has been reliant on an authoritarian style of government, partially to counter the alternative concepts of sovereignty, linked to ethnicity or pan-Islamic ideals, advanced by its political opponents.

Arguably, the failure of "democratic nationalist" leaders to achieve political power in Central Asia may have averted the kind of internal ethnic conflicts seen elsewhere in the former Soviet Union (Georgia, Azerbaijan), where "democratic nationalists" came to power. As a result, the identification of democratic movements with destructive nationalism and ethnic antagonism in the 1988–91 period provided Central Asian leaders with internal legitimation for repression of their political opponents and the establishment of authoritarian regimes. Nationalism was used by these new regimes, but as a carefully controlled and manipulated element in state-building policy, which was tempered by other imperatives.

Informal Structures, Networks and Post-colonial Power

The first legacy of empire – Soviet-era forms and bureaucratic understandings of sovereignty – made the emergence of authoritarian regimes in the post-Soviet period much more likely, assuming that the same kind of elites remained in control. The durability of those Soviet-era elites was partially the result of their role as informal leaders and patrons in social organizations and networks that combined Soviet informal groupings based on resource distribution with ethnic, kinship, regional and other affiliations in sub-state networks that have variously been termed "clans" or "power networks" or "patronage networks."

These patterns of social organization are the second major legacy of empire that has shaped the post-Soviet Central Asian state. This organizational form is a particular type of reinvented informal network that has been shaped by the Soviet experience, but also harks back to pre-colonial forms of social organization, or at least to pre-colonial cultural hierarchies and kinship patterns. These groups gained significant power by taking control of instruments of resource allocation, through patronage and through control of republican budgets. However, this aspect of localism, which was present throughout the Soviet Union, was augmented in the case of Central Asia by the role of such networks in resisting central Soviet encroachment on the relative autonomy that national elites had earned in specific areas, such as the economy. This autonomy was formed within specific national sovereign spaces (the Central Asian republics) and shared predominantly by the same ethnic or kinship group. Not surprisingly, in the context of the Soviet Union, these networks include some dynamics that echo mechanisms of resistance in other colonial structures. Informal networks of power and influence became even more influential after independence. They helped to manage the complex transition process, and have at times been an important stabilizing factor in the region. But there is also little doubt that these structures subsequently proved to be a major obstacle to economic modernization and political reform, and have contributed strongly to the emergence of Central Asian authoritarianism.

Soviet writing on Central Asia (sometimes mirrored in Cold War-era scholarship in the West) suggested that Soviet power had effectively destroyed so-called "feudal" social structures, and replaced them with a socialist identity that rose above both clan and nation. More recently, scholars have suggested that during the Soviet period, pre-Soviet feudal structures were transmuted into ethnic or regional identities.[15] In reality the situation seems to have been much more complex, with a wide range of social groups and elites emerging from the Soviet period.[16] However, in terms of political power and control over resources, the most important transformation appears to have been in these informal networks of power. The system of Soviet rule, while promoting a particularly controlled form of nation-building as a way of undermining feudal social structures, actually ensured a role for a range of informal networks of power, initially based on pre-revolutionary kinship groups but also rapidly adapting and changing to meet the needs of local elites acting within a new, centralized authoritarian state, in which the dynamics of colonialism remained very strong.

Debates continue about how to define these informal structures. Gleason called them "informal authority structures,"[17] while more recent work by Collins and Schatz has revived the term "clan" to define groups that have a significant element of kinship involved, but also contain new dynamics of fictive kinship. This use of the term clan, however, is much contested, with other scholars arguing that its narrow definition (a grouping based on kinship that traces its genealogy back to a single ancestor) does not have significant resonance among non-nomadic groups, such as the Uzbeks and Tajiks. Collins uses the term in a much broader sense to encompass non-kinship relations, but this does sometimes appear to over-stretch the concept, as Tuncer-Kilavuz argues.[18]

Tuncer-Kilavuz concludes that "these groups which are erroneously labelled as 'clans' are political power networks which aim to control political and economic power within the republic, and gain assets and privileges resulting from this control."[19] He goes on to explore the instrumental reasons why people join networks, and suggests that these are more akin to patron–client networks at the elite level, mixed with some elements of kinship and regionalism at lower levels. While scholars who focus on clans tend to suggest that pre-existing structures were reinforced or adapted by Soviet rule, Tuncer-Kilavuz argues that "the Soviet system played a central role in the formation of this network structure. Its centralised administrative system and lack of accountability allowed leaders to distribute resources under their control as they wished."[20] He points to *obkom* first secretaries as key figures in distributing state resources, and also emphasizes the importance of *kolkhoz* leaders in rural areas as the basis for patron–client relations (something also discussed earlier by Olivier Roy, who wrote of the "Kolkhoz as a new tribe").[21]

Although such networks were strongly shaped by the Soviet experience, they also seem to have differed from the regional party networks built up around district, *oblast* and republican party chiefs in other parts of the USSR. In each of these areas, similar informal networks also produced nepotism, corruption and localism, but the outcome in Central Asia was much more resilient and far-reaching because there were underlying social structures and kinship networks that informed many of these groupings. At the very least, dynamics of control, patronage and exchange within these groupings owed much on an everyday level to the underlying realities of social organization (including kinship groups or geographically defined networks at the level of village or region, for example) and the relationships and hierarchies on which these social organizations relied. In addition, at the republican or all-union level, these groupings might use common ethnicity as an organizing method and as a definition of membership of a network or group. However, these informal networks among Central Asians in the later Soviet period appear not to have been simply a reinvention or retention of pre-revolutionary social forms, but a new remaking of such organizational networks molded by the Soviet experience and the economic reality of a centralized economy.

Here the importance of empire, the colonial nature of the political system and the gradual coincidence of pre-existing loyalties with networks that reflected Soviet-era institutions and boundaries becomes significant. Networks of power in Uzbekistan, for example, consisted primarily of ethnic Uzbeks, many of whom had some kinship or regional affiliation in common, but acted within the boundaries of Uzbek republic and party structures. Only limited areas of the economy were the preserve of republican elites: valuable sectors such as the mining of gold and other precious metals were run from the center, as was much of the defense industry and other specialized areas of manufacturing. Foreign trade was also highly centralized until the late 1980s. However, agriculture and internal trade sectors were largely decentralized to republican level, ensuring that in these areas national elites could exert considerable control over resource collection and distribution. There were therefore rational economic reasons for the distribution of work along ethnic lines in Central Asia, where areas such as agriculture and services provided economic incentives through informal payments and other income that was made possible by the creation of closed networks of power in those sectors.

The idea that sub-ethnic groupings have been preserved, reinvented or reinforced by centralized colonial rule has been discussed in other post-colonial settings. Colonial regimes replace any central political authority, but often seek to reinforce local kinship or tribal groupings as a conservative and inexpensive means of indirect rule. The colonized, meanwhile, use such groupings as a limited refuge from the interference of the colonial power, a way to preserve internal areas of autonomy, such as culture, social hierarchies or spiritual life, but often at the expense of internal pluralism. In the African context, Mahmood Mamdani seeks explanations for post-colonial authoritarianism in these structures of late colonialism, particularly what he calls the "decentralized despotism" of indirect rule. He explores the contradictory policies present in several colonial polities, between the desire to break the power of tribal autonomy, and then to re-impose tribal identities and laws when autonomous individuals then threatened the power of the colonial regime.[22]

In the USSR, although the history and structures were very different, some similar processes can be noted. There was always a similar tension between the use of direct rule to effect social transformation – which inevitably provoked various forms of resistance and instability – and more indirect rule, through unacknowledged informal structures that ensured political control but limited the social (and sometimes the economic) impact of the metropolis. Central Asia experienced two periods of relatively indirect rule: first, in the 1920s, which was followed by the collectivization campaigns of 1928 onwards and the purges of elites in the late 1930s; and, second, in the 1960s and 1970s, which was also followed by the less brutal, but equally dramatic purges of 1984–8. The first of these shifts in policy, when a large proportion of Central Asian elites was physically destroyed, was a reaction to the apparent emergence of "bourgeois nationalism" among Central Asians; the second was couched in the language of a massive anti-corruption drive, but also became an assault on the autonomy of national elites and their resistance to central control and oversight.

Resistance and Corruption: Late Soviet Central Asia

Just as Stalinist purges ultimately resulted in the stasis of the Brezhnev period, the shock and fear experienced by Central Asian elites in the purges of the 1980s explains much of the search for political stability through authoritarianism after 1991. Between 1983 and 1986 all of Central Asia's Communist Party first secretaries were replaced; between 1984 and 1988 more than 58,000 Central Asian officials lost their jobs in purges,[23] many of them in Uzbekistan, which was at the center of a defining financial scandal of Union-wide proportions.

The cotton scandal uncovered in the early 1980s, and prosecuted with vigor by both Andropov and Gorbachev, demonstrated the reality of networked corruption that had developed around Uzbek Party leader Sharof Rashidov during his two decades in power until his death in 1983. Massive over-reporting of cotton production in the Uzbek republic netted Rashidov and his allies millions of rubles in illegal profit in transfers from the Soviet central state. These funds further contributed to a system of patronage and clientalism that almost completely undermined the formal institutions of state and party. The arrest of Rashidov and the almost complete purge of the Uzbek party and state elite was a significant shift in Moscow's policy toward Central Asia, but both policies echoed varieties of colonial rule: the massive corruption and significant autonomy of the Rashidov period was followed by an attempt by Moscow to impose direct rule and promote centralized Soviet policies of reform and modernization. There were also many non-Uzbeks who were involved in the cotton scandal, reaching the very top of the Soviet political elite, but for the most part the focus of Moscow was on Central Asian corruption, with investigations into major Moscow-based figures halted on the orders of Gorbachev, concerned at the potential ramifications of the investigations he had initially launched. The discourse of anti-corruption in this period also took on a profoundly ethnic and racial nature, with Central Asians being the primary targets of blame for a range of corrupt practices which were endemic throughout the Soviet system.

As Critchlow and others have argued, Uzbek corruption was not simply a method of self-enrichment, but a more complex response to Moscow's attempts to control both the political and economic life of Central Asians.[24] Uzbek leaders had effectively bought considerable autonomy from the center through their corrupt cotton scheme, and the subsequent dynamics of the affair can be viewed in a framework of colonial tensions between direct and indirect rule. Each leader in the Uzbek SSR could achieve durability in office only by both holding official office (maintaining good relations with Moscow) and also controlling informal resource distribution and patron–client networks. If he was unable to maintain this dual, mediating role he would lose power. Inomzhon Usmankhodjaev, Rashidov's replacement, was initially viewed as a pro-Moscow figure by local elites, meaning that he fulfilled only the first aspect of leadership, but his apparent attempts to rectify this imbalance resulted in his being charged with corruption, and he was dismissed in 1988. Soviet leaders then faced a typical colonial quandary: loyal party leaders, such as Rafiq Nishanov, a Foreign Ministry official, who took over after Usmankhodjaev, were unable to penetrate the informal structures of Uzbek politics. To try to change the dynamic, Moscow effectively imposed direct rule. Nishanov was accompanied by thousands of predominantly Slavic officials appointed to fill the top rungs of the party in Uzbekistan. This *krasnyi desant* (red landing) emphasized the ethnic lines being drawn in the corruption investigations, as viewed from Tashkent, with ethnic Russians or Russian-speaking Slavs coming in from outside the republic to take over key positions.[25]

The anti-corruption campaigns spread across the Central Asian republics. In Kyrgyzstan, in 1985 Turdakun Usubaliev was sacked for alleged embezzlement and corruption, and replaced as republican Communist Party leader by the southern political leader Absamat Masaliev. In Tajikistan a similar purge led to the removal of Rahmon Nabiev in 1985, but did not lead to the scale of dismissals experienced in Uzbekistan. In Kazakhstan a purge of the Kazakh Communist Party in 1986 resulted in the dismissal of long-term leader Dinmukhamed Kunaev, and his replacement by Dmitry Kolbin, a Russian from outside the republic, brought in to "clean up" widespread corruption in the Kazakh SSR. Kunaev's dismissal in 1986 provoked mass protests, involving as many as 60,000 people, against Kolbin's appointment. It is probable that the protests were partially organized by Kunaev himself, but nevertheless they demonstrated the extent to which popular mobilization against Moscow was possible even in 1986 by leaders of informal networks of power.[26]

These attempts by first Andropov and then Gorbachev to reassert a modernizing form of direct rule – controlled primarily by European officials – were viewed as profoundly destabilizing by Central Asian elites. They were followed by a wave of violence in Central Asia in 1989–90, in which ethnic minorities, in particular, were targeted in the Fergana valley region. There is no evidence for any direct provocation of the violence for political ends by local elites, but a lesson could easily be drawn that leaders loyal only to Moscow were unable to achieve the kind of social and political stability offered by informal leaders and networks. It was quickly understood in Moscow that it was impossible to achieve change in Central Asia by importing Slavic administrators and picking loyal pro-Moscow leaders with limited leverage in local communities. In 1989, Moscow resorted to what was effectively a resumption of indirect rule, appointing new heads of republican party structures in Kazakhstan (Nursultan Nazarbaev) and in Uzbekistan (Islam Karimov). Nazarbaev was already head of the republican Council of Ministers, but he clearly had much deeper roots in Kazakh society than his Russian predecessor. Although Karimov seemed to suit Moscow, he also appears to have represented a compromise deal among various powerful networks in Tashkent, who had discussed informally who to promote to this position.[27] According to Collins, "the Politburo had realized that it could no longer oppose internal Uzbek power networks and expect the situation to remain stable."[28]

These appointments may have averted violent conflict in the transition period to independence in Central Asia. In Tajikistan, where there was no informal pact among such groupings, political conflict quickly turned into civil war. In the other states, these informal networks of power produced quite durable regimes, in which the informal and formal elites were closely entwined, although in all states there was a continuing reliance on repressive internal security mechanisms to counter any opposition.

Networks of Power and Authoritarianism

The informal networks of the Soviet period in Central Asia, shaped and informed by an authoritarian-colonial political system, easily morphed into post-independence political and economic networks that controlled much of the state apparatus that was developed or inherited from the Soviet state. While these states developed formal processes of state-building, including the full derivative apparatus, symbols and spaces of a modern state (embassies, ministries, parliaments, political parties, flags and anthems, demarcated borders, visas, passports and so on), a parallel process of state capture continued in the informal sphere. Power became located primarily in the interactions and dynamics of informal leaders and networks. Real politics, for the most part, consisted of acts of balancing among different informal groupings. Conflict was linked to a break down in such informal pacts among elites, even if its root causes were located elsewhere, in social dislocation, economic deprivation and institutionalized and perceived group difference.

Although informal networks were important in shaping many aspects of the post-Soviet state in Central Asia, were they necessarily bound to result in the emergence of authoritarian political systems? Collins argues that "clan pacts" explain the durability or otherwise of political regimes, but not necessarily the type of regime that emerges.[29] However, the dominance of informal political structures over the formal has tended to make the development of more authoritarian political systems highly likely, particularly in the absence of strong countervailing forces. Here again, Mamdani's account of how the "decentralized despotism" of colonialism translated into post-colonial authoritarianism has some resonance in Central Asia. These decentralized networks of power captured the authoritarian state left behind by the Soviet collapse, and proceeded to design and implement policy informed by the methods of the former regime.

In addition to the obvious legacies of attitudes, behaviors and ways of thinking and operating, post-Soviet Central Asian elites also captured a huge range of repressive technologies and institutions within their new states, particularly republican interior ministry structures, with their powerful police service (*militsia*), and internal prison system and the prosecutor's office (*prokuratura*), a body which had remained largely unreformed since Stalinist times. But there were also other processes that encouraged the emergence of authoritarianism that arose from the power of informal networks inherited from the late Soviet period, and their subsequent effective capture of the post-Soviet state. The first issue – and one often discussed by those sympathetic to authoritarian political leaders in Central Asian – is that modernizing leaders surrounded by informal networks of power (whether termed clans, networks, regional elites or some hybrid) often use authoritarian methods to push through economic and political reforms against these powerful vested interests. This has been common in post-colonial states in the Middle East and Africa, where leaders have sought a variety of mechanisms to promote modernization of fragmented societies or to develop and enforce a national identity. Typically, the military or single political parties have been used to fulfill both these roles, but at best these attempts to use such mechanisms have been only partially successful, failing to overcome strong informal power networks and resistance to modernization. The result tends to be an ineffective and authoritarian state, in which the mechanisms of authoritarian modernization are enmeshed with informal tribal or kinship structures.

In Kyrgyzstan, President Akaev gradually increased the power of the presidency ostensibly to promote economic reform, which was opposed by parliament and by vested interests. However, he failed to achieve substantive reforms and instead created a centralized political system that was eventually captured by informal power networks that controlled the flow of economic resources. Continued centralization of power by Akaev finally undermined an informal pact among different power groups and resulted in his being ousted from power. This kind of "failed modernization" strategy has echoes in Uzbekistan's political trajectory in the early 1990s, while in Kazakhstan, arguably, authoritarian modernization has been more successful in achieving economic modernization, if not effective political development.

In all Central Asian states, presidents may have begun by balancing different groupings and acting as arbiter among them, but in most cases they also gradually consolidated power and took over the role of primary arbiter of resource distribution, of both public and private goods, albeit with continued contestation within the closed political circles of elites in Kazakhstan and Uzbekistan. In poorer countries, such as Kyrgyzstan and Tajikistan, where there were fewer central resources to be distributed in this way, the political elites constantly sought to control what resources were available, including illegal resources, such as those derived from drug trafficking. To achieve this level of control, ruling elites have consolidated their control over the political system, removed potentially powerful rivals and asserted almost complete control over key resource flows. In Tajikistan, several key informal leaders were arrested, killed or exiled during 2001–8 under the increasingly authoritarian regime of President Imomali Rahmon. In Kyrgyzstan, the post-2005 leadership gradually resorted to more oppressive political tactics to deal with political opposition, and a number of organized-crime leaders were killed in unclear circumstances in 2005–7, suggesting an increased centralization of power in both formal and informal networks. The explanations for President Bakiev's subsequent ousting in a popular revolt in 2010 might also be sought in the breakdown of this mixture of formal and informal political dynamics.

Authoritarian control is consistent with failed forced modernization strategies, but it has also become of instrumental convenience for consolidated elites, who seek to exclude political and business rivals from the business of the state. Authoritarian regimes undermine the rule of law, ensuring that all contracts are subject to arbitrary re-evaluation or re-negotiation. This is a vital instrument for informal elites to ensure their continued economic dominance, but it is possible only within an authoritarian political system coupled with a strong form of sovereignty that limits the influence of external actors. Authoritarian methods were used to defend sovereignty, understood in the ways outlined above, against ethnic nationalist or pan-Islamic movements, but also against major external economic forces which could upset the internal control and the balance among leading power groups. Authoritarianism thus became the most likely way for Soviet-era elites to promote short-term stability, because it appeared to be the only way in which the political system could incorporate informal elite pacts that ensured agreement on resource and power distribution. Elite support for authoritarianism presupposed a lack of any other significant pressure for a more pluralistic regime. International pressure on Central Asian states occasionally had some influence on internal dynamics, but it was never sufficiently strong to influence policies, nor was it aimed at the kind of economic resources that might have concerned power elites.

Both these aspects – failed modernization strategies and instrumental utility for elites – ensured that an authoritarian state was a likely outcome of state capture by such groups. The dominance of informal networks in the state ensures that authoritarianism is most likely to emerge in the specific form of the neo-patrimonial authoritarian state, of the type that has become increasingly familiar in Central Asia and the Middle East. In the Middle East, such states have emerged where attempts to modernize through statist authoritarianism (through one-party states or through military rule) or through some kind of political ideology (nationalism, socialism) have been largely abandoned, and replaced by a relatively durable authoritarian system, in which patron–client relations form the central political and economic dynamic (for example, Syria and Egypt). In Central Asia such states have emerged without a significant period of centralized, forced modernization, although it is arguable that the period of the 1920s and 1930s shares many common features with nationalist, military-led modernization campaigns in the Middle East. However, the resulting political systems in the two regions are similar, and combine the same kind of unlikely amalgam of relative political longevity and stability with poor socio-economic performance, significant political repression and high levels of popular discontent.

In neither region are these political systems perceived by their elites to be in a state of systemic transition, but are seen by their leaders as relatively successful and stable political entities. In reality, these regimes face significant internal and external obstacles, but so far in most cases they have found ways of overcoming such weaknesses: demands for more popular forms of sovereignty are diffused by co-option and coercion; many young people leave through mass labor migration, which tempers any significant social demands from the population; and external pressure is negated by using strategic arguments and geopolitical competition in their favor. These dynamics seem unlikely to change in the near future, although the eventual passing of the present Soviet-era generation of political leaders in Central Asia will undoubtedly produce different understandings of sovereignty and a re-examination of the legacy of empire.

Notes

1. For a range of views on the colonial roots of African authoritarianism, see Mamdani, *Citizen and Subject*; Cooper, *Africa since 1940*; Ekeh, "Colonialism and the two publics in Africa," pp. 91–112; Schneider, "Colonial legacies and postcolonial authoritarianism in Tanzania," pp. 93–118.
2. See, e.g., Khalid (ed.), "Introduction: locating the (post-)colonial in Central Asian history"; Northrop, *Veiled Empire*; Michaels, *Curative Powers* and also the articles in the special issue of *Russian Review* (April 2000), particularly Hirsch, "Toward an empire of nations," pp. 201–26.
3. Adams, "Can we apply post-colonial theory to Central Eurasia?," pp. 2–7.
4. Beissinger, "Soviet empire as 'family resemblance'," pp. 294–303.
5. Osterhammel, *Colonialism: A Theoretical Overview*, p. 61.
6. Hirsch, "Toward an empire of nations," pp. 201–26.
7. See Michaels, *Curative Powers*; Northrop, "Nationalizing backwardness."
8. On the resort to indirect rule to maintain control in French colonies, see Conkin, *A Mission to Civilise*, pp. 182–6.
9. Ilkhamov, "Nation-state formation," p. 321.

10. See Edgar, *Tribal Nation*; Sabola, "The creation of Soviet Central Asia," pp. 225–41; Hirsch, "Toward an empire of nations," pp. 201–26; Karasar, "The partition of Khorezm and the positions of Turkestanis on *Razmezhevanie*," pp. 1247–60.

11. See, *inter alia*, Karasar, "The partition of Khorezm and the positions of Turkestanis on *razmezhevanie*," p. 1254.

12 On early ideas of regional integration, see, Karasar, "The partition of Khorezm and the positions of Turkestanis on *Razmezhevanie*," pp. 1256–457. The Central Asian Economic Region lasted only for 18 months: Matley, "Industrialization (1865–1964)," p. 337.

13. Ilkhamov, "Nation-state formation," p. 320.

14. Allworth (ed.), *Central Asia*, p. 593.

15. For a discussion, see Collins, *Clan Politics*, pp. 56–60.

16. Ilkhamov, "Nation-state formation."

17. Gleason, "Fealty and loyalty," pp. 613–28.

18. Tuncer-Kilavuz, "Political and social networks," pp. 323–34.

19. Tuncer-Kilavuz, "Political and social networks," p. 328.

20. Tuncer-Kilavuz, "Political and social networks," p. 331.

21. Roy, *The New Central Asia*, p. 89.

22. Mamdani, *Citizen and Subject*.

23. Critchlow, "Corruption, nationalism and the native elites in Soviet Central Asia," p. 146.

24. Critchlow, "Corruption, nationalism and the native elites in Soviet Central Asia."

25. See Staples, "Soviet uses of corruption purges as a control mechanism', pp. 112–17.

26. Gennady Kolbin later told CPKa CC members: "Comrades, during the two days of rioting in the square, young people frankly expressed the view that they were not against a Russian as the leader of the Kazakh party organisation, but argued that this Russian should come from Kazakhstan. The names of likely candidates were given, Of course, those who expressed these views had not suddenly guessed at various options for the placement of cadres in the top echelon of the republican party organisation. How did they know this? It was quietly whispered to them." *Kazakhstanskaya Pravda*, March 15, 1987, cited in Gleason, "Fealty and loyalty." This suggests an interesting understanding of the extent of informal networks within the republic, and the complex role of ethnicity in these dynamics. It reinforces the idea that elites were networked not solely on the basis of ethnicity, but through their adherence to republican sovereign institutions.

27. For a good account of his rise to power, see Collins, *Clan Politics*, pp. 122–5.

28. Collins, *Clan Politics*, p. 123.

29. Collins, *Clan Politics*, p. 51.

Section IV

Empire and Popular Sovereignty

10

Culture, Colonialism and Sovereignty in Central Asia

Laura L. Adams

In 1970, the Uzbek Soviet Socialist Republic was preparing to celebrate the 2500th jubilee of the city of Samarkand.[1] As part of the official celebrations, the Samarkand Theater of Opera and Ballet had produced an opera, "The Legend of Bibihanum," based on a well-known local legend about one of the wives of the medieval ruler, Amir Timur (Tamerlane). The theater had chosen this theme because the legend had an epic quality well suited to opera, and because it resonated strongly with Soviet understandings of the importance of Samarkand's Timurid-era architecture. Samarkand's despotic history was problematic for Soviet ideology, but the symbols of civilizational achievements created by the despots (the name Bibihanum also refers to the architectural complex that is named after Timur's wife) were international icons of which the Soviet state was proud. Here, it would seem, was an ideal enactment of Soviet ideas about culture: the European high art genre of opera would facilitate the fullest expression of the cultural development of the local people, while the theme of the opera would synthesize perfectly the principle of "national in form, socialist in content," by communicating Soviet values through the medium of a local legend. However, in spite of the seeming acceptability of this theme given the dual constraints of Soviet ideology and common knowledge about the significant monuments and historical events of Samarkand, there was a fatal flaw in the story that halted the opera's production in its tracks. The flaw in the story was that it could not avoid the topic of the world-conquering Timur himself.

The opera, as it was presented to a review committee composed of officials from the Uzbek SSR Ministry of Culture, told the story of how Bibihanum had a beautiful mosque built in Timur's honor while he was away on one of his campaigns. However, Bibihanum and the mosque's architect fell in love and when Timur returned home, he killed them both and partially destroyed the building. The local legend upon which this story was based has many different variations, but this re-telling deliberately highlighted an interpretation that was stripped of its un-socialist mystical elements (such as the architect turning into a bird and flying away – a familiar trope in Persian literature), which was very much in line with the Soviet image of Timur as an unredeemable despot. This interpretation focused on Timur's cruelty to women and to the common people, portraying the architect as something of a populist hero. As a representative from the theater explained, the opera demonstrated that Timur was "a cruel warrior and a master of court intrigue, on the background of which the presence of the people and their talented representative, the architect Bakhram, is completely erased."[2]

The theater was required to give this explanation because during this review of the dress rehearsal, a sharp disagreement broke out about whether the fit between this legend and Soviet ideology was as perfect as it seemed. Representatives from the Ministry of Culture called the production "ideologically defiled" because Timur was not portrayed as being cruel enough to justify his appearance on stage in Soviet Uzbekistan. However, given that the opera was already in the dress rehearsal stage, the ideological unacceptability of depicting this medieval hero in a major Soviet production was not obvious, and even the representatives from the ministry disagreed amongst themselves about whether that ship had already sailed, so to speak. "History is history, and everyone knows it anyway," said one ministry official, prompting a discussion about the controversy that would ensue when the people of Samarkand noticed that the opera was absent from the festival. Culture Minister Kuchkarov (who had occupied his position since 1953), decided in the end that the production should be cancelled unless the libretto was completely rewritten – in three days – because "though built by Timur, these monuments belong to the Soviet people now and therefore the show should be contemporary, celebrating what we have spent so much to restore." As someone from the theater concluded grimly, "It's out of the question to present Timur on stage, but it is also out of the question to present this show without him."[3]

This glimpse of culture production on the periphery during an era that was the peak of Soviet power can be read in a number of ways, but the focus here will be on the way that this incident sets the stage for a discussion of the applicability of a colonial or post-colonial lens to the issue of cultural sovereignty in Central Asia. These kinds of incidents are often interpreted, both in Western scholarship and in contemporary Central Asian critique of the Soviet period, as examples of how "the Soviets" repressed "Central Asian" cultures. Through this lens, the interaction

between the ministry and the theater can be read as a case of cultural imperialism, of Moscow's attempt to subjugate artists in the Soviet periphery
by robbing them of their own culture and imposing a Russian culture
thinly disguised as Soviet values. In this admittedly simplistic scenario,
an assertion of cultural sovereignty would manifest as a rejection of
Soviet ideology and an affirmation of traditional cultural values. Indeed,
this is what happened throughout Central Asia after the collapse of the
Soviet Union: cultural content was stripped of its socialist symbolism and
replaced with a new, nationalist iconography.[4]

However, it would be incorrect to view struggles over cultural content
as the only arena for the exercise of sovereignty. A simplistic understanding of Soviet power as an imperial imposition must gloss over the fact
that most of the people involved in the debate about the opera were themselves non-Russians, that the debate was between representatives from
the local center (Tashkent, not Moscow), that the ideological demands in
this context were vague enough that even the ministry employees disagreed among themselves about what was acceptable, and not least, that
the defenders of local Samarkandi culture were also passionate defenders
of European-style opera. Central Asians today sharply dispute whether
they were "colonized" by the Soviet Union, and this ambivalence toward
Russian/European culture is part of such disputes. For many Central
Asians, it is not so easy to divide culture into "ours" and "theirs," in part
because Central Asians were active participants in the Soviet project,
creatively using their own national cultures to create a pluralistic – albeit
russocentric – Soviet culture. Cultural sovereignty in Central Asia is
also about struggles over the hegemony of European cultural forms and
modern ways of knowing, and in this sense the assertion of cultural sovereignty comes into conflict with the very institutions (such as participation
in a globalized economy) that make other kinds of sovereignty possible.
As other authors in this volume such as Morten Valbjørn point out, sovereignty itself is conceived of in Central Asia and the Middle East today
through concepts and institutions generated in the West.

Questions of cultural sovereignty are inherently questions of us/them
power dynamics. Unlike other kinds of sovereignty, the term cultural
sovereignty, as it is commonly used, does not have a meaning independent of a discourse of cultural imperialism. The term is usually invoked
as the assertion of a group's right to cultural expression free of external
imposition. Often the concept is linked to other kinds of sovereignty, as
in the legal sovereignty of indigenous peoples where issues of cultural
sovereignty might be tied to educational institutions and language use,[5] or
to refer to protectionism, resistance to how the group is represented in a

dominant cultural narrative, or to demonstrate a denigrated group's equality with others.[6] One thing these various approaches share is an analysis of how cultural sovereignty relates to the way the dominant culture becomes embedded in the very institutions (such as the law) that are then called upon to defend the embattled group's sovereignty.[7] Central Asian culture was both enabled and constrained by Soviet institutions and the question, as Winegar puts it, is not one of ideal types but of graduated, strategic and context-specific sovereignty.[8]

After Empire?

Clearly, in order to make sense of the incident with the Samarkand Opera and Ballet Theater, and to understand issues of cultural sovereignty in post-Soviet Central Asia, we need a more complex understanding of the ways that the Soviet Union was and was not like a colonial empire. Applying the term "empire" to the Soviet Union has been the subject of much debate among scholars in the last ten years. In the early 1990s, the lively discussion in Western scholarship about the nation-building policies of the Soviet Union gradually evolved into a debate about whether or not the Soviet Union should be considered an empire. Historians have tended to focus on the early Soviet period, where the consolidation of Soviet power in Central Asia often played out in ethnic and cultural terms that were directly linked to, and often in opposition to, Tsarist imperial policies and attitudes. Social scientists, who focus more on the late and post-Soviet periods, have attended to the instrumental use of the term empire by Central Asian elites and the very messy realities on the ground that at times confirm and at times reject the utility of post-colonial theorizing about Central Asia.

The term empire has been invoked in many historical studies of early Soviet policies, especially those polices that aimed to build nations in the name of Soviet progress. These scholars have argued that the Soviet Union was an "affirmative action empire" or an "empire of nations" that used nationality as an organizing principle to foster various kinds of centrally controlled development.[9] Even though these policies were designed to build nations and modernize Central Asia, they perpetuated the kinds of cultural hierarchy and core–periphery differences that characterize modern empires.[10] However, these historians are also cautious about the applicability of the term empire to the USSR, pointing out that early Bolshevik policies were self-consciously anti-imperial, and that Soviet modernization policies were just as brutal on the Russian peasantry as on, say, Kyrgyz nomads.[11]

Other historians reject outright the appellation empire as applied to Soviet Central Asia. Pointing to the important differences between the Soviet Union and other imperial powers of the twentieth century, Adeeb Khalid argues that the Soviet Union resembled an empire less than "a different kind of modern polity, the activist, interventionist, mobilizational state that seeks to sculpt its citizenry in an ideal image. [Conflating this kind of state with colonial empires] leads to a fundamental misunderstanding of modern history."[12] Furthermore, as Marianne Kamp has argued, casting early Soviet history in a colonial light runs the risk of painting an overly polarized picture in which European colonizers battle native anti-colonial resistance. Rather, her work demonstrates that violence and upheaval in the early Soviet period was part of an ongoing struggle between traditionalists and the indigenous modernizers who made use of Soviet policies to carry out their ongoing, pre-Soviet agenda.[13] Those who violently opposed Soviet policies in early Soviet Central Asia "were not victims of Russian colonialism; they were agents who decided to enact their opposition to the Soviet state and to the ideas of the Uzbek reformers (whom the Soviets had empowered)."[14] Similarly, other authors have argued against seeing the creation of European-style Soviet institutions as a result of a colonial imposition, but rather as part of an active effort on the part of local elites to adapt local culture to better serve the building of Soviet socialism.[15]

The framework used in this chapter to understand the colonial nature of the Soviet Union comes from the argument put forth by Adrienne Edgar, who shows that unlike other imperial states, the Soviet Union intended to effect real social change, intervening in realms of law and family (what Chatterjee calls the "inner realm" that nationalists stake out as their territory against imperialism) to an extent more characteristic of a modernizing state such as Iran or Turkey, than of a colonial empire.[16] However, she argues that the resistance to these interventions was much stronger in Central Asia than in these other modernizing states because Soviet rule was perceived as "fundamentally alien. The important point here is not that Soviet rule of Central Asia was *objectively* more 'foreign' than the Turkish and Iranian leaders' rule over their respective peripheries ... it was the popular impression of Moscow's foreignness that mattered" (original emphasis).[17] Whereas modernization in Iran and Turkey during this period was often perceived as the independent nation's best defense against European imperialism, Edgar argues, the backlash against modernization in early Soviet Central Asia more closely resembled that of the colonized populations of the Arab world which saw modernization as Europeanization and, therefore, these modernization policies were resisted by anti-colonial movements.

In this sense, the subjective perception of imperial rule in Central Asia is seen, especially by social scientists studying late and post-Soviet Central Asia, as more important than comparing the Soviet Union with a particular ideal type of empire. These scholars see the term empire as a discursive strategy worth studying on its own terms and examine changing local perceptions over time.[18] As Mark Beissinger put it:

> What needs to be explained is why "the world's first post-imperial state" was vulnerable to framing as an empire, how and why these framings varied over time and across a diverse population, why opportunities for constructing an alternative multinational space to empire failed, and what ultimately led to the amplification of the imperial charge and to its terminal political effect.[19]

What these debates have shown us is that the Soviet Union was like an empire in that a center dominated politically a geographically diverse territory as well as imposed a hierarchical culture (with not just Russian culture but the culture of Moscow and Leningrad at its center) over its ethnically diverse citizens. But scholars also tend to agree that the Soviet Union was unlike other European empires in a number of ways, the most significant of which was its emphasis on the modernization and political mobilization of the periphery. This helps us see why some scholars are uncomfortable applying the label "empire" to the Soviet Union, while at the same time raising the question of whether we can label the resistance to certain Soviet policies as anti-imperial or post-colonial. It is not correct to call the Soviet Union an empire and leave it at that. Nonetheless, it is analytically useful to view issues of sovereignty in contemporary Central Asia through the *theoretical* lens of comparative post-colonialisms, whether or not we agree that Central Asia was *really* a colony. A post-colonial analysis can help us understand the Bibihanum opera incident above, and power dynamics in Soviet culture more generally, as having little to do with the imposition of Russian culture. Rather, it shows us that Soviet institutions made opera (1) a prestigious cultural form, (2) a venue for the creative reinterpretation of locally meaningful content and (3) a venue for the exercise of modern disciplinary power.

As Partha Chatterjee argues, colonial practices are one among many techniques in the arsenal of modern disciplinary power:

> It is possible to give many instances of how the rule of colonial difference – of representing the "other" as inferior and radically different, and hence incorrigibly inferior – can be employed in situations that are not, in the strict terms of political history, colonial . . . This reason makes it necessary to study the specific history of the colonial state, because it reveals what is only hidden in the universal history of the modern regime of power.[20]

Drawing on the tradition of authors such as Michel Foucault, Edward Said and Partha Chatterjee, the definition of empire used in this chapter is one that focuses not on economic or political structures as much as on regimes of practices and ways of knowing. The kind of colonialism I am talking about is the institutionalization of the ways of knowing (epistemes) of the colonizer. These epistemes may not even be hegemonic in the colonizer's own society, but rather are considered to be the truth that the empire sees itself as charged with spreading. They may not be common sense, but they are the "good sense" that the imperial powers wish will become hegemonic, and often this wish is strong enough that the colonizer is willing to engage in the "irrational" expenditure of resources to ensure this episteme's institutionalization in the periphery. It is this kind of cultural imperialism that I will show is characteristic of the early Soviet period, but I argue below that as time passed, both the development of Soviet institutions and global influences greatly changed the relationship that Central Asians had to Soviet culture, such that it was no longer experienced as an alien imposition, but was instead an expression of their own cultural development.

Cultural Change in Soviet Central Asia through the Lens of Post-colonialism

In order to understand what practices and forms of knowledge became naturalized and internalized in Soviet Central Asia, it is useful to see how early Soviet policies are viewed today. Drawing on secondary sources based on archival and ethnographic research on Central Asia, as well as my own research on culture and identity in Kazakhstan, Kyrgyzstan and Uzbekistan,[21] I will provide a few examples of how we might view cultural sovereignty in Central Asia as an effect of empire as regimes of practices and ways of knowing. Some of these policies receive more public attention today than others and are critiqued from a post-colonial perspective, whereas others receive less attention and are part of a discourse of "progress" and "development." The most radical Soviet policies of the 1920s and 1930s, those that produced the greatest amount of what we might call anti-colonial resistance on the part of the local population at the time, are commonly viewed today as necessary progress and are not consistently marked in public discourse by the label "colonialism" or "imperialism." In fact, the institutions and norms produced by these revolutionary campaigns are sometime ones that the current regimes would like to preserve, and framing them in a discourse of progress helps to maintain the legitimacy of current state policies. On the other hand, many more minor policies, often those that dealt explicitly with the realm of language and culture, are often critiqued as cultural imperialism. This, too, is related to the legitimacy of the current governments, who inverted Soviet hierarchies and used nationalism and critiques of Russian hegemony to justify their consolidation of power after independence.

In contemporary Central Asia, cultural sovereignty is both constrained and enabled by Soviet legacies, the most important of which are not colonial legacies. Central Asians themselves have not developed particularly clear critiques of the Soviet period or particular schools of interpretation that might be termed post-colonial, post-modern, neo-liberal or anything else except nationalist. Rather than questioning the epistemology of a Russian–Uzbek dichotomy, for example, culture producers in Uzbekistan today tend to celebrate and elevate Uzbek culture in the same ways that Russian culture was lauded in the Soviet period.[22] This muddled response to Soviet cultural policies is in part due to a dependence on Soviet schemas of national identity and culture. But the particular kinds of critiques of the Soviet period that we find in Central Asia today are also in part the result of the ongoing lack of a public sphere for discussion that would allow people to form and articulate diverse critiques of the Soviet system.

THE LEGACIES OF STALINIST POLICIES IN EVERYDAY LIFE CULTURE

There are several examples of early Soviet policies that had a deep and lasting impact on Central Asian culture. Collectivization, sedentarization of nomadic peoples,[23] anti-religious campaigns[24] and efforts to "liberate the Eastern woman"[25] all, over the course of many decades, greatly transformed Central Asian societies. As Matthew Payne has shown, even though on paper many of these policies were in line with Soviet ideals of anti-colonialism, fraternity and class equality (for example, Russians working in Kazakhstan should learn Kazakh), in practice old colonial racist dynamics formed quickly on the ground.[26] During the terror and purges of the 1930s, Central Asian politicians, artists and scholars were put on trial for "nationalist deviation" from the Party line, leading to the destruction of a whole generation of indigenous leaders.[27] Other policies were more insulting than injurious: national histories of the 1950s and 1960s required that authors both glorify Tsarist-era anti-colonial struggles and portray the Tsarist conquest of Central Asia as the inevitable joining of the Central Asians to the Russian people.[28] There is as yet very little published primary source research on the post-Stalin era in Central Asia, but Sovietological analyses showed that from the 1950s to 1970s, struggles over the value of Russian culture versus local culture waxed and waned, with Russian cultural domination being embraced explicitly by official ideology at some points in time.[29] However, certain aspects of what Chatterjee calls the inner spiritual (as opposed to material) realm of culture were never abandoned and replaced with Soviet equivalents. The ongoing existence of Muslim norms and rituals (such as circumcision and funerary rites) in Central Asian Soviet culture is evidence of a kind of cultural sovereignty that is not just a kind of resistance to Russian cultural domination, but is also the active creation of a meaningful, living culture. Though the existence of such prevalent everyday life expressions of Muslim culture in the late Soviet period caused considerable dismay,[30] Central Asians in the late Soviet period had clearly created their own variant of Soviet yet Muslim culture.

The most profound and violent of the policies that transformed everyday life came not from a russification paradigm, but from the Bolshevik historical materialist worldview that demanded conformity to a particular (eurocentric) path of economic development. In the early 1930s, the sedentarization and collectivization of nomadic populations in Kazakhstan and Kyrgyzstan resulted in the deaths of hundreds of thousands and irrevocably changed what it meant to be Kazakh and Kyrgyz. Yet the history of collectivization was so traumatic, so divisive (Central Asians were both perpetrators and victims) and so repressed during the Soviet period, that this most profound of transformational policies is the subject of very little critique, post-colonial or otherwise, in contemporary Central Asia.[31] However, the legacies of these campaigns after they became fully-fledged Soviet institutions are seen with more ambiguity and from more diverse perspectives in contemporary Kazakhstan.[32] People who lived through the Soviet period may label these policies as "colonial," but at the same time most recognize that they were not targeted for collectivization or dekulakization because of racial or cultural difference. Stalinism was a trauma suffered by all Soviet peoples, and in this sense the shared critique of Stalinist repression is something that makes Central Asians all the more Soviet. This is changing, however, as the new nationalist histories tend to portray each Central Asian country's Soviet experience as unique and isolated from the others, or ignore the Soviet period almost completely, as in Turkmenistan's attempts to create an ahistorical national narrative.[33] Because of this nationalist finessing of the "us versus them" trope, the current post-Soviet generation in Central Asia may be more likely to see the Soviet Union as a colonial empire than did their parents.

One interesting example of the changing interpretations of Soviet policies is the case of the "hujum," the attack in the late 1920s on traditional gender roles in the urban areas of today's Uzbekistan and Tajikistan.

Northrop makes the case that this was perceived at the time as a colonialist policy that would do nothing less than destroy local culture, and was therefore confronted with violent anti-colonial resistance, including numerous murders of unveiled women.[34] The way that this campaign is understood today, however, is cast much more in the light of "progress" than of "alien imposition." In order to understand this shift, we need to see how the policy was institutionalized in the longer term and how it transformed from a colonial to a disciplinary technique of power. Although Northrop shows that the unveiling campaign failed largely in the medium term, Marianne Kamp and others show that during the early Stalin period, Soviet cultural policies were implemented quite unevenly with quite a bit of variation from place to place. They also show that there was a steady increase in the institutionalization of these policies, with pressure on families to send their children to schools that would inculcate the new generation with Soviet values.[35] The state – personified not just by Russian bureaucrats in Moscow but also Uzbek bureaucrats in Tashkent and idealistic teachers in the villages – gradually built its capacity to coerce and persuade families to let their women work outside the home, to marry after getting an education and so on. In other words, to become modern.

After the outbreak of the Second World War, cultural policies became much more lenient for a time, with the result that religion began to flourish again and some women re-veiled, but the general trend of modernization policies had been established.[36] We have very little evidence from this period because not much archival research has yet been done on Central Asia during and after the Second World War. However, it seems pretty clear that the war marked a turning point in the popular perception of Moscow's "foreignness." Central Asians were mobilized along with other Soviet peoples to defend the motherland against a foreign invader, restrictions on local cultural expression were relaxed during and after the war allowing a greater synthesis of "Soviet" and "local" culture, and post-war policies enabled Central Asians to make increasing demands on the state within the framework of their rights as citizens and as contributors to the war.[37] Through their participation in Soviet institutions, both at home and in far-flung locations such as Moscow or on the Western Front, Central Asians came to see that they had a stake in Soviet power, and institutions such as public education and party membership gave an everyday reality to an evolving Soviet identity. In many ways, this process was not so different from how political identities were built in any colonial empire, with the circulation of elites in ever-ascending institutions (from the local primary school to the metropolitan university) creating a sense of what the empire was and where one belonged in it.[38]

Although Soviet campaigns against "backward" practices were often imbued with orientalist rhetoric and were sometimes carried out by racist individuals, it is difficult to see such policies exclusively through the lens of colonialism. Indeed, Central Asians themselves mark these kinds of policies today as part of development and progress, in spite of the fact that they specifically targeted Central Asian culture for change. Today there is very little criticism of the hujum as an "alien" campaign imposed by "the Russians" or even "the Soviets." The complete seclusion of women as practiced in urban areas of Tajikistan and Uzbekistan in the 1920s is seen by most people today as not just impractical but distasteful, a way of life from a less civilized era. However, the idea that a woman, especially a young bride, should be obedient to her husband's family and should observe very strict rules of behavior, is a practice that persisted and evolved during the Soviet period, and is now openly justified with reference to the norms of Muslim societies.[39] Thus, the main aspects of such Soviet policies ceased to be seen as alien and became incorporated in a discourse of "our progress." But it was a local definition of progress that also incorporated Muslim norms.

The struggle between "traditionalists" and "modernizers" continues today, but unlike the "forward-to-the-past" advocates in the Middle East,[40] even the traditionalists are defending and expanding a particular Soviet approach to gender, undermining the post-colonial thesis that all things Soviet are seen as "alien impositions." Today's traditionalists are often Central Asians defending their particular Soviet way of life (including subsidies for mothers, income levels that allowed women not to work and patriarchical authority within the family), while reaching out to Islam to help them frame the legitimacy of this way of life.[41] The modernizers are also defending a Soviet way of life (emphasizing education, employment and political opportunities for women), but draw on liberal and international norms to make their case for individual liberties accruing to women and girls in Central Asia. Official state ideology in Uzbekistan, for example, "draws on the Soviet legacy, makes explicit references to Islamic discourses on motherhood, and is creating a newly emergent but rather ordinary nationalist linkage of women and the nation."[42]

Interestingly, it is not Soviet discourses about gender, but Western notions of individual liberty, domestic violence and sexual norms that attract the most critical public discourse today. This is more true in Uzbekistan than in Kazakhstan, which has embraced a more neo-liberal ideology. A particularly defiant article exemplifying this attitude was published in the main Uzbek-language newspaper in 2003:

We answer those who, behind the mask of democracy propagandize throughout the world the lifestyles and values of the West, with the defense of our eternal national heritage. What's more, we are persuaded that this heritage is not only compatible with universal trends towards democracy, but it in fact guarantees democracy's enrichment and improvement.[43]

The article went on to promote indigenous institutions as superior to foreign ones in achieving internationally valued goals ranging from internal security to the protection of the family. The author criticized "certain foreign organizations" for provoking a rise in extremism by attacking traditional institutions in the name of human rights. He also defended the mahalla (urban neighborhood administration), which was being portrayed by these organizations as an organ of the state that oppressed women, and criticized Western divorce rates and culturally biased assumptions about what constituted proper behavior for women and girls.

The "alien" imposition of Western norms is highly productive of state-supporting discourses in Uzbekistan and this is parallel to the responses to US "neo-colonialism" in the Middle East.[44] Unlike in the Middle East, it is not US consumerism or militarism that has been the main target of this neo-colonial critique, but rather the discourse of civil society and democratization, which many Central Asian leaders have accused of being an alien imposition that does not fit with local ways of life. As other authors in this volume have shown, some Central Asian states are willing to cede certain kinds of political sovereignty to Russia in exchange for Russia's support for the perpetuation of these Soviet styles of legitimation.[45]

LANGUAGE AND EXPRESSIVE CULTURE AS CONTESTED TERRAIN

While Soviet policies that aimed to change the culture of everyday life are widely seen as "normal development" today, policies related to language and expressive culture are more polarizing. Although many Central Asians look back on the 1970s and early 1980s as a time of stability and pride in Soviet achievements, they also remember with resentment their being told that the Russians were their "elder brother" and that Russian culture was superior to their own. Or – ironically, given our Samarkand opera adventure – that certain nations' despots were more admirable than others. As this actor and Uzbekistan Ministry of Culture official put it, in the Soviet period

all the shows had to answer to the politics of the Soviet Union. For example, we couldn't dream of putting on a show about Timur, but we could put one on about Peter the Great. Back then we hardly even studied Uzbek literature, it was all Russian.[46]

210

Thus, many early post-Soviet policies in Central Asia aimed to elevate national language, culture and cadres at the expense of their Russian counterparts. In Central Asia today, it is not uncommon to turn on a local television channel and find a poet or singer relating a story about what was and was not allowed during the Soviet era. For example, in a 2008 broadcast, a Kazakh opera singer (clearly someone who straddled the European/Kazakh cultural divide) related that he also sang songs in Kazakh, but they wouldn't play those on the radio. He went on to criticize the Soviet characterization of Kazakh music as "primitive" and to explain just how sophisticated the music actually is. On another channel that same evening a reporter said that although some Europeans look down on nomadic culture, a concert in the capital city, Astana, demonstrated "how rich and wonderful nomadic culture is."[47] Much of the promotion of local culture today is in a similarly close – and defensive – dialogue with Soviet discourse.

This "decolonizing" response was more severe immediately after the collapse of the Soviet Union because the political stakes were high: the russification of the Soviet Central Asian elite meant that the leaders of the newly independent republics had to reconcile their nationalist ideology with their hybrid identities. The presidents of Kazakhstan and Uzbekistan, for example, were not fluent in their respective national languages at the time of independence, yet for much of the 1990s they saw nationalism as their main platform for legitimacy. It was in this context that the terms "imperialism" and "colonialism" could most often be found as a scapegoat for both the political problems of the elite and the economic problems of the nation. However, these "us versus them" discourses of victimization that became enshrined in the new nationalist histories I mentioned above were often framed in imperial, but not ethnic terms. That is, "Moscow" or "Soviet power" and not "Russians" were to blame for repression and injustice.[48]

Nonetheless, in Kazakhstan and Kyrgyzstan these kinds of "us versus them" discourses created some unwanted tensions, complicating the relationship between the nationalizing states and the nationalists.[49] At the time of independence, the population of Kazakhstan was slightly less than half Kazakh, and there were also many non-Kyrgyz in Kyrgyzstan at the time of independence. Many Russian-speakers left for Russia, creating a brain drain. But the Russian-speakers who remained had citizenship rights and blatant discrimination against them created the specter of instability. Most importantly for my argument here, many ethnic Kazakhs and Kyrgyz themselves felt a sense of ownership over Russian language and culture and the indigenous non-nationalist intelligentsia felt that their experiences were not represented by a one-sided colonial critique of Russian culture. Soviet writers such as Kyrgyzstan's Chingiz Aitmatov and Kazakhstan's Olzhas Suleimenov were examples of the new Soviet Central Asian, respected across Soviet borders and rewarded by Moscow for their literary output in Russian, yet always in tension with the Party and the Writers' Union for their particular brand of political – not cultural – critique from the margins.[50] The popularity of these russified writers today shows that the point of building Soviet culture was not assimilation to Russian culture. People who assimilated completely are derisively called "mankurts," a term coined by Aitmatov to denote someone who has forgotten his own ethnic culture. Proper Soviet Central Asians did not try to become Russian, but instead tried to create their own version of Soviet identity.

As discussed earlier, one of the paradoxical features of cultural sovereignty is the problematic institutionalization of another culture's norms that govern the very institutions through which sovereignty is exercised.[51] Empires exert political power by colonizing knowledge, thus Beissinger's suggestion to recognize empires by their perception as "fundamentally alien" is only the first part of the equation. Equally interesting from the perspective of post-colonial cultural sovereignty are those practices and ways of knowing that have come to be hegemonic, that are seen as common sense or "normal development." The ways of knowing that shaped the subjectivities of Central Asians during the Soviet period included the internalization of otherness (nationality is a good example) that we might find fits well with a post-colonial interpretive lens, but they also included other practices (such as modern schooling) that emerged not out of colonial relations of power, but out of what Foucault calls modern disciplinary regimes. If such disciplinary regimes are hegemonic in the world today, it is difficult to make the argument that sovereignty involves their rejection. If the Soviet state instituted practices of governmentality in Central Asia, practices which are themselves indicators of sovereignty, then the question of cultural sovereignty in Central Asia involves the successful naturalization of these policies. While the legacies of Russian cultural imperialism are easily pointed out and critiqued by contemporary Central Asians, the critique of Soviet cultural development is more difficult to formulate because it would require a deconstruction of socio-economic development and modern subjectivity that are not seen as problematic by most Central Asians. An artist and official at Uzbekistan's Ministry of Culture whose grandparents had been killed during the purges in the 1930s articulately expressed both a materialist anti-colonial critique of Soviet power and an internalized sense of what makes for "good" art that depends on the adoption of European artistic techniques. He also makes clear the ways that Central Asians draw rapidly shifting distinctions between Europeans, Russians, and the Soviets in naming the "other" against whom they define themselves:

> There was an invaluable contribution to Uzbek culture from European culture, realism for example, enriched our high art. But on the other hand, our ecology of art was polluted. The masters started using non-traditional materials. There's nothing wrong with enriching the range of materials you work with, but don't lose your traditional materials. Don't lose what's your own ... The national culture should always use what has been used in the past because you can get cut off from Russia or the rest of the world and if you can't use what you have at hand you can't transmit your knowledge to the next generation ... There's a lot of damage to make up for and we can't recover it all at once. Russian culture was damaged, too, by the Soviets.[52]

What Soviet cultural policies are seen today as more or less natural parts of cultural development rather than as imperial impositions? In general, those policies that gave a form for the expression of local content, though it is important to recognize that these cultural forms themselves were not culturally neutral. Soviet institutions "developed" culture in Central Asia using the infamous "national in form, socialist in content" formula, using traditional genres of song, dance, art and theater to propagate communist themes.[53] However, as was stated in the introduction, it may be more accurate to speak of cultural development through international forms and national content. The content of the opera about Bibihanum was limited, but not determined, by socialist culture. At the time, the official argument about productions like Bibihanum was that Uzbek culture should be developed, elevated and advanced through the "internationalization of national culture," through the indigenization (both in terms of content and in terms of personnel) of high culture such as opera. What is questioned today is not the principle of development (which is part of hegemonic "ways of knowing"), but rather the importance of such "European" genres for national cultural development, and here Central Asians are divided. Some see opera and ballet as necessary arts for any civilized country, while others see them as symbols of an imposed cultural hierarchy that arbitrarily denigrates local high cultural forms.[54]

The codification and institutionalization of national cultures in the early Soviet era quite blatantly imposed a eurocentric hierarchy in the name of "development."[55] Displays of Kazakh musical culture in Moscow "highlighted the importance of European devices in order to 'properly' express Kazakh music ... [and] promoted the conversion of spontaneous Kazakh instrumental pieces into orchestral movements and operatic endeavours."[56] However, this Europeanization of local musical forms is critiqued today mainly by musicologists and cultural elites, while artists themselves see Soviet cultural policies as helping them to develop their national cultures.[57] In his oral history research, Ali Igmen interviewed artists and educators who expressed

> Strong convictions that Soviet culture helped Kyrgyz shape their own culture in "the modern world." They referred to the cultural and educational differences between their grandparents and themselves; they were grateful to be able to appreciate Western literature and arts; they proudly pointed out that "thanks to the Soviet education system" they were all bilingual or even trilingual.[58]

In order to understand how cultural forms became naturalized while cultural content remains a contested terrain, we need to view the development of Soviet cultural institutions as disciplinary regimes that made colonial hierarchies, and even Soviet practices, undetectable behind a conceptual matrix of development, progress and modernity. Archival research shows that artists, culture administrators and ordinary citizens in early Soviet Central Asia took the civilizing mission of Soviet institutions seriously, seeing them not primarily as a colonial imposition but as a path to modernity.[59] Of course, the historical record of Soviet cultural institutions largely neglects the point of view of those who did not participate in those institutions, so this evidence for the modernization argument must be taken with a grain of salt. Still, the resonance of this appeal to modernization and cultural development only grew as Soviet cultural institutions expanded in the post-war era, spreading the colonial ideology of the Russian elder brother, to be sure, but also creating real opportunities for artists to create authentic syntheses of local and Soviet culture.

During the post-war era, much of the "development" of Central Asian cultures took place through a historical accident, an improvisation, rather than as a direct result of Moscow's policy. During the war, a flood of refugees from the European part of the Soviet Union brought artists to Central Asia, many of whom stayed on and established a variety of cultural institutions which reflected, but were not designed by, Soviet attitudes about nationality and cultural development. The director of the ballet company from Karakalpakistan (an autonomous region within Uzbekistan located on the southern shores of the Aral Sea) talked to me in 1996 about how some of these elite refugees helped found not only the professional dance group that would go on to become the Karakalpak Ballet Theater, but also helped Karakalpaks form the first "national" theaters, as well.[60] Conversations with cultural elites in Central Asia often produce such stories of admiration for the ways that these refugee artists, not the Soviet state *per se*, helped locals to "develop culturally." For those artists who specialized in "European" cultural forms such as ballet, sovereignty means not the rejection of ballet as an alien cultural imposition, but rather the right to be seen as legitimate practitioners of the art, with support from the state and from the international community for the indigenization of ballet that is still, nonetheless, recognized as ballet.[61]

In understanding the epistemic dimension of contemporary cultural sovereignty, we need to understand that the second half of the Soviet period was a time when not just Soviet socialist ideology, but also an ideology of universalism, was a part of the way that institutions of expressive culture developed. During the 1950s and 1960s, there was a shift that resulted not just from Soviet policy, but from external cultural influences that are part of a larger global dynamic related to modernization.[62] Whereas in the 1930s the cultural "progress" of Central Asian nationalities was measured in terms of Europeanization, in the 1960s local cultures came to be appreciated through a modern, rather than an culturally imperialist lens. What I have in mind are things like the showcasing of Tashkent as a global model of industrialization, arts and sport from the late 1950s onwards,[63] the participation of Central Asia's rural, amateur artists in the worldwide folk culture movement,[64] a phenomenon that emerges from a modern sense of reflexivity: one has a folk culture, and it is something not just to be lived, but to be preserved. This reflexive consciousness, what Francois Bourricaud calls the "ethnographic approach" to mankind, is a defining feature of modern societies. It allows us to become culturally relativistic as well as allowing us "to discover the universality of a principle common to all men."[65]

In the 1960s and 1970s, Soviet institutions cemented Central Asians not just to their Soviet identity, but to the ethnic identity that both Soviet and global discourses validated. For example, an Uzbek composer told the story of how his national dance ensemble was formed in 1957 (on the model of the Moscow women's dance ensemble Beriozka) and went on to become recognized as a representative of Uzbek culture in the larger world. "Our government [by which he meant the Uzbek SSR] strongly supported this. And the ensemble became an instant success. We've been all over the world and the reception to this novelty, new national costumes, has been very good."[66] Thus, it is not clear what cultural sovereignty would look like in a nation-state that is trying to participate in a world system structured around universalistic discourses of ethnic cultures, human rights and neo-liberalism. Cultural sovereignty, the freedom to express one's culture free from outside interference is both made possible and paradoxically unrealizable by adopting the epistemology of Bourricaud's "ethnographic approach."

These trends of international influence on Soviet values helps to explain why sovereignty movements in Soviet Central Asia formed first around issues of language and expressive culture, areas where local sovereignty had been granted legitimacy by both Soviet and international institutions. In the 1980s and early 1990s, Central Asians mobilized mainly around issues of language, but also around environmental protection, another internationally legitimated discourse. It is significant that the term mentioned above, *mankurt*, is used in the popular press not just to critique so-called race traitors, but also bureaucrats who cannot think for themselves and ordinary people who fall into groupthink.[67] The critique of Soviet power that emerged in the mid-1980s in Central Asia had an anti-colonial element that confronted Russian cultural imperialism, but it also had an anti-totalitarian element that challenged Soviet policies that wreaked environmental havoc in the name of progress and crushed individual liberty in a hypocritical pursuit of ideological purity. However, these movements were short-lived, their agendas were often co-opted after independence by the former Communist Party elites of their respective countries, and they never developed the kinds of critiques or the forms of social mobilization that made anti-colonial movements elsewhere a force to be reckoned with. The "colonial elite" was handed power, promptly took over the as yet amorphous discourse of the "anti-colonial elite," and set about trying to make sure that the critique evolved no further. Thus, even though the maintenance of Muslim norms and practices in everyday life was one of the main ways that cultural sovereignty was exercised during the Soviet period, the absence of any kind of organized Islamist opposition meant that religion has not yet been able to serve as a discursive resource in critiquing issues of cultural sovereignty today.[68]

This lack of diversity in critique and interpretation is a common problem in environments where there is only one publicly available discourse (in this case, Communist Party ideology), because critique is formed in relation to that dominant discourse. As Mansoor Moaddel has argued, ideologies in pluralistic systems are enriched and diversified through competition with other ideologies, while monolithic systems tend to produce unitary and formulaic discourses because "in attacking a monolithic target, ideological producers often tend to reproduce in a different form an idea system similar to what they are criticizing."[69] Cultural sovereignty takes on a particular meaning therefore in monolithic ideological systems, where even political and economic independence do not have an immediate impact on the new ideology, which is still dependent on, and in opposition to, the old ideology. However, to the extent that there are now multiple "targets of discourse" in Central Asia (Soviet, Islamic and Western liberal ideologies), it is interesting to see the extent to which the same dynamics of "normal development" and "fundamentally alien" are applied to the transformative policies of both the Soviet Union and of international secular and religious actors.

Weighing the Contribution of Post-colonial Theory to the Central Asian Case

Post-colonial theory points out contradictions between the universalizing progress/modernization and the particularizing racist ideologies that legitimate colonial rule. Colonial powers justify their rule through an ideology of universally attainable enlightenment, development or liberty, while at the same time undermining the universal applicability of their ideology by institutionalizing categories of essential difference between colonizer and colonized such as race or ethnicity. So although programs designed to promote enlightenment and cultural development in early Soviet Kyrgyzstan were aimed at helping the "idle" and "backward" Central Asians,[70] the reification of the Central Asian "other" meant that cultural difference could always be invoked to explain the failure of the universal principle.

But did it fail in the Soviet case? The justifying ideology of the state in the Soviet case was not liberalism and enlightenment, as it was in the case of European empires where colonial subjugation put the lie to the center's ideology of liberty, for example. The justifying ideology of the Soviet state was socialism and its own form of enlightenment that would produce *homo Sovieticus*. However, Russia, too, was "backward," according to the Bolsheviks. Russians, too, had to transform themselves into new Soviet men.[71] What are the implications of this difference between the Soviet Union and European empires?

Homi Bhabha argues that the irresolvable contradiction between universal principles and racist ideology is produced by the colonizer's ambivalence over the success of the civilizing mission, by the fear that that racial inferiority will disappear and so will the justification for segregation and racial dominance; mimicry must always also produce its slippage.[72] So what was the slippage between the ideology and the realities of subjugation in the Soviet case? Did the Turkmen or Tajik mimicry of Russian culture create ambivalence on the part of Russians in power, which then led them to create institutions that perpetuated national differences? We don't really have evidence of this. Or did the ambivalence work the other way, perhaps, with the colonized striving to mitigate their own anxieties about assimilation by reifying the nationality principle? This seems more likely. In Central Asia, nationality was an organizing principle that may have been imposed initially but was subsequently reproduced locally.

Or was there no slippage necessary because there really was a "new Soviet (not just Russian) man?" There are elements of truth to this, but the marker of nationality remained too vivid to discount. However, there is an important distinction between European and American racism and Soviet calls for eradicating backwardness, and that is precisely the idea that the line of racial difference can and should be crossed. Soviet ideology in different eras emphasized that non-Russian peoples were different from, and often less than, Russians, but all peoples (from "backward" Russian peasants to "primitive" Kazakh nomads) could advance and participate in the building of socialism. Because there was no clear racial barrier, anyone on the Soviet periphery could contribute to the creation of Soviet culture, giving non-Russian peoples a stake in the Soviet social and political system. The Minister of Culture in the opening anecdote ruined the opera's production probably because he feared the reaction of his superiors should the forbidden Timur appear even tangentially in a performance he authorized. But this doesn't mean that all the others involved in the discussion were similarly driven by pure relations of domination. The fact that there was a vivid debate showed that these Uzbeks were invested and involved in their work not because they were commanded to be, or as a purely aesthetic exercise, but as part of their own elaboration and enhancement of Soviet Uzbek culture.

Precisely because the Soviet project was not primarily one of imperial domination, the contradictions of Soviet ideology were not as productive of resistance as they were in other empires. Few Central Asians aspired to become Russian, but many considered themselves Soviet and for them, the ambivalence produced by the "Russian elder brother" version of *homo Sovieticus* was expressed through their creative reproduction of nationality within the framework of Soviet culture. The protection of Chatterjee's "inner realm" of culture was not just a defensive move against Russian cultural imperialism, but rather a proactive and strategic choice to incorporate difference into Soviet culture. The Soviet man was a myth, but Soviet culture was a real and meaningful project that did not simply colonize its Central Asian subjects, but was produced by them. This creativity did not negate the reality that in some eras, Moscow's justifying ideology imposed an explicit rule of colonial difference via the elder brother discourse, and it did not subvert the historical materialist and eurocentric hierarchies of culture that denigrated Central Asian values and practices.

These Soviet legacies were the ones most productive of anti-colonial resistance, then and now. However, the reproduction of difference within Soviet culture also means that we must not view Central Asian cultural sovereignty only through the lens of post-colonialism.

Notes

1. Research presented in this chapter was supported by the International Research & Exchanges Board (IREX) with funds from the National Endowment for the Humanities, the US Department of State (Title VIII), and the US Information Agency. I would like to thank Sally Cummings, Ray Hinnebusch, Fred Lawson and Morten Valbjørn for their critical feedback.
2. O'zbekiston Markazi Davlat Arxivi (Central State Archive of Uzbekistan), f 2487 r. 3 y. 1974.
3. O'zbekiston Markazi Davlat Arxivi, f 2487 r. 3 y. 1974.
4. Adams, "Invention, institutionalization, and renewal."
5. Singel, "Cultural sovereignty and transplanted law."
6. Winegar, "Cultural sovereignty in a global art economy," p. 198.
7. El-Shibiny, *The Threat of Globalization to Arab Islamic Culture*; Singel, "Cultural sovereignty and transplanted law"; Winegar, "Cultural sovereignty in a global art economy."
8. Winegar, "Cultural sovereignty in a global art economy."
9. Hirsch, *Empire of Nations*, p. 145; Martin, *Affirmative Action Empire*; Suny and Martin (eds), *A State of Nations*.
10. Michaels, *Curative Powers*; Northrop, *Veiled Empire*; Suny, "The empire strikes out."
11. Martin, *Affirmative Action Empire*; Martin, "An affirmative action empire"; Slezkine, "Imperialism as the highest stage of socialism."
12. Khalid, "Backwardness and the quest for civilization," p. 232.
13. Kamp, *The New Woman in Uzbekistan*.
14. Kamp, *The New Woman in Uzbekistan*, p. 13.
15. Igmen, "Building Soviet Central Asia"; Rouland, "Music and the making of the Kazak nation," pp. 358–60.
16. Edgar, "Bolshevism, patriarchy, and the nation."
17. Edgar, "Bolshevism, patriarchy, and the nation," p. 269.
18. Adams, "Modernity, postcolonialism and theatrical form in Uzbekistan"; Adams, *The Spectacular State*, pp. 105–10; Beissinger, "Soviet empire as 'family resemblance'"; Beissinger, "The persistence of empire in Eurasia"; Dave, *Kazakhstan*, ch. 1.
19. Beissinger, "Soviet empire as 'family resemblance,'" p. 302.
20. Chatterjee, *The Nation and Its Fragments*, p. 33.
21. I know the case of Uzbekistan the best, having spent more than 15 months doing research there since 1995. I have spent nearly three months in Kyrgyzstan since 2003 and visited Kazakhstan for a month in 2008.

22. Adams, *The Spectacular State*.
23. Loring, "Building socialism in Kyrgyzstan."
24. Keller, *To Moscow, not Mecca*; Khalid, *Islam After Communism*.
25. Kamp, *The New Woman in Uzbekistan*; Northrop, *Veiled Empire*; Massell, *The Surrogate Proletariat*.
26. Payne, "The forge of the Kazakh proletariat."
27. Khalid, *The Politics of Muslim Cultural Reform*.
28. Keller, "Story, time and dependent nationhood in the Uzbek history curriculum," pp. 266–7.
29. Martin, "An affirmative action empire," pp. 80–2.
30. E.g., Poliakov, *Everyday Islam*.
31. Benjamin Loring, personal communication, March 1, 2010.
32. Dave, *Kazakhstan*, ch. 3.
33. Keller, "Going to school in Uzbekistan," pp. 248–65; Denison, "The art of the impossible."
34. Northrop, *Veiled Empire*.
35. Kamp, *The New Woman in Uzbekistan*; Keller, *To Moscow, not Mecca*; Keller, "Going to school in Uzbekistan."
36. Kamp, *The New Woman in Uzbekistan*; Keller, *To Moscow, not Mecca*.
37. Stronski, *Tashkent*.
38. Anderson, *Imagined Communities*.
39. Harris, *Control and Subversion*; Kamp, "Between women and the state," pp. 52–3.
40. Valbjørn, this volume.
41. Kamp, "Between women and the state."
42. Kamp, "Between women and the state," p. 52.
43. Abduazimho'ja Sherzodho'ja o'g'li, *Xalq So'zi*, December 16, 2003, translated as "Vernost' Natsional'nomu Dukhu" on http://www.tribune-uz.info/society/index.php?id1=427, accessed September 3, 2004.
44. Said, *Orientalism* (and others in this volume).
45. Lewis, this volume and Atkin, this volume.
46. Interview (paraphrased), Tashkent, Uzbekistan, September 12, 1996.
47. Field notes, Karaganda, Kazakhstan, July 2, 2008.
48. Adams, "Tashkent museum."
49. Dave, *Kazakhstan*.
50. Qualin, "Searching for the self"; Ram, "Imagining Eurasia."
51. El-Shibiny, *The Threat of Globalization*; Singel, "Cultural sovereignty and transplanted law"; Winegar, "Cultural sovereignty in a global art economy."
52. Interview (paraphrased), Tashkent, Uzbekistan, October 28, 1996.
53. For a discussion of how this balance of form and content was accomplished in Kyrgyz Soviet film, see Cummings, "Soviet rule, nation and film."
54. Adams, "Modernity, postcolonialism and theatrical form in Uzbekistan."
55. Djumaev, "Power structures"; Igmen, *Building Soviet Central Asia*;

Rouland, *Music and the making of the Kazak nation*; Tomoff, "Uzbek music's separate path."

56. Rouland, *Music and the making of the Kazak nation*, p. 375.
57. Adams, "Modernity, postcolonialism and theatrical form in Uzbekistan."
58. Igmen, *Building Soviet Central Asia*, p. 145.
59. Igmen, *Building Soviet Central Asia*.
60. Field notes, Tashkent, Uzbekistan, August 24, 1996.
61. Adams, "Modernity, postcolonialism and theatrical form in Uzbekistan."
62. Bourricaud, "Modernity"; Giddens, *The Consequences of Modernity*; Robertson, "Glocalization."
63. Stronski, *Tashkent*, ch. 8.
64. Adams, "Globalization, universalism and cultural form."
65. Bourricaud, "Modernity," p.16.
66. Interview (paraphrase), Tashkent, Uzbekistan, May 16, 1996.
67. Ciaramella, "A linguistic analysis of the term mankurt."
68. Volpi, this volume.
69. Moaddel, "Conditions for ideological production," p. 675.
70. Igmen, *Building Soviet Central Asia*, p. 7.
71. Slezkine, "Imperialism as the highest stage of socialism'; Stronski, *Tashkent*, ch. 2.
72. Bhabha, *The Location of Culture*.

11

Culture in the Middle East: The "Western Question" and the Sovereignty of Post-imperial States in the Middle East

Morten Valbjørn

The "Western Question"

> To those living in the Middle East the Eastern Question became a "Western Question" – how to deal with intrusive Europe while coping with the ever-present perils and prospect within the region itself . . . should we Middle Easterners seek to gain needed strength by adopting Western ways that have produced powerful states in Europe and North America? Or does our salvation lie in resisting alien ways and returning to our own religious and cultural heritage? . . . Should we rally around the existing states ruling over us? Or should we seek a new political community with either different borders or different organisational principles (if not both). If so, should that new state be based on religion, ethnicity, or language?[1]

In the broader discussion of this volume on "sovereignty after empire," this chapter turns attention to the impacts of imperialism on the Middle East as they are related to culture. While references both to culture and an imperial(ist) legacy frequently appear in discussions on the Middle East, both terms are also highly contested. Culture may refer to a "bar" dividing humanity or a "bond" uniting it, so that instead of speaking of a "world of cultures" we should refer to a (emerging) "World Culture" in the singular.[2] Similarly, an "imperial legacy" may refer to the impact of European imperialism or the influence of successive Islamic empires.

This diversity of meanings is also reflected in the Western academic literature on the contested nature of the post-imperial states and the salience of the sovereignty institution in the Middle East. In simplified terms, three positions can be identified.[3] According to a "vanguard" position,[4] the twentieth century is marked by the "expansion of international society."[5] At the time of decolonization the European territorial-state had become the "compulsory model" for any polity aspiring to independence, and today the Westphalian state system has gained global reach and is universal. Hence, it is assumed that "the West is what the Middle East seeks to become,"[6] as reflected in Fouad Ajami's obituary for Arab nationalism, in which he prophesied the emergence of fully sovereign states within a "normal state-system," where transnational forces would not play any role.[7] This is rejected from an "exceptionalist" position, which argues that the formal globalization of the (Western) Westphalian state system has neither brought real homogenization nor given rise to some all- human "World Culture." On the contrary, the lack of legitimacy among these "imported states"[8] has only caused a return to what is perceived as pre-modern traditional sub- and supra-national solidarities, leaving us with "a [global] plurality of diverse political systems, each an outgrowth of culture-specific concepts."[9] In the Middle East, the very logic of sovereign territorial-states is thus supposed to be incompatible with the prevalent political thoughts of the region.[10] The apparently modern Middle East states established in the context of European imperialism are from this perspective nothing but "tribes with flags" or "external, formal, legal skeletons," whose relations are less defined by notions about territory or sovereignty than non-territorially bound ancient identities and rivalries between sects (e.g., Shia/Sunni), religions (Islam/Christianity/Judaism), dynasties (Hashemite/Sa'ud) or ethnic groups (Arabs/Kurds/Persians).[11] In between these two extremes one finds a "syncretist" position.[12] While acknowledging that the European state model has become "the compulsory model" for establishing new political units worldwide,[13] these new post-colonial states are only considered as "like but not same as" their European predecessors. Hence, Middle East states are only "modern but not Western."[14] In terms of organization, administration and rule they are modern and, moreover, real, relevant and "here to stay."[15] As "late-comers" having a different relationship with their populations and born in a different era and in another regional and global context it is, however, neither anticipated that they will follow the same pattern of state formation nor that the resulting states or regional society of states will be identical to the European model.[16] This is also reflected in the sovereignty institution, which due to state–society incongruence is expected to be marked with ambiguity and a low salience.[17]

One strategy to explore the cultural dimension of how an imperial legacy has impacted the salience of sovereignty among Middle Eastern states would be to go further into this *Western* debate between these three positions. Instead, attention in this chapter will be directed to how these issues have been discussed *within the Middle East*. Thus, the bulk of the chapter is devoted to the still ongoing debate about the so-called "Western

Question,"[18] which emerged in the context of the fragmentation and ultimate collapse of Islamic empires and the parallel growing influence of
imperial Western powers. This is done through an examination of how
the questions about "what went wrong," "where should we now be going"
and whether the West should be perceived as a "promise," a "peril" or
just as an "example" have been answered in this Middle Eastern debate.
Besides showing how the views on culture and imperialism have been no
less contested in a Middle Eastern context, where positions equivalent to
the aforementioned three Western ideal types can be identified, the ways
these questions have been answered are relevant to discussions about the
salience of sovereignty among the post-imperial states in the Middle East.
Thus, following Barry Buzan, a state can be conceptualized as consisting not only of material capabilities and institutions but also of ideas.[19]
While being the most abstract of the three components, the latter is, Buzan
argues, also the most central.[20] Thus, it is "the idea of the state that both
provides the major bindings holding the territorial–polity–society package
together and defines much of its character and power as an actor in the
international system."[21] It is, moreover, so that

> unless the idea of the state is firmly planted in the minds of the population,
> the state as a whole has no secure foundation. Equally, unless the idea of the
> state is firmly planted in the "minds" of other states, the state has no secure
> environment.[22]

Against this background, it becomes crucial for a discussion of the
post-imperial state and the salience of sovereignty in the Middle East to
examine whether and how this "idea of the state" has been contested in the
Middle East, and the "Western Question" debate provides a perfect tool
for doing this. Thus, as L. C. Brown reminds us in the opening vignette,
the varying ways in which the "Western Question" has been addressed
are closely related to different views about the optimal organizational
principle for the region, how borders should be drawn, whether the object
of loyalty and identification should be existing polities or new political
communities and finally to what extent these polities should be based on
ethnicity, religion or language.

What Went Wrong and Where Should We Now Be Going?

In parts of the Western post-9/11 debate one can easily get the impression that the question "what went wrong" in the Middle East has only
been asked quite recently and by "elderly British gentlemen" rather than
people in the region, as Karen Elliott House stated in her laudatory review

of Bernard Lewis' *What Went Wrong? The Clash between Islam and Modernity*.[23] This is, however, far from the case. On the contrary, this very question constitutes one of the prominent themes within the regional debate since at least 1798, when Napoleon defeated the Mamluks outside Cairo.[24] Although the French adventure was short-lived, it was, as the first modern major incursion of a European power into the Middle East heartland, a landmark event. It symbolized the shift in the balance of power between the northern and southern shores of the Mediterranean not only in military, but also in economic, scientific and intellectual terms.[25] In a European context this triggered a debate on the so-called "Eastern Question": how should the European states orchestrate a dismembering of the Ottoman – and the Persian Qajar – Empire without upsetting the European balance of power?[26] To those living in the Middle East it instead set off a process of soul-searching in terms of the aforementioned "Western Question" debate. Basically, this was a debate partly about why the region had lost its former dynamism and strength as reflected in the shift in the balance of power with Europe, and how the region should regain its former glory. In simplifying terms it is possible to make a distinction between three ideal-typical positions in the debate *in* the Middle East corresponding roughly with those previously identified in the Western academic debate *on* the Middle East.

The West as a Peril: "Forward-to-the-Past"

The first of these ideal-typical positions attributes the problems of the region to the growing foreign influence and a blind mimicking of the West by the Middle Eastern elites. This has led the region away from the "straight path" outlined by God, resulting in the degeneration of its own culture. Thus, it is no coincidence that it was before the region was corrupted by these foreign influences that the Middle East, during the reign of Prophet Muhammad and the first caliphates, experienced a "golden age." At that time, the balance of power with Europe had favored successful Middle Eastern empires. The answer to the question of "where should we now be going" is, against this background, straightforward: in order to revive this glorious past one must purify the region from all the pernicious foreign influences and return to the original and uncorrupted form of society.

One of the most well known and clearest exponents of this "forward-to-the-past" position is the Wahhabist movement, whose puritan and orthodox interpretation of Islam stems from the doctrine that Muhammed ibn Abd al-Wahhab advocated during the eighteenth century in parts of the

Arabian Peninsula. Based on a narrow interpretation of the unity of God (*tawhid*) and a literal approach to the Qur'an and the *hadith* considered as the only legitimate sources for guidance, he and his followers called for a purification of Islam from what they saw as illicit innovation (*bidah*) and foreign influences, so that Muslims could return to an original Islamic order as existed at the time of the Prophet Muhammad.[27] During Islamic history it is possible to identify a range of figures and movements – sometimes disagreeing in most other regards – calling for a return to some form of "original uncorrupted Islam," including the Kharijites' critique of ͨAli and the Kadizadeler ͨ*ulama*'s campaign in the seventeenth century against foreign influence and the moral laxity of the Ottoman elite. More recently, this position can be found in the Wahhabi-inspired part of the salafist movement, which, particularly since the 1970s, has gained ground in large parts of the Middle East. Their struggle to "command what is proper and forbid what is reprehensible" can be pursued through peaceful missionary activism or violence, but common to quietist- and jihadi-salafism is a rejection of political concepts about democracy and nationalism and participation in elections or the establishment of political parties, which all are perceived as Western and un-Islamic.[28] In addition to these examples, which stress how the restoration of an "original" Islam should take place through a strict and literal adherence of Islamic law, another more mystical way to an original Islam without temporal decadence and foreign influence can be found in various Sufi movements, including the eighteenth- to nineteenth-century Libyan Sanusi order and the Sudanese Mahdi movement, which at the end of the nineteenth century led a revolt against the British.[29]

Against this background, it may be tempting to agree with the so-called "exceptionalist" position in the aforementioned Western academic debate, according to which the Middle East is resistant to reform, anti-Western and marked by a backward-oriented longing for the restoration of some long gone political order. Although it is necessary to acknowledge the existence of this forward-to-the-past position, this does not, however, mean that it is the only or most prominent position in the Middle Eastern "Western Question" debate.

The West as a Promise: "The West is What the Middle East Seeks to Become"

The remark by Daniel Lerner, a leading American modernization theorist that "the West is what the Middle East seeks to become,"[30] also fits well with the second ideal-typical Middle East positions on the "Western question." The weakness and decline of the Middle East is attributed to the region's own blind adherence to a frozen tradition, which is not able to provide solutions to the challenges faced by modern(izing) societies. To regain its former strength the legacy of an obsolete past must therefore be abandoned. Instead, attention should be turned to the organization of Western societies, which to some proponents of this position "not only represented a technical model but also a moral ideal."[31]

This growing attention to the West was in the beginning often based on the narrow and instrumental principle of "using the enemies' trick to overcome them." In an attempt to counter the growing European threat, Selim III, for example, tried at the turn of the eighteenth century to reform the Ottoman military according to French principles.[32] During the nineteenth century it is, however, also possible to identify an attitude where the West is perceived as "less of a threat than a promise,"[33] as Rifa al-Tahtawi concluded after a stay in Paris where he translated into Arabic European classics by Rousseau, Voltaire and Montesquieu in order to "awaken the peoples of Islam – both Arabs and non-Arabs – from the sleep of indifference." Al-Tahtawi's visit was part of an ambitious Western-inspired reform program of the Egyptian ruler, Muhammad Ali, who in the first half of the nineteenth century challenged the suzerainty of the Ottoman Empire in an attempt to turn Egypt into an independent power. In parallel with this development, Istanbul had, with the Gülhane edict in 1839, launched its own series of reforms. These were further radicalized by another edict in 1856, which was almost cleared of any honorific references to Islamic law (*shari^{c}a*) or the glorious tradition of the empire.[34] During this *Tanzimat* era, religious institutions as well as the Janissaries were challenged through the establishment of state-supported and European inspired modern counterparts, including a military re-organized according to European principles, new secular schools, a centralized bureaucracy, fiscal and land reforms, new European-inspired legal codes and courts – all resting on the overall idea "of Europe as the exemplar of modern civilisation and of the Ottoman Empire as its partner."[35]

In the twentieth century even more radical versions of this contempt for the past and unrestrained fascination for the West can be identified. The most obvious example is the Kemalist reforms carried out in the decades following the Ottoman collapse. According to the Turkish president Mustafa Kemal, or Atatürk, Western civilization was the only universal civilization and to secure the independence of the young Turkish republic it was necessary to "catch up with and become part of this civilization." This meant a full-scale Westernization of the Turkish way of life. Changes in political, legal and economic institutions also signified a cultural break from the Ottoman past, notably in the abolition of the caliphate, the relocation of the capital from Istanbul to Ankara, the introduction of the European calendar, changing the alphabet from Arabic to Latin letters and the imposition of a dress code, where the fez and the veil were banned. A similar ambition was found in Iran, where, in the 1920s, Hasan Taqizadeh concluded that Iran had "to be Europeanized in appearance and in reality, body and soul, that's all."[36] Although Reza Shah was not as successful in curbing the ᶜulama as his Turkish counterpart, his reform program was in a comparable way based on the idea that "the West is what Iran should become."

The West as an Example: "A Middle East Like but not Same as the West"

In addition to these two answers to the question about "what went wrong" and suggestions as to "where should we now be going," the "Western Question" debate offers a third ideal-typical position which has some resemblance to the "syncretic" position in the Western academic debate. Instead of being perceived either as a promise or a threat, the West is "thought [of] as an example, but not as a goal"[37] for a Middle East, which should be "like but not same as" the West. A need for change and renewal is recognized, but modernization should not be identical to Westernization. Instead of blind mimicry, the Middle East must turn to its own history and culture to find the principles on which a reform strategy for a revitalized "modern but not Western" Middle East can be based. In reality, this vision of some kind of "indigenous" modernization does not, however, imply a full rejection of all forms of Western influence. A selective import of Western technology and science is welcomed as necessary for the renewal of Middle Eastern societies. Based on a distinction between "civilization" (*medeniyet*) – in the material sense of technology and science – and "culture" (*hars*) – referring to morals and values – Zia Gökalp, for example, argued that he was "of Turkish nationality, of Muslim religion, and of Western civilization."[38] This "culture–civilization" distinction and the references to "nationality" reveal another important but implicit form of Western influence. Thus, the distinction between modernization and Westernization, the reference to Middle Eastern culture(s) different from but equal to Western culture, and the argument about how Middle Eastern people belong to different nations entitled to a particular piece of land, self-determination and independence – all of these statements bear witness to the influence of ideas and notions from various Western intellectual currents and debates. Put differently, the various claims about the non-Western nature of the Middle East are expressed in a language and rest on ideas clearly influenced by the very same West. Although the most prominent in the Middle Eastern "Western Question" debate, this third and more syncretistic position is also marked by a huge internal diversity.

Besides different views on the precise mix between Western "civilization" and Middle Eastern "culture," this diversity is also related to differences about the exact nature of the supposed "indigenous" culture on which the distinct principles for a revived "modern but not Western" Middle East should be based. The Islamic Modernist movement in its various disguises represents one variant. What is considered as an obsolete *ulama* is rejected, but without embracing the secularism of the Western model.[39] Instead, the aim is to "marry Islam with modernity" based on the claim that Islam consists of some essential doctrines with universal validity as well as social teaching and laws, which are specific applications of these general principles to particular circumstances.[40] When the latter change so must the laws and customs, and in doing so the Middle East should, according to the Islamic modernists, apply the example of the "pious ancestors" of Islam (*as-salaf al-salih*) to the contemporary context through *ijtihad*. Along with Muhammed Abdou, who at the end of the nineteenth century formulated these ideas about essential and contextual elements of Islam, Jamal al-din al-Afghani constitutes another famous figure in this attempt to promote a rebirth (*nahda*) of strong and dynamic Muslim societies through a distinctly *Islamic* modernization. Inspired by European nationalism, Al-Afghani's pan-Islam saw all Muslims regardless of ethnic and linguistic differences as part of the same nation to be united as a way of countering European imperialism and reviving the Muslim community (*ummah*).[41] During the second half of the nineteenth century these overall ideas about marrying Islam and modernity appeared in different kinds of political projects for the revival of the decaying Ottoman Empire, such as Sultan Abdülhamid II's attempt to promote material modernization of the empire while legitimizing it through an Islamic revival; indeed, he promoted the empire as a modernized version of the caliphate.[42] Symptomatic of this was Abdülhamid's building of the famous Hijaz railway (the symbol of modernity) connecting Damascus and Medina as a way of making it easier for Muslims to perform the holy Muslim duty of *hajj*. A more liberal version is represented by Young Ottomans such as Namik Kemal, who wanted to save the Ottoman Empire by means of Ottoman identity and liberal constitutional democracy. The Young Ottoman's use of Islamic notions of *umma*, *ijma* and *ijtihad* as equivalents to Western liberal ideas about the nation, a social contract and parliamentary legislation[43] was also found in an Iranian context, where

Mirza Malkom Khan argued that "whatever good laws the European have they have taken from the sacred books of Islam."[44] This attempt to marry Islam and modernity can also be seen in the Muslim Brotherhood, which has, since its foundation in Egypt in 1928, worked to Islamize modernity within the context of the modern nation-state through, in different periods, missionary, political, social and violent activism.[45] In Iran, Jalal Al-e Ahmad tried in the 1960s to "reimagine modernity in accordance with Iranian-Islamic tradition, symbolism and identities" based on a critique of the "Westoxification" (*gharbzadegi*) of society.[46] Despite the popular depictions of the Islamic Republic of Iran as anti-modern and a "return to the Middle Ages," this ambition can also be found in the Shi^cite Islamism of Khomeini as reflected in the famous slogan "neither East nor West, but Islamic republic," which is closer to Islamic modernism than a "forward-to-the-past" vision.[47]

It is, however, also possible to identify a number of other variants of this third influential position on the Middle Eastern "Western Question" debate. These are marked by different views on who "we" are when answering the question "where should we now be going." Contrary to al-Afghani's idea about Muslims constituting one single nation, others have placed more emphasis on ethnicity, language or history as the key cultural ingredients of a "modern but not Western" Middle East. At the turn of the twentieth century the Young Turks, for example, tried to transform the crumbling multi-ethnic Islamic Ottoman Empire into a modern and strong secular Turkish empire and through this become "the Japan of the Near East," that is, to modernize without losing cultural distinctiveness.[48] In 1920s' Egypt there arose a distinct Egyptian nationalism calling for Egyptian independence and self-determination based on a claim about the existence of a distinct Egyptian nation. "We Egyptians," Ahmed Lufti al-Sayyid argued, "must hold fast to our Egyptianness and must not profess allegiance to any other fatherland than the Egypt from which we originate."[49] This Egyptian fatherland was neither Islamic nor Arab, as its roots could be traced all the way back to the Pharaohs, who had become an object of huge interest after the discovery in 1922 of the tomb of Tut-Ankh-Amon.[50] While not necessarily rejecting Islam as such, in the view of al-Sayyid – as well as Ali ^cAbd al-Raziq – religion belonged in the private sphere and should not constitute the basis for national identity or politics: "Religion is for God, the Fatherland is for Everyone" as the famous slogan from the 1919 revolt by the *Wafd* party goes.

Against such state-specific identities (*al-wataniyya*), Arab national-ism (*al-qaumiyya*), inspired by German nationalist thinkers such as J. G. Herder and J. G. Fichte, saw the common Arabic language as the basis of nationhood.[51] According to Sati al-Husri "every Arabic-speaking people is an Arab . . . he is an Arab regardless of his own wishes."[52] This emphasis on a distinct Arabness is reflected in the way, on the one hand, he criticized figures such as the Egyptian Taha Hussein for an unreserved fascination and acceptance of Europe, leading to what al-Husri saw as an unacceptable passive-imitative acculturation.[53] On the other hand, he also rejected various more state-specific nationalisms (*al-wataniyya*), such as the existence of a distinct Egyptian nation, while also maintaining that if (Muslim) Arabs ceased to be Muslims, they would still be Arabs.[54] Despite claims that Arab nationalism "was born in the arid desert of Arabia in the seventh century,"[55] its origins can in fact be traced to the late nineteenth century[56] where it embodies the idea that special bond exists between Arabic-speaking peoples, who are assumed to belong to the same distinct Arab nation once united but later divided by foreign powers.[57] This general notion found different expressions during the twentieth century when it came to the specific interpretation of belonging to one Arab nation.[58] The ultimate goal of "pan-Arabists" is the territorial unification of what are considered to be artificial Arab territorial-states into a "true" Arab nation-state, and until then the "*raison de la nation Arabe*," that is, that common Arab interests and security concerns, should always take precedence over a narrow "*raison d'état*."[59] To "cultural Arabists," the Arab world is a cultural space in the sense that Arabs feel a degree of cultural proximity and share common habits and customs, but without implying any substantial political commitments or obligations. In between these two extremes one finds the "political Arabists."[60] They perceive the Arab world as an international society, where Arabs living in different states are linked by special bonds. Arab politics should reflect this reality and accordingly should be informed not only by a narrow state self-interest, but should also comply with a number of distinct Arab norms, rules and values including certain obligations and a commitment to solidarity among Arabs.[61]

The "Western Question" and the (varying) Salience of Sovereignty among Post-imperial States in the Middle East

Recalling Buzan's argument that the state will lack a secure foundation and environment if "the idea of the state" is not planted in the "minds" of the population and other states, an examination of the "Western Question" provides us with a number of insights on how imperial legacies have impacted the salience of sovereignty among the post-imperial states in the Middle East.

On the one hand, it appears that the European territorial-state and the Westphalian state system have been much more contested in the Middle East than is assumed by the "vanguard" position; yet, despite calls for going "forward-to-the-past," this does not mean that the very logic of sovereign territorial-states is completely incompatible with political thought in the region as claimed by the Western "exceptionalist" position. Thus, in the regional debate it is also possible to identify positions which want to combine Western "civilization" with some allegedly indigenous regional "culture" as a way of revitalizing a Middle East that is "modern but not Western." Instead of perceiving the Middle East as marked by a clash between, on the one side, Western modernity and the Westphalian state and, on the other side, some pre-modern Middle Eastern tradition and ancient supra-/sub-national identities – as the case (sometimes) has been in the Western academic and popular debate – the defining feature of the regional debate appears, instead, to be the existence of parallel but contending novel visions about "where should we now be going" partly responding to and partly inspired by the growing Western influence since (at least) the late eighteenth century.[62]

At the same time, however, it is necessary also to pay attention to how the importance and strength of the various regional visions of "where should we now be going" vary across time and space. As for the *variance in time*, it thus appears that the nature of the debate on the aspired-to form of organizational principle for the region changed in the 1920s. Before that time, and in particular at the turn of the century, it is possible to identify a huge variety of suggestions on this issue. Some wanted to revive the caliphate institution either within the context of the Ottoman Empire (e.g., Abdülhamid II), in the form of a new Arab caliphate (e.g., Sharif Hussein's declaration of himself as caliph in 1916)[63] or as a kind of supra-national moral leadership within a state system quite similar to the Catholic papacy model (e.g., Rashid Rida).[64] Others wanted instead an imperial organization based on a liberal-constitutional form of Ottomanism, or around some form of pan-Islamic nationalism (e.g., Afghani) or in the form of a secular Turkish empire (e.g., the Young Turks). Still others called for the organization of the region into smaller territorial-states (e.g., Egyptian nationalism and other forms of *wataniyya* nationalism) or into a larger Arab nation-state, where Arabic-speakers live under a secular constitutional regime (e.g., the pan-Arabism of Negib Azoury).[65]

Although al-Raziq's debunking of the caliphate institution turned into a huge controversy in the mid-1920s, with various attempts at countering his argument that the caliphate was without any Qur'anic foundation,[66] this row did in many ways mark the end of the caliphate debate. Except for marginal voices, such as the call for the restoration of the caliphate institution by Hizb-ut Tahrir which has been much weaker in the Middle East than Central Asia, few have since then espoused a revival of the caliphate. As for the various forms of imperial organization, this option was in reality rendered mute with the collapse of the Ottoman Empire. Thus, the real controversy regarding "where should we now be going" has, since Atatürk's abolition of the sultan and caliphate institution in 1924 and the post-Ottoman re-organization of the region as a (proto) state-system, been less about the state institution as such, which to a large extent has been accepted as the "compulsory model" for political units today. This does not, however, imply agreement on what kind of state and for whom. The important controversies in the twentieth century were about whether one should rally around the existing territorial-states or work for the establishment of new ones with different borders, and over what purpose and nature this state should have, which is a question related to the key issue in the "Western Question" debate on whether the West should be perceived as a peril, promise or just as an example.

In order to grasp the complexity of this controversy, it is useful also to turn attention to the *variance in space* as the relative importance and urgency of these two issues vary across the region. In the non-Arab parts of the Middle East the controversy has less been about the "we" than the "where" in the question "where should we now be going." Thus, Turkey and Iran have a long history as separate imperial centers and have been quite successful in constructing modern nations around their dominant ethno-linguistic cores, although an unfinished task exists of integrating a multitude of minorities, including the Kurds.[67] Although Israel does not have a similar history, it is nevertheless also marked with quite a strong fit between state and nationhood with the exception of the Arab minority. Here the controversial issue has been over whether Israel should be a distinct religious Jewish state or a secular state for the Jewish people just like any other. In a similar way, a key controversy in Turkey and Iran has been about whether one should strive for a model in which modernization is identical to Westernization – as in the Kemalist and Pahlavi eras – or if one should seek to combine Western "civilization" with some indigenous "culture" resulting in a "modern but not Western" Turkey or Iran. This is most clearly the case for the Islamic Republic of Iran, but the AKP's synthesis of Islam, capitalism and political reforms in Turkey can also be interpreted in this way.[68]

In the Arab world also, "where" has been contested. This is reflected in the variety of state models ranging from traditional monarchies, where tribal chiefs-turned-state elites have sought legitimacy through traditional versions of Islam or the manipulation of tribal and kinship links, to secular revolutionary republics combining a distinct form of nationalism and socialist modernization in their praetorian form of rule, and in between these one also finds the Libyan "state of the masses," *jamahiriya*, and the Lebanese consociational model based on confessionalism.[69] However, in contrast to the non-Arab Middle East, the "we" has been even more contested. Thus, in addition to various sub-state communities the state identity has also been challenged by supra-national claims advanced by Arab nationalists arguing that the interests of the Arab nation should take precedence over what is presented as artificial territorial-states made by European imperial powers.[70] This does not mean that identification with the territorial-state has been completely absent or insignificant. But owing to a much weaker fit between territory and identity, it has been far less obvious what kind of political community and identification should take precedence. This is also reflected in the way and degree to which the "idea of the state" has been planted in the "minds" of the population and among other Arab states. As for the internal state–society dimension, Shibley Telhami and Michael Barnett have argued that state-building can be per-ceived as a social engineering exercise intended to generate the very state–nation conflation simply assumed in the Westphalian nation-state model. They point out that while "other Third world leaders have attempted to fill up the state with a national identity derived from sub-national particles," for example, Persian in the Iranian case, "Arab leaders have attempted to shrink the national imagery from its transnational status to the confines of the state."[71] This has been paralleled by a long tradition among Arab leaders of seeking domestic legitimacy by presenting themselves as being in the service of a higher "Arab cause" at the regional level, which at the same time has undermined their attempts to shape a better territory–identity fit.[72] As for the external state–state dimension, it may come as a surprise as why all the Arab nationalist rhetoric about Arab unity and the illegitimacy of the existing territorial-states has not led to significant border changes and even less to any permanent unions between Arab states; the merger between Syria and Egypt in the United Arab Republic, for example, only lasted from 1958 to 1961. This does not, however, mean that the contested nature of the "we" has been without impact on the rela-tions between Arab states. During the twentieth century the conflicting behavioral expectations associated with a status of being, respectively, Arab and sovereign[73] paved the road for a distinct form of inter-Arab rivalry. Aspiring Arab powers have tried to meddle in the domestic poli-tics of other Arab states based on claims of acting on a mandate from the entire Arab nation, as reflected in an almost "habitual willingness to act across international borders that seems unparalleled elsewhere in the non-European world."[74] Contrary to the Arab–non-Arab conflicts, such as the Arab–Israeli conflicts and the Iran–Iraq War,[75] this rivalry has however seldom evolved into "hot" militarized warfare. Instead, it has taken the form of a dueling with Arab symbols, where the purpose has been to monopolize the meaning of being Arab, while discrediting rivals as acting at variance with the Arab cause. In this distinctly Arab kind of rivalry that has taken place in a complex interplay between regional and domestic theaters, "soft power" derived from ideological appeal and from being perceived as protecting the Arab interest has often constituted a much more important commodity than "hard" military power.[76]

While it is important to pay attention to the features that place the Arab world apart not only from an European model of statehood, but also from other parts of the Middle East, it is at the same time also necessary to pay attention to how the importance of this supra-national challenge compared with other identities has varied across time and space. Based on the observation that multiple levels of identity co-exist in Arab states in quite different ways, Raymond Hinnebusch suggests, for example, that the Arab states can be placed on a kind of *wataniyya–qawmiyya* continuum. Kuwait and the Maghreb countries represent Arab states where identification with the existing territorial-state (*wataniyya*) overshadows without wholly displacing an Arab identification (*qawmiyya*), whereas the opposite has long been the case for the Mashriq countries, while in between Egypt and Yemen figure as examples of a kind of balance between these forms of identification.[77]

In addition to this variance across space, it is similarly possible to identify an evolution in the salience of the sovereignty institution among the Arab states. Thus, since the 1950s and 1960s Arab Cold War,[78] which took place in the heyday of pan-Arabism, the balance between a concern for a *raison d'état* versus a *raison de la nation Arabe* slowly shifted in favor of the former. To the extent Arab nationalism still informs the relations between the Arab states it takes the form of a kind of "intergovernmental political Arabism,"[79] where grand pan-Arab unity schemes have been replaced by mutual recognition and a growing respect for the principle of non-intervention. The fact that "the idea of the state" in this way increasingly appears to have been planted in the "minds" of other Arab states does not, however, mean that Ajami's prophesy – referred to in the introduction – has at last come true. By turning attention to the degree to which "the idea of the state" has been planted in the "minds" of the population, it thus appears that Paul Noble has a point when he maintains that it is still "premature to talk of the end of permeability and the full consolidation of the Arab state system along the lines of the post-Westphalian European system."[80] While a sense of local national identity (*wataniyya*) and a concern for narrow *raison d'état* increasingly prevail among Arab state elites, within Arab societies it is still possible to identify a sense of attachment to a larger Arab community.[81] This, for example, appears in Arab opinion polls according to which large majorities of Arabs still rank the Palestine issue as one of the most important political issues to them personally and, moreover, they evaluate non-Arab countries on a basis of those countries' policies toward key regional Arab issues, that is, Palestine and Iraq, rather than on their specific behavior toward the country of the respondent.[82] Instead of seeing this as an expression of the persistence of pre-modern loyalties, this should rather be understood in the context of, on the one hand, poor territory–identity fit in the post-imperial Arab world and, on the other hand, the rise of new trans-Arab media and the emergence of a "new Arab public sphere."[83] The paradigmatic, but far from only example, is *Al Jazeera*, which in contrast to previous Arab satellite channels, emphasizes Arab news and political debate thus making it a perfect platform for political deliberation revolving around regional issues. *Al Jazeera* and similar trans-Arab satellite channels are as (quasi)-commercial channels concerned with reaching the largest possible audience in the Arabic-speaking world. They, therefore, emphasize matters with a common Arab interest, such as Iraq or Palestine, or they situate local issues in a larger Arab framing. By tying distant events together in a common Arab narrative and by bringing Arabs into the same virtual space united not only by the Arabic language but also a common Arab news agenda revolving around "Arab issues," these new trans-Arab media are playing an important role in (re)producing an "imagined Arab community" within an Arab world that as recently noted by Noble still – or more precisely once again[84] – "resembles a large sound chamber in which currents of thoughts as well as information circulate widely and enjoy considerable resonance across state frontiers."[85] The use of this metaphor, which was originally applied to the 1950s and 1960s Arab world, where another trans-Arab media, the radio, played an important role, does not, however, mean that the dynamics of today's Arab world are identical to the heydays of pan-Arabism. In comparison with its predecessor, what may be described as a new societal Islamic political Arabism[86] does, on the one hand, hold a stronger Islamic dimension, but is, on the other hand, neither state-led nor about grand pan-Arab unity schemes based on a vision of a radical transformation of the existing society of Arab states. Instead, it is related to the growing de-link between states and societies in the Arab world, where people are dissociating themselves from increasingly de-legitimized authoritarian Arab regimes. Following Rami Khouri, it is more about the emergence of a kind of parallel non-statist Arab order, which is dominated by societal actors propagating Arab-Islamic resistance (*muqawama*) and exists side-by-side, but in a tense relationship with the Arab society of states.[87]

Conclusion

As a way of exploring the impacts of imperialism that relate to culture on the post-imperial states and salience of the sovereignty institution in the Middle East, this chapter has delved into one of the great debates within the Middle East. Based on an examination of answers in the "Western Question" debate concerning "what went wrong," "where should we now be going" and whether the West should be perceived as a "peril," "promise" or "just an example," the chapter has shown that instead of perceiving the Middle East as marked by a clash between, on the one side, Western modernity and the Westphalian state and, on the other side, some pre-modern Middle Eastern tradition and ancient supra-/sub-national identities, the defining feature of the region seems rather to be the existence of a range of parallel but contending novel visions about "where should we now be going" partly responding to and partly inspired by the growing Western influence since (at least) the late eighteenth century. This holds implications for whether and how "the idea of the state" has been planted in the minds of the populations and other states in the region. The overall picture is, on the one hand, that the basic idea of the state – compared with alternative forms of regional organizations, including various forms of imperial organizations – seems to have taken root in the region since the European orchestrated post-Ottoman re-organization of the region into a (proto-)state system. But on the other hand, what this state should be like and who it should be for has been highly contested. The question of "where should we now be going" has therefore remained a prominent topic in the twenty-first-century debate, although the degree of urgency varies across the region. While the "we" has been less disputed than the "where" in the non-Arab states, the opposite has been the case in the Arab world partly owing to a quite different imperial legacy. This has been reflected in a distinct form of inter-Arab relations, where the sovereignty institution has held a very low salience. Although, from the end of the twentieth century it appeared that in the Arab world this institution had also gained a growing prominence among the Arab state leaders, it has to a lesser extent been the case at the popular level, where it still – and maybe even increasingly – is possible to find a sense of attachment to a larger Arab community. In particular, in the Arab world it therefore still seems to be premature to talk of the end of permeability or about a full consolidation of the post-imperial states along Westphalian lines.

Notes

1. Brown, *Diplomacy in the Middle East*, p. xi.
2. In this chapter I am only making a distinction between "culture-as-a-bond" and "culture-as-a-bar." The concept of culture is, however, more complex than that and I could – but have decided not to – frame this discussion on culture and the imperial legacy based on some of the other possible conceptualizations of culture I have suggested in a typology elsewhere. Based on a genealogical reading of the transformation of the concept of culture this typology makes a distinction between "the signifying idea of culture," "the aesthetic idea of culture," which can be subdivided into "culture-as-the-best-that-is-thought-and-said" and "popular/mass-culture," and "the anthropological idea of culture," which can be subdivided into the aforementioned "culture-as-a-bond" and "culture-as-a-bar." For an account of these various ideas of culture and their place in international relations theory, see Valbjørn, "There are clearly cultural issues at play" and also Valbjørn, *A "Baedeker" to IR's Cultural Journey*.
3. For a more thorough discussion of these three positions see Valbjørn, 'Culture blind and culture blinded', pp. 39–78; Valbjørn, "Toward a 'Mesopotamian Turn'," pp. 47–75. For a similar distinction see Zubaida, "The nation state in the Middle East."
4. On the "vanguard" concept see Buzan, *From International to World Society*, pp. 222ff.
5. Bull and Watson (eds), *The Expansion of International Society*.
6. Lerner, *The Passing of Traditional Society*, p. 47.
7. Ajami, "The end of Pan-Arabism," pp. 355–73.
8. Badie, *The Imported State*; see also Leander, "Bertrand Badie: cultural diversity changing international relations?," pp. 145–69.
9. Bozeman, "The international order in a multicultural world," pp. 387–406; see also Bozeman, "Statecraft and intelligence in the non-Western world," pp. 158–79.
10. Kedourie, 'The Nation-State in the Middle East', pp. 1–9; Vatikiotis, *Islam and the State*; Lewis, "The Middle East in world affairs (1957)," pp. 232–9.
11. Salzman, "The Middle East's tribal DNA"; Salamé, "The Middle East: elusive security, indefinable region," pp. 17–35.
12. See, e.g., Buzan, "Culture and international society," pp. 1–25.
13. Owen, *State, Power and Politics*, p. 3; Zubaida, "The nation state in the Middle East," p. 121.
14. Zubaida, "The nation state in the Middle East."
15. Korany, "Alien and besieged yet here to stay," pp. 47–74.

16. Lustick, "The absence of Middle Eastern great powers," pp. 653–83.
17. See, e.g., Hinnebusch, "The politics of identity in the Middle East international relations," pp. 151–71; Halliday, "The Middle East and conceptions of 'international society,'" pp. 1–23. Barnett, *Dialogues in Arab Politics: Negotiations in Regional Order*; Gause, "Sovereignty, statecraft and stability in the Middle East," pp. 441–69.
18. Brown, *Diplomacy in the Middle East*, p. xi. See also, Yurdusev, "From the Eastern Question to the Western Question," pp. 323–32.
19. Buzan, *People, States & Fear*, p. 65. See, e.g., Sørensen, *Changes in Statehood: The Transformation of International Relations*, p. 20.
20. Buzan, *People, States & Fear*, p. 69.
21. Buzan, *People, States & Fear*, p. 64.
22. Buzan, *People, States & Fear*, p. 78.
23. Eliott House, "Why Islam fell from grace." As for the subtitle of Lewis' book it changed from *Western Impact and Middle Eastern Response* in the original version to *The Clash Between Islam and Modernity in the Middle East*. As a forerunner to the book Lewis had presented his argument in a short version, "What went wrong?," pp. 43–5.
24. See, e.g., Cole, *Napoleon's Egypt: Invading the Middle East*.
25. For a discussion on reasons for this change see Hourani, *A History of the Arab Peoples*, pp. 258–62.
26. Brown, *Diplomacy in the Middle East*, p. x.
27. See, e.g., Ayoob and Kosebalaban, *Religion and Politics in Saudi Arabia*; Tibi, *Arab Nationalism*, pp. 88–90.
28. Wiktorowicz, "Anatomy of the Salafi movement," pp. 207–39. For the complexity of salafism see also Meijer (ed.), *Global Salafism: Islam's New Religious Movement*.
29. Esposito, *Islam and Politics*, pp. 36–9.
30. Lerner, *The Passing of Traditional Society*, p. 47.
31. Behnam, "The Eastern perception of the West," p. 185.
32. Black, *The History of Islamic Political Thought*, p. 274.
33. Niva, "Contested sovereignties and postcolonial insecurities in the Middle East," p. 155.
34. Zubaida, *Law and Power in the Islamic World*, p. 129.
35. Hourani, *A History of the Arab Peoples*, p. 272.
36. Behnam, "The Eastern perception of the West," p. 186.
37. Bahnam, "The Eastern perception of the West," p. 183.
38. Behnam, "The Eastern perception of the West," p. 187; see also Davison, "Ziya Gökalp and provincializing Europe," pp. 377–90.
39. On Islamic modernism see Hourani, *Arabic Thought in the Liberal Age 1798–1939*.
40. Hourani, *A History of the Arab Peoples*, p. 308
41. Tibi, *Arab Nationalism*, p. 90.
42. Zubaida, *Law and Power in the Islamic World*, pp. 138–40.

43. Black, *The History of Islamic Political Thought*, p. 293.
44. Black, *The History of Islamic Political Thought*, p. 290.
45. "Understanding Islamism,"; see also Mandaville, *Global Political Islam*.
46. Mirsepassi, 'Islam as a modernizing ideology: Al-e Ahmad and Shari'ati', pp. 96–128.
47. "Understanding Islamism," p. 20.
48. Niva, 'Contested sovereignties and postcolonial insecurities in the Middle East," p. 156.
49. Tibi, *Arab Nationalism*, p. 186. See, e.g., Esposito, *Islam and Politics*, p. 65.
50. See, e.g., Reid, *Whose Pharaohs?*
51. See, e.g., Dawisha, *Arab Nationalism in the Twentieth Century*, p. 60.
52. Dawisha, *Arab Nationalism in the Twentieth Century*, p. 72. See also, Tibi, *Arab Nationalism*, p. 189.
53. Tibi, *Arab Nationalism*, p. 188
54. Dawisha, *Arab Nationalism in the Twentieth Century*, p. 70.
55. Viorst, *Storm over the East*, p. 9.
56. For a discussion on the origins of Arab nationalism see Valbjørn, "Arab nationalism(s) in transformation," p. 149.
57. For a critique of the claim about some original Arab unity destroyed by the Europeans, see Harik, "The origins of the Arab state system', pp. 1–28.
58. For an elaboration of this distinction between forms of Arab nationalism: see Valbjørn, "Arab nationalism(s) in transformation," pp. 142–4.
59. Khalidi, "Thinking the unthinkable," pp. 695–713.
60. Khalidi, "The origins of Arab nationalism: Introduction," p. vii. On the notion of an anarchical society see Bull, *The Anarchical Society*.
61. Khalidi, "The origins of Arab nationalism: Introduction," p. vii.
62. For a similar argument, see Niva, "Contested sovereignties and postcolonial insecurities in the Middle East," p. 150.
63. Black, *The History of Islamic Political Thought*, p. 314.
64. Black, *The History of Islamic Political Thought*, p. 315.
65. Dawisha, *Arab Nationalism in the Twentieth Century*, p. 25.
66. See, e.g., Skovgaard-Petersen, *Al-Azhar 1922–2006*.
67. Hinnebusch, "Chapter 2: the Middle East regional system," p. 33.
68. See, e.g., Nasr, *Forces of Fortune*.
69. For different suggestions for typologies of state-models in the Arab world see Hinnebusch, "State formation and international behaviour," pp. 73–90; Ayubi, *Overstating the Arab State*; Harik, "The origins of the Arab state system"; Hudson, *Arab Politics*; Luciani, 'Allocation vs. Production States', pp. 63–82; Owen, *State, Power and Politics*.
70. On this twin pressure on the Arab states from below and above see Gause, "Sovereignty, statecraft and stability in the Middle East', pp. 441–69. Hinnebusch, *The International Politics of the Middle East*.
71. Telhami and Barnett, 'Ch. 1: Introduction: Identity and foreign policy in the

Middle East," p. 9. See, e.g., Gause, "Sovereignty, statecraft and stability in the Middle East," pp. 441–69.

72. Telhami, "Power, legitimacy and peace-making in Arab coalitions – the New Arabism," pp. 43–60.
73. Barnett, *Dialogues in Arab Politics*.
74. Owen, *State, Power and Politics*.
75. The key exceptions are the Saudi–Egyptian clashes in Yemen in the 1960s and, of course, the Iraqi invasion of Kuwait in 1990s, which can, however, also be interpreted as a symbol of the weakening of this distinctly Arab game.
76. See, e.g., Barnett, *Dialogues in Arab Politics*; Valbjørn, "Arab nationalism(s) in transformation," p. 146.
77. Hinnebusch, "The politics of identity in the Middle East international relations," p. 158.
78. Kerr, *The Arab Cold War*.
79. For an elaboration see Valbjørn, "Arab nationalism(s) in transformation," p. 158.
80. Noble, "From Arab system to Middle Eastern system?," p. 87.
81. Noble, "From Arab system to Middle Eastern system?," p. 85.
82. Furia and Lucas, "Determinants of Arab public opinion on foreign relations," pp. 585–605; Lynch, *Voices of the New Arab Public*.
83. For a discussion on the role of the new trans-Arab media see Lynch, *Voices of the New Arab Public*; Rinnawi, *Instant Nationalism*; Pintak, "Border guards of the 'Imagined,'" pp. 191–212. For a more sceptical view, see Murphy, 'Theorizing ICTs in the Arab world," pp. 1131–53.
84. In the last quarter of the twentieth century, the role of trans-Arab media was decreasing partly as a consequence of the growing state capacity in terms of infrastructural power. This was reflected in an improved ability to control and insulate the society, making the regimes less susceptible to trans-Arab currents. At that time, the Arab authoritarian regimes controlled the media to the point where little real public sphere remained, either within the individual states or at the Arab level.
85. Noble, "From Arab system to Middle Eastern system?," p. 92.
86. For a further elaboration of this point see Valbjørn, "Arab nationalism(s) in transformation," pp. 162–7, and Valbjørn and Bank, *Disentangling the New Arab Cold War*.
87. Khouri, "Heed the changes in Arab public opinion."

12

Pathways of Islamist Mobilization against the State in the Middle East and Central Asia

Frédéric Volpi

Concepts and Approach

How far are contemporary forms of Islamist mobilization in the Middle East and Central Asia presenting differences that can be attributed to the role played by different colonial experiences?[1] This is not an issue that is particularly well integrated in contemporary regional debates dominated by discourses about the securitization of Islamism. Even if there is no immediately obvious way of framing complex post-colonial legacies in an international security debate primarily concerned with violent forms of Islamist mobilization against the state, comparative reflections on such socio-historical transformations may nonetheless shed some new light on dilemmas in current affairs. The analysis that follows is not intended to provide a comprehensive account of the scholarship on the relations between political Islam and the state in the Middle East and Central Asia. Rather, it draws some parallels between discourses and practices of governance and opposition in the two regions, and proposes some tentative suggestions regarding a common rationale for the contemporary framing of post-colonial Islamism. Clearly, such a large comparative project is always open to charges of being too broad and of missing some distinctive traits and dynamics of the individual countries or regions concerned. The purpose and ambition of the analysis is to contribute to the discussion on the implications of inclusion–exclusion for the "radicalization–moderation" of Islamist groups.[2] By positioning my narrative in relation to general political science debates and by highlighting the more structural insights provided by this cross-regional comparison, I recognize that there is a price to be paid in terms of details and nuances.

The comparative perspective developed in the following account presents the imperial/colonial system primarily as a set of practices of governance that indigenous societies consider to be framed by the needs and demands of an external political order. It is evidently possible for external practices to become associated over time with indigenous rule, as in the case of the heritage of early Islamic empires viewed from the perspective of contemporary Muslim populations. Indeed, the frame of reference corresponding to the establishment of "Islam" as the main religious tradition in both regions provides a nominally common ideational background for assessing certain practices of governance across polities.[3] Yet the ideational relevance of such framing of an Islamic *longue durée* is tightly connected to contemporary efforts at asserting the relevance of the Islamic tradition to modern social and political practices and identities in the Middle East and Central Asia.[4] In this context, the notion of post-imperial, post-colonial or post-Soviet order also must be problematized in relation to such an Islamic narrative.

The colonial and post-colonial predicament cannot neatly be encapsulated by references to the actual transformation of governing institutions. As Mark Beissinger suggests, "Empire must be understood not as a thing, but as a set of practices that give rise to perceptions and claims that the polity represents a fundamentally alien rule, an 'other.' "[5] What matters are not merely the actual structural and functional aspects of imperial rule, but equally, and perhaps ultimately, the extent of the perception that a system is imperial (or not), at home and abroad. Hence, the modern imperial period does not simply signify the factual collapse of an indigenous "Islamic-framed" rule in much of the Middle East and Central Asia, and the concomitant establishment of colonial networks of governance (British, French and Russian). Indeed, if we were to focus on the details of the historical construction of these colonial practices of governance, we would uncover complex hybrid imbrications of foreign and indigenous logics and methods of social ordering.[6] In a similar way, the formal recognition of the institutional system of an independent nation-state does not necessarily indicate that state practices and national narratives cease to be dictated by external actors. In contemporary Islamist discourses, the Westernization of formal and informal institutions – economic, political and cultural – is commonly presented as a form of neo-colonialism that does not fundamentally alter the colonial nature of the rule. Evidently, such narratives about an Islamic authenticity that could/should provide a significantly different form of governance are framed, much like nationalism, in the context of a prospective societal project and not as a pragmatic account of historical practices.[7]

Governance (or governmentality in a Foucauldian sense) is used in the following account to characterize the mechanisms of rule rather than the institutional framework of government. The structures of governance are not fixed centers of authority operating in a top-down fashion, but rather dynamic formalizations of the self-governing networks that compose the system. In what follows, therefore, terms like "the administration" or "the state" are short-hand for a particular set of practices and rationales, which may or may not be fully institutionalized. In a similar way, even though it is commonly portrayed as a return to the "fundamentals" of Islam, Islamism or political Islam does not refer here to a predefined set of ideational and practical elements. Because the core meanings of political Islam are defined inter-subjectively, the discursive strategies of ideological dominance in contemporary Islam are what most immediately define Islamism today.[8] In this context, by Islamist mobilization I mean the social and political articulation of societal demands and projects of action in a conceptual framework and in practices reflectively viewed as "true" expressions of the Islamic faith and tradition. In the following, I frame the trajectories of interactions between the state and Islamism by comparing evolving sets of Islamist rationales and practices of governance with those of the state. More specifically, contemporary Islamist mobilization in the Middle East and Central Asia is analyzed in relation to a key difference between the traditional forms of colonial governance implemented by the French and British empires – indirect rule – and those of the Soviet model deployed by the USSR. In functional–structural terms, the former tended to include local Islamic "authorities" in their networks of governance of the indigenous population, while the latter excluded them in their capacity of "religious authorities."[9]

The analytical value of such distinctions is meaningful principally for a comparative perspective concerned with the trajectory of modern Islamism. If one were to focus on more geopolitical concerns, as Olivier Roy does, it may be more meaningful to stress the continuities between Russian and Soviet rule in Central Asia.[10] From the perspective of the transformation of Islamism, however, it is important to note that although the Russian and Soviet administrations shared the same overall approach to Islam – that is, a marginalization and instrumentalization of the local religious authorities – the dramatic re-articulation of the networks of governance between the Russian and Soviet systems make the two periods qualitatively different for political Islam. Put simply, the Soviets were involved in a form of social engineering on a scale that traditional imperial powers never attempted even in their most extensive colonial schemes (like the French in Algeria).[11]

In this perspective, it is also important to note how the traditional networks of governance that the French, British and Russian empires had produced at the end of the nineteenth century showed their limitations in dealing with mass politics in the post-First World War period. While the Soviet system provided a new organizational model for Central Asian politics at the time, other imperial systems slowly ground to a halt in the face of rising structures of national governance. The shift from external to domestic dominant political institutions marks the distinction between imperial and national governance, between colonial and post-colonial systems. In its turn, the "nation-centric" character of the post-colonial and post-Soviet regimes that emerged after countries formally gained independence created new constraints and opportunities for Islamist mobilization. Yet from the perspective of modern Islamism, this formal transfer of sovereignty does not signify that the post-colonial state's approach to Islam is necessarily qualitatively different from that of the colonial/ Soviet administration. As Beissinger suggested, perceptions about what kind of political rule is implemented is crucial as "empires and states are set apart not primarily by exploitation, nor even by the use of force, but essentially by whether politics and policies are accepted as 'ours' or are rejected as 'theirs.'"[12] In this perspective, therefore, what greatly matters is the inter-subjective assessment of how national governments are able to legitimately organize mass politics.

New and Old Techniques of Imperial Governmentality

At the end of the First World War, the mandate system put in place after the collapse of the Ottoman Empire formally sketched the mechanisms of colonial governance that the French and British empires had developed in the Middle East and North Africa (MENA).[13] In Central Asia, the expansion of the Soviet area of influence laid the foundation for a centralized policy-making system that would increasingly format political (and religious) processes in the region.[14] At this historical juncture we can more clearly distinguish a traditional Western (including Russian) imperialist approach to Islam, which concerned itself with maintaining the political quiescence of indigenous religious authorities – while expecting Muslims to "enlighten" themselves through their contacts with "civilization" – from a Soviet one concerned with implementing a roots-and-branch transformation of the indigenous social and political system.

In the Middle East and North Africa, the French and the British administrations commonly relied on local religious leaders to act as the transmission belts for the colonial administration. The formal recognition of indigenous elites in their "tribal" or "religious" role simultaneously empowered and marginalized Islamic structures of authority by emphasizing and strengthening their traditional character. These processes of power redistribution also applied to situations of direct colonization like that of Algeria, where the colonial administration only partially undermined the economic and political viability of indigenous elites through military control and land reform.[15] Formally and institutionally, this approach created and entrenched over time a situation of legal pluralism (citizens–colonizers versus natives–colonized) that limited the interactions between the two groups while maintaining a clear pattern of ethno-national subjugation.

Despite their rhetorical commitments to a "civilizing mission," colonial administrations kept the issue of the management of religious and educational establishment at arms' length for a long time.[16] Colonial powers did not directly challenge established Islamic theological centers such as al-Qayrawan (Morocco) or al-Azhar (Egypt), which remained the main providers of traditionally trained religious scholars. Although these institutions were not directly challenged, their authority was undermined by the new legal frameworks devised by the colonial administration, which bypassed Islamic regulations; thereby rendering them less relevant to the domestic organization of society.[17] In a similar way, in the educational sector the colonial administration encouraged indigenous political elites to reform the religious-dominated schooling system to develop literacy and numeracy skills as well as the teaching of modern sciences. Yet the French and British administrations never sought directly to address the basic schooling requirements of the bulk of the indigenous population. Indeed, a too great access to education by the colonized was perceived to be risky for the rule of the colonizer. So, instead, they supplemented traditional education with an elitist Westernized school system for the children of indigenous notables.[18]

These approaches to the organization of power among indigenous elites can be contrasted to the system that the Soviets implemented from the 1920s onward. Four main policy periods can be crudely identified in Central Asia: Soviet penetration; Stalinist modernization; maintenance of the status quo (mainly under Khrushchev and Brezhnev); and liberalization (mainly under Gorbachev). Importantly, under the impulse of Stalin the Soviet administration developed a quite systematic and sustained campaign of elimination of (formal) religious-based authority structures, as well as an ideological reformation of the role played by traditional religious leaders in local Muslim communities.[19] The Soviet approach in the late 1920s and 1930s in particular was less concerned with maintaining the status quo through an instrumentalization of the local Islamic leadership than were earlier tsarist policies (or than their British and French counterparts at the time). Instead, it constituted an attempt to mobilize the local social structures into a larger Soviet project and system of governance articulated by different ideational and organizational principles. Peter Blitstein remarks:

> Like the colonial regimes of interwar Africa, Soviet nationality policy emphasised "indigenisation" of the institutions of local government. But the fundamental purpose of Soviet indigenisation policies was precisely the opposite of the European policy of colonial indigenisation in Africa. Soviet policy was not designed to preserve 'traditional' content, but to replace it.[20]

Such policies did not merely invoke rhetorically a putative "enlightenment" of the colonized people, but they sought to practically ensure that the category of the colonized was dissolved into that of *homo Sovieticus* – just as the traditional model of the nation-state was meant to be transformed into that of a union of Soviets.[21]

These differences in modes of governance had a direct impact at the ideational level on the process of articulation of political Islam as an alternative model of social organization in the two regions. While in the late nineteenth and early twentieth centuries there were clear signs that similar reformist trends in Islamic thinking were on the ascendancy in both locations – for example, the Islamic Reform movement in the Middle East and Jadidi movement in Central Asia – this convergence was disrupted by the entrenchment of Soviet rule.[22] In Central Asia all Islamic networks, reformist and traditionalist alike, were eventually repressed by the Soviet regime. By contrast, in the MENA context, colonial policies created a space where a contest between different Islamic elites could take place. There, proponents of more "traditional" practices of Islam, often endorsed by the colonial administration, competed for influence with reformist (and thereafter revolutionary) forms of Islamism that opposed the established religious and political elites. In the MENA this contest meant that beside the anti-colonial struggle spearheaded by nationalist movements there were Islamic discourses that emphasized, for example, the primacy of the sovereignty of the sacred law (*shari'a*) in substantive debates about independence.[23]

In Central Asia, in a context far less conducive to the articulation of religiously-framed ideological debates, internal rivalries between various Islamic networks (reformists, Sufis and so on) were overshadowed by a more pressing struggle for survival in the face of harsh Soviet campaigns against the religious establishment.[24] Even those trends, such as the Jadidi, which had initially sought to use the anti-imperialist policies of the USSR to develop a modernist Islamist discourse, could not, in the main, survive

the Stalinist purges of the 1930s. The adaptation of Islamic authority networks in the face of the far-reaching modernization policies and repressive
tactics of the Soviet administration generally led to a displacement of their
formal political and social activism toward activities centering on private
and local practices.[25] This diminishing visibility of Islamic authority networks was accompanied by the rise of new state-supported networks of
governance – for example, workers' unions and women's organizations –
articulated around new socio-economic policies that modified the regional
economic power distribution.[26] Over time, this power redistribution and
the growth of "national" authority structures – designed in part to avoid
the perception that the Soviet Union was an empire[27] – coupled with state
repression of religious networks, meant that the circumstances were most
unpropitious for the articulation of a grand, politically explicit Islamic
discourse. This de-structuring process would have important implications
for the post-Soviet context, as it created a need for a reorganization of the
Islamic public sphere, both at the grassroots level (to enable mass participation) and at the elite level (to re-validate claims to religious legitimacy
and expertise).

Partly as a result of these different modes of governance, and partly
as a result of their different sequencing, the way in which Islamist
movements challenged the religious authorities endorsed by the state –
and in this way indirectly challenged the state itself – in the final days
of the colonial period in the MENA could not be replicated during the
collapse of the Soviet system. While the formal inclusion of traditional
Islamic networks in French and British models of colonial administration brought to the fore rivalries between reformist and traditionalist
Islamic trends, the more systematic process of social engineering backed
by repression adopted by the Soviets eclipsed the tensions between different Central Asian Islamic tendencies. The articulation of Islamism
from roughly the 1930s to the 1970s was thus quite different in the two
regional contexts, as movements could not express themselves in the
same way or tap into the same constituencies. While modern Islamist
organizations like the Muslim Brotherhood increasingly defined themselves in opposition to the official religious authorities supported by the
colonial and then the secularized post-colonial state, reformist movements in Central Asia went through a phase of "de-modernization," to
use Khalid's terminology, not least because they were cut off from the
debates taking place in rest of the Muslim world.[28] Here, de-modernization did not mean that there simply remained "traditional" authority
networks – as much of the Soviet scholarship on Islam in Central Asia
has suggested – but rather that these networks did not contribute to the

construction of political modernity in the region in the same way as Islamist movements in the Middle East.

Functional Adaptations in the National Post-colonies

The post-colonial dimension of governance in the MENA does not fundamentally change the terms and parameters of the internal struggle for the ideological higher ground between competing Islamic trends. The slow end of empire, mediated by mandates and other forms of quasi-sovereignty, increased the ability of the national elites to organize and strengthen their governance skills and networks prior to independence. The struggle for power among indigenous elites intensified as the process of withdrawal of the colonial powers became more advanced. The Islamist movements that had associated themselves with nationalist forces in anti-colonial fronts progressively became marginalized as movements commonly spearheaded by military elites strengthened their grip on power during the transitional period. In the new populist republics of the region, marginalization could occur through co-optation, as in the case of Algeria's Association of Ulama inclusion in the National Liberation Front in the 1950s. It could also be obtained by direct repression, as with the Muslim Brotherhood in Egypt, after it withdrew its support for the Nasserite project.[29]

As networks of governance became more state-centric, two state strategies were noticeable, sometimes clearly demarcated in time and space, sometimes feeding into one another. Some nationalist regimes engaged in intense efforts at state-led modernization, akin to the efforts of the Soviet administration in the 1930s. The policies of the Nasserite regime in the late 1950s to early 1960s were indicative of this trend. During that time, al-Azhar came under full state control, and Nasser tried to present Islam as a kind of proto-socialism. Usually such efforts at roots and branch modernization of societal structures in the face of opposition from religious networks are not sustained for very long. There are nonetheless polities where there have been prolonged efforts at secular modernization; namely, Tunisia, Syria and Turkey.[30] More commonly, post-colonial regimes followed in the footsteps of the departing colonial powers in instrumentalizing traditional Islamic authority networks; that is, they provided them with institutional recognition and financial support in exchange for political quiescence. In the 1960s, the king of Morocco used religious authority networks to gain the upper hand over the dominant nationalist movement of the day, only to undermine other Islamic actors once he established his own religious and political power base. In the Gulf region, the transformation of tribal leaders into institutionalized national elites also involved co-opting entrenched religious authority networks when creating state structures and policies, though trajectories of institutionalization display notable intra-regional differences (for example Kuwait versus Saudi Arabia).[31]

The second key aspect of the post-colonial redefinition of governance in national terms is, from a structural perspective, the turn to mass politics (most commonly via the institutionalization of anti-colonial movements). In this respect, there is a distinction to be made between the new populist republics with a considerable degree of (controlled) mobilization in the 1950s and 1960s (for example, Egypt and Algeria) and the more traditional monarchies, particularly in the Gulf region. From a state perspective, despite a turn toward mass political mobilization, one element that hardly changed in the post-colonial context is the pervasive use of strong-arm political tactics. Post-colonial regimes have insisted that harsh measures were required precisely to ensure the full independence of the country from departing colonial powers and emerging regional competitors (and their domestic agents).[32] The ideological effectiveness of these "nationalist" arguments decreases over time as regimes are seen not to deliver "real" independence amidst economic crises, lost wars and so on. Indirectly, faltering state efforts at modernization validate the opposition discourses and practices of Islamism at both grassroot and elite levels. The 1967 defeat of the Arab armies by Israel is often presented as the turning point for the changing fortunes of nationalist/pan-Arabist and Islamist trends. Organizationally, political Islam at that time increasingly articulated itself as the primary form of political opposition to secularized or traditional (that is, monarchic) state institutions.[33] In the 1970s and early 1980s, as Islamism recast itself as an inescapable domestic opposition movement, its interactions with the state apparatus often turned violent. Starting in the late 1980s, however, this confrontation began to take a more routine political turn as many Islamists sought to make the most of the processes of partial democratization that various regimes initiated at the time (both to cope with pressure and to entrench their rule).[34] Clearly, beside these general tendencies, to understand the differences between how different Islamist movements have evolved in the region it is necessary to pay careful attention to the specificities of the varied "official Islam" policies that were put in place by specific post-colonial regimes. In its turn, the relative importance of the colonial legacy is affected by the strength of the new post-colonial legacy constructed through these different national policies.

The articulation of Islamism in Central Asia is structurally different due to the introduction of mass political mobilization during the Soviet period. This sequence of events is the reverse of that obtained in the MENA, where mass participation came through national liberation movements. In this context, the important repression of public forms of Islamic activism prevented an explicit competition between reformers and traditionalists. Competing perspectives on the political role of Islam were mainly available in the late 1910s and early 1920s when the Soviet Union was still trying to impose its authority on the region. At that time, traditionalist Islamic leaders connected to the so-called Bashmachi revolt could oppose Jadidi and other Islamist reformers who, like Sultan Galiev, associated themselves with the progressive political agenda proposed by the Soviets and contemplated a rapprochement between Islamic and Marxist thinking.[35] The reformers, like the Soviets, were keen on the modernization of Muslim communities (and on fighting off ignorance and superstition) in order to enable the Central Asian Muslims to play a greater role in world affairs. From the 1930s onward, however, under Stalin and then under Khrushchev, reformist Islamic networks of governance were progressively dismantled and replaced by secular networks of Soviet governmentality. As disagreements about the type of modernization that was required for the region emerged, the Islamic networks that had sought to ally themselves to the Soviets were either suppressed or, at best, allowed to perform a purely cultural function in a Moscow-controlled directorate of religious affairs.

The political disempowerment of explicitly religious power structures in Central Asia did not, of course, signify that all channels of governance in the region lost their religious character. As the scholarship on Soviet Muslims in the 1980s indicates, there were intense debates about the role played by "parallel" and "traditional" or "informal" Islam in the Soviet Union.[36] It was noted that Sufi networks continued to operate in the social sphere – like Christian Orthodox networks in Russia – and that even party apparatchiks could retain a strong commitment to Islam. What this religious activism lacked, however, was a sound organizational basis for political activism. Stressing the structural divide between the political–doctrinal demands of Islamists in the Middle East and the practice-oriented articulation of Islamic religiosity in the Soviet Union in the early 1980s, Olcott concludes that in the Soviet context, Islam was a social force but not a political one.[37]

In the mid-1980s when the process of *perestroika* loosened up the repressive structures that had constrained religious activism, Islamic religiosity quickly became noticeable in the public sphere once more. Bennigsen points to a survey conducted in Uzbekistan indicating that while in 1973 over 98 percent of the respondents declared that they were either atheists or non-believers; in 1986 less than 36 percent did so.[38] In this context, perhaps more than an indication of a revival of public religiosity, such trends indicate a general increase in freedom of expression concerning a religious situation that was only tacitly acknowledged previously. "Parallel" or "informal" Islam not withstanding, the domestic repression that undermined the internal debate among Islamic currents in Central Asia, coupled with Soviet policies restricting freedom of movement, greatly contributed to the disconnection between Islamic activism in the region and in the rest of the Muslim world. The articulation of an Islamist identity and practice thus remained fragmented and low-key until the late 1980s, when a liberalization of state policies and a relaxation of ideological norms enabled Islamic actors progressively to revitalize authority networks based on religious identity.[39]

The speed at which the Soviet Union disintegrated and the *ad hoc* production of authoritarian post-Soviet regimes in Central Asia contributed to the ideological and political fluidity of Islamist movements in the region post-1991. Unsurprisingly, in recent years there has been a multiplication of (diverging) explanations of the key dynamics of Islamism in the region.[40] Contemporary scholars have used a wide range of explanatory perspectives to account for recent transformations in the region – anything from an insistence on the significance of externally-supported violent militancy, to an emphasis on the importance of hybrid secular–traditional forms of Islamic religiosity.[41] Hence, while some analysts suggest that the secularization of societal and ideational structures initiated by the Soviets would continue to reduce durably the relevance of Islamism in the region, others point to events like the Tajik civil conflict to illustrate the ever-present potential for Islamist revolt in such authoritarian post-Soviet settings.[42]

If the overall direction taken by Islamism in the region remains to this day difficult to estimate with precision, what is clear is that the nationalist elites that took over from the departing Soviet establishment used the same technique of governance to retain and entrench their power – not least because they themselves were commonly part of the Soviet *nomenklatura*.[43] This situation helped to produce very similar policies regarding Islamism across the region: a co-option of the more traditionalistic and nationalistic Islamic groups, and a repression of reformist and revolutionist Islamic trends. From the perspective of the state, this situation resembles the one obtaining in the Middle East and North Africa after the departure of the French and British colonial powers. Yet, unlike in the MENA, post-Soviet elites did not face an ideologically and organizationally well-structured Islamist opposition. Hence, in the two decades that followed independence, Central Asian regimes were generally able to manage political and socio-economic development by nationalizing the governance tools of the Soviet Union sufficiently well to diffuse frontal challenges to their legitimacy – except, to a degree, in Tajikistan. In its turn, relative stability in the region, especially in the context of troubles in neighboring countries like Afghanistan, facilitated the external validation of stable authoritarian systems. In this context, while a few Islamist organizations turned to direct action strategies to challenge the regime, for example, the Islamic Renaissance Party (for a while) and the Islamic Movement of Uzbekistan, increasingly significant movements chose to refocus their activities on grassroots Islamization below the political radar of the state (for example, Hizb-ut-Tahir and Fethullah Gulen).[44]

As stable forms of post-Soviet authoritarianism became entrenched in Central Asia, the mechanisms of confrontation and of instrumentalization of the structures of Islamist networks in the region became similar to those operating in the MENA. This homogenizing trend has been reinforced in the last decade by the international politics of the "War on Terror."[45] Yet, at the ideational level, the lack of solid ideological and organizational structure of the Central Asian Islamist constituencies contributes to a more haphazard pattern of co-optation and radicalization of movements – a trend reinforced by the importance of transnational connections for the viability of specific movements and strategies in this region. The post-1991 articulation of Islamism in Central Asia remains connected to the Soviet experience in two principal ways. First, Soviet policies weaved into the republics' national identity the notion of Islam, but only as a cultural artifact and not as a blueprint for social and political organization. This ensured that the post-Soviet regimes were able to endorse various "national Islams" as a legitimating component of their independent political system, while feeling threatened by the demands of Islamist movements for implementing more concretely Islamic policies. The initial uneasiness of regimes with Islamists would quickly produce highly intolerant and repressive policies toward movements that were perceived to challenge the ideational unity of the nation, as well as being political challengers. The second specific impact of Soviet policies has been on the emptying of the substantive social and political content of the Central Asian Islamic discourses and practice, at least beyond the level of the local community. This ideological and organizational weakening of the Islamic public sphere facilitated the penetration of Islamist ideas and organizations from other parts of the Muslim world in the post-1991 context.

Cross-regional Trends: Functional and Ideational

In the Middle East and North Africa, the political dynamics that were set in motion inside the Islamic field in the final stages of imperial domination directly structured conflict and dialogue between regimes and Islamist movements in the post-colonial period. In the MENA, the relatively sound grounding of Islamist discourse among the citizenry over time ensures that whether Islamists are co-opted by the local regimes or whether they remain fully in the opposition, their views influence the way in which the state exercises sovereignty. In Central Asia, by contrast, the emerging debate on Islamic normativity offers more possibilities for the post-Soviet regimes to portray their actions as being in tune with the requirements of both an independent nation-state and a "true" (national) Islam. In the two regions, the reluctance of regimes to tolerate a form of Islamism that engages in formal electoral politics equally facilitates the rise of a nominally apolitical (grassroots) conservative salafism. Across the two regions, the continuing ideological strength of Islamism also has similar implications for the evolution of the sovereignty dilemmas of the post-colonial/Soviet regimes. Despite the posturing of the incumbent elites, there is a widespread popular perception that "real" independence and sovereignty have not been fully achieved. This situation is not simply caused by the perception that the policy decisions that matter are not taken at the national level, but also by the assessment that when they are, the state elites are representing the views and interests of foreign powers and not those of the population. In this context, Islamist discourses and practices of "authenticity" are redeployed as mass mobilizers in a project to achieve "genuine" sovereign independence. From an ideational Islamic perspective, political actors in the Central Asian republics are still considering the issue of what alternative forms of sovereign power could and should be established. In the MENA states, political actors are already considering the issue of the practical implementation of Islamist proposals.[46]

The transnational articulation of Islamist discourses and the practices of grassroots activism have produced similar dynamics in recent years in the two regions. While the MENA has been both a producer and a recipient of these transnational activities, Central Asia has thus far been only a recipient (for example, Hizb-ut-Tahir, Gulen and Wahhabism). In both regional contexts, the main internal tensions within the Islamist field remain between the more conservative, neo-scripturalist movements and the more modernist ones. In this context, besides organizational issues, the ideological weakness of the Central Asian movements can be attributed to contemporary socio-historical dynamics favoring neo-scripturalist forms of Islamic activism. The relative weakness of Islamist movements in formal politics in the two regions is more directly a consequence of the authoritarian models put in place by all the post-colonial and post-Soviet elites. At the state level, competitive forms of authoritarianism reproduce similar models of governance and control of the Islamist opposition despite being rooted in different institutional and ideological traditions. In the post-colonial and post-Soviet period, we can note an uniformization of the discursive practices of government and opposition that relativizes the inputs of the diverse historical formations of the political field. However, in the MENA, even when there is exclusion from high politics, the more informal influence that Islamists are able to exert on the regime via popular mobilization in favor of greater Islamization mitigates the situation.[47] In Central Asia, by contrast, in a context where the process of grassroots Islamization of the citizenry is less elaborate, such bottom-up influences on state policies remain relatively weak today. As Dale Eickelman and James Piscatori note, to understand the political dynamics of the Muslim world one has to appreciate how much the Islamic tradition – or more precisely what is deemed to be properly Muslim – constitutes "the language of politics," while at the same time remain aware of the "politics of language" in different socio-historical contexts.[48] When considering the extent to which Central Asia differs from the Middle East in terms of Islamist mobilization, it is therefore important to stress not only that there is a quantitative difference to how much the Islamic tradition constitutes "the language of politics," but also that the "politics of language" in the post-Soviet context are not articulated in exactly the same way as in the MENA. Hence, it cannot be a case of Islamism simply "catching up" in Central Asia.

Notes

1. I am particularly grateful to Sally Cummings, Raymond Hinnebusch and Morten Valbjørn for their suggestions on the framing of the issues addressed in this chapter in the context of the comparative narrative developed in the book.
2. Classic references to this debate include Anderson, "Lawless government and illegal opposition," pp. 219–32 and Schwedler, *Faith in Moderation.*
3. As Cole and Kandiyoti remark in another comparison of the Middle East and Central Asia, "the 'universalism' of the great religious traditions is, on closer examination, limited to a few abstract themes. In fact, the 'universal' religions act as umbrellas for diverse local beliefs and social practices, binding them together rather loosely by appeal to some simple common themes, myths, and rituals. Insofar as religion is predominantly localistic in nature

despite its apparent universalism, it can usually be co-opted for nationalist purposes." Cole and Kandiyoti, "Nationalism and the colonial legacy in the Middle East and Central Asia," p. 197.

4. See particularly, Eickelman and Piscatori, *Muslim Politics*.

5. Beissinger, "The persisting ambiguity of empire," p. 155.

6. See Mitchell's insightful account of the construction of governance in British-administered Egypt in Mitchell, *Colonising Egypt*.

7. For a useful account of the articulation of Islamism in the face of alternative secularizing projects of governance see Sayyid, *A Fundamental Fear*.

8. For an elaboration of this inter-subjectivist perspective see, in particular, Volpi, *Political Islam Observed*. In the following I use the terms "Islamism" and "political Islam" interchangeably.

9. As scholars of the colonial/post-colonial condition from Chatterjee to Mamdani indicate, the main objective of indirect rule was to formalize an unequal form of citizenship in the colony (despite gestures in the direction of assimilation). See Chatterjee, *The Nation and Its Fragments* and Mamdani, "Historicizing power and responses to power," pp. 859–86.

10. Roy, *The New Central Asia*.

11. Khalid remarks that "while tsarist Central Asia was indeed directly compara-ble to other colonies of modern European empires, early Soviet Central Asia cannot be understood as a case of colonialism. In terms of both the scope and the nature of state action, the Soviet remaking of Central Asia makes sense only as the work of a different kind of modern polity, the activist, inter-ventionist, mobilizational state that seeks to sculpt its citizenry in an ideal image." Khalid, "Backwardness and the quest for civilization," p. 232.

12. Beissinger, "Demise of an empire-state," p. 99.

13. For the continuities in the French colonial approach compare Prochaska, *Making Algeria French* with Khoury, S*yria and the French Mandate*.

14. See, in particular, Martin, *The Affirmative Action Empire* and Suny and Martin (eds), *A State of Nations*.

15. Outside those areas with dense *colon* populations, traditional religious and tribal leaders remained key implementers of the colonial policies, even as they were made more dependent upon French financial and military support to maintain their position. Compare, e.g., Hoisington, "French rule and the Moroccan elite," with Hounet, "Des tribus en Algérie?," pp. 150–71.

16. This "hands off" approach was equally noticeable in relation to women's rights – the family code of the "natives" being left as the responsibility of the indigenous Muslim elites. See Thompson, *Colonial Citizens* and Charrad, *States and Women's Rights*.

17. These institutions were also weakened by power struggles between indigenous political leaders (sultan of Morocco, khedive of Egypt) and the religious establishment. See, e.g., Raineau, "Des tableaux noirs à l'ombre du minbar," pp. 90–104 and Vermeren, "Une si difficile réforme," pp. 119–32.

18. See in particular, Tignor, *Modernization and British Colonial Rule in Egypt, 1882–1914*; Berque, *French North Africa*; Starrett, *Putting Islam to Work*; and Segalla, *The Moroccan Soul*.

19. Parallels can be drawn with the process of construction of the Turkish Republic at about the same time. The evolution of the social and political situation of Turkey can be framed as an attempt by the Atatürk regime to remove Turkey from the "Middle East" and to reposition it as a "modern" European country. For this analogy see, e.g., Khalid, "Backwardness and the quest for civilization."

20. Blitstein, "Cultural diversity and the interwar conjuncture," p. 287. Blitstein also notes that, "this distinction between a Soviet universalist project and the colonial project is especially vivid in labor policy and education policy. While European policy in Africa was designed to prevent, or at least limit, the formation of an urbanized, 'detribalized' working class, for example, the Stalinist authorities consistently bemoaned the slow process of working-class formation among the Central Asian peoples . . . The fundamental principle of Soviet education policy was to implement mandatory universal primary and, ultimately, secondary instruction . . . The universal Soviet curriculum also had an economic and political logic, albeit a completely different one from the colonial approach: to create a loyal, modern, interchangeable population suitable for rapid industrial development" (p. 288).

21. See in particular, Martin, *The Affirmative Action Empire*. Importantly, this process of modernization addressed directly the issue of women and of religion. See, respectively, Northrop, *Veiled Empire* and Khalid, *Islam after Communism*.

22. About Central Asia, see, Khalid, *The Politics of Muslim Cultural Reform*. Regarding the "global" dimension of reformist trends, see the collection of texts in Kurzman, *Modernist Islam*.

23. E.g., in the 1930s the Algerian Association of Ulama debated with the Young Algerians whether it would be possible to retain Algeria as a part of the French Republic if the French granted full status to Islamic law and full citizenship to all the Algerians then ruled by the indigenous code. See Berque, *French North Africa* and Merad, *Le réformisme musulman en Algérie de 1925 à 1940*.

24. See particularly, Keller, *To Moscow, Not Mecca* and Khalid, *Islam after Communism*.

25. For the debate about informal and parallel Islam in the Soviet Union see, in particular, Bennigsen and Wimbush, *Mystics and Commissars*; Poliakov, *Everyday Islam*.

26. Regarding the Soviet efforts at empowering women's organizations as a means of weakening Islamic/traditional networks of authority – and their failings – see Northrop, *Veiled Empire*; Kamp, *The New Woman in Uzbekistan*; Edgar, "Bolshevism, patriarchy, and the nation," pp. 252–72. Evidently, confronted with an often dysfunctional Soviet bureaucracy,

Islamic-based networks, alongside clans and reconstructed *asabiyya*, remained empowered and active as patronage networks in the Central Asian republics. See, e.g., Roy, *The New Central Asia*.

27. As Martin notes in connection with Beissinger's argument about the subjective dimension of the notion of empire, Communist leaders were very aware of the risks associated with such imperial ascriptions, and the "affirmative action" dimension of the nationality policies was in part at least, "a strategy designed to avoid the perception of empire." Martin, *The Affirmative Action Empire*, p. 19.

28. Khalid, *Islam after Communism*. While in the MENA, Islamism and Arabism stressed that Arabic was an important element of their common pre- and post-colonial condition, in Central Asia the Soviet policies of modernization and indigenization (*korenzatsiia*) resulted in the progressive imposition of the Latin (1920s–1930s) and then Cyrillic (1940s onward) scripts in replacement of the Arabic script; thereby creating further impediments to the articulation of a common "Islamic bond." See, *passim*, Suny and Martin (eds), *A State of Nations*.

29. Compare Burgat, *L'islamisme au Maghreb* with Mitchell, *The Society of the Muslim Brothers*.

30. See, e.g., Murphy, *Economic and Political Change in Tunisia*; Hinnebusch, *Syria: Revolution from Above*.

31. See in particular, Zeghal, *Islamism in Morocco*; Brand, "Al-Muhajrin w-al-Ansar"; Herb, *All in the Family*.

32. This process led to the entrenchment of what Ayubi called "hard" states, relying heavily on coercion to remain in power, rather than "strong" states able to mobilize effectively the resources at their disposition. Ayubi, *Overstating the Arab State*.

33. See, e.g., Zubaida, *Islam, the People and the State*.

34. For an early account of this re-articulation see, Salamé (ed.), *Democracy without Democrats?*.

35. This strategy was not merely the outcome of an ideological rapprochement, but also a pragmatic political move in circumstances where Jadidi scholars were often loosing out against more traditionalist or conservative Islamic leaders. See Khalid, *The Politics of Muslim Cultural Reform*.

36. Compare the more subversive role attributed to Islam in Bennigsen's and Wimbush's *Mystics and Commissars* with its more traditional function described in Poliakov's *Everyday Islam*. See also Atkin, "The survival of Islam in Soviet Tajikistan," pp. 605–18.

37. Olcott, "Soviet Islam and world revolution," pp. 487–504.

38. Bennigsen, "Unrest in the world of Soviet Islam," pp. 770–86.

39. For an analysis of the historical evolution of these trends see, Ro'i, *Islam in the Soviet Union*.

40. Just like the scholarship on Islamism was found to be wanting at the time of the Iranian revolution, so too an understanding of the significance of

Islamism in Central Asia was limited in the aftermath of the collapse of the Soviet Union. See, Eickelman (ed.), *Russia's Muslim Frontiers*.
41. Compare the more sensationalist arguments in Rashid, *Jihad* with the more sober assessments in Rasanayagam, "I'm not a Wahhabi: state power and Muslim orthodoxy in Uzbekistan," pp. 99–124, and in Khalid, "A secular Islam: nation, state, and religion in Uzbekistan," pp. 573–98
42. In the Tajik context, the changing objectives of the Islamist opposition and its shifting alliances with other political and military forces also illustrated the weak ideological organization of the Islamist movement there – a situation which in its turn facilitated post-conflict accommodation of their demands within the secularized political system.
43. These included the co-option of "moderate" Islamic leaders in the apparatus of official Islam – where they resumed a primarily "cultural" role – and the repression of those Islamist movements that were deemed to present a socio-political challenge to the ruling elite. See, e.g., Rasanayagam, "I'm not a Wahhabi"; Khalid, "A secular Islam."
44. See, e.g., Collins, "Ideas, networks, and Islamist movements," pp. 64–96; Akcali, "Islam as a 'common bond' in Central Asia," pp. 267–84; Karagiannis and McCauley, "Hizb ut-Tahrir al-Islami," pp. 315–34; Balci, "Fethullah Gülen's missionary schools in Central Asia and their role in the spreading of Turkism and Islam," pp. 151–77.
45. For illustrations of the framing of Islamist militancy in the region by Central Asian governments and by international players during the "war on terror," see Horsman, "Themes in official discourses on terrorism in Central Asia," pp. 199–213; Perthes, "America's 'Greater Middle East' and Europe," pp. 85–97.
46. See, e.g., Browers, *Political Ideology in the Arab World*.
47. See in particular, Bayat, *Making Islam Democratic*.
48. Eickelman and Piscatori, *Muslim Politics*.

Section V

Empire and External Sovereignty

13

Empire and State Formation: Contrary Tangents in Jordan and Syria

Raymond Hinnebusch

Empire matters for post-imperial sovereignty and variations in imperial impact make for variations in post-colonial states. Indeed, the initial differential impacts of imperial experiences have put Middle East states on divergent pathways that have endured for decades after independence. This chapter will compare the cases of Syria and Jordan, showing how the era of Western empires set them on enduring differential tangents that resulted in quite divergent regimes and contrary foreign policy orientations that persist to this day.

The analysis is in the tradition of historical sociology which assumes that each individual state's formation reflects some quite specific combination of local and external (international) agency; hence, there is a constant interaction as the external shapes the internal and the internal responds to the external. In this case, the decisive interaction is between, first, imperialism and local actors, resisting or collaborating; and, second, in the post-colonial period between the regional states system (protected or dominated by Western great powers) and differently constituted regimes in Jordan and Syria. State-building was in both cases intimately shaped by the post-First World War Versailles settlement, but responses to it differed, varying between rejection and acceptance. This depended on such factors as: (1) whether identity was satisfied or frustrated by boundaries imposed under imperialism; and (2) whether a regime originated in external imposition/protection by imperialism or revolution against imperialism and its residues. These factors, in turn, affected whether satisfied or dissatisfied social forces were incorporated or excluded at regime formation, whether elite and popular identity were congruent, hence, whether state-building responded to threats from within or without, and whether a regime saw the ex-imperial powers as threats to or protectors of its sovereignty. This is not to say that states were inexorably set on pre-determined paths. Indeed,

under sovereignty the continuing interaction of agent (state) and structure (international system) might either dilute or reinforce the original
tangent; and, in fact, there are several successive watersheds which did
so. However, what is striking is that many of the systemic forces and the
domestic reactions were themselves residues or consequences of empire.

Imperialism and Regime Origins: The Roots of Regime Divergence in Hashemite Jordan and Ba^cathist Syria

The contemporary Syrian and Jordanian states were initially parts of the
same country, *bilad ash-sham*, a geographical and cultural, albeit not
political, entity that was dismembered and divided between the Western
imperial powers, Britain and France. Yet, despite the fact that what
became the two states was hitherto a nearly undifferentiated socio-cultural
space, almost at birth they embarked on quite opposite state formation
paths and opposing foreign policy tangents: an increasingly radicalized
republic followed a revisionist nationalist foreign policy in Syria while
a conservative monarchy followed a status quo foreign policy in Jordan.
What explains this contrary response to what was, across the region, a
fairly uniformly despised Versailles settlement? This section will explore,
as an explanation, the varying impact of imperialism on the two states-in-
formation.

OTTOMAN INHERITANCES AND EXPERIENCE

Under the Ottomans, the two parts of historic Syria had slightly different
experiences. The north with its large trading cities, arable land and emerging landed notables, had a more complex social structure compared with
the more tribal south, where arable land was scarce and land holdings
more fragmented. Syria also had many more minorities, both Islamic and
Christian sects and non-Arabs; secular Arabism was the one identity most
(not all) of them shared and most of the minorities embraced it as a way
of achieving integration on equal status into the political community. The
emergence of Arabism was a key factor in the rejection of French rule. By
contrast, Jordan had only the Muslim Circassian minority, settled by the
Ottomans, and the greater weight of the Bedouin – two non-politicized
social forces that would not contest the British power in Jordan. Finally,
while Syria was fairly integrated into the Ottoman Empire through state
schools, elite recruitment and local self-government, with the result that
Syria remained largely loyal to the empire in the First World War and
largely unresponsive to the British and certainly never to the claims of

French tutelage, Jordan was open to the Arabian peninsula, less solidly incorporated into the empire and, hence, more welcoming of rule by the Hijazi Hashemites, even if under the umbrella of the British.

INCORPORATION INTO WESTERN EMPIRE: A TALE OF TWO BROTHERS

The British had promised Sharif Hussein of Mecca an independent Arab state in greater Syria if he revolted against the Ottomans, but also secretly plotted to divide up the area, taking Palestine and Iraq for themselves and allocating northern Syria, including Lebanon, to the French. Hussein's son, Prince Faisal, arrived in Syria under the banner of Arab nationalism but sponsored by the British. Most Syrians had remained loyal to the Ottomans and widely rejected a Western takeover, and when Faisal summoned a Syrian general congress to strengthen his hand at Versailles, it was dominated by the nationalist al-Fatat movement which demanded the independence of greater Syria. Abandoned by Britain, Faisal was pushed into accepting French patronage for his kingdom, but this was rejected by the congress. Even more radical grassroots organizations pressured Faisal and prepared to resist a French takeover. The French were, therefore, only able to take Syria by military conquest, defeating the Arab army at Maysalun, in part because of aerial bombardment. For Syrian nationalists, Britain was as much to blame as France for this dashing of the promise of independent statehood.[1]

Meanwhile Faisal's brother, Abdullah, at the head of a column headed for Syria, was prevailed upon by the British to remain in Jordan and assume governance of the area for which the British could not spare forces. Churchill saw him as an ideal agent since, not a popular native, he would be dependent on Britain; yet he was shrewd in dealing with tribal leaders and would restrain anti-Zionist and anti-French elements. In short, the British created Jordan as a buffer state to protect the unfolding Western/ Zionist projects in Palestine and in Abdullah found a ready collaborator.[2]

CONTRASTING EXPERIENCES UNDER IMPERIALISM

The French initially attempted to rule Syria through directly appointed Syrian officials shadowed by advisors who could veto their actions. Pacification of the country required a large army of 70,000 at its height for extended periods, mostly composed of Africans, and a minority-recruited *Troupes Spéciales*, with Syrians' taxes used to pay for their own occupation. The French practiced divide-and-rule, dividing the country into regional segments and fostering separate minority identities.

French rule generated a multitude of grievances. Economic links with Turkey were broken, Lebanon separated and later Iskandarun conceded to Turkey. A private French bank was given the concession to issue Syrian currency pegged to the French franc which depreciated heavily; the land tax was doubled; the lack of an adequate tariff led to decline of artisan manufacture, halving between 1913 and 1937 and leading to mass urban unemployment; peasants feared land registration and that French encouragement of commercial agriculture would threaten security of their tenures.

There was serious discontent throughout the mandate period that burst out in regular uprisings, which, however, were usually not coordinated enough to force the French out. Risings began with one by the Alawis in 1920 and another by Ibrahim Hananu in Aleppo. In Damascus, Abdul Rahman Shabandar led mass marches of students, religious leaders and quarter bosses, and an effective strike closing down the city gave national-ists some negotiating cards and showed the precariousness of French rule. In the Great Syrian revolt of 1925–7, well-armed Druze mountain fighters linked up with urban uprisings and it took France 50,000 troops using the most brutal methods to pacify the country.[3]

Hated by most Syrians, French rule depended on coercion and col-laborators whom they co-opted from the biggest landlords whose control over their estates was consolidated under the French at the expense of the peasantry and who needed French protection against radical social forces. However, these collaborators never enjoyed enough support to make them very useful and the 1925–7 rebellion showed the French that they had to compromise with Syrian opinion. They experimented with co-opting moderate nationalist elements who enjoyed support and were also willing to enter a power-sharing deal; hence, allowing the forma-tion of parties and elections to a national assembly. A National bloc (*al-kutla al-watani*) emerged, dominated by great landowning families and wealthy merchants from Damascus and Aleppo, which, by linking the clientalist networks of many notables, won every fair election. The nationalists demanded the reunification of the country including the return of Lebanon, tariff protection of Syrian industry, a national currency, an education system and army, and a treaty giving limited independence like that conceded by the British in Iraq – all measures unacceptable to France. The moderate nationalists had to prove to the population that they could win increasing independence through political means and thereby marginalize both the overt collaborators and the radi-cals who rejected any compromise short of full independence. In 1936, demands for a treaty took the form of a general strike and riots; fearing disorder would spread from the city to the countryside, the French undertook to negotiate for a treaty but were determined to maintain commercial privileges, military bases, oil rights and control of foreign policy which the Syrian parliament and public opinion rejected. In the event, the French were never willing to concede real powers to Syrian politicians, knowing full well that they would use them to push for total independence. What ended France's rule in Syria was its weakening in the Second World War and the post-war Soviet, US and British recognition of Syrian independence. When Syria rejected French efforts to keep special privileges after sovereignty, the French bombarded Damascus, sparking British intervention that forced their withdrawal.[4]

The new Transjordanian regime, by contrast, worked closely with Britain from the start to pacify society. Abdullah was wholly dependent on the British to consolidate his authority: his British subsidy was greater than any resources extractable from a resource-poor society, ensuring his dependence on the British would be matched by his autonomy of his own people.[5] He called on the Royal Air Force to break resistance from the tribes, then used British subsidies to co-opt their shaykhs; he was dependent on the British for protection from the Zionists who coveted Transjordan and to turn back an invasion by the Wahhabi Ikhwan.[6] The pillar of the state was the Arab Legion, British officered and recruited from the tribes and Circassian minority, hence, immune to nationalist currents.[7] By contrast to Syria where conflict between great landlords and the peasantry created social ferment fuelling nationalist rebellion, similar tensions were absent from Jordan's more egalitarian social structure. Having inherited the least urbanized part of historic Syria and finding its strongest support in the pre-national tribal Bedouin, the monarchy forged the state around this social force and used it, under British pressure, to marginalize weaker urban nationalist elements.

The contrasting experiences of these two parts of Greater Syria set them on different pathways from the outset. If in some ways Jordan's founder, King Abdullah, "claimed" Jordan from Britain, the French conquered Syria by military force. In Jordan, co-optation predominated over coercion; in Syria it was the reverse. In consequence, France would never enjoy special or treaty relations with an independent Syria, while the Hashemites valued their British, and later American, connection. Britain's indirect rule in Jordan was far more successful than France's more direct rule in Syria; in Syria's more nationally mobilized society, finding a collaborator comparable in stature to Abdullah proved impossible, at least after the French expelled Faisal and imposed a proto-republican regime.

CONTRARY PERCEPTIONS OF IMPERIAL IMPACT

If the Hashemite regime was the beneficiary of Jordan's separation from Syria, Damascus felt itself a victim of the fragmentation of historic Syria. Damascus had memories of imperial greatness under an Arab Umayyad dynasty, making for an Arab nationalist identity, while Amman was a provincial backwater and Jordan's pre-Islamic polity at Petra enjoyed no comparable historical resonance. This had inevitable consequences for their attitudes toward the Versailles settlement. Although Emir Abdullah had viewed Jordan as a launching pad for reuniting historic Syria and intrigued until his death to bring about "Greater Syria" under his leadership, his utter dependence on the British, who sternly discouraged such ventures, meant that this quintessential realist ended up acquiescing not only in the permanent dismemberment of historic Syria, but in the transformation of Jordan into a buffer state at odds with its official Arab identity.[8] It is widely accepted (Salibi; Adelson) that Abdullah received British support on condition that he allowed Jordan to be a buffer zone against the Wahhabis and avoided troubling the French in Syria, the British in Iraq and the Zionists in Palestine.[9] Abdullah came to be regarded by the British as their "only sure ally,"[10] especially when, during the Second World War, his army fought alongside them in their suppression of the nationalist Rashid Ali government in Iraq. By contrast, Syrian volunteers, many of whom would later surface as leaders of Arab nationalist parties, including future Ba^cath party leader Akram Hawrani, traveled to Iraq as volunteers to defend Rashid Ali against the British. The only chance Abdullah got to enact his ambitions was when the British abandoned Palestine and he reached a 1948 deal with the Zionists to divide the country, an act which, far from endowing him with Arab nationalist legitimacy, made him a pariah in the Arab world. This also ended in the incorporation of the Palestinian "West Bank" into Jordan, making an intensely irredentist and Arab nationalist population the majority in the new state. From this the Hashemite regime acquired a shared interest with Israel in keeping its big Palestinian population politically demobilized.[11] If in rhetoric the dynasty continued to proclaim its Arabism, in practice Jordan's was the Arab regime most incompatible with, and threatened by, Arab and Palestinian nationalism, hence, its very survival was utterly dependent on external protection.[12]

The impact of Syria's imperial experience on its politics was quite the opposite. Imperialism, in radically truncating historic Syria, created a deep-seated irredentism. Syrian irredentism was further inflamed when the French ceded the Arab-majority province of Iskanderun to

Turkey in 1939 in order to win its favor against Nazi Germany. The Zionist colonization of Palestine, viewed as a lost portion of historic Syria, also deepened Syrian irredentism, expressed in an utter rejection of Israel's legitimacy. Anti-imperialist pan-Arabism and pan-Syrianism, expressing impulses to reconstruct historic *bilad ash-sham* and/or merge the Syrian state (seen as an artificial creation of imperialism) in a wider Arab nation became the most widely shared political sentiments in Syria. For the first quarter of a century of its independent existence, the Syrian state, unable to count on the identification and support of its population, was weak, insecure and the victim of acute domestic instability and vulnerable to pan-Arab appeals.[13] If the Hashemite regime benefited from the 1948 war with Zionism (by incorporating the West Bank), Syria's republican oligarchy suffered a mortal blow to the precarious legitimacy won in the independence struggle against France for its perceived failure to defend Palestine. While no Syrian politician could hope to gain or keep power without affirming his commitment to pan-Arabism and rejection of Israel, the state initially remained too weak to be an actor rather than a victim of the regional power struggle, and foreign policy took the form of a rhetorical rejectionism meant to appease the public.[14]

Path Dependency under Sovereignty

Well after formal empire, Syria and Jordan remained profoundly affected by its permanent consequences: imperialism left behind a flawed states system with high levels of insecurity that allowed the British and then US hegemons to try to replace formal with informal empire in the region. Yet, faced with multiple threats from within and without, Jordan and Syria initially chose diametrically opposite foreign policy responses to this. Jordan bandwagoned with the West – Britain, then the United States – to acquire protection and the continuance of economic subsidies; Syria, by contrast, sought nationalist legitimacy within by a revisionist foreign policy, while diversifying its dependencies and seeking protection during the Cold War from the world's revisionist counter-hegemon, the Soviet Union. If in the initial years of independence contrary reactions to empire consolidated the divergent tangents of Syria and Jordan, at a later point, the quite different costs incurred on both tangents and their efforts to respond to similar systemic (regional and international) threats and take advantage of similar opportunities (oil revenues) drove a certain limited convergence.

POLITICAL MOBILIZATION AND ARAB NATIONALISM: 1950S–1960S

The era of pan-Arab political mobilization impacted differentially on the two states, propelling them further in contrasting directions. As artificial states with no history of statehood or separate identity, both were uniquely vulnerable to the appeal of Arab nationalism, especially as it was power-fully propagated from Nasser's Egypt. The Arab nationalist mobilization of the emerging middle classes soon threatened the very foundations of oligarchic and monarchic rule, but while the latter survived in Jordan, in Syria revisionist forces seized power, freezing the two states into diametrically opposite positions.

In Jordan, while the youthful King Hussein may have aspired to an Arab identity, Nasser viewed Arabism and Jordan's Western alignment as incompatible and Arab nationalists saw Jordan as an artificial and ille-gitimate obstacle to Arab unity and, later, to the formation of an effective eastern front against Israel. They and Palestinian nationalists saw Jordan's attempts to pacify its border with Israel as preventing the mobilization of the Palestinian population in the struggle to recover their homeland. Arab nationalism was thus chiefly a threat against which Hussein was consistently on the defensive, not a role to be embraced.[15]

As Arab nationalism spread, the regime's British alignment became incompatible with domestic political stability and legitimacy. Each time King Hussein attempted to incorporate the rising middle class into the regime through political liberalization, the resultant mobilization of Arab nationalist opinion threatened to force Jordan out of its Western alignment. To appease the public, free elections were permitted in 1956, resulting in a nationalist–leftist government under Suleiman Nabulsi that abrogated the Anglo-Jordanian treaty and attempted to steer Jordan toward diplomatic relations with the USSR and China and into the Arab collective security agreement as a substitute for the Western-sponsored Baghdad Pact. It is telling that Nabulsi was able to take these initiatives only after security promises from the Arab states to replace the British subsidy (which were not kept). When Hussein's dismissal of Nabulsi over his resistance to the Eisenhower Doctrine precipitated an attempted coup by nationalist officers, a general strike and massive demonstrations, the king suspended democracy and unleashed his Bedouin-staffed repressive apparatus.[16] Upon the 1958 overthrow of the Hashemites in Iraq, he called on British military intervention which enabled him to consolidate a royal dictatorship. Thus, a combination of repression and foreign interven-tion kept Jordan's Western alignment intact. Yet no political normality was possible in Jordan as long as it stood against Arab – and the rising

Palestinian – nationalism. Moreover, surrounded on all sides by often hostile states, an insecure regime had no alternative to bandwagoning – only whether it would bandwagon regionally or rely on Western global patrons. When the 1967 crisis with Israel aroused the powerful pan-Arab sentiment of the populace, the king had to choose and was swept into an alliance with Egypt on the eve of the war. This move, at odds with the interests and normal disposition of the regime, ended in the loss of half his kingdom (the "West Bank"); the dynasty survived, having learned the lesson of regional bandwagoning.

In Syria, by contrast, radical forces successfully challenged and swept away the old order. Oligarchic-dominated political institutions failed both to absorb the political mobilization of the middle class and to address the growing agrarian unrest. In contrast to Jordan, where conservative tribes dominated the army, in Syria, the military, expanding to meet the Israeli threat and recruited from middle-class and peasant youth, was a hotbed of populist dissent, radicalized by the conflict with Israel and Nasser's anti-imperialism. The West's backing of Israel inflamed the people and de-legitimized pro-Western politicians and the Western economic ties of the landed–commercial oligarchy. This fuelled the rise of radical parties – notably the Ba^{c}ath Party – and the military coups and counter-coups that de-stabilized the state and gradually pushed the oligarchic elite from power.[17]

Domestic instability coincided with perceptions of a rising threat from Israel as border skirmishes over the de-militarized zones left over from the 1948 war escalated. Syria could not do without protective alignments, but Syrians were deeply divided between the conservative politicians who advocated adhesion to the Western-sponsored Baghdad Pact and Egypt's Nasser who opposed the pact in the name of non-alignment and Arab collective security. Since the fate of the Baghdad Pact was believed to turn on Syria's choice, a regional and international "struggle for Syria" took place (1954–8). The mobilization of Syria's nationalist middle class swung the balance in favor of Egypt and those aligned with Cairo – above all, the Ba^{c}ath Party – leading to the 1956 formation of a pro-Egyptian, anti-imperialist National Front government. The West's sponsorship of several abortive conservative coups against it and a 1957 attempt to quarantine Syrian radicalism under the Eisenhower Doctrine, backed by Turkish threats, precipitated Soviet counter threats against Turkey and a backlash of pro-Communist feeling inside Syria. It was this sense of interlocking external siege and internal polarization which led Ba^{c}ath leaders to seek salvation in a short-lived (1958–61) union with Egypt.[18]

The coup that brought the Ba^{c}ath Party to power in 1963 was an outcome of Syria's previous nationalist mobilization. However, once in power the Ba^{c}ath Party, facing opposition not just from the oligarchy it had overthrown, but also from middle-class political rivals such as the Nasserites and Muslim Brothers with whom it would not share power, suffered a precipitous narrowing of its support base. On top of this, the regime itself was wracked by a power struggle along sectarian, generational and ideological lines in which "ex-peasant" radicals, in particular Alawis, assumed power at the expense of middle-class moderates. Foreign policy was an issue in this struggle, with the Ba^{c}athi radicals seeking nationalist legitimacy by sponsoring Palestinian fedayeen raids into Israel and a pan-Arab revolution against pro-Western monarchies like Jordan. This, however, ignoring Israeli military superiority, brought on the 1967 defeat, the Israeli occupation of the Syrian Golan Heights, and the discrediting of the radical Ba^{c}athists.[19]

The occupation of the Golan Heights made Syria a permanently dissatisfied power and further locked into the struggle with Israel; yet Syria had learned the hard way the costs of ignoring the regional power balance. This dilemma provoked the rise to power of a new "realist" wing of the Ba^{c}ath under Hafiz al-Asad. The "system" level had socialized the radical regime into the realist rules of international politics in which ideology had to be subordinated to the power balance. The actual issue that precipitated Asad's coup and which signaled the triumph of prudence over revolutionary zeal was his opposition to the radicals' attempted intervention in the Jordanian civil war of 1970 in the hope of protecting the Palestinian fedayeen and overthrowing the monarchy.[20]

WAR, RENT AND REGIME CONSOLIDATION: 1970s–1980s

In both states, the unstable regimes of the 1950s and 1960s were by the 1970s seemingly stabilized. This consolidation was, ironically, a by-product of the shared disaster of the 1967 war and of the oil boom unleashed by the 1973 war.

In Jordan, consolidation was abetted by the discrediting of Arab nationalism in the 1967 war, the main ideological opposition to Hashemite rule. The war also precipitated the rise of a state-within-a-state, the Palestinian fedayeen movement. However, the regime was consolidated by the smashing of this challenge in 1970, the subsequent purge of Palestinian and nationalist elements from the army and state, sharply reinforcing their tribalist East Bank composition, and the American and Israeli threats which, in helping to defeat the Syrian intervention in support of the fedayeen, reinforced the belief that outside powers would not permit the regime's overthrow. Equally crucial was the increasing availability of rent (Arab aid) after the post-1973 oil boom, allowing the state apparatus to incorporate a significantly larger trans-Jordanian segment of the population, giving it – as a privileged element – an enhanced stake in the status quo against the excluded Palestinians. However, the Palestinians, pushed into the private sector, thrived on the remittances of the oil boom years, helping to reconcile them to the status quo; simultaneously, the Muslim Brothers were cultivated by the monarchy as a counter to the nationalist left. The regime, able to rely on repression and external protection, did not invest in a society-penetrating political infrastructure. Instead, standing above and arbitrating among this divided society, the king was enabled to co-opt old enemies and heal old wounds, permitting a relatively mild version of authoritarianism by comparison with that in neighboring republics.[21]

King Hussein's post-1967 foreign policy focused on coping with the loss of the West Bank, but his strategy was much more ambivalent than Syria's drive to recover the Golan Heights. Unable to trust the Palestinian and urban majority of the population, the regime could not create the mass conscription military that might have enabled it to deal with Israel from a position of strength or to relieve its security dependence on the United States. Amman could rely only on diplomacy to maintain its claim to the West Bank and not just against Israel's occupation of the territory but also against the PLO, which, by the mid-1970s, sought to claim it as the locus of a Palestinian state (with Gaza). Indeed, Jordan, isolated by its 1970 repression of the fedayeen and left out of the 1973 war, lost, as a result, the legitimacy battle in the inter-Arab arena and the PLO was designated by Arab summits as having the sole legitimate claim to the West Bank. After Sadat's separate peace with Israel, which temporarily brought Syria and Jordan together, the king alternated between sticking with the Arab consensus against further separate deals with Israel (for which Jordan was rewarded with large Arab rent transfers after the 1980 Baghdad summit) and exploring one, such as the Reagan Plan which excluded Syria; the latter antagonized Damascus which brought Jordan to realign with Syria's rival, Saddamist Iraq. In the Iran–Iraq War, King Hussein supported Iraq against Iran, which he saw as a revolutionary threat to all conservative monarchies and which put Jordan on the same side as Washington at a time when Syria embraced Iran as a valuable counter to Israel and was deeply at odds with Washington.[22]

Ultimately, however, the failure of negotiations with Israel led the king to relinquish Jordan's claim on the West Bank to the PLO, enabling a reconciliation with the Palestinians that was a watershed in the further consolidation of the Jordanian state. Another watershed took place when the decline of oil rent after 1986 forced the regime into IMF-imposed austerity measures which unleashed the 1989 riots, shaking the regime's hard-won stability. But the regime turned a liability into an advantage, opting to trade a restoration of political liberalization for public acceptance of economic austerity, a bargain for which the political opposition recognized, in return, the legitimacy of the monarchy. The regime's stand with Iraq against Western intervention in the 1990–1 Gulf War won the king an additional nationalist legitimacy windfall at home. The very longevity of King Hussein's rule had endowed him with a certain patriarchal prestige, acknowledged even by the opposition. The Hashemite regime entered the 1990s relatively consolidated and more at peace with civil society than ever hitherto – its foreign policy temporarily congruent with nationalist opinion.[23]

In Syria, consolidation took a different form in the country's more intractable society: the Ba'ath regime, facing powerful urban upper class and Islamic opposition, relied on a complex strategy to survive. In the first stage, the radical Ba'athists launched a "revolution from above" aimed at securing the social bases of power through land reform, nationalizations and government control over the market that broke Syria's economic dependency on the West. The regime also forged a strong ideological party which mobilized a largely rural base of support and institutionalized the Ba'ath's socialist and Arab nationalist ideology. After his 1970 seizure of power, al-Asad forged a hydra-headed security apparatus recruited from his Alawi kin and clients that gave the regime a neo-patrimonial core similar to Jordan's tribalist one; additionally, a regime-dependent segment of the Sunni bourgeoisie, appeased by economic liberalization and state patronage, became another pillar of the regime. Clientele networks serviced by the rent from domestic oil revenues and aid from the Arab oil states widened the circles with a stake in the regime. The regime's role as the most steadfast defender of the Arab cause in the battle with Israel became the basis of its wider domestic legitimacy and of the regional stature that entitled it to the financial backing of other Arab states.[24] The regime harnessed the public sector and external rent for the construction of a huge partly conscript military establishment buttressed by Soviet arms and designed to contest Israel's occupation of the Golan Heights.[25] If the Hashemite monarchy had acquired some Islamic legitimacy through its Hashemite roots and alliance with the Muslim Brotherhood, for Syria's Alawi elite, the Muslim Brotherhood was an irreconcilable opponent which mounted an uprising that was only repressed with great brutality that hardened the regime's authoritarianism; the regime had all the more to prove its Arab nationalist credentials against Israel while also trying to link the Ikhwan to those seeking to weaken Syria against Israel.

The consolidation of the regime was accompanied by the concentration of power in Asad's hands, allowing him to mobilize the resources and attain the autonomy of domestic constraints needed to pursue a rational foreign policy that matched goals and capabilities, turning Syria from a victim into a regional actor which had to be reckoned with by its much more powerful opponents, Israel and the United States. Asad's foreign policy after 1970 reflected a combination of realism and tenacity in the struggle with Israel. He had the autonomy to enforce a reduction in the publicly expected aims of Syria's policy from liberating Palestine to the limited, but still very ambitious, goals of recovering the Golan Heights and achieving a Palestinian state in the West Bank/Gaza. He welcomed US brokerage of a peace settlement with Israel, but refused for a quarter of a century to settle for a partial or separate peace abandoning the Palestinians. He struck the alliances, regardless of ideology, with both the Soviet Union and the conservative Gulf oil states needed to build up the military capabilities to back his challenge to Israel's hold of the Golan Heights in the 1973 war and to avoid bargaining from weakness in the periodic subsequent peace negotiations. Backed by his Soviet patron and an alliance with Islamic Iran, he also engaged in risky resistance to the 1982 US and Israeli penetration of Lebanon, while sending the message to Washington that without accommodating Syrian interests no peace could be imposed in the region.[26]

Thus, systemic forces – war defeat, the need to recover occupied territory and the oil boom – drove parallel internal consolidations, giving ex-plebian elites in Syria a stake in the status quo similar to Jordan's Hashemites and endowing both king and president with the security and autonomy to pursue "pragmatic" foreign policies. There was thus a certain convergence between them – Syria's abandonment of radical revisionism and Jordan's accommodation with regional and domestic opinion. But differential state-building had reversed their original relative strengths: Jordan, which under Abdullah had been the militarily stronger state, eschewed further military build-up, while Syria pursued it. Differential capabilities meant that while Jordan was dependent on the appeasement of Israel and the good offices of its US patron, Asad could combine openness to US diplomacy with power-balancing against it and Israel. In addition, different leadership styles reflected different state tangents originating in imperialism and resistance to it. At the helm in Syria was a "provincial," Hafiz al-Asad, a product of the Syrian village, school and military, who seldom left Damascus and saw Syria as the "beating heart of Arabism," bearer of a revolution against imperialism and Zionism; in the other ruled King Hussein, a "cosmopolitan," the product of British boarding schools and attuned to metropolitan culture, who saw Jordan as a force for moderation against nationalist extremism and a bridge between the West and the Arab world.

THE END OF BIPOLARITY, THE IRAQ WAR AND THE MIDDLE EAST PEACE PROCESS

The end of the Cold War and the emergence of American hegemony in the region put Arab states, especially former Soviet clients like Syria, under pressure to "bandwagon" with – that is, appease – the US hegemon. Syria initially reacted to the decline of its Soviet patron by trying to trade adhesion to the Western coalition against Iraq during the Gulf War for American pressure on Israel to evacuate the Golan Heights. Jordan, however, unexpectedly defied its Western and Gulf patrons in the Gulf War, tilting toward Iraq; this won King Hussein legitimacy at home but cost him patronage abroad: a course at odds with the regime's historic choices and interests. There was thus a certain convergence in regime tangents as Baᶜathist Syria moved toward accommodation with the West, while Hashemite Jordan moved toward accommodation with Arab nationalist opinion. The entry of both states into the Madrid peace process seemed to consolidate this convergence, but its differential outcome – success for Jordan, failure for Syria – reversed this tendency. After the Iraq War, King Hussein opted for a separate "warm peace" with Israel (even though the Palestinians and Syrian tracks soon stalled). This was the price Washington demanded for Jordan's rehabilitation as a US ally after its defiance during the Gulf War, allowing a restoration of the economic aid Jordan could not live without. This sacrificed domestic support among non-tribal civil society, both secular nationalist and Islamist. The regime promoted a "Jordan-first" (that is, not Arab) identity, signaling Jordan's return to its historic role as a buffer state against Arab nationalism. Syria's Asad had also entered the peace process, but Syria and Israel failed to reach a settlement: without the Golan Heights, Syria remained a dissatisfied power and could not adhere to the West-centric world order Jordan was embracing. The different outcomes of the peace process led to a disengagement of both regimes from the anomalous positions at odds with initial regime identities that they had assumed in the exceptional situation of the 1991 Gulf War, and restored them to their original opposing tangents.

At century's end, however, leadership succession again promised a convergence in regime tangents. Long-serving leaders passed on power to their sons, King Abdullah II (February 1999) and President Bashar al-Asad (June 2000), both of whom been socialized at a time of liberal ideological hegemony and saw the solution to their counties' economic crises in "modernization" and globalization. The first priority of Jordan's King Abdullah was economic modernization, which he believed depended on investment from Israel and aid from the United States, requiring close foreign policy alignment with both of them. However, after the al-Aqsa intifadah and Israeli violence against the Palestinians, Jordanian opinion turned so anti-Israeli that this policy was impossible without a further reversal of Jordan's earlier partial democratization. In Syria, Bashar al-Asad's priority was also economic modernization, accompanied by realignment with the West. However, this required peace with Israel, which was impossible after the rise of Israel's hard-line Sharon government and Washington's disinterest under George W. Bush in the peace process. Bashar opted for an alternative quick fix solution to Syria's economic problems, a tilt toward Saddam Hussein who was offering cheap oil and business opportunities in exchange for helping Iraq evade UN sanctions. This, however, brought Syria onto a collision course with the United States which was trying to isolate Iraq.

As a result, the historic foreign policy divergence between the regimes on the big issues in Arab politics was restored. While Jordan sought to dampen down the Palestinian intifadah, cracking down on the Jordanian branch of Hamas, Bashar advocated the breaking of relations with Israel and support for the intifadah and gave refuge to Hamas leaders. Under US pressure, Jordan broke its intimate economic ties with Iraq, allowing Syria to step into the gap and take them over. In the 2003 US war on Iraq, Abdullah permitted anti-Iraqi US deployment on its territory, while Syria supported the resistance to the US occupation of Iraq. The consequent US siege of Syria reversed the limited political liberalization with which Bashar had experimented on coming to power. At the end of the first decade of the twenty-first century, therefore, both regimes had reverted to authoritarian governance at home, but this was combined with diametrically opposing external policy orientations. Jordan's regime was at peace with the Versailles settlement and Syria's still at odds with it.

Conclusion

Empire can affect what comes after in at least two contrary ways: it can leave behind residues incorporated into the post-imperial order (Jordan) and it can provoke reactions leading to rupture with that order (Syria).

Which predominates will depend on the imperial experience. Table 13.1 summarizes and underlines the differential impact of imperialism on Syria and Jordan.

Table 13.1 Differential impact of imperialism on Syria and Jordan

	Syria	**Jordan**
Imperialism and state founding	Conquest of existing regime, identity violated	Creation of new regime, identity created
Coercion – co-optation balance	Coercion – divide-and-rule	Co-optation
Perceived impact of imperialism for regime	Victim, high damage but lesser dependency	Beneficiary, low damage but high dependency
Relation with imperialism	Rebellion against imperialism	Protection by imperialism
Nationalist mobilization and outcome	Middle-class and peasant mobilization – oligarchy overthrown	Middle-class repression – monarchy survives
Social forces incorporated	Plebeian ex-peasants	Tribal elites
Leadership style	Provincial Arab-centric	Cosmopolitan West-centric
After empire foreign policy orientation	Revisionist, balancing against the West	Status quo, bandwagoning with the West
Power structures	Strong	Weak

The Versailles settlement that imposed empire in MENA was widely seen, there as in Europe, as a victor's *dictat* by its victims, at odds with the norm of self-determination. Yet even within the region there were big variations in whether post-imperial states saw themselves as empowered or disempowered for sovereign statehood by the imperial experience. This depended on several factors. One was the amount of damage done under imperialism: populations in both Jordan and Syria suffered from the creation of Israel, but Syria suffered more from the forced fragmentation of the Mashriq and the imperial consolidation of big landed classes compared with the lesser class stratification in Jordan. Another is whether there was a strong prior identity that was violated by imperialism; this was certainly the case in Syria, where the infant Arab nationalist regime was destroyed by imperialism and in Jordan for much of the population but, importantly, not for Abdullah who, regardless of his Arabist discourse, ended up endowed with a kingdom owing to the break up of Syria. In consequence, the third factor, the balance between imperial coercion and co-optation, differed, with lighter touch British imperialism in Jordan contrasting with the heavy French use of repression and divide-and-rule in Syria. It also mattered whether the imperial impact advanced or crippled the economic viability of the state, with the outcome in Jordan more damaging, but generating instead of revolt a total dependency on external subsidies that has never been overcome. Finally, variations in imperial experience translated into different intensity and social depth of nationalist mobilization, with much higher levels in Syria driven by imperialism's greater damage and harsher methods of rule combined with a more developed and class-divided society explaining greater rupture with empire after statehood. Thus, the path from empire to sovereignty set the two states on different tangents from their very founding.

Even after empire, Syria and Jordan remained profoundly affected by its permanent consequences. Imperialism left behind a flawed states system, riven with irredentism from the incongruity of boundaries and identity, with both high levels of inter-state conflict and high domestic legitimacy deficits and instability. This system of weak states afflicted with economic dependency and high levels of insecurity allowed the British and then US hegemons to use divide-and-rule to try to replace formal with informal empire in the region. Yet, faced with multiple threats from within and without, Jordan and Syria chose diametrically opposite responses to this: Jordan bandwagoned – "omni-balanced"[27] – with the core hegemonic states to acquire protection and the continuance of economic subsidies; Syria by contrast chose "reverse omni-balancing," seeking nationalist legitimacy within by a revisionist foreign policy that challenged the Versailles settlement, while diversifying its dependencies and seeking protection during the Cold War from the world's revisionist counter-hegemon, the Soviet Union. These choices were most immediately a function of the contrary identities assumed by the two states – in spite of being essentially severed parts of the same country – moderate buffer state versus militant Arab nationalist state, as a result of their differential experiences under imperialism: what was for Syria a national disaster, spelled for the Hashemites the birth of the state. These identities also reflected the contrasting origins of the two states' regimes: Hashemite Jordan established and protected by imperialism, Baᶜathist Syria established in revolt against it. These contrary state formation experiences incorporated different kinds of social forces: during the pan-Arab 1950s, the mobilization of the nationalist middle class in Syria and its repression in Jordan hardened initial tangents; in the 1960s and 1970s, the rise from below of plebeian radicals in Syria and the co-optation of a pre-nationalist tribal elite in Jordan consolidated them. Elite identity also reinforced this path dependency: for example, the Hashemites' identity allowed them and Israeli leaders to construct a less threatening relationship than that which grew up between Syria and Israel, deepening the two contrary tangents. Finally, the differential origins and composition of the two regimes made for very different structures of power. Because the Ba^{c}ath regime, rising out of an anti-imperialist and anti-oligarchy revolution from below and engaged in conflict with Israel, could not depend on external intervention for protection, it had to establish mass incorporating political institutions capable of mobilizing the rural majority and compatible with a large mass conscription military. The Hashemite regime, able to depend on Western protection and, facing a majority Palestinian population whose loyalty was suspect, survived by demobilizing the nationalist majority and tribalizing the army. This meant that Syria could continue its nationalist tangent and Jordan could not, except briefly, even had the king so wanted. Defeat in war and the oil boom, driving state consolidation, started a convergence between the two states that was reinforced by the end of bipolarity and the beginnings of the peace process; but the differential outcome of the latter propelled them back onto divergent paths. Thus, to this day, both states remain products of the original sin – the breakup of *bilad ash-Sham* – accompanying their births.

Notes

1. Fromkin, *A Peace to End All Peace*, pp. 435–3; Yapp, *The Making of the Modern Near East 1792–1923*, pp. 301–51; Gelvin, *Divided Loyalties*.
2. Fromkin, *A Peace to End All Peace*, pp. 504–6, 510–11.
3. Fieldhouse, *Western Imperialism in the Middle East, 1914–1958*, pp. 246–62, 287–9.
4. Fieldhouse, *Western Imperialism in the Middle East, 1914–1958*, pp. 277–87.
5. Piro, *The Political Economy of Market Reform in Jordan*, pp. 17–18, 24–31; Robins, *A History of Jordan*, pp. 5, 15, 63.
6. Fromkin, *A Peace to End All Peace*,
7. Robins, *A History of Jordan*, pp. 5, 15, 63.
8. Salibi, *The Modern History of Jordan*, pp. 73–119.
9. Salibi, *The Modern History of Jordan*, pp. 86–95 and Adelson, *London and the Invention of the Middle East*, p. 200.
10. Monroe, *Britain's Moment in the Middle East 1914–1956*, pp. 156–60.
11. Salibi, *The Modern History of Jordan*, pp. 144–67.

12. Salibi, *The Modern History of Jordan*, pp. 144–67; Brand, *Jordan's Inter-Arab Relations*, p. 157; Robins, *A History of Jordan*, pp. 49, 69.
13. Dawn, "The rise of Arabism in Syria," and Maoz, "Attempts at creating a political community in modern Syria."
14. Seale *The Struggle for Syria*; Hinnebusch, *Syria: Revolution from Above*, pp. 139–40, 143–5.
15. Lynch, *State Interests and Public Spheres*, p. 25.
16. Salibi, *The Modern History of Jordan*, pp. 187–92; Lynch, *State Interests and Public Spheres*, p. 25; Robins, *A History of Jordan*, pp. 99–102.
17. Seale, *The Struggle for Syria*; Torrey, *Syrian Politics and the Military*.
18. Seale, *The Struggle for Syria*; pp. 164–306.
19. Hinnebusch, *Syria: Revolution from Above*, pp. 52–7.
20. Yaniv, "Syria and Israel: the politics of escalation," pp. 157–78.
21. Piro, *The Political Economy of Market Reform in Jordan*, pp. 59–63; Salibi, *The Modern History of Jordan*, pp. 243–49; Brand, *Jordan's Inter-Arab Relations*, pp. 153–6; Salloukh, "State strength, permeability, and foreign policy behavior."
22. Lynch, *State Interests and Public Spheres*, p. 26; Salibi, *The Modern History of Jordan*, pp. 250–63.
23. Lynch, *State Interests and Public Spheres*, pp. 71–165; Brand, *Jordan's Inter-Arab Relations*, pp. 149, 159; Brynen, "The politics of monarchical liberalization," pp. 71–100; Shyrock, "Dynastic modernism and its contradictions," pp. 60–1.
24. Hinnebusch, *Syria: Revolution from Above*.
25. Clawson, *Unaffordable Ambitions*.
26. Seale, *The Struggle for Syria*, pp. 226–66, 267–315, 344–49, 366–420; Maoz, *Asad: The Sphinx of Damascus*, pp. 113–24, 135–48.
27. David, "Explaining Third World alignment."

14

Rentierism, Dependency and Sovereignty in Central Asia

Wojciech Ostrowski

Twenty years after becoming independent states, all five Central Asian republics can be broadly characterized as either rentier or semi/quasi-rentier states. The "classic" rentier states – Kazakhstan and Turkmenistan – rely on rent (wealth) derived directly from the sale of oil and gas. Kyrgyzstan and Tajikistan rely on rent from a combination of indirect taxation on labor remittances from Kazakhstan and Russia, international aid, the leasing of access to their territory and the drug trade. Uzbekistan, relying heavily on the sale of cotton, gold and gas on the international market, along with labor remittances and to a lesser degree leasing access to territory, falls somewhere in between. The economic composition of the Central Asian region, which began taking its current shape with the unprecedented increase in oil prices at the beginning of 2000s, has started to mirror the Middle Eastern-style "division of labor" that developed between oil-rich Gulf and oil-poor Arab countries, as well as Pakistan and other states which have remained greatly dependent on labor remittances earned in the oil-rich states.[1]

The dependency of the Central Asian republics on rent has a far-reaching impact on these countries' foreign policies, their relationship with Russia and state sovereignty. In the case of Kazakhstan and Turkmenistan, the lack of viable alternatives to oil and gas exports and full dependency – until very recently – on the Russian-controlled pipeline system, have substantially narrowed their room for maneuver and allowed Russia to maintain the upper hand in its relationship with Central Asian oil and gas exporters. In sharp distinction to Kazakhstan and Turkmenistan, Uzbek over-reliance on cotton has allowed the ruling regime to pursue the most independent foreign policy in the region, the durability of which, however, is highly questionable due to unstable cotton prices on the international markets. Kyrgyz and Tajik dependency on foreign aid, labor remittances and leasing access to territory has forced ruling regimes to largely subordinate their foreign policies to the politics of the regional or international powers on which its economic survival currently depends. Their dependency on outside "patrons" explains both the presence of the US and Russian military bases on Kyrgyz territory, and Tajikistan's strong ties to Russia. In short, the key role that rent plays in the survival of the Central Asian states has either hampered these countries' sovereignty or made its maintenance very difficult.

Rentierism and Sovereignty

The rentier state concept attempts to elucidate the impact that rent derived mainly from the sale of oil and gas on the international markets has on the nature of the states and the political systems of resource- and energy-rich countries. Thus, those researchers working within the rentier state tradition focus on states in which the economy is dominated by rents rather than by productive enterprises like agriculture and manufacturing, and where the origin of the income is external. In addition, the rent is generated by a small elite, wherein the majority are involved in its distribution or utilization, and the state itself is the principal recipient. A rentier state accordingly plays a central role in distributing this wealth to the population.[2]

The rentier state concept was initially crafted by scholars of North African and Middle Eastern politics,[3] but over time has been applied to other areas of the world, including sub-Saharan Africa[4] and South America.[5] In recent years, with various degrees of success, the rentier state concept has also been applied to post-Soviet Central Asia and the Caucasus[6] and even to Russia.[7] The fact that the rentier state concept has traveled across space and time and endured as a valid notion is testimony to the initial analysis by Middle Eastern scholars who correctly decoded and described the dynamics of the rentier state and its impact on the political systems of the non-Western, post-colonial states.[8] Terry Karl, in the study of Venezuela written almost thirty years after the rentier state concept was first applied, argues that in essence all rentier states can be characterized by the same fundamental economic policy pattern: "maximizing the external extraction of rents for subsequent distribution through public spending according to a political logic."[9]

At the same time, the success that the rentier state concept enjoys has led to a situation in which the notion has been overstretched. Critics have pointed out that the concept was applied to various cases that did not necessarily meet Hazem Beblawi's criteria and, hence, faced the danger of losing its intellectual appeal.[10] One of the key problems has been the states whose economies over-rely on remittances and outside aid (rent), and for these reasons have been quickly grouped together with the oil- and gas-rich countries. Giacomo Luciani correctly notes that while remittances are an important flow of income – and contain a rent component – they do not accrue directly to the state, and therefore the term "rentier state" is not fitting here. He goes on to argue that the state may attempt to tax the income of economic migrants, but is in no position to do so before the income is repatriated. Thus, economies which rely on remittances, according to Luciani, do not constitute a full-blown rentier state but rather a rentier economy.[11] Beblawi calls these sorts of states "semi-rentiers without oil."[12]

The distinction between oil- and gas-rich rentier states and semi-rentier states that rely on remittances and international aid has important implications for the state–society relationship, and arguably also impact a country's foreign relationships. In the traditionally understood rentier state, rent provided the state with an extremely large and powerful economic and social role that fostered the long-term stability of the ruling regime and allowed it to survive internal as well as external crises.[13] The ruling elites of the semi-rentier state, which do not have access to abundant income, are expected to be affected by changes in the regional as well as the global economy and are inevitably less stable, and thus more likely to adapt to the changing environment.[14] For instance, they are more likely to liberalize some aspects of their economies and at times political life, but do not go so far as to fully democratize.[15] By the same token, the foreign policy of the semi-rentier state is more prone to change and also much more dynamic. This is due to the simple fact that labor remittances and international aid constitute the basis for a much weaker and less stable alliance between ruling regimes and regional, international powers than oil and gas. Hence, semi-rentier states can attempt to switch alliances from one patron to another.[16] The oil- and gas-rich rentier states are different in this respect, since they are often interlocked in long-term economic and military relationships with outside powers. These relationships tend to endure – mainly due to the physical nature of oil and gas – regardless of major political shifts at the regional or global level.[17] At the same time, the existing difference between rentier states and semi-rentier states should not obscure the fact that, at its most fundamental level, both foreign policies are entangled and shaped by various types of dependencies: dependencies which inevitably pose vital questions concerning state survival, state security and, ultimately, the sovereignty of rentier and semi-rentier states, as the example of Central Asia confirms.

Rentierism, Dependency and Central Asia

The rentierism and economic dependency in post-Soviet Central Asia is a direct result of two legacies: (1) the Soviet Union; and (2) the neo-liberal project that reached its high point with the collapse of the communist regimes in Europe and, in all but name, in Asia. The Soviet Union, due to its long-term domination of Central Asia, shaped it economically and politically, while the neo-liberal enterprise allowed the post-Soviets elites to consolidate key structural elements of the Soviet system vital to their rule – networks based on patronage and favor. Consequently, the collapse of the Soviet Union in Central Asia, at the time a much hailed "rupture," over time came to signify merely a launch of a post-Soviet narrative – where stress from the outset was firmly placed on the Soviet element – rather than the creation of something intrinsically new and unique.

Today's dependency of the key post-Soviet Central Asian economies on rent income, the origins of which are external, rather than on productive enterprises, is largely a legacy of the role that Central Asian republics played in the Soviet economy as suppliers of cotton, oil, gas and minerals to existing manufacturing centers located primarily in the Russian areas of the USSR. The role of Central Asia in the Soviet Union economy was further entrenched by the network of transport infrastructure that was built to serve the larger Soviet project.[18] The resource-dependent nature of the Central Asian economy on the eve of independence was actively reinforced by post-Soviet ruling elites. Their actions were motivated by two factors: (1) lack of any apparent alternatives to commodity based economies; and (2) their unbridled lust for power and wealth.

From the late Khrushchev era until early into Gorbachev's rule, regional Central Asian cadres were groomed and controlled by Moscow through an elaborate system of patron–client relationships.[19] The prime function of the Soviet Central Asian elites, who sat firmly at the top of their own patron–client pyramid, was to ensure that the republics met their quotas (something that they often failed to do) and to keep the population in check and under control (something that they never failed to do successfully). The Central Asian Soviet elites, who much to their own surprise overnight became rulers of the newly independent states,[20] chose to rely on existing industries and patron–client-based political structures as long as these allowed them to maintain relative social peace and successfully keep them in power.[21]

Whereas the Soviet Union set the material and political stage on which Central Asian elites have since been operating, it is important to recognize that the post-Soviet economic structure was also significantly shaped by the nature of the economic order that developed outside the Soviet Union and the larger socialist world in the late 1970s and 1980s. It should be remembered that 1991, a year in which the Central Asian republics gained their independence, was also one of the high points of the neo-liberal project, a project which (1) significantly aided the transformations of the Soviet Central Asian republics into rentier and semi-rentier economies, and (2) reinforced and deepened separations in the Central Asian economy which today are reflected in the regional "division of labor."

In reference to the first point, the price liberalization that followed the disintegration of the USSR, and which was actively encouraged by the advocates of the neo-liberal enterprise, instantly rewarded countries rich in natural resources and their rulers. The amounts of money to which yesterday's apparatchiks gained access was unimaginable to them only a few years earlier – the "success" was dazzling. Thus, the benefits that liberalization brought, along with the prospects of opening global markets, ensured that the foundations of a rentier post-Soviet economy and its specific mentality were firmly put in place.

In reference to the second point, the key Central Asian republics of Kazakhstan and Uzbekistan, which during the Soviet Union were vital to the regional economy and its economic future, managed largely to maintain and consolidate their dominant positions in the 1990s, whereas Kyrgyzstan and Tajikistan – resource-poor and heavily subsidized by Moscow – were in steady decline. The "winners" in the global neo-liberal "casino" were those Central Asian republics that could offer commodities (mainly oil and gas) that Russia and the external world still wanted. As a result, two decades after the collapse of the Soviet Union, Kyrgyzstan and Tajikistan are widely grouped together with the regions of the global South "excluded" from the neo-liberal project,[22] relegated to relying on a shadow criminal economy to re-integrate themselves back into the global economy. Philip Le Billion argues that the activities of those excluded from the neo-liberal enterprise revolve around tax evasion, tax havens and smuggling schemes, with some involved in drug trafficking, money laundering and illegal migration.[23] All of the above are a firm feature of today's Kyrgyzstan and Tajikistan, and are largely responsible for their political and economical decline as well as systemic political violence.

UZBEKISTAN AND TURKMENISTAN

The legacy of Soviet patterns of development have been most visible in Uzbekistan, where cotton constituted a vital part of the economy from the Second World War onward, and in Turkmenistan which besides being a cotton producer, also became an important exporter of natural gas from the 1970s. At the beginning of the 1990s, both countries substantially benefited from buoyant cotton prices, which allowed ruling regimes to maintain the status quo without any major economical and political reforms. In the 2000s, both regimes tried to preserve the situation from the 1990s. Hence, Uzbekistan deepened its dependency on cotton and in later years gold, gas and labor remittances, and Turkmenistan turned almost fully to gas exports. The Turkmen regime's concentration on gas exports accelerated after the rise in gas prices at the beginning of the 2000s, along with the failure of the Import Substitution Industrialization (ISI) program introduced by the government in the late 1990s.

In Uzbekistan, cotton production can be traced back to the nineteenth century when it was one of the key suppliers of cotton to Tsarist Russia. Cotton production rapidly expanded in Soviet Uzbekistan in the 1950s and 1960s, and by the 1980s the republic was qualified as a "monocultural economy" with some 65 percent of cultivated land being devoted to cotton production. The so-called "white gold" accounted for about two-thirds of the republic's agricultural output, and the Uzbek SSR produced 62 percent of all cotton grown in the Soviet Union in late Soviet times. On the eve of independence, Uzbekistan was the fourth biggest cotton producer in the world and the second leading exporter.[24]

The much talked about mechanization of the countryside – part of the so-called equalization policy aimed at balancing the levels of economic development and living standards of the country's diverse nationalities and regions[25] – did not take place. In the late 1980s more manual workers – largely woman, children and students – were picking cotton by hand than twenty years before. According to one author, in 1981 about 35 percent of the overall harvest was hand-picked.[26] In mid-1980s' Uzbekistan, more than half (around 58 percent) of the population worked in agriculture. The overwhelming majority of those living in the countryside were ethnic Uzbeks, whereas industrial management and the skilled labor sector were primarily composed of Russians and other Slavs who populated two urban centers.[27] Finally, most of the cotton output during Soviet times went to cotton mills in the Russian republic and was then sold on the international markets through centralized foreign trade agencies – "with little benefit to the growers."[28]

On face value, the relationship between the imperial core and the colonized periphery closely mirrored the type of dependency relationship that could be found in the Middle East.[29] However, in the Soviet Union the actual situation on the ground was much more complicated than, and not as clear-cut as, other parts of the world (that is, post-colonial sub-Saharan Africa or South America). It should be kept in mind that at the time of independence, the Uzbek economy was more diversified than the economies of other Central Asian republics. It included agriculture, light and heavy industry and branches of primary products.[30] Furthermore, in Uzbekistan the level of literacy, public health and education for women exceeded regional levels.[31] Yet the preservation of those Soviet "achievements" proved to be highly problematic to the Uzbek post-Soviet regime, which in the face of the post-Soviet chaos, largely abandoned other sectors of industry in favor of cotton and thus began a process of the steady retreat of the state, with far-reaching consequences for education, public health and the role of women in society.[32]

The turn toward the cotton industry in the post-Soviet period was significantly accelerated due to favorable cotton prices on the international markets in 1992–6, a move which left a lasting legacy on today's Uzbekistan.[33] Deniz Kandiyoti argues that in order to fully understand post-Soviet trajectories of the Central Asian republics, students of the region should not only take into account "the historical specificities of their colonial encounters but also very different modalities and temporalities of their insertion into world capitalist markets."[34] It is argued here that the initial policies and choices of the post-Soviet regime firmly linked the future of the country to the volatile commodity prices on the international markets. This argument is supported by the fact that despite the collapse of cotton prices toward the end of the 1990s, at the beginning of the 2000s the primary commodities, together with cotton fiber, still accounted for 75 percent of merchandise exports, with cotton alone accounting for about 40 percent.[35] In the second decade of independence, the Uzbek government attempted to cushion the fall in cotton prices with a partial liberalization of its economy. Yet the cotton industry remained subject to state orders and state control.

The winners in the new Uzbekistan have been those at the apex of power and their clients.[36] According to a report by the International Crisis Group, money obtained from the sale of cotton circulates within a small elite, and rarely if ever enters the agricultural financing system: "one estimate is that as little as 10 to 15 per cent of the income generated by the sale of cotton goes back into agriculture thus to the farmers."[37] The development of the oligarchy that governs today's Uzbek cotton industry goes back to the 1970s when a "clear-cut cotton *nomenklatura* had developed, with 'cotton-barons' dominating the [cotton] complex, making use of falsified output and yield data, illicit trade practices and forced labour."[38] The effects of the so-called "cotton curse" are most visible in the large numbers of labor migrants to Kazakhstan and Russia. In 2004–8 as many as 2.5 million Uzbeks left the country – a fact that the Uzbek government has officially denied – and by 2008 remittances consisted of 13 percent of the Uzbek economy.[39] The workers, who until the recent introduction of Western Union, carried their earnings back home in cash, were subject to indirect taxation by the state agencies at various stages of their journey.[40]

Other important sectors of the post-Soviet Uzbek rentier economy are gold and energy sales – mainly gas – which currently account for 14 percent of export value. Gas is transported through the Russian-owned Gazprom pipeline network via Kazakhstan.[41]

Finally, toward the end of the 1990s and in the first half of the 2000s, the Uzbek government established strategic alliances with the United States, which further deepened the rentier character of the Uzbek state and economy.[42] In 2000, Uzbekistan received considerable amounts of equipment under the Foreign Military Financing program. Military alliances deepened on the eve of the "war on terror," which led to the establishment of a small US military base in Uzbekistan in which around 1,000 personnel were stationed. During the first year the base earned the Uzbek government around US$450 million in grants and credits,[43] however, the military alliance was abruptly terminated by the Uzbek regime in 2005,[44] prompting a turn towards Russia and China and search for new grants, credits and deals.[45]

Today's Uzbekistan is a well-diversified rentier state whose roots can be directly traced back to the Tsarist and Soviet period. The regime survives primarily due to rent obtained from the sale of cotton, gold and gas, which allows it to fuel patrimonial networks and to pay for a fairly large military and security apparatus. In this respect the Uzbek regime is very similar to neo-patrimonial regimes which have ruled various parts of the Middle East[46] as well as sub-Saharan Africa.[47] The remittances indirectly allow the government to maintain social peace and subsidize wages of the local bureaucracies even though the regime does not want to acknowledge it.

Turkmenistan is another Central Asian state with a rentier character, which, even more than Uzbekistan, took its shape during the Soviet period and blossomed in the post-independence period. The critical juncture in the development of the Turkmen rentier state was the period toward the end of the 1970s and the beginning of the 1980s when natural gas came to dominate the republic's economy. According to one author, as early as 1970 the Turkmenistan SSR supplied 24 percent of natural gas in the Soviet Union, and by 1975 it supplied just under 33 percent.[48] Today, Turkmenistan ranks as the world's fourth largest potential gas producer, after Russia, the United States and Iran. Outside the natural gas sector, the industrial base of Soviet Turkmenistan was grossly underdeveloped and traces of modern industry (particularly textile enterprises) that existed survived solely thanks to the Soviet central subsidies. The Soviet planners left the republic underdeveloped largely due to its remote geographical position.

Another important element of the Turkmen economy – similar to Uzbekistan – was cotton production. In the 1980s, more than 50 percent of the republic's population was employed on the cotton fields,[49] its sole major agriculture product. A major boost to cotton production was provided by the completion of the Karakum Canal (over more than 1,200 km) which diverted water from the Amu Darya into the southern desert regions of Uzbekistan and Turkmenistan. On the eve of independence, cotton, oil and gas made up 80 percent of Turkmenistan's industrial economy.[50] Furthermore, the cotton industry was still the largest employer in the country, whereas gas guaranteed the most significant revenues to the national government.[51]

Leading on, similar to Uzbekistan, the bulk of the cotton produced in Turkmenistan during Soviet times was processed and manufactured outside the republic in the northern industrial centers of Russia and the Ukraine. Similarly, gas was sent through an inter-Union pipeline system, "to the European zone of the Soviet Union, whose high demand for fuel could only be satisfied by massive imports of oil and gas from other regions of the USSR."[52] The collapse of the Soviet Union strengthened the regime's dependency on gas and cotton as well as on pre-existing relationships with its economic partners. As in the case of Uzbekistan, the key to Turkmenistan's quick transition toward a rentier economy was price liberalization which followed the disintegration of the Soviet Union: "this enabled Turkmenistan to charge world market prices for the gas it supplied to its former Soviet era customers in Ukraine, Georgia, Russia, and other countries."[53] In the first two years of the post-Soviet Union period, Turkmenistan was second only to Russia in benefiting from the adjustment of prices to world levels.[54] On the negative side, Turkmenistan, like Uzbekistan, very quickly became over-exposed to volatile – or cyclical – energy prices on the international markets[55] and firmly linked their post-Soviet fate with the Russian-controlled pipeline system, a dependency which was only recently broken.

It appears that the new Turkmen regime was acutely aware of the situation in which it found itself. For instance, at the beginning of the 1990s the Turkmen government actively participated in efforts to build a pipeline which would run under the Caspian Sea and connect Turkmenistan to non-Russian markets. Those efforts had largely failed by 2000. In the next phase, Turkmenistan, in classic rentier-state-style, embarked on an economic program of ISI. Since the mid-1990s the government has financed the development of a modern textile industry processing domestic cotton and silk, which became the centerpiece of ISI.[56] However, the much hyped modernization resulted in the production of low-quality manufactured goods that could not compete on the international market.[57] The main reason for this failure was a lack of technical capacity.

At the same time, the Turkmen regime did not attempt far-reaching economic liberalization. Rather, the two key sectors of gas and cotton stayed in government hands, with accompanying strict administration and financial control. State controls over the economy allowed the ruling regime to fuel and uphold a vast patronage system.[58] Kiren Chaudhry argues that historically, rulers of the rentier states in the Middle East were also extremely hostile to the free market, which they viewed as being politically dangerous because:

> A functioning market provides opportunities for mobility that undercut lineages and traditional rights of privileges, thus threatening the status quo. Market creates inequalities in wealth that may not match existing patterns of income distribution, status, power, and entitlements; they dislocate groups in both the political and economic realms.[59]

Following the same strategic logic of non-liberalization and upholding existing structures, the Turkmen regime also successfully attempted to sustain parts of the Soviet welfare system throughout the 1990s, as argued by Richard Pomfret: "the universal benefits from the Soviet era, such as pensions at 57 for woman and 62 for men, were supplemented by free provision of gas, electricity, water, and slat for residential use."[60] Again the behavior of the Turkmen regime mirrors that of the Middle Eastern and North African regimes. John Entelis argues that in the Middle Eastern and North African states "a sort of 'ruling bargaining' was struck by the leadership with its people at independence under which the populace gave up its rights to independent political activity in return for the state's provision of social welfare."[61]

This does not mean, however, that an ordinary person or every region in the country is a winner. In rentier states, state investment funds often are disproportionately directed toward the provision of services and infrastructure to those areas of the country which are predominantly populated by the ruler's tribe. Already in 1970, H. Mahdavy, who first advanced the rentier-state concept, warned that oil states create an impression of prosperity and growth, whereas in reality "the mass of the population may remain in a backward state and the most important factors for long-run growth may receive little or no attention at all."[62] In Turkmenistan by the end of the 1990s, the heavily subsidized agriculture sector still employed about half of the economically active population. Students above grade five were forced to harvest cotton and the number of students in higher education "fell from 40,000 in 1991 to less than 10,000 by 2004."[63] An argument could be made that the quasi-Sultanistic Turkmen regime[64] was pursuing an active policy of de-diversification of its economy reminiscent of the politics of Mobutu in Zaire – also a rentier state – in the 1970s and 1980s which has since had tragic long-term consequences for the country.[65]

Finally, the Turkmen regime has been hostile to all forms of regional cooperation,[66] pursuing a policy of virtual isolation from the outside word. Again the rentier effect largely explains why this is the case. Historically, key energy-rich states in the Middle East – for example, Saudi Arabia or Kuwait – have also been hostile to regional cooperation. In the context of the Middle Eastern states it resulted in the fiercely negative attitude of Saudi Arabia and the Gulf states to the idea of pan-Arabism. The issue of artificially drawn colonial border lines does not interest those elites whose states have been "blessed" with petro-dollars. Hence, the movements which strongly rely on symbols that emphasize the unity of all Arabs have been most unwelcome in the oil-rich states.[67] Instead, rulers strongly support movements that use Islamic symbolism. Nazih Ayubi asserts that an important function of what he calls petro-Islam – which stresses an interpretation of religion that is both excessively ritualistic in style and conservative in socio-economic content – "is to keep the oil wealth away from other Arabs."[68]

KAZAKHSTAN

The resource-based economies that Turkmen and Uzbek rulers inherited from the Soviet Union, coupled with an autocratic regime and a lack of human capital to diversify their economies, made the turn toward rentierism somewhat inevitable. Kazakhstan, which today also closely resembles a rentier economy, started its transformation toward rentierism from a very different point when compared with its regional counterparts. The disintegration of the Soviet Union hit Kazakhstan, a middle income country at the beginning of the 1990s, incomparably harder than its southern neighbors as the country's entire industrial structure was inseparably intertwined with that of Russia. In response to the crisis, the Kazakh regime decided to privatize huge, collapsing enterprises (to very mixed effect), while turning its own attention to oil and gas. The oil and gas sectors were largely underdeveloped during the Soviet era, but had the potential to attract foreign oil companies and much needed foreign direct investment, which they did. The increase in oil prices in the 2000s strengthened the Kazakh dependency on resources and led the regime to largely abandon other sectors of the economy. By the end of the 2000s, the turn toward rentierism was complete.

As discussed in the previous section, the relative economic success of Uzbekistan and Turkmenistan at the beginning of the 1990s can be largely explained by the interest of the outside world in the commodities they had for sale. Kazakhstan, despite its overwhelming wealth in natural resources, initially found itself on the other end of the equation. This was largely due to three reasons: (1) the remote location of many of the deposits; (2) inadequate or non-existent transport links to the outside markets; and (3) shifting interests of the global mining industry which at the beginning of the 1990s chose to turn its attention to South American, not post-Soviet, deposits.[69]

In the Soviet Union, the development of the republic's extractive industries followed an enclave-type pattern which mirrored the experience of colonial Africa or nineteenth-century South America. Thus, development was regionally concentrated but with little, if any, investment in ancillary industries. The large extractive enterprises were closely linked to enterprises in other part of the USSR or "imperial" core. It should be added that the same was true for Kazakhstan's industrial economy, which mainly concentrated in primary sectors like ferrous and non-ferrous metals, fuels, electricity generation, metallurgy and machine building and chemicals. The industrial economy was built around "one-company towns" in which production concentrated on intermediate products, which had to be sent to factories in Russia for further processing and manufacturing.[70] In short, without the Soviet economy there was hardly any Kazakh economy one could speak off.

The overwhelming economic problem that Kazakhstan faced at the beginning of the 1990s was exacerbated by two additional factors. The enterprises within the borders of the newly independent Kazakhstan were old and suffered from chronic under-investment during the late Soviet era. Thus, the enterprises needed huge funds in order to become commercially attractive. Furthermore, the Russian, German and Slavic managerial and engineering classes which worked on major enterprises in the north of country began migrating back to Russian and other republics. In the first decade of independence almost two million people left Kazakhstan.[71]

The response of the Kazakh government to the mounting economic crises, which followed the collapse and disintegration of the Soviet economy, was to privatize existing enterprises in the mid-1990s. The Kazakh ruling elite hoped that through privatization it would be able to shift responsibility from itself to the private sector for running the enterprises and maintaining social peace in "one company towns." Yet the proposed privatization did not generate much interest among multinationals. Instead, the country's key assets were bought at a very low price by little known outside companies whose real identity was disguised by the company's off-shore registration. In the years to come, most of them failed to meet their commercial or social obligations and instead engaged in widespread asset striping.[72] The privatization, the so-called "sale of the century," deepened the existing economic and social crises in the country[73] and fully opened the doors to crony capitalism which was accompanied by rampant corruption.[74] As a result, according to one author, the Kazakh political system throughout the 1990s began retreating to a pre-Soviet logic of *zhuz* (horde), tribes and clans.[75]

In the face of a collapsing economy and growing social problems, the Kazakh ruling elite turned its full attention to oil and gas, which were the only two sectors able to attract the interest of major international companies from the beginning of the 1990s. Kazakhstan, in which production on major oil fields began only in the 1980s and where there was enormous potential for future development, presented foreign oil companies with a unique opportunity they were not going to miss. The regime on its part created institutional structures – an early version of the National Oil Company along with oil laws – which best suited the interests of the outside companies. The regime further allowed companies to entrench their position in post-Soviet Kazakhstan by signing a whole host of Production Sharing Agreements which clearly favored outside companies.[76] The bond forged in the 1990s between oil companies and the Kazakh regimes, to some extent, mirrors the relationships forged between Saudi Arabia and the Western oil companies in the 1950s and 1960s.[77]

The gamble which the Kazakh elites took in the first decade of independence – staking their future largely on oil – paid off in 2000 when a consortium of Western companies discovered the Kashagan oilfield, which is the largest oil find in the past thirty years. Coincidentally, the discovery was followed by a rapid rise of oil prices on the international commodity markets throughout the 2000s, finally bringing much needed revenues.[78] This in turn allowed the regime to increase social spending as well as the all important public sector salaries.[79] What is more, the increase in revenues also gave the regime leverage in its relationships with the foreign oil and gas companies.[80] At the same time, Kazakhstan's growing dependency on oil and gas exports meant that the country would have to heavily rely on Russian-controlled infrastructure for some time to come. According to one assessment, around 84 percent of Kazakhstan's oil exports still pass through Russia to the international markets.[81]

Today's Kazakhstan strongly resembles a classic rentier state.[82] Its full dependency on commodity markets became all too visible during the financial crises in the late 2000s, which in Kazakhstan manifested themselves in an almost instantaneous collapse of the country's banking and building sectors. The Kazakh political system largely follows a regional pattern of neo-patrimonialism, while its economy is shaped and dominated by a few oligarchs and their cliques.[83] However, there are two important differences between Kazakhstan and Uzbekistan and Turkmenistan. First, the Kazakh regime is much more liberal and less oppressive than its regional counterparts,[84] and, second, it recognizes the limits of politics based on informal networks. It has been argued that the regime's long-term ambition is to create a political and economical system in which formal institutions would play a much bigger role.[85] This should facilitate the rise of much more stable political structures which, however, will not be democratic in outlook.

KYRGYZSTAN AND TAJIKISTAN

Kyrgyzstan's economy, similarly to that of Kazakhstan, was badly affected by the collapse of the Soviet Union, but it is not rich in exploitable and exportable natural resources. Hence, at the beginning of the 1990s it decided to liberalize its economy and, at least partly, the political system. This maneuver allowed the post-Soviet regime to obtain sufficient foreign aid/rent from various Western governments and agencies, which helped to smooth its transition from the USSR. However, this source of rent inevitably dried up, and in the second decade of independence the Kyrgyz state began relying on the in-flow of remittances and rent derived from leasing territory. The economy of Tajikistan, the poorest republic in the Soviet Union, was almost completely devastated and looted during the civil war at the beginning of the 1990s. Today, Tajikistan is held together by remittances sent by labor workers that migrate predominantly to Russia, as well as foreign aid. That said, it is also estimated that as much as a third of the population depends on the drugs and weapons trade.

Kyrgyzstan and Tajikistan on the eve of independence found themselves in a much more difficult economic situation than any of the other three Central Asian republics discussed so far. This was due to two factors: (1) both are resource-poor, thus they could not benefit from price liberalization at the beginning of the 1990s in the same way as did Turkmenistan and Uzbekistan; and (2) neither of the two had a developed and well-functioning economic base. In the Soviet Union the Kyrgyz economy was not highly industrialized and "much of the industry that the republic did have was tightly integrated into the Soviet military–industrial complex, which left the republic especially vulnerable after the dissolution of the USSR."[86] Tajikistan was the poorest of the Soviet republics, with 40 percent of its budget coming from subsidies.[87]

The response of the Kyrgyz elites to the disintegration of the Soviet Union, which had far-reaching social and economical effects, was to fully embrace the discourse of democracy and the free market economy as advocated by the IMF and the World Bank at that time. This in turn won the country the support of ideologically driven major international donors and some Western governments.[88] Both parties between 1992 and 2000 poured US$1.7 billion into Kyrgyzstan, a substantial amount of money which greatly aided the Kyrgyz government in smoothing out the transition from the Soviet Union.[89] However, the outside aid/rent slowly came to an end by early 2000s as donors became increasingly disillusioned with Kyrgyzstan's ever more authoritarian political regime and the lack of liberal economic reforms.[90]

Tajikistan did not go through the process which is normally understood as a "transition" from a Soviet to a post-Soviet system. On the eve of independence, the country collapsed into a civil war, which formally lasted from 1992 to 1997, although significant political violence continued until 2001.[91] According to some accounts, the civil war came about as a result of the collapsing Soviet economy in the late 1980s, which was no longer able to subside Tajikistan to the same levels as it had in the past. Thus, in the early 1990s, poverty, youth unemployment, corruption and competition for resources between regionally defined groups were seen as the key reasons for the outbreak of hostilities.[92] The war took the lives of 50,000–100,000 people and had a devastating impact on the country's economy.[93] By the mid-1990s the industrial sector, state property and bank assets had been looted and much of what had any productive value left the country. The physical infrastructure was also largely destroyed. On the eve of the new millennium, Tajikistan was ranked among the poorest countries in the world.[94]

Since the early 2000s Kyrgyzstan's and Tajikistan's economies have followed very similar trajectories. First, today both countries rely overwhelmingly on labor remittances which Kyrgyz and Tajik workers send home from Russia and Kazakhstan. According to recent studies, "Tajikistan has the world's highest proportion of remittances to GDP.

In 2007 remittances comprised 36% of its GDP, or $1.8 billion, while Kyrgyzstan ranked fourth in the world, with 27% of GDP or $322 million."[95] Second, the ruling elites of Kyrgyzstan and Tajikistan greatly rely on income obtained from leasing land to foreign powers. Kyrgyzstan is home to both a Russian and US military base. The Manas US Air Base, since its creation in the early 2000s, has become increasingly important to the Afghanistan war effort, something that the Kyrgyz elite tried to use to extract more rent through playing – rather unskillfully – Russia and the United States against one another.[96] In 2004, Tajikistan agreed to become host to a Russian base after the Russian government agreed to write off a large part of its bilateral debt. Third, both countries are slowly falling prey to organized crime, which is playing a growing role in their economical and political life.[97]

Today, Kyrgyzstan and Tajikistan are semi-rentier states. In essence, their internal stability is indirectly linked to the oil and gas prices which shape the economic fate of Russia and Kazakhstan and in turn determine the level of remittances that Kyrgyz and Taijk workers are able to send home. The place that Kyrgyzstan and Tajikistan have in the regional economy is largely the outcome of an insignificant role that both countries played in the Soviet economy, which with its collapse left them with a reservoir of cheap, young labor and little more.

The Foreign Policy of Central Asian (Rentier and Semi-rentier) States

The Kazakh and Turkmen autocratic regimes from the first years of independence attempted to translate the advantage of having substantial natural resources on their territory into consolidating their rule and their countries' sovereignty. The pursuit of greater independence resulted in diametrically opposed foreign policies, with Kazakhstan coining the term of a so-called "multi-vector" foreign policy,[98] whereas Turkmenistan opted, uniquely in the post-communist space, for a policy of "positive neutrality."[99] In both cases, post-independence foreign policy became an important part of the state ideology and aided rulers in strengthening their grip on power. However, in neither case have they led to a limiting of the countries' dependency on Russia, in fact, quite the contrary. The growing reliance of both states on oil and gas resources, reinforced by a lack of economic diversification, strengthens Kazakh and Turkmen dependency on the Russian-controlled pipeline system, a dependency which both ruling regimes have found extremely complicated to overcome for various internal and external reasons. Yet it has to be said that this relationship of dependency in the case of Turkmenistan has been partly balanced by growing Russian reliance on Turkmen gas.[100]

In the case of Kazakhstan, its reliance on the Russian-controlled infrastructure, reinforced by geographical proximity and an ethnic Russian minority living in Kazakhstan, has led to the decision by the ruling regime to largely follow the Russian lead on the international stage.[101] Thus, the Kazakh regime pursues the long-term goal of not antagonizing Russia, but to rather grow in strength next to it, at least for the time being. Rather tellingly, Kazakhstan only began consolidating its relationships with China in the mid-2000s after Chinese–Russian rapprochement, whereas the influence of Western oil companies has been largely limited to oil enclaves. Turkmenistan, in contrast to Kazakhstan, engaged, on the one hand, in a series of disputes concerning the price of gas sold to Russia and the Ukraine through Russian-controlled pipelines, and, on the other hand, chose to pursue a policy of virtual isolation from the outside world. The change at the apex of power of the ruling regime in the second half of the 2000s was marked by a continuation of foreign policy rather than a meaningful shift toward greater openness.[102]

The situation has been very different in the case of Uzbekistan, which overwhelmingly relies on cotton and gold, and whose exports to international markets do not depend to the same extent on Russian controlled infrastructure as is the case for Turkmenistan and Kazakhstan. This situation has allowed the Uzbek regime to maneuver rather freely between Russia, the United States, European states and China.[103] This highly flexible foreign policy allows not only for the consolidation of the ruling regime and suppression of internal dissent, but also greatly increases Uzbek sovereignty. Thus, when compared with Kazakhstan and Turkmenistan, Uzbekistan emerges as a unique case in Central Asia, since it is the only state that has managed to end its direct dependency on Russia. At the same time, Uzbek independent foreign policy is built on very weak foundations. Over the last two decades, the ruling regime has failed to diversify the country's economy away from cotton, the prices of which are highly unstable, and instead have become increasingly reliant on indirect taxation of labor remittances by different levels of the state bureaucracy. Hence, the maintenance of the Uzbek version of "multi-vector" foreign policy and state sovereignty is a serious challenge to the authoritarian regime.

In recent years, Kyrgyzstan and Tajikistan, similar to Kazakhstan and Uzbekistan, have also declared an intention to pursue a "multi-vector" foreign policy. However, while in the Uzbek context the multi-vector policy has been framed as an outcome of strategic re-positioning and in

Kazakhstan as an expression of the regime's inspiration to achieve full sovereignty, in the Kyrgyz and Tajik cases the "multi-vector" policy has rather been a reflection of a position in which those states find themselves on the regional "chessboard."[104] In both cases, the almost full dependency on aid and labor remittances significantly narrows a leader's room to maneuver and inevitably undercuts these states' sovereignty.

Conclusion: Rent and Sovereignty in Central Asia

Twenty years after the fall of the Soviet Union, the Central Asian republics are still shaped by Soviet policies – the legacy of which has been chiefly upheld and reinforced by the neo-liberal project. In the new post-Soviet reality, the rulers of the three Central Asian states of Turkmenistan, Uzbekistan and Kazakhstan largely embrace the role that was envisioned for their republics by the Soviet planners. The privatization of state assets by the elites in the 1990s has guaranteed them access to rent, the constant flow of which quickly became their main preoccupation. As a result of this, the interest of the ruling cliques in state sovereignty has been directly and unbreakably linked to the issue of rent and its control. This is to say, that whoever guarantees a steady flow of rent is also largely seen as a strategic partner and a best guarantor of a country's sovereignty. In the cases of Kazakhstan and Turkmenistan, Russia has successfully fulfilled this role.

The direct dependency of Kazakhstan and Turkmenistan on the old "imperial" core has been underpinned by geography and the existing infrastructure. As in the case of the other "classic" rentier states, Turkmenistan and Kazakhstan are interlocked into a relationship with an outside patron, a situation which is unlikely to be easily changed due to the physical nature of oil and gas. This physical link is strengthened by the countries' elite, which on a political, economic, cultural and personal level[105] have more in common with Russia and Russians than with either the broadly understood "West" or China, which are seen as potential competitors. It is important to keep in mind that the Central Asian key producers of oil and gas do not only share a communist past, but also the experience of "transition" which resulted in the installation of variants of post-Soviet authoritarian regimes and in crony capitalism.

Furthermore, Kazakhstan and Turkmenistan have been keen on retaining their links with Russia since venturing into unknown territories – foregoing alliances with other powers can be a risky enterprise as the case of Uzbekistan and its attempts to cut or limit its ties with an old imperial power demonstrate. Uzbekistan has been the most successful state in crafting a multi-vector foreign policy. In the last twenty years it has not been firmly linked to one outside patron. Yet by doing so the country's elites have exposed themselves to a changing international environment with which they are now forced to interact and to respond. Effectively, neither isolation (Turkmenistan) nor growing in strength next to a patron (Kazakhstan) is an option for Uzbekistan. Rather, the Uzbek elites have to engage in a politics of "balancing," which is inherently precarious because the resources- and remittances-dependent economic structure makes punching above the country's weight on the regional stage much more problematic.

Kyrgyzstan and Tajikistan played a peripheral role in the Soviet economy. Their status did not change with the collapse of the Soviet Union. Today both countries remain dependent on Russia, which is a major source of remittances and is vital for the survival of the post-Soviet semi-rentier states. Furthermore, these countries' dependency on Russia is deepened by the fact that there is a lack of any real alternative to the old imperial "core," since the interests of European countries and the United Sates are inherently short-term and limited to the war in Afghanistan. Thus, underdevelopment and geography will keep both countries closely tied to Russia in the years and more likely decades to come.

Notes

1. Chaudhry, "The price of wealth"; Addleton, *Undermining the Centre*; Hinnebusch, *The International Politics of the Middle East.*
2. Beblawi, "The rentier state in the Arab world," pp. 51–3.
3. Mahdavy, "The patterns and problems of economic development in rentier states"; Beblawi and Luciani (eds), *The Rentier State*; Skocpol, "Rentier state and Shiᶜa Islam"; Chaudhry, "The price of wealth"; Crystal, *Oil and Politics in the Gulf*; Brynen, "Economic crisis and post-rentier democratization in the Arab world"; Shambayati, "The rentier state"; Okruhlik, "Rentier wealth, unruly law, and the rise of opposition."
4. Yates, *The Rentier State in Africa.*; Clark, "Petro-politics in Congo"; Frynas, "The oil boom in Equatorial Guinea"; Soares de Oliveira, *Oil and Politics in the Gulf of Guinea.*
5. Karl, *The Paradox of Plenty.*
6. Kuru, "The rentier state model and Central Asian studies"; Ishiyama, "Neopatrimonialism"; Franke, Gawrich and Alakbarov, "Kazakhstan and Azerbaijan."
7. Jones Luong, "The 'use and abuse' of Russia's energy resources"; Kim, *The Resources Curse*; Wood, "Contours of the Putin era."
8. Ross, "Does oil hinder democracy?"

9. Karl, *The Paradox of Plenty*, p. 197.
10. Okruhlik, "Rentier wealth, unruly law, and the rise of opposition"; Smith, "Oil wealth and regime survival."
11. Luciani, "Allocation vs. production states," pp. 68–70.
12. Beblawi, "The rentier state in the Arab world," p. 59.
13. Anderson, "The state in the Middle East and North Africa"; Ayubi, *Over-Stating the Arab State*; Karl, "Ensuring fairness"; Omgba, "On the duration of political power in Africa."
14. Brynen, "Economic crisis and post-rentier democratization in the Arab world."
15. Hinnebusch, "Liberalization without democratization."
16. Clapham, *Africa and the International System.*
17. Noreng, *Crude Power*; Shaxson, *Poisoned Wells.*
18. Odum and Johnson, "The state of physical infrastructure in Central Asia."
19. Roy, *The New Central Asia*; Dave, *Kazakhstan*; Khalid, *Islam after Communism.*
20. Olcott, *Kazakhstan. Unfulfilled Promises.*
21. Jones Luong and Weinthal, "Prelude to the resource curse."
22. Rotberg, "The failure and collapse of nation-states."
23. Le Billon, "The political ecology of war," p. 576.
24. Spechler, *The Political Economy of Reform in Central Asia*, pp. 19–20.
25. Rodgers, "The location dynamics of Soviet industry"; Liebowitz, "Soviet investment strategy"; Ozornoy, "Some issues of regional inequality."
26. Gleason, "The political economy of dependency under socialism," p. 348.
27. Jones Luong, *Institutional Change*, p. 68; Lubin, *Labor and Nationality in Soviet Central Asia.*
28. Pomfret, *The Central Asian Economies since Independence*, pp. 143–4.
29. Hinnebusch, *The International Politics of the Middle East*, p. 35.
30. Gleason, *Markets and Politics in Central Asia*, p. 117.
31. Spechler, *The Political Economy of Reform in Central Asia*, p. 26.
32. Kamp, "Between women and the state,"; Spechler, *The Political Economy of Reform in Central Asia.*
33. Jones Luong and Weinthal, "Prelude to the resource curse."
34. Kandiyoti, "Post-colonialism compared," p. 282.
35. Gleason, *Markets and Politics in Central Asia*, p. 119.
36. Collins, "Economic and security regionalism," p. 270; Ilkhamov, "Neopatrimonialism, interest groups and patronage networks."
37. "The Curse of Cotton," pp. 4–5.
38. Spoor, "Transition to market economies," p. 11; see also Rumer, *Soviet Central Asia*; Vaksberg, *The Soviet Mafia*; Khalid, *Islam after Communism.*
39. "Central Asia: Migrants and the Economic Crisis," p. 3.
40. Collins, "Economic and security regionalism," p. 268.
41. Spechler and Spechler, "Uzbekistan among the great powers," pp. 358–9.
42. Hiro, *Inside Central Asia*, pp. 173–6.

43. Spechler and Spechler, "Uzbekistan among the great powers," p. 366.
44. Rumer, "The US interests and role in Central Asia after K2."
45. Hiro, *Inside Central Asia*, p. 190.
46. Hinnebusch, "Authoritarian persistence, democratization theory and the Middle East."
47. Le Vine, "African patrimonial regimes"; Bratton and van de Walle, "Neopatrimonial regimes and political transitions in Africa"; Bratton and van de Walle, *Democratic Experiments in Africa*.
48. Ebel, "Introduction," p. 4.
49. Gleason, "The political economy of dependency under socialism," p. 342.
50. Gleason, *Markets and Politics in Central Asia*, p. 107.
51. Anceschi, *Turkmenistan's Foreign Policy*, p. 66.
52. Anceschi, *Turkmenistan's Foreign Policy*, p. 66.
53. Gleason, *Markets and Politics in Central Asia*, p. 109.
54. Anceschi, *Turkmenistan's Foreign Policy*, p. 72.
55. Stevens, "Oil wars."
56. Pomfret, *The Central Asian Economies since Independence*, p. 93.
57. Anceschi, *Turkmenistan's Foreign Policy*, p. 75.
58. Collins, *Clan Politics*, p. 303.
59. Chaudhry, "Economic liberalization and the lineages of the rentier state," p. 4.
60. Pomfret, *The Central Asian Economies since Independence*, p. 90.
61. Entelis, "The emergence of civil society in Algeria," p. 45.
62. Mahdavy, "The patterns and problems of economic development in rentier states," p. 437.
63. Pomfret, *The Central Asian Economies since Independence*, pp. 97–9; see also: Lewis, *The Temptations of Tyranny in Central Asia*, pp. 80–1.
64. Cummings and Ochs, "Turkmenistan-Saparmurat Niyazov's inglorious isolation"; Chelabi and Linz, *Sultanistic Regimes*.
65. Young and Turner, *The Rise and Decline of the Zairian State*; Dunning, "Resource dependence."
66. Olcott, *Central Asia's Second Chance*.
67. Other states such as Syria or Libya, which do not have large oil revenues at their disposal, have tried to inspire loyalty among their people through non-state ideologies, i.e., pan-Arabism.
68. Ayubi, *Over-Stating the Arab State*, p. 233.
69. Bridge, "Mapping the bonanza."
70. Peck, *Economic Development in Kazakhstan*, pp. 60–2; Pomfret, *The Central Asian Economies since Independence*, p. 43; see also Cummings, *Kazakhstan: Center–Periphery Relations*; Olcott, *Kazakhstan. Unfulfilled Promises*.
71. Sinnott, "Population politics in Kazakhstan"; Dave, "Entitlement through number."
72. Ostrowski, *Politics and Oil in Kazakhstan*.

73. Nazpary, *Post-Soviet Chaos.*
74. Cummings, "Kazakhstan: an uneasy relationship"; Cummings, "Independent Kazakhstan"; Furman, "The regime in Kazakhstan"; Murphy, "Illusory transition?"; Dave, *Kazakhstan.*
75. Schatz, *Modern Clan Politics.*
76. Ostrowski, *Politics and Oil in Kazakhstan.*
77. Vitalis, *America's Kingdom*; Yessenova, "Tengiz crude: a view from below."
78. Pomfret, "Kazakhstan's economy since independence," pp. 867–8.
79. Ostrowski, "The legacy of the 'coloured revolutions,'" pp. 348–51.
80. Nurmakov, "Resources nationalism in Kazakhstan's petroleum sector"; Ostrowski, *Politics and Oil in Kazakhstan.*
81. "Central Asia's Energy Risks," p. 9; see also Ipek, "The role of oil and gas."
82. Kazakhstan anticipates a total investment of US$52 billion in its oil and gas sector by the second decade of 2000s. Olcott, *Central Asia's Second Chance*, p. 88.
83. Kjærnet, Satpaev and Torjesen, "Big business and high-level politics in Kazakhstan."
84. Olcott, *Central Asia's Second Chance.*
85. Ostrowski, "The legacy of the 'coloured revolutions.'"
86. Pomfret, *The Central Asian Economies since Independence*, p. 71.
87. "Tajikistan: On the Road to Failure," p. 1.
88. Gleason, "Foreign policy and domestic reform in Central Asia," pp. 173–4.
89. Pomfret, *The Central Asian Economies since Independence*, pp. 82–3.
90. Lewis, *The Temptations of Tyranny in Central Asia*, pp. 123–4; Hiro, *Inside Central Asia*, pp. 296–8.
91. Heathershaw, *Post-Conflict Tajikistan.*
92. Lynch, "The Tajik civil war"; Akiner, "Conflict and post-conflict Tajikistan."
93. Nakaya, "Aid and transition from a war economy," p. 260.
94. Pomfret, *The Central Asian Economies since Independence*, pp. 65–9.
95. Marat, "Labour migration in Central Asia," p. 7.
96. "Kyrgyzstan: A Hollow Regime Collapses."
97. Marat, "The state–crime nexus in Central Asia"; Kupatadze, "Organized crime before and after Tulip Revolution."
98. Cummings, "Eurasian bridge or murky waters"; Bukkvoll, "Astana's privatised independence."
99. Anceschi, *Turkmenistan's Foreign Policy,*
100. Kandiyoti, *Pipelines.*
101. Cummings, *Kazakhstan: Power and the Elite*; Dave, *Kazakhstan.*
102. Anceschi, "Analyzing Turkmen foreign policy."
103. Spechler and Spechler, "Uzbekistan among the great powers."
104. Spechler, *The Political Economy of Reform in Central Asia.*
105. Gammer, "Post-Soviet Central Asia."

15

Tajikistan: From *de facto* Colony to Sovereign Dependency

Muriel Atkin

People disagree about whether the Soviet Union was an empire and even about the definition of empire. Yet several points are clear. The concepts of empire and colony had negative connotations in Soviet rhetoric. Despite or even because of that in the last years of the Soviet era, advocates of change and even members of the political establishment in various non-Russian republics began to assert what had hitherto been absolutely taboo: that relations between the central government and the non-Russian republics had an imperial-colonial character. The motives for such declarations were varied, not solely to speak truth to power, but breaking the taboo was a dramatic change regardless of the motives. After the demise of the Soviet Union, the Union republics became sovereign states under international law, but the discussions of colonial grievances retained some utility. At the same time, some measure of dependence on Moscow persisted in the formally independent states. The characteristics of this dependence resembled those of former Western colonies on their imperial metropolis.

The Soviet Union as Empire

The debate about whether the Soviet Union was an empire is complicated by the polemical use of the term, especially in the context of the Cold War. The Soviet Union accused the major Western powers of imperialism, while some Western critics of the Soviet Union reciprocated by calling it an empire to highlight its oppressive character. One may, in fairness, object, as Adeeb Khalid does, that in its rule over Central Asia, the Soviet Union was "a different kind of modern polity, the activist, interventionist, mobilisational state that seeks to sculpt its citizenry in an ideal image," and do so more pervasively than Europe's overseas empires.[1] However, that does not mean that the Soviet Union, for all its differences from self-described empires, did not, in its own way, exhibit some significant traits of empire. Although any term ought to be used with due considera-tion of its meaning when defining categories, concepts like the existence of quasi-colonial relations in a self-proclaimed anti-empire need not be defined with the precision of an indictment in a trial. Sometimes it is the inconsistent and paradoxical which are the most illuminating.

For example, Partha Chatterjee sees one of the most important charac-teristics of British rule in India as the "rule of colonial difference," accord-ing to which the transformation brought by imperial rule could never be allowed to erase "the alienness of the ruling group," while making "race" (broadly construed) as "perhaps the most obvious mark of colonial difference."[2] In one sense, this would seem not to apply to the Soviet Union, given the presence of non-Russians in high office in Moscow, Stalin most of all. In the period between Stalin's death in 1953 and 1990, when the situation changed dramatically, a number of non-Slavs who were Communist Party first secretaries in the southern republics of the Soviet Union were represented at the highest political level, the Politburo in Moscow. There were, albeit in some cases only briefly, one Uzbek, one Kazakh, one Azerbaijani, one Armenian and two Georgians who were full members and two Azerbaijanis, one Uzbek and two Georgians who were candidate (non-voting) members. In mid-1990, in the context of Mikhail Gorbachev's attempt to defuse nationality problems, many non-Slavic first secretaries were added to an expanded Politburo; for the first time, all five Central Asian republics were represented. The Soviet system accepted the idea that non-Russians who spoke fluent Russian and exhibited "at least external ideological conformity and acceptance of the Party's behavioural norms" could become part of the Soviet elite.[3] Yet non-Russians were not the equal of Russians. In a lesser purge of Central Asians in the early 1930s and especially at the height of the Stalin Terror (1937–8), when so many Soviet citizens of any nationality were perse-cuted for so many reasons, prominent Central Asian political figures, like other non-Russians, were accused of bourgeois nationalism, a charge not levelled against ethnic Russians.[4] When the Soviet Union was created, its structure was designed to demonstrate to the non-Russian inhabitants that this would not be a new version of the tsarist empire, with Russians dominating the non-Russians. However, during the 1930s, the Soviet leadership began to adopt a more positive assessment of pre-revolutionary Russian cultural and scientific achievements, with emphasis not only on the value of those achievements but also on the fact that they were made by Russians. The regime also hailed the Russians for their role in the October Revolution, their receptivity to socialism and their battles over the centuries against external enemies.[5] Themes developed in the 1930s had long-lasting influence on official rhetoric and unofficial perceptions of the relative status of nationalities within the Soviet order. Thus, Russian culture and social practices were equated with progress, while Russians were depicted as exemplars of Sovietness whom other Soviet nationalities ought to emulate. Coupled with this was the argument that the other Soviet nationalities owed the Russians a debt of gratitude for all the Russians had done for them.[6] As Dominic Lieven summed up this elevation of Russians to a special place of honor among the Soviet nationalities:

> Russian history was . . . uniquely progressive, even before the Russian masses and intelligentsia joined together to create the world's first socialist society, thereby becoming mankind's vanguard and model. This society was the most modern, just, equal and powerful in the world. It was a story of unique success whose benefits existed for all Soviet citizens to share and all foreigners to admire.[7]

Linked to this was a longstanding theme of Soviet propaganda, that Russians helped the backward peoples of the Soviet Union to build social-ism.[8] Thus, praise for the official interpretation of the Russians' achieve-ments carried with it the message of the inferiority of the non-Russians and their obligation to show deference to their betters.

At least as important as whether the Soviet Union fits any definition of empire is the fact that many non-Russians and some Russians, too, con-sidered the Soviet Union an empire by the last years of its existence. This holds true even for some members of Mikhail Gorbachev's inner circle.[9]

The Stigma of Empire and Nationalism

The case of Tajikistan illustrates several aspects of the controversy over the imperial traits of the Soviet Union. In the era of *glasnost'*, the open discussion of the republic's colonial relationship to Moscow addressed a range of subjects, including the exploitation of the republic as a producer of raw materials, the denigration of and lack of access to the Tajik cultural heritage, and the failure of the Soviet system to bring, in substance, not just name, the progress that was part of the justification for Moscow's rule over the periphery. Many of the motives for making such arguments survived in independent Tajikistan and so did the expression of colo-nial grievances. At the same time, independent Tajikistan, especially its ruling elite, remained heavily dependent on Moscow for military, politi-cal, financial and economic support. Although this impoverished, fragile country received help from other external sources as well, including several countries, international bodies and non-governmental organizations, it continued to rely on Russia above all. Tajikistan's leadership routinely depicted cordial relations with Russia as its highest priority in international affairs. For example, the foreign minister in the short-lived coalition government of 1992, Khudoiberdi Holiqnazarov, a historian associated with the opposition, remarked late that year that Tajikistan had "very strong economic, political, and trade relations [with Russia] inherited from" the Soviet era and that Tajikistan had to maintain those. Failure to do so would result in "chaos and ruin" for Tajikistan's economy.[10] Imomali Rahmonov, who came to power at the end of 1992 and has remained in power ever since, has repeatedly endorsed close relations with Russia. He did so when the two countries signed a treaty of friendship and mutual aid in 1993 and on many subsequent occasions, as, for example, in 2007, when he commented that the United States could never eclipse Russia's importance to Tajikistan because "Russia has always been and remains our dependable strategic partner today."[11] Many thousands of ordinary inhabitants of Tajikistan looked to Russia for employment. In crucial ways, Tajikistan still needed the former Soviet core.

The official Soviet stance on imperialism and colonialism defined these phenomena as antithetical to the Soviet system. According to this line, imperialism was an attribute of capitalist societies. Pitted against it was the world socialist movement, begun by Russia's October Revolution. The Soviet-led socialist camp, allied with national liberation movements, would defeat imperialism and colonialism as the world advanced toward socialism and communism. Colonialism entailed the way the capitalist bourgeoisie ruthlessly exploited underdeveloped countries. The fate of Central Asia, according to this argument, was a prime example of the way the Soviet Union was leading colonial peoples to freedom and defeating capitalism. Thanks to the October Revolution and the help of the "Great-Russian people," the Central Asian republics went from backwardness to rapid economic, political and cultural gains.[12] A Central Asian (or other non-Russian) who had the temerity to challenge the official line and liken the Soviet Union to an empire or characterize the Kremlin's treatment of the republic as colonial exploitation faced dire consequences. How could the expression of nationalism be legitimate when the Central Asian peoples had already achieved their national liberation by their inclusion in the Soviet Union? Even with *glasnost'* and *perestroika* underway in the second half of the 1980s, and the greater latitude to speak more openly about some of the Soviet Union's problems, the inhabitants of Tajikistan were still warned against "nationalism and chauvinism," which Soviet rhetoric routinely deplored and which republican leaders linked to "illegal activity" and anti-Soviet subversion.[13] Any problems in relations among the Soviet nationalities were deemed the fault of deviations from the authentic Leninist nationality policy, not systemic defects.[14] The republican leadership faulted Tajiks for showing too much interest in their own culture and traditions. The Soviet policy of "national in form, socialist in content" had been launched in the 1920s not for the sake of promoting national cultures as an end in itself, but as a pragmatic way to spread the new regime's message to people for whom a national form still meant far more than a socialist content. In Tajikistan, as elsewhere in Central Asia, this meant intellectuals who were party members played a major role in defining what the officially acceptable version of the "national" culture would be. That included choosing which Persian-language writers of centuries past would be classified as Tajik and which dialects of Persian in Central Asian would become the basis for the written Tajik language. Along with this went a change of alphabet from Arabic to Latin and finally Cyrillic, which made it impossible for most Tajiks to read anything written in the Arabic alphabet, and the introduction of new cultural forms, such as novels, ballet and films. However, the traditionally favored literary form, poetry, never lost its pre-eminent place.

Whatever the form, cultural production remained subject to the regime's political oversight. In the late Soviet era, as before, the republican leadership decried interest in taking a fresh look at the Tajik cultural heritage and history as narrow-minded and inwardly focused, contrary to the ethos of "internationalism," a much-touted virtue under the Soviets, but something which had a decidedly Russian coloration to many non-Russians.[15] In the words of Tajikistan's leader when the Soviet Union dissolved, nationalism was one of the "grave diseases of our day."[16] Even in the changed climate that existed in the last years of the Soviet era, there were many people, especially settlers in Central Asia from elsewhere in the Union, who believed in the civilizing mission of Soviet rule, which established "unselfish friendship and mutual aid" among the Soviet nationalities. From this perspective, the non-Central Asians who came to Tajikistan "created by their joint labour industry, agriculture, science – all practically from nothing." This was said to have brought Tajikistan out of its "medieval stagnation."[17]

Criticism of the Imperial Order

Yet the discussion of problems proved impossible to keep as safely confined as the regime would have liked. People in Tajikistan were aware of the growing calls for change in the Soviet Union as a whole.[18] For example, a 1989 article about a visit to Vilnius, the capital of Lithuania, complied superficially with the requirements of "internationalism" in that it said positive things about a Soviet nationality other than the Tajiks. However, the substance of the article was anything but suitably "internationalist," since it praised the way Lithuanians respected and sustained their pre-Soviet heritage through such things as an ethnographic museum, historic preservation, publishing literature in Lithuanian and knowledge of their national language, and argued that Tajiks in Tajikistan did not do nearly as well.[19]

Tajiks were also aware of the strength not only of national pride but also of active nationalist movements in the Baltic and Caucasian republics, which pressed, among other things, for enhanced status of the language of eponymous nationalities and increased control at the republican level over local economic assets.[20] This affected not only Tajikistan's advocates of change, but also those in the ruling elite who were concerned with preserving their own power – although not necessarily with substantive reform; they saw the effectiveness of nationalism as a tool to mobilize popular support and its usefulness as a way of blaming outsiders for the republic's problems. Criticism of the Soviet status quo did not have to be couched in terms of colonialism; many Russian reformers also found much to criticize in the way the system functioned. However, by about 1989, the debate began to take on an additional dimension, an especially provocative one in the Soviet context: that the root of Tajikistan's problems was its position as an exploited colony of the Soviet empire. Many of the same arguments continued to be made in 1992, as people in the newly independent Republic of Tajikistan still grappled with the questions of how much of the Soviet order to preserve and what course the country ought to follow, while competing factions began a power struggle that culminated in civil war.

Some of the arguments along these lines were implicit, noting how far Tajikistan trailed behind the rest of the Soviet Union, especially Russia and other "European" republics, in terms of its standard of living and various specific criteria, including the number of inhabitants living below the poverty line, the infant mortality rate, access to health care and an adequate diet and the rate of housing construction.[21] The message was that Moscow favored European parts of the Soviet Union over Tajikistan when investing in social needs.

Other arguments alluded more directly to colonial exploitation. The economy was an inviting target for such arguments, whether by the republic's leading officials or advocates of change. To people in both camps, Tajikistan's place in the Soviet economy embodied classic traits of colonialism. A theme that had obvious appeal to the ambitions of the republic's high-ranking officials was that the Kremlin, not Tajikistan's leaders, controlled the republic's economy. Moscow, though it determined virtually all aspects of the republic's economy, ignored its characteristics and needs, over-emphasized the production of raw materials and prevented the republic from selling the raw materials it produced at world market prices.[22] The central government's exploitation of Tajikistan as a producer of raw materials hinged upon turning those materials into finished goods elsewhere in the Soviet Union and denying the republic a fair share of the income derived from such commodities. Products made from raw materials which had originated in Tajikistan were sold back to it at much higher prices than the republic had received for the components.[23] At the same time, Tajikistan was becoming increasingly dependent on consumer goods that were made elsewhere in the Soviet Union, even though Tajikistan was capable of making them itself.[24] It is worth noting that the Kremlin's position was that many of the southern republics contributed much less to the Soviet economy and were essentially subsidized by the most productive ones, especially Russia. That view was deeply entrenched in Moscow and continued to be heard at the end of the Soviet era, despite the complaints from the southern republics that they were treated like raw-materials colonies.[25] This interpretation of core–periphery relations found a responsive audience among Russians, too. By the eve of the Soviet Union's collapse, many ethnic Russians in the Russian Republic believed that they would be better off without the burdens of empire.[26]

Of all the raw materials produced in Tajikistan, the one that aroused the most ire there was cotton. People from various political factions, who might not agree on much else, denounced the cotton monoculture as something harmful imposed on the republic by Moscow. In this predominantly agricultural place, which paradoxically has only a little arable land, more than 80 percent of that land was used for cotton cultivation.[27] The anti-cotton argument sounded much like a classic theme of criticism of how empires exploit their colonies. The complaint was that the Soviet state paid Tajikistan too little for the cotton it grew and took about 90 percent of the crop for finishing elsewhere in the Soviet Union. Therefore, much of the money made from turning the cotton into finished goods went to others. At the same time, Moscow's emphasis on cotton cultivation combined with industrial mass production killed off the skilled artisanry of Tajikistan and the rest of Central Asia. Clothing made from Tajikistani cotton was difficult to find in the republic's shops, but readily available in Moscow or the Baltic republics. Such finished cotton goods manufactured elsewhere in the Soviet Union as were sold in Tajikistan carried disproportionately high prices.[28] The people who grew the cotton did back-breaking labor and lived in poverty, not only paid inadequately but also lacking adequate health care, a safe water supply and housing. The heavy demand for labor in cotton cultivation required taking children out of school for several months a year to work in the fields; as a result, the level of education and knowledge of the Tajik cultural heritage suffered.[29] In newly independent Tajikistan it became possible to say openly what had been known but not acknowledged before: Russians living there did not work on the cotton farms or endure such arduous conditions.[30]

Soviet policies brought some industry to Tajikistan but not, said the critics, in ways that benefited the inhabitants of the republic. The growth of industry required a labor force, but Moscow was indifferent to training the local population to fill such jobs. Instead, it relied heavily on workers sent there from outside Central Asia. This was true not only in the early years of rapid industrialization but also in the 1970s and 1980s. According to the critics, the authorities in Moscow consigned the indigenous population, which was predominantly rural, to agriculture. Down to the last years of the Soviet era, young Tajiks who wanted to learn skilled industrial trades had difficulty doing so because of the dearth of vocational textbooks in Tajik. Tajiks, and indigenous peoples in Central Asia as a whole, were substantially under-represented in a variety of industrial jobs as well as in various professions.[31] The influx of non-Central Asians of various ethnicities, known collectively as "Russian-speakers," employed in Tajikistan's industries led to their concentration in the cities, where they appeared to receive preferential treatment in access to housing. As a result, some critics said, young Tajiks who went to the cities felt like foreigners in their own country.[32]

Complaints about discrimination in employment went much further, to the upper reaches of power in the republic. The longstanding "second secretary" policy came under attack. At issue was the established practice of making Russians or other non-Central Asians second secretaries, the position in charge of personnel matters among other things, at various levels of republican Communist parties. This criticism was part of a broader objection to the role of non-Central Asians in a range of important positions in Tajikistan. In government ministries and other bodies, Tajiks comprised only a small fraction of the personnel.[33] One Tajik who worked on the staff of Tajikistan's Council of Ministers complained that the appointment of many of these outsiders to high office could not be justified on the grounds that they were more qualified than Tajiks. They knew no Tajik and were unfamiliar with Tajik customs and the republic's conditions; sometimes they had no evident expertise at all, he charged.[34] Russians living in

Tajikistan were indeed unlikely to know Tajik. A survey of several Union republics at the close of the Soviet era included two hundred Russians living in two cities in Tajikistan; virtually none of them claimed to know Tajik reasonably well.[35]

Although the transformation of Tajikistan under Soviet rule brought virtually universal public education and the establishment of several institutions of higher learning to the republic, many educated Tajiks of the late Soviet era interpreted these changes as less positive than they might seem and lamented their impact on the Tajik cultural heritage. One university-educated Tajik summed up the complaint of many: his education had stressed the Russian revolution, the role of Russians in the friendship among Soviet peoples and how much the Tajiks owed the Russians, but ignored the history of Bukhara or Iran. He judged that he had been educated "in the spirit of self-rejection."[36]

Efforts to improve the status of the Tajik language and cultural heritage began long before the demise of the Soviet Union, and were not necessarily couched in terms which conjured up images of Tajikistan as a Soviet colony.[37] However, at the end of the Soviet era, the issue could be presented as an example of imperial abuse. One of the people who did so most emphatically was Tohir Abdujabbor, the head of Rastokhez, a coalition of various groups of intellectuals which became part of the political opposition. He described the Soviet Union as a "semi-feudal colonial empire," which reduced the republics to subject provinces. Its ethnic groups were brought to the brink of extinction by the destruction of their languages and cultures, though the regime claimed to have brought about the "development of socialist nations" and their linguistic and cultural flourishing.[38] In the last months of the Soviet Union's existence, he turned Soviet rhetoric about empire against Moscow by arguing that many people were seeking a way out of "imperial rule" through national liberation movements.[39] Another intellectual characterized Soviet treatment of Tajikistan as an imperial policy meant to deprive the Tajiks of their entire cultural heritage, in effect, "cultural genocide."[40] According to that argument, Soviet book-burning was even more destructive of Tajik culture than the Mongol conquest had been.[41] "Moscow's empire" discriminated against the Tajik language and taught infatuation with what was foreign, leaving the Tajiks "without rights, without language" in their own home.[42]

Persistence of the Imperial Critique

Tajikistan became an independent state at the end of 1991, a transformation brought about by the Soviet Union's collapse, without Tajikistan's involvement. Even proponents of the imperial critique of the Kremlin's treatment of Tajikistan would no longer call it a colony of Moscow. In some ways, those who ruled in independent Tajikistan found it convenient to sustain the imperial critique as a way of playing on the rising tide of nationalism at the end of the Soviet era and blaming the Soviet empire for Tajikistan's problems. For example, an officially endorsed history of the country, presented as a guide for teachers of the subject, painted a negative picture of Soviet rule over Tajikistan and used the imperial critique to do so. In this account, Soviet rule in Central Asia was established by brute force, without the support of the inhabitants; many civilians were killed and national liberation movements crushed when the Red Army conquered the region. The Soviet Union was an empire in which Tajikistan had no autonomy. What was called "internationalism" in the Soviet Union was really Russification. The "Soviet Empire" tried to prevent the development of national awareness among young people, seeking to instill a slave mentality instead. The Kremlin also directed Tajikistan's economic development along lines which benefited the "empire," not Tajikistan's inhabitants.[43]

Dependent Independence

Yet Tajikistan continued to rely heavily on Russia even after becoming a separate state. The nature of the relationship was not identical to what it had been in the Soviet era, but it remained unequal, affecting especially the political, military and economic spheres. Tajikistan, like all the former Soviet republics, had to grapple with the difficult legacy of the Soviet economic system, including the way that it had molded republican economies to be interdependent, not self-sufficient. Tajikistan's economic weakness was especially severe because it was the poorest of all the successor states. Compounding the new country's problems was the power struggle which escalated into civil war. The conflict was at its most intense in the second half of 1992 and early 1993, but it continued until 1997, involving not only the two sides of the original conflict but also new rivalries among erstwhile members of the victorious coalition. The result was untold tens of thousands of dead, hundreds of thousands of refugees and virtual economic collapse. By 1998, Tajikistan's GDP had declined by 57 percent from what it had been in 1990 as a result of the civil war, the break up of the formerly integrated Soviet economy and natural disasters.[44]

The faction which prevailed in the civil war and has ruled Tajikistan ever since won with Russia's help. The coalition of groups comprising the other side had hoped in vain for support from Russia, counting on

President Yeltsin to support reformers in Tajikistan.[45] Units of the Russian 201st Motorized Rifle Division (formerly part of the Soviet military and stationed in Tajikistan in the late Soviet era) began aiding the anti-reformist coalition as the civil war intensified. By late 1992, Russia ignored the request of the short-lived coalition government to send more troops to protect the capital, Dushanbe, from anti-reformist fighters, but responded favorably to the calls for help from the anti-reformists and directly aided their final advance on the capital.[46] Uzbekistan, too, aided the anti-reformists' drive to victory, although it soon became disaffected with the new regime in Tajikistan and relations between the two countries cooled.[47] In subsequent years, Russian army and border troop units in Tajikistan occasionally fought opponents of the regime that Russia had helped to install in Dushanbe.[48] Russian border troops also remained along the Tajikistan–Afghanistan border until 2005.[49] Even after that, Russians stayed on as advisors to Tajikistan's border guards and Russia continued to train those troops. Some Western countries, notably the United States, also began to assist the country on border security, providing equipment and training.[50]

Russians played important roles in the upper levels of Tajikistan's own security forces after independence. The minister of defense and deputy minister of internal affairs in the government that took power at the end of 1992 were both Russians.[51] Other Russians did not hold formal office in Tajikistan's government, but advised it from the Russian embassy in Dushanbe or military units in the country or by attachment to Tajikistan's ministry of defence.[52] Russia helped arm and train the newly established army of Tajikistan.[53] Eventually, Tajikistan diversified the countries to which it sent soldiers for military training, adding the United States, Canada, India, Ukraine and Iran to the list, and joining the NATO Partnership for Peace in 2002, although it reportedly consulted with Moscow before signing the Partnership pact.[54] Military links to Russia remained significant, including Tajikistan's decision to continue to use Russian standards for its military hardware rather than NATO's.[55] In 1999 and 2004, Moscow and Dushanbe concluded agreements to establish a Russian military base in Tajikistan, to consist of about 5,000 contract servicemen, primarily ground troops, with a smaller contingent of air force personnel. That level of staffing would make it Russia's second largest military presence in the Commonwealth of Independent States (CIS) outside the Russian Federation itself; only the base of the Black Sea Fleet on the Crimean Peninsula, in what had become part of independent Ukraine, housed a larger number of Russian military personnel in the CIS.

At the time of the 1999 agreement and in subsequent years, the Dushanbe government maintained that Russia occupied the paramount position in its diplomatic, security, economic and other affairs. Tajikistan made a point of stating that the increased dealings with the United States after 2001 had not displaced Russia from its position as the crucial partner.[56] As a show of this devotion, Tajikistan's leadership even sided with Vladimir Putin's Russia in a controversy over the interpretation of Soviet expansion in Eastern Europe during the Second World War. In 2007, Estonia removed a Soviet-era war memorial which, from the Soviet perspective and that of the Putin administration, honored the Soviet liberation of that country from Nazi Germany, but from the Estonian nationalist perspective symbolized the Soviet conquest and annexation of a sovereign state. In the wake of Russian expressions of outrage over the monument's removal, the head of Tajikistan's ruling People's Democratic Party denounced the act as "blasphemous" and "immoral."[57]

Tajikistan also received vital political and diplomatic support from Russia after independence. The government in Dushanbe made a point of expressing its goodwill toward Russia and its desire for close relations.[58] With Tajikistan's government starved of revenue amid the crises of the early years of independence, Russia kept it afloat by an infusion of funds. By one estimate, Russia subsidized 70 percent of Tajikistan's state expenditures in 1993.[59] In 1994, Russia not only supported Imomali Rahmonov's campaign for the presidency against a former ally in the anti-reformist coalition, but also sent Rahmonov's government 15 billion rubles on the eve of the election, enabling the regime to ingratiate itself with voters by paying long-overdue wages in a country where most economic activity was still state-owned. Russia also declared that the 1994 presidential vote and the legislative elections the following year were a victory for democracy, despite international objections to the unfairness of the process.[60] Peace talks between the Rahmonov government and the opposition coalition began in 1994 and resulted in an agreement signed in 1997. As the negotiations proceeded by fits and starts, Moscow backed the Dushanbe government both diplomatically and by the use of Russian troops in operations against bands of opposition fighters. In addition, it supported an unyielding stance by Dushanbe, despite occasional exasperation with its clients there and concern about the cost to Russia of this involvement. The Dushanbe government sought to encourage Moscow to continue this support not only by its repeated expressions of good will toward Russia, but also by depicting the opposition as anti-Russian Islamic extremists.[61] This concerted stance on the peace process continued until the gains made by the Taliban in northern Afghanistan in 1996 altered the context of the dispute and drove the parties to a settlement. At that point, Russian pressure on Tajikistan played an important role in Dushanbe's willingness to come to terms with the opposition coalition.[62] By the opening years of the twenty-first century, Tajikistan no longer received the kind of support from Russia that it had for most of the 1990s. As more countries began to pay increased attention to Tajikistan, the government there sought to maximize what it could obtain from all of them, not to the exclusion of Russia, but in addition to that.[63] Nonetheless, Russia and Tajikistan continued to cooperate in military exercises related to preventing incursions from the Afghan side of the border.[64]

Nearly twenty years of independence did not make Tajikistan stronger or more self-reliant economically. The country remained poor, with an economy dominated by the production of raw materials and semi-finished goods, most of which it continued to export, as it had done in Soviet times. Although its poverty rate declined from a peak of 82 percent in 1999, it remained woefully high for the next decade. Tajikistan was the poorest of the post-Soviet states in Central Asia, just as it had been in late-Soviet times.[65] As a result, Tajikistan depended on humanitarian aid from abroad. In 2004, the value of such aid was nearly US$60 million. It came from numerous countries, including Russia and Kazakhstan, as well as several members of the European Union, the United States, some thirty other countries and several non-governmental organizations.[66] Hard times in Tajikistan drove many of its citizens to seek employment in other countries, the lion's share of them in Russia. The exact number is uncertain, since many of these migrant workers endeavored to avoid official notice and did not have work permits in Russia. The Dushanbe government held to the figure of 600,000 migrants for years, but other estimates were substantially higher, 800,000 to 1.5 million as of 2009.[67] That was a strikingly large number for a country with a total population of under seven million. The migrant workers' remittances home played an important role in sustaining Tajikistan's economy.[68] One estimate valued the remittances from Russia at 5 to 10 percent of Tajikistan's GDP in the opening years of the twenty-first century.[69] Russian politicians complained about the presence of so many Tajiks in Moscow and elsewhere in the country, likening them to beggars and linking them to drug trafficking and other crimes. Tajiks in the Russian Federation were also the target of violence. Russia began rounding up and deporting Tajiks in the country without work and residence permits, but that barely altered the number.[70]

Cotton cultivation remained the dominant component of Tajikistan's agriculture after independence, at the expense of food crops, and the country's largest source of employment, just as in Soviet times. It still suffered, as it did before independence, from inadequate mechanization and a flawed irrigation system.[71] Harvesting the cotton still relied heavily on child labor, to the detriment of the children's education and health.[72] Tajikistan's cotton exports still went primarily to states that used to be part of the Soviet Union; in 2004, just over 61 percent went to Latvia, Russia and Ukraine.[73] Independence brought Tajikistan the opportunity to sell its cotton on the world market for prevailing prices, but this proved not to be the panacea it had seemed in late-Soviet times, given the drop in prices for this commodity during the early years of independence.

Aluminum production was the other pillar of Tajikistan's economy in Soviet times and after. Not until 2004 did the output of aluminum finally return to the level it had achieved in 1991, the last full year of peace before the collapse of the Soviet Union and the start of Tajikistan's civil war. As in the Soviet era, nearly all the aluminum produced was exported. By the beginning of the twenty-first century, only about 1 percent was used in manufacturing within the country; the rest went elsewhere. Russia was no longer the primary market; the Netherlands occupied that position by a wide margin, although Russia and other countries still bought some of Tajikistan's aluminium.[74]

After 2001, Tajikistan's import and export trade with countries outside the CIS grew faster than trade with CIS members.[75] Even though several countries outranked Russia as a purchaser of Tajikistan's exports, overall Russia remained its single most important trading partner, with almost 31 percent of Tajikistan's imports and exports in 2004. Nearly two-thirds of Tajikistan's imports (64.3 percent) still came from six successor states of the Soviet Union, Russia first among them.[76] President Rahmonov remained a proponent of expanded trade and business dealings with Russia.[77] In other ways, too, Tajikistan's economic relations with Russia remained important, even though Dushanbe was able to develop some alternatives for aid, trade and investment as more time passed following the dissolution of the Soviet Union. Tajikistan negotiated urgently with Russia in 1993 to be able to use the new Russian ruble as its own currency. Tajikistan's minister of finance at the time acknowledged that, as a consequence, Russia would control much of Tajikistan's economy.[78] The Dushanbe government would gladly have kept the country in the ruble zone but for Russia's not sending it enough currency to make that possible; only at that point did it launch its own currency in 1995.[79]

Independent Tajikistan received loans from sources other than Russia, including the World Bank, International Monetary Fund, Asian Development Bank and several countries. What is particularly important in a discussion of Tajikistan's continued dependency is the size of its foreign debt. By 2005, according to official sources, its national debt amounted to US$953 million, over 40 percent of the country's GDP.[80]

Russia offered it some debt relief in exchange for maintaining another kind of security presence there. In return for control of a Soviet-era space-tracking post at Norak, in southern Tajikistan, in 2004 Russia wrote-off US$250 million of the US$300 million Tajikistan owed it.[81] By the early twenty-first century, China had become another important source of loans to Tajikistan.[82]

Russia's role in Tajikistan's economy included attempts to sustain some aspects of Soviet economic policy there. For example, in 2004, Russia and Tajikistan concluded an agreement by which the Russian aluminum company, RusAl, would invest US$1.5 billion in various projects in Tajikistan, including one to upgrade the existing, Soviet-era aluminum plant in the west of the country as well as build a second smelter in the south.[83] At least some people in Tajikistan objected to the deal in terms that borrowed from contemporary critiques of the effects of globalization. According to this argument, RusAl was behaving like a typical transnational company, shifting manufacturing operations to a poor country where labor and natural resources cost little and the company would not face pressure from the local government to protect the environment. The deal was characterized by its critics as being not only about business, but also about increasing Russia's influence over Tajikistan.[84]

The same agreement also called for RusAl to fund construction of the massive Roghun hydro-electric dam in the south of the country. This was a Soviet-era project left uncompleted when Tajikistan became independent. A combination of civil war and flood damage halted work. Attempts during the 1990s to obtain outside funding for the project from Pakistan or Russia fell through. Even in the Soviet era, the plan provoked controversy. The lake behind the dam would force the relocation of thousands of villagers and drown thousands of hectares of scarce farm land, while the electricity produced was alleged to exceed Tajikistan's needs and would be exported to other republics.[85] When the project was revived by RusAl's involvement, similar objections were raised anew.[86] After a few years, the RusAl deal fell through, not because Tajikistani officials accepted the standing criticism of the concept but because they charged that RusAl had not lived up to its part of the bargain; that included the failure to provide the promised funding and support for Uzbekistan's objections to the project.[87] Russia remained involved in another major hydro-electric project in Tajikistan, the first of the dams at Sangtuda, in which Russia acquired a 75 percent share.[88] It began operations in 2008. In keeping with Dushanbe's practice of seeking diverse external support, while maintaining close relations with Russia, Tajikistan launched construction of a second hydro-electric dam at Sangtuda in 2006 with Iran providing most of the funding and having ownership of the facility for several years before it would revert to Tajikistan.[89]

For all the Dushanbe government's readiness to adopt some of the cultural nationalism which originated with criticism of the Soviet system, there were ways in which it continued to favor the Russian language and culture in the post-Soviet era. In newly independent Tajikistan, the ruling establishment decried the Russian-speakers' unwillingness to learn Tajik as indicative of the Soviet imperial mentality.[90] In 2007, the president announced that he was changing his name from the Russianized form to the more Persian Imomalii Rahmon and encouraged other Tajiks to make similar changes. Yet the Russian language, for ethnic Tajiks, not just the Russian-speaking minority, continued to occupy a prominent position. The number of Russians and other non-Central Asian nationalities in Tajikistan dropped sharply from the late-Soviet to the post-Soviet era. For example, the Russian population declined both in absolute numbers and as a percentage of the total population, from 388,500 (7.6 percent) according to the 1989 census to 68,200 (just over 1 percent) according to the 2000 census.[91] Yet independent Tajikistan established a Russian–Tajik university in Dushanbe and Russian remained the most studied language in the country other than Tajik.[92] For all the talk and legislation since 1989 about promoting the use of the Tajik language in various public spheres, Russian continued to be the preferred language of many government offices. In addition, new legislation made the study of Russian obligatory in Tajikistan's schools as of the 2003–4 school year.[93] The official rationale for the promotion of Russian, and English as well, was the importance of both languages to diplomacy and expertise associated with development.[94] However, the context suggests that there were other considerations as well. The first half of 2003 saw increased discussion by Russian and Tajikistani officials of increased cooperation between the two countries in a range of areas. The highpoint of this was a visit to Tajikistan by President Vladimir Putin in late April. The two presidents' public pronouncements on that occasion included an optimistic assessment of the prospects for expanded ties between the countries.

Conclusion

The broadened range of political discourse at the close of the Soviet era made it possible for Tajiks and many other peoples of the Soviet Union to criticize the status quo in terms which had hitherto been impermissible. One consequence of that was the widespread practice of peoples transforming the way they characterized the effect of Soviet policies upon them. They went from obligatory beneficiaries to righteous victims. This was part of a widespread pattern in the Union republics in the last years of the Soviet Union's existence. Nationalist movements among the eponymous nationalities criticized policies that Moscow characterized as bringing them progress as in fact harming their interests in the areas of language and the environment, among others. Kazakhs criticized sedentarization, collectivization and the Virgin Lands scheme as nearly destroying the Kazakhs. The Lithuanians, Latvians and Estonians decried what Moscow called liberation in the Second World War as the end of their independent statehood.[95] Once that happened, the Soviet order lost its legitimacy to the degree that the regime could not be sustained without the use of greater coercion than its leaders proved either willing or capable of using. For Tajiks and various other non-Russian peoples, a central component of this victimhood was their newly proclaimed status as colonial subjects of a Soviet empire. Regardless of whether the Soviet Union truly was an empire, a striking characteristic of post-Soviet Tajikistan was the way its relations with the new Russian Federation resembled those of many former colonies of various Western empires with their erstwhile metropolis. Military and strategic ties remained strong. Russia's diplomatic support was important to the government in Tajikistan, which, in turn, usually voiced support for Russia's policies. Economic relations with Russia were significant for Tajikistan in such areas as trade and investment. Many inhabitants of Tajikistan went to Russia in search of work. The Russian language remained the most important foreign language in Tajikistan.

There were also ways in which Tajikistan's experience was different from that of Europe's former colonies. For example, there was no struggle for independence that could become part of a heroic creation myth of the new state. Tajikistan, like the other Central Asian states, had not pressed for independence from the Soviet Union but achieved it inadvertently because of developments elsewhere. The establishment of Soviet rule had not brought extensive religious proselytizing, although there certainly was an attempt to inculcate a new secular ideology, in the form of Marxism–Leninism, throughout the Soviet Union, but that proved unable to sustain much credibility in the wake of the Soviet Union's demise, if not before then. The concept of an authoritarian state run by a self-selected elite had much greater staying power than the ideology which justified it. The fact that many Russians regarded the term "empire" an insult when applied to the Soviet Union made it harder for them to grapple with the aftermath of loss-of-empire than was the case in Western European countries with avowed empires.

To say that independent Tajikistan relied heavily on Russia is not to argue that it was wholly dependent. It broadened its range of international dealings in its first twenty years of independence and acquired some leeway to bargain for agreements which would best serve its interests, or at least what those in power believed was in their best interests. Yet its options were limited because of its modest attractions to others. As a result, even on the level of declarations of intent, it was not able to obtain as many commitments as the government would have liked. Actual implementation was considerably less than what those declarations predicted. Tajikistan's leaders showed some ability to adapt to the changing international situation, but in international as in domestic affairs they also carried over the habits of mind of the old order which molded them.

Notes

1. Khalid, "Backwardness and the quest for civilization," pp. 232–3.
2. Chatterjee, *The Nation and Its Fragments*.
3. Lieven, *Empire*, p. 318.
4. Martin, *The Affirmative Action Empire*, pp. 359, 423; Simon, *Nationalism*, p. 158.
5. Martin, *The Affirmative Action Empire*, pp. 451–3.
6. Martin, *The Affirmative Action Empire*, pp. 452–4; Lieven, *Empire*, p. 317.
7. Lieven, *Empire*, p. 308.
8. Simon, *Nationalism*, p. 149.
9. Beissinger, "Soviet empire as 'family resemblance,' " p. 295.
10. FBIS, Al-Majallah, *Daily Report, Central Eurasia*, p. 68.
11. ITAR-TASS, March 17, 2007, retrieved by Nexis.
12. "Imperializm," pp. 569–70 and "Mustamlikaho va siyosati mustamlikadorī," pp. 592–3.
13. "O prakticheskikh," p. 19; "Rech' Predsedatelia Verkhovnogo Soveta Tadzhikskoi SSR K. M. Makhkamova," p. 3.
14. Dadabaev, "Edinstvo mnozhit sily," pp. 12, 13.
15. Dadabaev, "Edinstvo mnozhit sily," pp. 12, 13; "Za aktivnuiu politiku," p. 3; "Politicheskii kharakter," p. 2.
16. "Murojiatnomai raisi Shūroi Olii Jumhurii Tojikiston Rahmon Nabiev ba mardumi Tojikiston," p. 1.
17. Iushin, "Ot totalitarnogo internatsionalizm–k obshchinnomu mnogoobraziiu," p. 2.
18. Subhonov, "Dardi mo nogufta mond," p. 5; Berdieva, "Hama rostī jūyu mardonagī," p. 7; Khudoiev, "Gotovnost' k dialogu," p. 1; Tadjbakhsh, "The a-Soviet Woman of the Muslim East," p. 159; "DPR on the nation-wide scale,"; Dudoignon, "Political parties and forces in Tajikistan, 1989–1993," pp. 57–8; Gretsky, "Russia and Tajikistan," p. 234.
19. Toshbekov, "Dar Vil'nius chiro didem?," p. 15.

20. Vahhobov, "Khomūshī be ki lozim?," p. 2; Subhonov, "Dardi mo nogufta mond"; "Zachem poety novoi vlasti," p. 2; Rahimov, "Talabi aiyom," p. 2; Tadjbakhsh, "The a-Soviet Woman of the Muslim East," p. 159; Dudoignon, "Political parties and forces in Tajikistan, 1989–1993," pp. 59, 62.

21. Istad, "Iqtisod – sarchashmai mas"alahoi millī," p. 3; Berdieva, "Hama rostī jūyu mardonagī,"; Vahhobov, 'Khomūshī ba ki lozim?"; Alimov, Shoismatulloev and Saidov, "Migratsionnye protsessy i natsional'nyi vopros," p. 13; "Voprosy prinstipal'nogo znacheniia," p. 3; Umarov and Matqulov, "Protsesshoi kūchidani aholī," pp. 147, 148; Umarov and Matkulov, "Migratsionnye protsessy: motivy i otsenki," p. 2.

22. Sultonov, "Maromnomai partiya," p. 2; Kholiqov, "Oilai barodaronai mo," p. 3; "Voprosy prinstipal'nogo znacheniia," p. 3; Davlatov, "Vaqti mala ast," p. 3.

23. "Nuzhnyi obshchesoiuznye programmy," p. 4; Vahhobov, "Mo Tojikon magar soddaiyu gumrohem?," p. 2; "Shifo boyadat, dorui talkhnūsh," p. 2; Subhonov, "Dardi mo"; Murodov, "Chor andesha va shash peshnihod piromuni halli yak problema," p. 2.

24. "Durnamoi rushdi mo," p. 2.

25. FBIS, *Daily Report, Soviet Union*, April 12, 1991, p. 48; Tursunov, "Natsional'nyi vopros," p. 17.

26. Zaslavsky, "The Soviet Union," p. 90; Tuminez, "Nationalism, ethnic pressures, and the breakup of the Soviet Union," pp. 128–30.

27. Mir-Akilov, "Ot unifikatsii," p. 46.

28. Tursunov, "Natsional'nyi vopros," pp. 15–16; Mir-Akilov, "Ot unifikatsii," p. 46; "Voprosy prinstipal'nogo znacheniia," pp. 3–4; Muhammadiev, "Barodari man boshī, barobari man bosh!," p. 3; Kholiqov, "Oilai barodaronai mo"; Rahimov, "Talabi aiyom"; Panfilov, "Opiraias' na traditsii," p. 3; "Nuzhnyi obshchesoiuznye programmy," p. 4.

29. Olimova and Olimov, "Obrazovannyi klass Tadzhikistana v peripetiiakh XXv," p. 97.

30. Fathullohzoda, "Iloji voqea pesh as vuqu'' boyad kard," p. 1.

31. Sattorov, "Dardhoi miyonshikan," p. 4; Umarov and Madqulov, "Protsesshoi kūchidani aholī," p. 146; Kholiqov, "Oilai barodaronai mo"; Institut Etnografii, Akademiia nauk SSSR, *Sotsial'no-kul'turnyi oblik sovetskikh natsii*, pp. 87, 89; "Rohi rizoiyat," p. 2; "Soobshchenie komissii prezidiuma Verkhovnogo Soveta Tadzhikskoi SSR," p. 3.

32. Sattorov, "Dardhoi miyonshikan," p. 4.

33. Kholiqov, "Oilai barodaronai mo"; "Natsional'nyi vopros i mezhnatsional'nye otnosheniia v SSR: Istoriia i sovremennost'," p. 86.

34. Rahimov, "Talabi aiyom."

35. Gudkov, "Attitudes toward Russians in the Union republics," p. 20.

36. Halimshoh, "Safar az olami saghir ba olami kabir," p. 13.

37. Atkin, "Religious, national, and other identities in Central Asia," pp. 51–9, 62; Atkin, "Tajiks and the Persian world," pp. 127–43.

38. Abdujabbor, "Moro ma''rifat meboyat . . . [sic]," p. 2.
39. Abdujabbor, "Moro ma''rifat meboyat . . . [sic]," p. 2.
40. Shukurov, "Ravshanfikron kujoed?," p. 13.
41. Shukurov, "Ravshanfikron kujoed?," p. 13.
42. Vahhobov, "Mo Tojikon."
43. Kholiqzoda, "Ta''rikhi siyosii Tojikon," pp. 4, 46, 66, 97, 102, 105.
44. United Nations, *Tajikistan Human Development Report*, p. 4,
45. Atovullo, "Za chto gibnut russkie solday v Tadzhikistane," p. 3.
46. Atovullo, "Za chto gibnut russkie solday v Tadzhikistane," p. 3; ITAR-TASS, September 17, 1992, in *Russia & CIS Today*, p. 22; *Reuter Library Report*, December 6, 1992; Zviagelskaya, "The Tajik conflict," pp. 163–4; Khodjibaev, "Russian troops"; Gretsky, *Russia's Policy Toward Central Asia*, pp. 12–13; Atkin, "Islam as faith," p. 263; Atkin, "Thwarted democratization in Tajikistan," p. 303.
47. Atkin, "Tajikistan: a case study for conflict potential," pp. 197–9.
48. Atkin, "Tajikistan: a case study for conflict potential," p. 196; *Current Digest of the Post-Soviet Press*, 45(21); Gubarev, "Pamirskie zarisovki," p. 8; FBIS, *Daily Report, Central Eurasia*, March 4, 1993, p. 61; Khodjibaev, "Russian troops"; Agence France Presse, May 18, 1995; Melchin, "Za osobuiu rol' Rossii v Tadzhikistane," p. 3.
49. RFE/RL *Newsline*, Vol. 8, No. 225, and Vol. 9, No. 167, www.rferl.org/newsline.
50. RFE/RL *Newsline*, Vol. 10, No. 46; Vol. 10, No. 104; Vol. 11, No. 109; Heathershaw, *Post-Conflict Tajikistan*, pp. 127, 135; Bohr, "Regionalism in Central Asia," p. 490.
51. Atkin, "Thwarted democratization in Tajikistan," p. 303.
52. Atkin, "Thwarted democratization in Tajikistan," p. 303; *Current Digest of the Post-Soviet Press*, Vol.48(33), p. 13; Interfax, April 16, 1999.
53. Interfax, April 16, 1999; Atkin, "Tajikistan: a case study," p. 196; Khodjibaev, "Russian troops"; Federal Information Systems Corp., September 21, 1995.
54. Panfilova, "Na Zapad"; RFE/RL *Newsline*, Vol. 12, No. 43.
55. RFE/RL *Newsline*, Vol. 7, No. 98; Vol. 10, No. 59; Vol. 10, No. 236.
56. Interfax, April 16, 1999; FBIS, *Daily Report, Central Eurasia*, April 19, 1999, October 20, 2004 and November 12, 2004; ITAR-TASS, May 17, 2007.
57. ITAR-TASS, April 27, 2007.
58. Atkin, "Tajikistan: a case study," pp. 195–6; "V reserve," p. 4; ITAR-TASS, March 28, 1996; Interfax *Presidential Bulletin Report*, April 28, 2003.
59. Erlanger, "In ex-Soviet lands"; Atkin, "Tajikistan: a case study," pp. 196–7.
60. Atkin, "Thwarted democratization," p. 303; Atkin, "Tajikistan: a case study," p. 196.
61. FBIS, *Daily Report, Central Eurasia*, January 12, 1993, p. 62; FBIS, *Daily Report, Central Eurasia*, February 23, 1993, p. 49; *Russian Press Digest*, August 9, 1996; "Kazhetsia, v Tadzikistane," p. 1.

62. Atkin, "Thwarted democratization," p. 304; Atkin, "Tajikistan: a case study," p. 197; *Current Digest of the Post-Soviet Press*, 48(33), p. 13; *Russian Press Digest*, October 5, 1996; Federal Information Systems Corp., June 15, 1994 and December 14, 1995; Khodjibaev, "Russian troops."

63. Heathershaw, *Post-Conflict Tajikistan*, p. 140.

64. RFE/RL Newsline, Vol. 11, No. 30; Vol. 12, No. 15.

65. Asian Development Bank, "Asian Development Outlook 2004," pp. 2, 5.

66. *RIA Novosti*, December 19, 2004.

67. RFE/RL *Newsline*, Vol. 8, No. 185; Human Rights Watch, Tajikistan; *Asia Plus*, December 18, 2009; Institute for War and Peace Reporting, Tajikistan.

68. Asian Development Bank, "Asian Development Outlook 2004," p. 1.

69. *Regional Cooperation for Development of Human Capacity*, p. 17.

70. Jonson, *Tajikistan in the New Central Asia*, pp. 60–1, 210, n. 27.

71. "Asian Development Outlook 2004," pp. 1, 2.

72. RFE/RL *Newsline*, Vol. 8, No. 136.

73. *BBC Monitoring International Reports*, January 18, 2004..

74. *BBC Monitoring International Reports*, April 22, 2005.

75. Interstate Statistical Committee of the Commonwealth of Independent States, "Main macroeconomic indicators. Tajikistan."

76. US Department of State, "Background Note: Tajikistan"; *RIA Novosti*, December 19, 2004; *BBC Monitoring International Reports*, January 24, 2004 and February 6, 2005.

77. *Interfax Presidential Bulletin Report*, April 28, 2003.

78. Reuters, December 3, 1993.

79. *Reuters European Business Report*, July 27, 1993 and July 21, 1994; *Reuters Library Report*, November 25, 1993; Tett, "Mourners for the Soviet empire."

80. Agence France Presse, July 29, 2005; *Regional Cooperation*, p. 9.

81. Asian Development Bank, "Asian Development Outlook 2004"; Foreign Broadcast Information Service, October 20, 2004.

82. Heathershaw, *Post-Conflict Tajikistan*, p. 140.

83. FBIS, *Daily Report, Central Eurasia*, November 23, 2004; Zvezda TV, Moscow, June 4, 2005; Jonson, *Tajikistan in the New Central Asia*, pp. 77–8.

84. *BBC Monitoring International Reports*, April 14, 2005.

85. "Voprosy prinstipal'nogo znacheniia," p. 4.

86. Agence France Presse, October 9, 2005.

87. RFE/RL *Newsline*, Vol. 11, No. 15 and Vol. 11, No. 78; Najibullah, "Tajiks buy into state power plant initiative."

88. Najibullah, "Tajiks buy into state power plant initiative."

89. RFE/RL *Newsline*, Vol. 10, No. 31.

90. Mūminzoda, "Ei mardum, hushyor boshed!," p. 1.

91. Tajikistan Development Gateway.

92. ITAR-TASS, May 4, 2007.

93. Jonson, *Tajikistan in the New Central Asia*, p. 171; IRNA (Tehran), July 14, 2001; RFE/RL *Newsline*, Vol. 7, No. 97.

94. ITAR-TASS, April 7, 2003.
95. Senn, "Lithuania: rights and responsibilities of independence," pp. 355–6, 359; Muiznieks, "Latvia: restoring a state, rebuilding a nation," pp. 382–4, 386–7, 389; Raun, "Estonia: independence redefined," pp. 412–14; Motyl and Krawchenko, "Ukraine: from empire to statehood," pp. 245, 247–8, 251; Olcott, "Kazakhstan: pushing for Eurasia," pp. 551–3; Nissman, "Turkmenistan; just like old times," p. 640; Huskey, "Kyrgyzstan: the politics of demographic and economic frustration," pp. 660–3.

16

Conclusions

Sally N. Cummings and Raymond Hinnebusch

This volume has argued that empire matters for post-imperial outcomes. In the introduction we observed that the similarity in the imperial creation of states in the Middle East and North Africa (MENA) and Central Asia (CA) seemed to explain similarities in the successor states. We also hypothesized that differences in imperial heritages explain the greater instability of the MENA states system and the lesser legitimacy of informal hegemony over that region compared with CA. Here, in the conclusion, we review the evidence and incorporate the findings of the chapter studies regarding these issues. We view the impact of empire on post-imperial sovereignty as mediated through intervening variables and, hence, organize the evidence under these categories: we examine effects of the drivers of transition from empire; we then summarize the evidence on the imperial transmissions left behind by empires. We then examine the extent of rupture after empire, with its implications for post-imperial hegemonies. We end with a summary of the outcome for the various dimensions of sovereignty, highlighting the similarities and differences between the cases.

Drivers of Transition and Post-imperial Outcome

Differences in post-imperial states and states systems could be expected to be partly a function of differences in the drivers of sovereignty, that is, the forces propelling the transition from empire to sovereignty. Decolonization is driven by both external forces (such as the international system) and internal forces (nationalist mobilization), which together shape the particular direction it takes. These patterns have differed in MENA and CA.

If the international system is an intervening variable in the creation of empires, as Doyle argues, it also affects the end of empire, with pathways to sovereignty shaped both by imperial competition and global resistance to empire, which drive contests over normative hegemony.[1] This allows subject peoples to choose from ideologies that express their experiences under empire and their views of how best to achieve sovereignty. Since the international power balance and the norms dominant at the time the Middle East was making its transition to sovereignty were different from those accompanying the transition in CA, one would expect the new orders to be different.

The Versailles settlement that imposed empire in MENA was widely seen, there as in Europe, as a victor's *dictat* by its victims, at odds with the norm of self-determination the allies used to legitimize their fight against enemy empires during the First World War, but which now de-legitimized their own empires. In her contribution, Michelle Burgis traces the evolving effect of international law on empire and decolonization. She shows that international legal personality was constructed to justify empire, but also how the international norm of self-determination was both manifested in and diluted by the legal institution of the mandate. The mandate system was an effort to make empire more acceptable, but ultimately it legitimated the demand for independence if peoples could show that they were prepared for it. Thus, empire generated its antithesis, nationalism, and the demand for sovereignty. Still, despite new norms it took the emergence of bipolarity to fully empower the new norms: the anti-imperialist policy of the two post-Second World War superpowers, combined with the economic exhaustion of the old imperial powers, which nevertheless still fought tenaciously (Suez, Algeria) to keep their empires.

In CA the norms at the time of transition were rather different. The "scripts of sovereignty" explored by Mohira Suyarkulova were decisive in the fall of the Soviet Union. She focuses on the specificity of the emergence of the Central Asian republics as sovereign states within the broader context of the all-Union discourse on sovereignty, anti-imperialism and nationalism, and she identifies the events, laws, institutions and debates that shaped this discourse. In late Soviet discourse sovereignty denoted decentralization, power sharing and confederation, well short of full independence and, as she shows, Central Asian elites wanted greater autonomy only within the existing Soviet federation. The 1991 New Union Treaty negotiated with the leaders of the Union republics carved out a middle ground between full sovereignty and full subordination to Moscow, with republics allowed to opt in, and had it been allowed to structure relations between the republics, "sovereignty within the Soviet Union might have taken on a new and unique meaning in the international system of states."[2] But the Moscow coup of August 19, 1991 pre-empted its adoption, with the emerging Russian leader, Yeltsin, declaring Russia to be a sovereign state, with considerable popular support; this precipitated the break-up of the Soviet Union, with the right to secession enshrined in the Soviet constitution then becoming operative and legitimizing the transition to sovereignty on the periphery. As McFaul argued, the "rules of the game regarding sovereignty in today's international system . . . eventually helped to suppress . . . alternative models" that could have replaced the Soviet Union.[3] Traditional understandings of sovereignty endowed the Union republics with it, but not smaller units within them, and marginalized creative larger constructions, such as the CIS, whose function was reduced to presiding over a "civilized divorce." The outcome validated the argument of Krasner that "if decision makers are unable to voluntarily construct new rules [of federal cooperation] either unilaterally or multilaterally, or to use coercion to establish such rules, then sovereignty is the default."[4] Being congruent with shared understandings of sovereignty, the 1991 settlement enjoyed legitimation that Versailles never acquired.

Ultimately, in both regions the norm of sovereignty was embraced by the state elites that inherited power after empire, as a protection against stronger neighbors and interference by the ex-empire, although initially with reluctance in CA and in MENA with considerable ambivalence by would-be regional hegemons and public opinion insofar as sovereignty sanctified artificial boundaries at the expense of pan-Arab identity. Burgis shows, however, that the embrace by post-imperial states of the imported Western notion of sovereignty has been an element of stabilization in a turbulent region and, in particular, their acceptance of Western-shaped international law in dealing with the border conflicts left over from empire. In both regions "international society" confirmed the sovereignty of the new states by extending "recognition," with its assumptions of non-interference, membership in international organizations and the right to exploit their own natural resources and adopt their own particular development paths, at least until US hegemony and globalization started forcing all states onto similar neo-liberal paths.

If empire generated its antithesis, nationalism, whether the latter was combined with liberal and market values or with communitarian religions (Islam) or ideologies such as socialism/populism depended on the global power balance at the time of transition. At the time of transition to sovereignty in MENA, socialism, promoted by the Soviet counter-empire, was mounting a strong challenge to liberal capitalism and, in promising a more egalitarian road to development free of dependence on the West, was widely embraced in the region, in various mixtures with nationalism. Economic nationalism viewed global market integration under imperialism as reproducing dependency (neo-imperialism) after independence and advocated a diversification of economic relations and a turn from primary product exportation to import substitute industrialization, both of which were facilitated by Communist bloc aid and markets. Socialism also de-legitimized the expropriation under empire of land and oil by Western-fostered oligarchies and, once their imperial protectors departed, they were widely overthrown and their assets redistributed in revolutions.

By contrast, the market-centric norms of globalization that dominated the transition to sovereignty in CA had the reverse effect.[5] This was reflective of the triumph of Western liberalism accompanying Soviet collapse, itself attributed by Lieven to a loss of faith in the socialist ideology that cemented the empire owing to economic failure under the stress of military competition with the United States. Neo-liberal norms legitimized a "counter-revolution" compared with the Soviet period, with elites' private expropriation of public assets generating enormous new inequalities. Yet, while the ideal of independent national development once prevalent in MENA is no longer an alternative to neo-liberal hegemony, CA leaders are not enthusiastic liberalizers; and they have similarly sought to diversify economic relations, opening up to the West to reduce dependency on Russia, but not breaking with Russia (as did the Baltic states).

NATIONALIST MOBILIZATION

The pathway to sovereignty is also shaped by nationalist mobilization against the imperial power and the parallel creation of a national identity among the often diverse peoples inherited by new states from empire.[6] The intensity of nationalist mobilization is shaped by the imperial experience: the more alien, politically exclusionary and economically damaging the empire, the more at odds with emergent norms; the more incorporation into the empire violated pre-existing identity, the more nationalist movements will likely arise; and the more intense and extended the nationalist struggle, the greater the social depth of popular mobilization and the more radical the variant of nationalism.

Levels of nationalist mobilization were much higher in the Middle East than CA, although it was by no means uniform: it was most intense and radical in countries such as Algeria and Palestine, where colonial settlement drove indigenous people off the land; in Iraq and Syria, which

329

suffered from the forced fragmentation of the Mashreq and the imperial consolidation of big landed classes at the expense of peasants and tribesmen; and in Egypt and Iran, which endured long periods of foreign control. Region-wide, it was also stimulated by British-sponsored Zionist settlement in Palestine from the 1930s, poisoning Arab relations with Britain.

Nationalist mobilization was shaped by the particular context of imperial rule. In periods of imperial weakness and to avoid the costs of higher repression, Western empires in more nationally mobilized states such as Egypt promised or conceded greater self-government, which, however, provided space for nationalist elites to develop an organized mass base and gather momentum. Yet, because the autonomy granted indigenous elites was conceded over mainly internal matters while foreign and security affairs remained under imperial control, "high commissioners" and "advisors" retained authority over indigenous ministers, and the empire could intervene forcefully from military bases inside the country if its sway was challenged, this tended to discredit elites that accepted such terms, leading to the emergence of more radical nationalist counter-elites that attempted to more thoroughly mobilize mass strata.

In the Gulf emirates, a lighter touch imperialism imposed political advisors, resource concessions and military bases or ports, but not conquest and occupation *per se*, and client elites acquired a share of the growing oil wealth, which was generously distributed to their small populations who did not suffer from colonial-created big landed classes. Independence was granted for British economic reasons, without a struggle and accepted with reluctance, in view of the threats these weak but super-rich mini-states faced from their neighbors. The consequent lack of nationalist mobilization in the Gulf meant minimal rupture after empire and economic ties – the recycling of petro-dollars – to the core deepened after "independence."

Similarly, mobilization in CA was limited because sovereignty was devolved without a struggle once the core no longer found it profitable to maintain the empire; nationalism was a project of intellectuals and political elites rather than mass society. That CA resembles the Gulf countries in spite of much higher levels of social mobilization (for example, literacy) takes some explanation. A series of grievances against the Soviet center certainly existed in CA,[7] but these largely took the form of demands for cultural or environmental rights within the Union rather than mass Soviet anti-imperialism. Anti-imperial discourse surfaced in late Soviet times, for example, in Tajikistan (Atkin, Chapter 15), where Moscow was criticized for creating a cotton monoculture and preventing the republic from selling its products at world-market prices, but such grievances remained a fairly fleeting intellectual phenomenon. Indeed, CA populations had voted to maintain the Union just before its break up and the Central Asian republics were excluded from the dissolution negotiations and their leaders disappointed by the outcome.[8] Semi-sovereignty had preceded the development of nationalism, which had to be generated after empire. Indeed, nationalism since independence has been elite-driven and largely pragmatic; for example, in Uzbekistan it was stimulated by Gorbachev's crackdown on corruption in the regional party apparatus and in Kazakhstan by the ex-communist Kazakh elite's determination to appropriate the country's energy resources and not let them fall to Russians (see Ostrowski in this volume). Although the relatively strong "stateness" inherited from the Soviet era provided the basic foundation of sovereignty, the weakness of national mobilization in CA means that states may not enjoy much of the nationalist legitimacy bonus usually accruing from a struggle for independence.

Imperial Transmissions

While differences in empire matter, it is the particular experience of specific areas of the periphery, which may differ in different parts of the same empire, that shapes the effect of empire on sovereignty. Empire can affect what comes after in at least two contrary ways: it can leave behind positive legacies incorporated into the post-imperial order and it can provoke reactions leading to rupture with that order. Which predominates depends greatly on whether the impact of the imperial heritage is positive or negative for state formation inheritances, nation-building and economic development.

STATE FORMATION INHERITANCE

State formation inheritance refers to the effect of the colonial experience on the strength and nature of the post-imperial state, that is, whether or not the empire contributes to state formation. This is affected by whether under the empire itself the periphery is politically empowered through bureaucratic and representative institutions and accorded local self-government (autonomy).

Certainly, the successive empires in both regions variously provided key requisites of statehood (boundaries, state apparatuses) that have endured almost without exception. Empires also transmitted political practices used in post-imperial state-building, notably the

331

overdevelopment of autocratic, bureaucratic and patrimonial practices at the expense of political institutions. Although there were similarities in outcome, it was not uniform or without exceptions and pathways varied.

According to Barkey, the ex-imperial core inherits the strongest institutions, sense of identity and the most developed economy, while the periphery tends to turn to anti-imperialist nationalism as a substitute for institutions.[9] Fortna examines the emergence of MENA's strongest post-Ottoman state in Turkey, observing how Western encroachment stimulated the rise of the Young Turks and later of Atatürk, who sought to imitate the West in order to fight it off. He argues that the stress on rupture after empire underestimates continuity under the republic; hence, Turkey's successful adaptation to the age of nation-states can be traced both to its inheritance of core institutions of the Ottoman empire and to the nationalist legitimacy derived from the expulsion of Western imperialism from Anatolia in the post-First World War war of independence. This dual heritage also allowed Turkey to democratize, hence, strengthen the legitimacy of the post-imperial state. Lieven contrasts the ease with which Turkey shed its empire with the humiliation and identity crisis suffered by Russia with the collapse of the Soviet Union. Although Russia, he argues, has no wish to reassume the burdens of governing the lost lands and Russian revanchism has been quite restrained, the existence in the "near abroad" of Russians and of instability make it inevitable that Moscow would attempt to extend informal post-imperial influence in CA and the Caucasus through military intervention, treaties and "pipeline politics."

In the Arab lands,[10] the main Ottoman inheritance was the "notable" clientelist style of politics that was combined with the power apparatuses transmitted by Western empires. James McDougall sees the British and French establishment of empires as necessarily involving a compromise with local agents, the outcome of on-going contestation produced and reproduced by agents with access to unequal resources. The differences between French and British rule is, he argues, exaggerated, with both combining coercion and co-optation of local elites, and each empire transmitting to sovereign states permanent heritages such as borders that, however contested, were eventually naturalized and aspects of education and law that have also endured. The imperialists also created armies in each colony and inadvertently stimulated nationalist movements that both gave rise to the new elites that inherited power.

Elites gained some preparation for governing in periods of semi-sovereignty (such as the mandates explored by Burgis) under which representative institutions had been conceded by the colonizers. However, the latter could not be consolidated because of their domination by imperial-fostered landlords and tribal chiefs, whose clientele networks kept the middle classes excluded and the masses unmobilized. Under European rule, the Arab militaries had been recruited from non-nationalist Turkic, tribal or minority elements, but as independence approached, the dominant Sunni notables shunned military careers and officer corps came increasingly to be recruited from the nationalist-minded rural lower middle classes; as a result, the military and the politicians of the urban oligarchy came to represent different social classes, unleashing instability after independence until a new generation of elites found a formula for constructing durable regimes.

Initially, in reaction against the non-egalitarian heritage of Western rule, a wave of revolutions gave birth to populist authoritarian regimes in the more developed Arab lands. This was a reversion to the combined egalitarian legitimacy norms and authoritarian practices of Islamic empires reinforced by the hierarchical inclinations of the military elites trained under imperialism that almost everywhere assumed power. Their rule was modernized via diluted versions of bureaucratic centralism, single-party systems and etatism borrowed from the Soviet Union. These states could not, however, be consolidated until the new elites learned to draw on the patrimonial and clientelist practices of past nomadic-constructed Islamic empires, notably elite cohesion through primordial *asabiyya* (solidarity) and clientelism, thereby producing hybrid neo-patrimonial regimes. The exception to this post-imperial revolution was the survival of ruling monarchy in more tribal parts of the Arab world, where a lighter touch imperialism froze existent social structures and growing oil resources energized an effective clientelism; here British imperialism engineered an anomaly in the modern world, ruling monarchy.

In CA the transition to sovereign statehood was much smoother than in MENA, because the Soviet Union republics were sovereign states in embryo with recognized borders and robust levels of institutionalization and societal penetration from Soviet times, and they had just acquired legitimacy from the 1990 elections. David Lewis employs the term "bureaucratic sovereignty" to underscore how Central Asian states in the Soviet period already enjoyed some autonomy and how, in the absence of independence movements, this autonomy simply moved from a Soviet to independent vessel. Also, because there were no separate colonial armies or independence wars to generate an indigenous one, the military was weak and subordinate to civilian leadership, allowing CA to avoid the coups typical of the Middle East. In late Soviet times, various forms of corruption and clientelism, somewhat pre-modern forms of association, had come to empower local elites and mediate the relation to the imperial center; with the collapse of the Communist Party ideology and organization that had been the motor of the state, such patrimonial practices from the imperial past filled the vacuum. Hybrid neo-patrimonial regimes mixing bureaucratic structures with rent-lubricated clientalism emerged, very similar to those in the Middle East. Under such regimes, as Ostrowski shows, state capacity contracted after independence, resulting in falls in education and health levels; rentierism loomed larger, resulting in a certain de-diversification of the economy; while de-mobilization of a population more dependent on patron-states maintained stability in the region. The exception to this peaceful transfer to sovereignty was Tajikistan, where a civil war of anti-communist, Islamic and regional forces against the ex-communist elite ended in a stalemate and power-sharing.[11] Statehood in oil-poor Kyrgyzstan has also proved less robust.

By contrast to the cosmopolitan mixing of un-politicized ethnicities under empires, the modern counter-norm of nation-state congruence legitimates the creation of homogeneous nations, resulting in ethnic un-mixing after empire, sometimes through violent conflict.[12] Important for post-imperial outcomes is whether there is a strong prior identity that was violated by the original imperial incorporation and whether the sub-state units created within the empire frustrate or satisfy, even constitute, identity. This determines whether the post-imperial states are congruent with popular identity and, hence, provide positive contexts for nation-building or whether their creation inflicts national identity deficits.

In Turkey, Atatürk, by fighting imperialism to a standoff, was able to negotiate boundaries relatively congruent with an emerging Turkish nation, albeit accompanied by population transfers (paralleled by a longer history of in-migration of Turkic peoples from the Balkans and Caucasus); in the process, he acquired the legitimacy to reconstruct the core of the empire as a Turkish nation-state. This legitimacy allowed Turkey to eschew irredentism, turning its back on the Arab provinces in a way similar to Yeltsin's post-1991 abdication of responsibility for the Russian "near abroad."

It is no accident that the two peoples denied statehood in the Versailles settlement, the Kurds and Palestinians, would become centers of enduring conflict. Assimilationist nation-building projects in Turkey, Iraq and Iran have confronted and denied demands for Kurdish self-determination. In Palestine, empire-sponsored settler colonialism shifted ethnic balances, ending in the expulsion of Palestinians, with fraught consequences for regional stability. Also, where imperialism had created artificial communally-divided states, there was a strong tendency once the mediating imperial power departed for one communal group to seize the state for its own ends, for example, in Lebanon and Iraq, at the expense of national cohesion.[13]

What made the Arab world's experience unique, however, was the poor fit between territory and *supra*-state identity resulting from the imposition of a Western-style states system from without. The new states froze the region into a permanent fragmentation contrasting, in indigenous memories, to periods of greatness under Islamic empire, including the recent Ottoman experience, and/or came at the expense of pan-Arab identity that was emerging even as Western empires took over the region. Resentment at this outcome, further inflamed by the loss of Palestine, de-legitimized the first generation ruling elite and made pan-Arab issues the main preoccupation of social movements and army colonels for two decades at the expense of institution-building, much as Barkey suggests.[14]

Several of the authors in this volume address the impact of Western imperial encroachment on the Arab-Islamic world and its imposition of a formally Westphalian style states system in place of Islamic empire. Morten Valbjørn examines the variations in how intellectuals responded to the West, their views of it ranging from model to threat, and also how variations in identity from state-centric (*watani*) to supra-state (*qaumi*) were shaped by the impact of imperialism and the response of nationalists to it. The result was a situation of multiple identities in which post-colonial Arab states have had to compete for the loyalties of their populations with supra-state identities that may be used by opposition movements to contest their legitimacy. Ruling elites cannot wholly rely on "national" identities attached to the state for their legitimacy; rather, legitimacy depends, to an extent not seen elsewhere, on their being seen to act in the interest of the larger supra-state (Arab, Muslim) community against what are widely seen as threats from Israel and the West; this, however, contradicts with the contemporary economic- and security-dependence of most ruling elites on the West. Unlike in the West, where the rise of nationalism was combined with the achievement of sovereignty, hence, a stabilizing legitimacy,[15] in the Arab world, sovereignty was used to deny pan-Arab or Islamic (and Kurdish) self-determination, with a consequent legitimacy deficit attaching to the states system.[16]

However, despite this, the actual impact of identity frustration varies considerably. McDougall argues that the negative effect of

Western-imposed fragmentation has been exaggerated and it certainly varies among the Arab states, and the durability of the state boundaries is undeniable. Still, there is no doubt that identity remains a fraught issue in the Arab world. Louise Fawcett examines the impact of imperialism and post-imperial informal empires on the kinds of post-imperial state which emerged in MENA, specifically, their non-democratic character. For her, much of this outcome can indeed be traced to aspects of the imperial impact, including legitimacy deficits rooted in incongruities of identity and territory and continuing external intervention. Hinnebusch demonstrates how the dismemberment of historic Syria and quite different perceptions of it set the Syrian Ba‘athist and Jordanian Hashemite regimes on opposing tangents that have largely endured to this day. Frédéric Volpi shows that Islamic identity has been embraced as the main opposition discourse in the MENA region; this reflects the fact that even as Arab nationalism weakened after the 1970s it was more supra-state Islamic identity than individual state identities that filled the vacuum.

In CA, rather than frustrating identity, the Union republics fostered proto-national identities and the achievement of sovereignty largely satisfied them.[17] The Union accorded to Kazakh, Kyrgyz, Tajik, Turkmen and Uzbeks a land that for the first time bore their name. While the Western empires drew MENA borders for strategic convenience frustrating identity, Soviet ethnographers meticulously took identity and language into account when drawing CA borders.[18] Some authors have stressed how local elites participated in border drawing.[19] Nevertheless, none of the CA states have deep historical memories to support national identity and all suffer from sub-state divisions: Uzbekistan has some historical roots in the emirates of Bukhara and Khiva, but Tajikistan also has historical claims on the emirates. The nomadic states, such as Kazakhstan, have memories of tribal and clan division rather than national unity and politico-economic localism is strong, especially when energy and foreign investment is concentrated in certain regions. In spite of this and even though there had been substantial ethnic mixing under empire, a shallow territorial-focused identity was generated and, as Critchlow argued for Uzbekistan, the population within state borders, whatever their ethnic origins, had, after seven decades of schooling and media in the Uzbek language, come to see themselves as Uzbek.[20] The titular majorities who dominated the post-Soviet states sought to continue the type of state-building begun under the Soviets, nurturing, on the one hand, a state identity (Soviet now becoming a "-stani" identity) and, on the other hand, an ethnic one (the titular). There was some ethnic unmixing, particularly Russian exit, but it proceeded without serious ethnic conflict. Lewis further argued that part of the reason for the emergence of five territorially defined sovereign states lies in the legacy of the Soviet state, understood as an imperial construct (a "structurally centralized political system," in Motyl's definition),[21] with an underlying discourse and structural mechanisms that reflected racial and cultural difference. The place where irredentism has had some purchase in CA is the Ferghana Valley region, where Soviet national delimitation resulted in a mismatch of ethnic and political boundaries but even here conflict has been contained.[22] Nor have the individual states been de-legitimized by strong competing pan-Turkic or pan-Islamic identities.

There is evidence that the Soviet experience forged a hybrid culture in the CA states. For Beissinger the sign of empire is that it is seen to be fundamentally "alien" by the ruled, against whom the imperial center uses its political power to colonize knowledge.[23] However, in the Soviet case, Laura Adams argues, local cultures, albeit dominated by Soviet interventionism, actively and strategically participated in the production of difference. The peculiarity of the Soviet experience lay in the fact that "Soviet culture was a real and meaningful project that did not simply colonise its Central Asian subjects, but was produced by them" with the result that "we must not view Central Asian cultural sovereignty only through the lens of postcolonialism."

Frédéric Volpi, comparing the impact of empire on Islamic identity in both regions, shows how different imperial experiences have carried different implications for the ways in which political Islam has been mobilized in Central Asia and the Middle East. What was a single Islamic cultural area was bifurcated under different imperial experiences into different tangents. Islam has to be part of the identity of the new Central Asian states and, since independence, Islamic revival has been stimulated by the re-opening of contact with the Middle East, but it has not, for the most part, taken a revolutionary or a very politicized form and elites, fearing political Islam, have fostered a controlled moderate form of cultural Islam.[24] By contrast, in MENA Islam takes many forms, both a co-opted establishment Islam that legitimizes states, and oppositionist Islam which contests them, sometimes in the name of a pan-Islamic alternative. While many Islamic movements in MENA are moderate and seek incorporation into governing bargains, others are revolutionary and violent. While some of these have spilled over from MENA to CA, the experience of education and secularization under the Soviets, similar to the nation-building project in Turkey, has produced a similar moderate form of Islam.

ECONOMIC DEVELOPMENT AND DEPENDENCY

Another variable of imperial transmission worth exploring is whether imperial economic practices and relations advance or cripple the economic viability of the periphery, specifically whether a classic colonial division of labor is established under empire or efforts are made to break down core–periphery economic gaps through industrialization and mass education.[25] This will have important consequence for whether post-imperial sovereignty remains sharply qualified by dependency on the ex-imperial core.

Fred Lawson examines the economic heritage of the late Ottoman empire, stressing the growth of economic interdependence, the emergence out of semi-official tax farmers of a partly autonomous bourgeoisie in certain areas and a state-determined concentration of industrial development in the imperial core areas. These three factors determined the constraints and opportunities that confronted post-imperial states as they set out to manage not only their respective domestic economic arenas, but also their economic relations with one another. While emergence of a bourgeoisie left Syria better prepared for statehood than tribal and less-developed Iraq and eastern Turkey, the imposition of new borders under Western empires snapped the economic interdependencies generated under the Ottomans, forcing post-imperial states to reconstruct state-bounded national economies. While this began in Turkey, Western imperialism's incorporation of the Arab Middle East into a colonial division of labor and fostering of client elites invested in this system led to an ongoing struggle for indigenous control over economic borders. Western imperialism was perceived as designed to foster dependency, generating a reaction in the statist revolutions that followed independence.

A similar division of labor in the Soviet empire led to less core exploitation of the periphery, although the debate continues over which part benefited most, the core or periphery. However calculated, the Soviets invested much more in the non-Russian periphery than Western empires did in their colonies, and spread mass literacy, urbanization and industrialization that eroded rather than accentuated core–periphery differences. Nevertheless, as Muriel Atkin explains, after the demise of the Soviet Union, a measure of dependency on Moscow persisted in the formally independent states, not dissimilar to dependency in MENA former colonies on their ex-imperial metropolis. In the era of *glasnost'*, the open discussion of Tajikistan's colonial relationship to Moscow addressed the exploitation of the republic as a producer of raw materials, the denigration of and lack of access to the Tajik cultural heritage, and the failure of the

Soviet system to bring, in substance, not just name, the progress that was part of the justification for Moscow's rule over the colonial hinterland. Many of the motives for making such arguments survived in independent Tajikistan and so did the expression of colonial grievances. At the same time, post-Soviet Tajik elites remained heavily dependent on Moscow for military, political, financial and economic support. Although this impoverished, fragile country received help from other external sources as well, it continued to rely on the former Soviet core above all.

In both regions, states inherited hydrocarbons, making them rentier states. This is famously so in the MENA region, especially the Arab Gulf where single-product economies in tiny city-states are based on the export of hydrocarbons; the vast revenues earned are used to pacify privileged state citizens (while migrants without rights do much of the work) and are expended on expensive imported arms or re-cycled to Western banks and financial markets, rather than invested in the region. The outcome is vast income inequalities between rich and poor and between oil and oil-less states, creating resentment that makes the rich Gulf monarchies clients dependent on the United States for their security, sharply limiting their foreign policy sovereignty. Ostrowski characterizes all of the independent Central Asian republics as rentier states and sees this as a direct legacy of Soviet rule. He argues that the "direct dependency" of Kazakhstan and Turkmenistan on the old "imperial" core has been underpinned by geography and the existing infrastructure. In sharp distinction, Uzbekistan's reliance on cotton allowed the ruling regime to pursue the most independent foreign policy in the region, the durability of which is, however, highly questionable due to unstable cotton prices on the international markets. Kyrgyz and Tajik dependency on foreign aid, labor remittances and leasing access to territory forced ruling regimes to largely subordinate their foreign policies to the politics of regional or international powers.

The main shared economic liability of post-imperial regimes in both regions is that the insufficient differentiation between political and economic realms typical of and partly transmitted from non-capitalist empires, whether the Ottoman or Soviet, has made economies vulnerable to exploitation for distributional, patrimonial and military ends which retards capital accumulation. Even before CA independence, military over-investment in the Soviet Union, spurred by Cold War competition, had retarded growth; this was paralleled in the Middle East by capital-dissipating militarization spurred by intense regional conflicts (Arab–Israel, Iran–Iraq). Post-colonial regimes in both regions and at about the same time, parallel to the global hegemony of neo-liberalism beginning in the 1980s, have sought ways of re-stimulating capitalist development.

Where regimes enjoyed hydrocarbon resources, rentier states emerged, more responsive to the demands of global markets or their protector hegemons than their own populations; where such resources were absent, regimes tried to solve the capital accumulation problem by adopting non-egalitarian capitalist practices promoted by the global hegemon, such as cuts in welfare and privatization of public sectors which generated stark increases in inequality and hence legitimacy deficits that necessitated increased repression. Thus, the political economy of integration into world markets under US hegemony helped sustain authoritarian rule in both MENA and CA.

Rupture or Post-imperial Hegemony

Empire can survive the transition to sovereignty in the form of new hegemonies exercised by imperial cores and new dependencies in the ex-colonies. But whether this is legitimized or results in attempted rupture and enduring conflict and instability varies sharply between MENA and CA. Arguably, the imperial experience, transition drivers and imperial transmissions together shape the degree of rupture after empire. Rupture refers both to internal order and external relations – whether anti-imperialism shapes relations with the ex-empire or whether the post-imperial states are content to remain informal dependencies.

The main difference between the two regions is the greater attempted rupture in MENA. Internally this can be seen in the waves of revolutions in MENA against the inequalities established under Western imperialism. In manifest contrast to the way the Arab provinces only reluctantly accepted the break up of the Ottoman Empire and the CA republics only reluctantly separated from the Soviet Union, many Arabs fought to end the Western empires and after independence sought to efface their remnants and consequences. Externally, the greater degree of legitimacy attached to association with the ex-empire in CA compares with the enduring persistence of anti-imperialism in MENA.

This contrast can be traced partly to differences in the transition to sovereignty: the high levels of nationalist mobilization and a hegemonic anti-imperialism within MENA colonies parallel to the global advance of egalitarian and nationalist norms compares with low mobilization levels in CA paralleled by the global hegemony of neo-liberal globalization which legitimized trans-national economic penetration by both the West and the ex-empire, defusing anti-imperialist impulses.

Underlying the differences in transition and further accounting for the continuing contrasts between the regions' levels of rupture and receptivity to new hegemonies, however, is arguably the different experiences of empire. The damaging experience, and enduring consequences, of empire in MENA, including the considerable frustration of identity, regional fragmentation, economic dependency and empire's most fraught residue, the Palestinian–Israel conflict, generated an enduring anti-imperialism. Yet attempts to restructure core–periphery relations, such as Egypt's brief pan-Arab hegemony and Iran's Islamic revolution, all failed to establish a viable alternative order, largely because the residues of the Western imperial era – borders, client elites, inter-regional conflicts, Israel – combined with external intervention and the continued incorporation of the oil-rich part of the region into the core, blocked such projects and instead resulted, especially since the end of the Cold War, in the even more overt and unchecked hegemony of the United States over the region. The Middle East, as Brown argues, is the most penetrated Third World region and has experienced the most chronic and unwelcome external intervention; it is, as Buzan observes, the one classical civilization that has not recovered its historical greatness after (Western) empire.[26] This explains why anti-imperialism, obsolete in much of the post-colonial world, remains alive in MENA and external hegemony, lacking legitimacy, continues to stimulate resistance, keeping the region unstable. The exception is Turkey, which, having successfully fought off imperialism, could engage with the West on a more self-confident basis, with anti-imperialism much diluted.

MENA's enduring anti-imperialism can be compared with CA, where modernization sufficiently empowered the region, nationhood was a product of imperial rule and de-development came after imperial break-up, resulting in more benign perceptions of the imperial era. In striking contrast to MENA, where imperial association was a liability, in CA leaders' Soviet identity initially give them the legitimacy to continue to rule. The idea of a Commonwealth (CIS) joining the ex-empire and ex-colonies was accepted by the Central Asian states, as well as subsequent security pacts joining them to Moscow, indicative of shared Soviet political culture (by contrast to MENA where similar schemes, such as the Baghdad Pact, were legitimacy liabilities and the British Commonwealth was never accepted).[27] Also distinctive of CA is the gap between the more state-centric identities of elites and popular attachment to the supra-state post-Soviet space manifest in support for open borders and trade, nostalgia for the Soviet era, emigration to Russia and a backlash against the inequalities fostered by Western-promoted neo-liberal globalization (issues partly explored by Adams in this volume). While the greater mass-level embrace of supra-state identity in CA is similar to MENA, its pro-imperial (pro-Russian) thrust contrasts sharply with the anti-imperial thrust of such identities in MENA.[28]

Outcomes: A Krasnerian Tally of Different Degrees of Sovereignty

While eventually the imperial relation to an external metropole came to an end, the social patterns and institutional practices forged in these relationships remained; some only as traces, but others that endured in the transformation of empire into something else, a national sovereignty which should be seen as more than "neo-colonialism" but less than "total independence." This challenges the view of an automatic linear progression from empire to sovereignty and, indeed, suggests the two conditions can co-exist. The full complexity of this "semi-sovereignty" can be measured by a rough tally of where the two regions stand on Krasner's four dimensions of sovereignty.

International legal sovereignty through external "recognition" was the least problematic for regional states to acquire, with the important and notable exception of Palestine. But we can say that states in both regions currently share, to all intents and purposes, the same international legal sovereignty (Iraq being a presumably temporary anomaly).

Domestic sovereignty is predominantly about "stateness" and authority (or lack thereof). MENA and CA share most domestic sovereignty attributes, referring to whether public authority operates effectively. In both there is enough "stateness" that, with some exceptions for certain periods (Lebanon and Tajikistan during their civil wars, and Kyrgyzstan in 2010), the states have possessed the bureaucratic and military capabilities to maintain order, an inheritance of empire or enabled by hydrocarbon rent. On the other hand, in terms of infrastructural power to deliver public goods and services or promote development, states in both regions are weak. This can be attributed to their particular neo-patrimonial versions of authoritarian rule that typically combine authoritarian personalistic leadership and clientelism with institutional underdevelopment. Un-incorporated oppositions are also typical: Islamic opposition is stronger in MENA, liberal opposition in CA – a product of more thorough modernization under Soviet empire (and similar to Turkey). Both regions have ended up with domestic sovereignty that is negative rather than positive.

Both regions share substantial challenges to interdependence sovereignty, taken to mean control over territorial borders, a variable that overlaps considerably with the congruence between territory (state) and identity (nation). In both regions, nation-building suffered from some-what arbitrary borders and competing sub-state and supra-state identities. Nevertheless, the extent of the problem varies considerably between the regions.

Despite some border disputes, borders have acquired a fair amount of legitimacy in CA. No minority has to date asked for a separate state and no ethnic group has adopted violent irredentist practices, although borders have had devastating effects on the livelihoods of cross-border communities and also on the cultural cohesion and strength of ethnic groups that are spread across borders, particularly in the Ferghana Valley (the recent Osh conflict, however defined, attesting to these challenges).[29] Nevertheless, in CA there are no supra-state identities with the power of pan-Arabism and pan-Islam in MENA and no stateless nations comparable with the Kurds and Palestinians.

In MENA, states have established control of their borders but these, in cutting across ethnic groups and violating supra-state identities, lack the same legitimacy as elsewhere and are vulnerable to penetration by tribal and trans-state movements. As a result of weak state–nation identity congruence, the Middle East contains a higher concentration of disputes around territory, borders and self-determination, frequently issuing in armed conflict.

Westphalian sovereignty, taken to mean freedom from penetration of policy processes by external actors, above all the ex-empire(s), and similar to the autonomy–dependency dichotomy, has been compromised in both regions. In both cases, elites installed in the imperial period tended to survive the collapse of the empire, remaining, to varying extents, clients of the center, hence, alienated from their populations and based on privileged access to office and/or appropriation of property (land, oil resources) facilitated under the empire. In MENA many of the initial client elites were overthrown in the post-independence revolutions, but even here clientage was later re-established (for example, in Egypt after Nasser). In both cases economies remain peripheries of imperial cores, with primary product production, combining hydrocarbons and agriculture/pastoralism, being the norm and import substitute industrialization failing to break the hold of dependency.

In both cases foreign policy autonomy is also limited. Kyrgyzstan's dependence on Western aid and the stationing of Russian and American troops and bases amount to a breach of Westphalian sovereignty. Periphery states, however, have more autonomy when there are competing hegemons. In CA, Russian, Western and Chinese competition maximizes options and autonomy. In the Middle East, by contrast, many states are profoundly dependent for security or foreign aid on the United States, US military bases and treaties are widespread and an overt US conquest of a Middle East state – Iraq – has seemingly turned the clock back to the imperial era. As a result, resistance to US hegemony is high in the MENA, albeit concentrated at the level of trans-state radical Islamic movements and manifest in the ongoing instability of the region. There is no comparable anti-imperialism in CA.

Coming back to the initial hypothesis, these comparisons enable us to understand the fundamental similarities and differences between the two regions. While legal and domestic sovereignty are similarly established at high to medium levels, in good part a result of similarities in imperial heritages, the two regions diverge considerably on territory–identity congruence, hence, in conflict and instability, as a result of differences in imperial practices. While in both regions Westphalian sovereignty has been compromised, that the resultant anti-imperialism is so much more marked in MENA is arguably a function of the regions' quite different experiences of empire. MENA's greater instability compared with CA issues in part from its greater rejection of the greater external domination to which it is subjected.

Notes

1. Doyle, *Empires*, pp. 232–56; see also Parrott, "Analyzing the transformation of the Soviet Union," pp. 14–24.
2. McFaul, "The sovereignty script: red book for Russian revolutionaries," p. 202.
3. McFaul, "The sovereignty script," p. 213.
4. Krasner, *Problematic Sovereignty*, pp. 2, 29.
5. Atkin, Lewis and Suyarkulova, this volume.
6. Doyle, *Empires*, pp. 369–72.
7. Smith, *Nations and Nationalism in a Global Era*, p. 18.
8. Lieven, *Empire: the Russian Empire and its Rivals*, p. 289.
9. Barkey, "Thinking about consequences of empire," pp. 99–114.
10. Fawcett and McDougall, this volume.
11. Lieven, *Empire: the Russian Empire and its Rivals*, pp. 390–5; Lewis, this volume.
12. Brubaker, "Aftermaths of empire and the unmixing of peoples," pp. 155–80.
13. Lieven, *Empire: the Russian Empire and its Rivals*, p. 369.
14. Hudson, *Arab Politics*.
15. Smith, *Nations and Nationalism in a Global Era*.
16. Valbjørn, this volume; Lawson, *Constructing International Relations in the Arab World*.

17. Critchlow, *Nationalism in Uzbekistan*; Lewis, this volume.
18. Lieven, *Empire: the Russian Empire and its Rivals*, p. 315.
19. Haugen, *The Establishment of National Republics in Soviet Central Asia.*
20. Critchlow, *Nationalism in Uzbekistan.*
21. Motyl, *Revolutions, Nations, Empires*, p. 126.
22. Indeed, if it was associated with some cross-border interference chiefly by Uzbekistan, this was defensive, with no irredentist ambition to create a "Greater Uzbekistan."
23. Beissinger, "Soviet empire as 'Family Resemblance.' "
24. Olcott, "Islam in Central Asia in a global context."
25. Parrott, "Analyzing the transformation of the Soviet Union," pp. 14–24; Tsygankov, "Defining state interests after empire."
26. Had the ex-(Islamic) empire been preserved, as in the cases of India and China, the region might have been comparably situated to be a player in the world political economy.
27. Despite its symbolic importance, however, the CIS has remained of limited importance with most cooperation confined to the military and security sectors.
28. Adams and Lewis, this volume.
29. Lubin and Rubin, *Calming the Ferghana Valley.*

Bibliography

Court cases, international agreements, legal documents

Application for Revision and Interpretation of the Judgment of February 24, 1982 in the Case Concerning the Continental Shelf (Tunisia/Libyan Arab Jamahiriya), *ICJ Rep.* 1985, p. 192.

Article 22, Covenant of the League of Nations, 225 CTS 188, June 28, 1919.

Article 3, paragraph 2 of the Treaty of Lausanne (Frontier between Turkey and Iraq), (Turkey/Britain), *PCIJ*, Ser. B, No. 12, 1925.

Case Concerning Maritime Delimitation and Territorial Questions between Qatar and Bahrain (Qatar/Bahrain) (Merits), *ICJ Rep.* 2001, p. 40. The pleadings can be accessed on the ICJ's website at http://www.icj-cij.org/docket/index. php?p1=3&code=qb&case=87&k=61.

Case Concerning the Continental Shelf (Libyan Arab Jamahiriya/Malta), *ICJ Rep.* 1985.

Case Concerning the Territorial Dispute (Libyan Arab Jamahiriya/Chad), *ICJ Rep.* 1994.

Case of the Readaptation of the Mavrommatis Jerusalem Concessions (Greece/ Britain), *PCIJ*, Ser. A, No. 11, 1927.

Case of the SS *Lotus* (France/Turkey), *PCIJ*, Ser. A, No. 10, 1927.

Covenant of the League of Nations, 225 CTS 188, June 28, 1919.

Customs Regime between Germany and Austria (Advisory Opinion), *PCIJ*, Ser. A/B, No. 41, 1931.

Frontier Dispute (Burkina Faso/Mali), Judgment, *ICJ Rep.* 1986, p. 554.

General Act of the Conference of the Plenipotentiaries of Austria-Hungary, Belgium, Denmark, France, Germany, Great Britain, Italy, the Netherlands, Portugal, Russia, Spain, Sweden-Norway, Turkey (and the United States) respecting the Congo, 165 CTS 485, February 26, 1885.

Great Britain–Trucial Sheikhdoms, Exclusive Agreements, 176 CTS 457, March 6/8, 1892.

Island of Palmas Case, *RIAA*, April 4, 1928.

Legal Consequences of the Construction of a Wall in the Occupied Palestinian Territory (Advisory Opinion), *ICJ Rep.*, 2004, p. 136.

Legal Status of Eastern Greenland (Denmark/Norway), *PCIJ*, Ser. A/B, No. 53, 1933.

Legality of the Threat or Use of Nuclear Weapons (Advisory Opinion), *ICJ Rep.* 1996, p. 26.

Letter from Captain T. Hickinbotham, British Political Agent (officiating), to the British Political Resident, Bahrain, Counter-Memorial, May 9, 1936, Vol. 2, Annex 73, at 236.

Letter from Lt. Col. Loch, British Political Agent, to Lt. Col. Fowle, British Political Resident, Bahrain, Memorial, May 6, 1936, Vol. 5, Annex 247, at 1074. All memorials are available at: http://www.icj-cij.org/docket/index. php?p1=3&k=61&case=87&code=qb&p3=1.

Libya/Chad (separate opinion Shahabuddeen), *ICJ Rep.* 1994, p. 44.

Nationalities Decree Issued in Tunis and Morocco (French Zones) on November 8th, 1921, *PCIJ*, Ser. B, No. 4, 1923.

O'zbekiston Markazi Davlat Arxivi (Central State Archive of Uzbekistan), f. 2487 r. 3 y. 1974.

Phosphates in Morocco (Italy/France), *PCIJ*, Ser. A./B, No. 74, 1938.

Qatar/Bahrain (Merits) (dissenting opinion Bernádez, at para. 311), (separate opinion Kooijmans, at para. 4), (separate opinion Kooijmans, at para. 4), (dissenting opinion Bedjaoui, Ranjeva and Koroma, at para. 42), 2001.

Qatar/Bahrain (Merits), CR 2000/7, Mr Bundy, at paras 1–78, May 31, 2000.

Qatar/Bahrain (Merits), CR 2000/8, Qatar, Sir Ian Sinclair, at para. 15, June 5, 2000.

Reparations Case (Advisory Opinion), *ICJ Rep.* 1949, p. 174.

The Mavrommatis Palestine Concessions Case (Greece/Britain), *PCIJ*, Ser. A, No. 2, 1924.

The Mavrommatis Jerusalem Concessions Case (Greece/Britain), *PCIJ*, Ser. A, No. 5, 1925.

Treaty Guaranteeing the Independence and Integrity of the Ottoman Empire, 114 CTS 497, April 15, 1856.

UNGA Resolution 3292. The full text of the resolution is reproduced in the Opinion: Western Sahara (Advisory Opinion) *ICJ Rep.* 1975, p. 12.

Media and other sources

Abduazimho'ja Sherzodho'ja o'g'li, *Xalq So'zi*, translated as "Vernost' Natsional'nomu Dukhu," December 16, 2003, available at: http://www. tribune-uz.info/society/index.php?id1=427, accessed September 3, 2004.

Abdujabbor, T., "Moro ma"rifat meboyat . . . [sic]," *Dunyo*, May 1991, p. 2.

Adabiyot va san"at

"Durnamoi rushdi mo," July 13, 1989, p. 2.

"Shifo boyadat, dorui talkhnūsh," December 7, 1989, p. 2.

Halimshoh, S., "Safar az olami saghir ba olami kabir," August 6, 1992, p. 13.

Istad, A., "Iqtisod – sarchashmai mas"alahoi millī," September 7, 1989, p. 3.

Kholiqov, Q., "Oilai barodaronai mo: tajriba, problema, peshomadho," April 13, 1989, p. 3.

Muhammadiev, H., "Barodari man boshī, barobari man bosh!," September 7, 1989, p. 3.

Rahimov, I., "Talabi aiyom," September 14, 1989, p. 2.

Shukurov, Sh., "Ravshanfikron kujoed?," May 14, 1992, p. 13.

Toshbekov, M. "Dar Vil'nius chiro didem?," June 15, 1989, p. 15.

Agence France Presse

May 18, 1995

July 29, 2005, retrieved by Nexis.

October 9, 2005, retrieved by Nexis.

Asia Plus, December 18, 2009, available at: www.asiaplus.tj/en/news/39/60572. html.

Asian Development Bank, "Asian Development Outlook 2004 – Tajikistan," available at: www.adb.org/Documents/Books/ADO/2005/taj.asp.

Associated Press, The

Brumley, B., "Two duelling Soviet leaders able to claim victory in referendum," March 18, 1991.

Rosenblum, M., "AP Newsfeature: Samarkand, USSR," September 16, 1990.

Rosenblum, M., "Islam, economics, ecology: recipe for unrest in the Soviet south," July 23, 1990.

BBC Monitoring International Reports

April 14, 2005, retrieved by Nexis.

January 18, 2004, retrieved by Nexis.

April 22, 2005, retrieved by Nexis.

January 24, 2004 and February 6, 2005, retrieved by Nexis.

BBC Summary of World Broadcasts

"Congress of Communist Party of Uzbekistan" (Soviet television report), 1600 GMT, December 7, 1990.

"Discussion of 'General Principles' for Republican Self-Management," editorial report of phone-in program, "Restructuring problems and solutions" (Soviet television), 1500 GMT, March 29, 1989.

Niyazmatov, V., Interview with Islam Karimov, President of Uzbekistan, *Sovet Uzbekistoni* (in Uzbek), March 12, 1991.

Text of broadcast of a speech by the president of Uzbekistan, Islam Karimov, Moscow home service, 1600 GMT, December 18, 1990.

Zherebenkov, Y., "Kyrgyz president on status of Union Treaty," report from USSR Supreme Soviet Session, Russian radio, 1530 GMT, August 26, 1991.

Zvezda, TV, Moscow, June 4, 2005, retrieved by Nexis.

Dildyaiev, G., "A Union treaty must be signed immediately," *Pravda*, February 12, 1991, p. 2.

Eliott House, K., "Why Islam fell from grace," *Wall Street Journal*, January 11, 2002.

Erlanger, S., "In ex-Soviet lands, Russian army can be a protector or an occupier," *New York Times*, November 30, 1993, retrieved by Nexis.

Federal Information Systems Corp., transcript of official Kremlin international news broadcast, June 15, 1994 and December 14, 1995, retrieved by Nexis.

Foreign Broadcast Information Service
"Daily Report, Central Asia, 4–10 November," Al-Majallah, November 10, 1992, p. 68.
"Daily Report, Central Eurasia," January 12, 1993, p. 62.
"Daily Report, Central Eurasia," February 23, 1993, p. 49.
"Daily Report, Central Eurasia," March 4, 1993, p. 61.
"Daily Report, Soviet Union," April 12, 1991, p. 48.
April 19, 1999, retrieved by World News Connection.
October 20, 2004, retrieved by World News Connection.
November 12, 2004, retrieved by World News Connection.
November 23, 2004, retrieved by World News Connection.
Gray, J., "Gorbachev upbeat on union, rest of country apparently oblivious to President's concern," *The Globe and Mail*, September 2, 1991.
Human Rights Watch, "Tajikistan," available at: www.hrw.org/en/world-report-2010/tajikistan.
Entsiklopediayai Sovetii Tojik
"Imperializm," Vol. 2 (Dushanbe: Sarredaktsiyai ilmii Entsiklopediyai Sovetii Tojik, 1980), pp. 569–70.
"Mustamlikaho va siyosati mustamlikadorī," Vol. 4 (Dushanbe: Sarredaktsiyai ilmii Entsiklopediyai Sovetii Tojik, 1983), pp. 592–3.
Institute for War and Peace Reporting, "Tajikistan: No Jobs for Returning Migrants," July 12, 2009, RCA No. 583, available at: http://iwpr.net/report-news/tajikistan-no-jobs-returning-migrants.
Interfax
April 16, 1999, retrieved by Nexis.
Interfax Presidential Bulletin Report, April 28, 2003, retrieved by World News Connection.
International Crisis Group
"Asia Briefing: Kyrgyzstan: A Hollow Regime Collapses," April 27, 2010, No. 102.
"Asia Report: Central Asia: Migrants and the Economic Crisis," January 5, 2010, No. 183.
"Asia Report: Central Asia's Energy Risks," May 24, 2007, No. 133.
"Asia Report: Tajikistan: On the Road to Failure," February 12, 2009, No. 162.
"Asia Report: The Curse of Cotton: Central Asia's Destructive Monoculture," February 28, 2005, No. 93.
"Middle East Report: Understanding Islamism," March 2, 2005, No. 37.
International Monetary Fund, "Tajikistan," available at: www.imf.org/external/np/country/notes/tajikistan.htm.
Interstate Statistical Committee of the Commonwealth of Independent States, "Main Macroeconomic Indicators: Tajikistan," available at: www.cisstat.com/eng/tad.htm.
Islamic Republic News Agency, Tehran, July 14, 2001, retrieved by World News Connection, July 17, 2001.

ITAR-TASS

September 17, 1992, photocopied in *Russia & CIS Today*, September 17, 1992, p. 22.

March 28, 1996, retrieved by Nexis.

April 11, 2003, retrieved by World News Connection, April 14, 2003.

April 17, 2003, retrieved by World News Connection, April 18, 2003.

March 17, 2007, retrieved by Nexis.

April 27, 2007, retrieved by Nexis.

May 4, 2007, retrieved by World News Connection.

May 17, 2007, retrieved by Nexis.

Iushin, V., "Ot totalitarnogo internatsionalizm – k obshchinnomu mnogoobraziiu," *Vechernyi Dushanbe*, July 11, 1990, p. 2.

Javononi Tojikiston

Fathullohzoda, S., "Iloji voqea pesh as vuqu" boyad kard," October 15, 1992.

Vahhobov, A., 'Mo Tojikon magar soddaiyu gumrohem?', March 3, 1992, p. 2.

Jumhūriyat

"Murojiatnomai raisi Shūroi Olii Jumhurii Tojikiston Rahmon Nabiev ba mardumi Tojikiston," September 25, 1991, p. 1.

"Rohi rizoiyat," October 18, 1992, p. 2.

Mūminzoda, M., "Ei mardum, hushyor boshed!," February 22, 1992, p. 1.

Murodov, A., "Chor andesha va shash peshnihod piromuni halli yak problema," August 19, 1992, p. 2.

Karimov, I., speech at the session of the Khorazm Regional Council of People's Deputies, March 16, 1996, available at: http://2004.press-service.uz/rus/knigi/9tom/4tom_21_3.htm.

Kazakhstanskaya Pravda

"Agreement on economic, scientific-technical, and cultural cooperation of the Uzbek, Kazakh, Kirgiz, Tajik and Turkmen SSRs," June 23, 1990.

Isinaliyev, M., "An anxious time, a time of hope," December 2, 1990.

Khouri, R., "Heed the changes in Arab public opinion," *Agence Global*, July 28, 2006.

Kommunist Tadzhikistana

"Appeal of the Extraordinary Session of the Supreme Soviet of the Republic of Tajikistan to the Congress of People's Deputies of the USSR and to the Supreme Soviet of the RSFSR," September 3, 1991.

"O prakticheskikh merakh po realizatsii v respublike reshenii sentiabr'skogo (1989 g.) Plenuma TsK KPSS," February 1990, No. 2, p. 19.

Dadabaev, A., "Edinstvo mnozhit sily," May 1989, 5, pp. 12, 13.

Khudoiev, M., "Gotovnost' k dialogu, no na printsipial'noi osnove," July 3, 1990, p. 1.

Mir-Akilov, T., "Ot unifikatsii – k mnogoobraziiu," January 1990, No. 1, p. 46.

Tursunov, A. "Natsional'nyi vopros i natsional'naia intelligentsiia," March 1989, No. 3, p. 17.

BIBLIOGRAPHY

Komsomolets Tadzhikistana
"Nuzhnyi obshchesoiuznye programmy," December 27, 1989, p. 4.
Panfilov, O., "Opiraias' na traditsii," August 11, 1989, p. 3.
"Politicheskii kharakter partiinogo rukovodstva: opyt i problemy," April 14, 1989, p. 2.
"Rech' Predsedatelia Verkhovnogo Soveta Tadzhikskoi SSR K. M. Makhkamova," April 15, 1990, p. 3.
"Za aktivnuiu politiku, perestroiku, obnovlenie partii, demokratizatsiiu i gumanizatsiiu obshchestva," May 25, 1990, p. 3.
Umarov, Kh. and Matqulov, N., "Migratsionnye protsessy: motivy i otsenki," November 22, 1989, p. 2.
Komsomol'skaya pravda
"Kazhetsia, v Tadzikistane oboidutsia bez 'golubykh kaso,'" January 12, 1993, p. 1.
Mursaliyev, A. and Sorokin, Yu., "Firm hand as lever of perestroika," interview with A. Pulatov and P. Akhunov of the Birlik Uzbekistan Opposition Movement, July 27, 1991.
Solzhenitsyn, A., "How to rebuild Russia," September 18, 1990.
Solzhenitsyn, A., "Kak nam obustroit' Rossiyu" (How we should rebuild/develop Russia), Special supplement/brochure, translation from Russian by Mohira Suyarkulova, September 18, 1990.
Mahkamov, K., President of the Tajik SSR, speech to the 4th Congress of People's Deputies of the USSR, Official Kremlin International News Broadcast, December 20, 1990.
Melchin, L., "Za osobuiu rol' Rossii v Tadzhikistane prikhoditsia platit' slishkom doroguiu tsenu," *Izvestiya*, February 12, 1994, p. 3.
Nadler, G., "Gorbachev's gamble: what is Soviet referendum all about?," *United Press International*, March 11, 1991.
"Natsional'nyi vopros i mezhnatsional'nye otnosheniia v SSR: Istoriia i sovremennost'," *Voprosy istorii*, No. 5, May 1989, p. 86.
Omūzgor
Berdieva, B., "Hama rostī jūyu mardonagī," July 25, 1989, p. 7.
Subhonov, E., "Dardi mo nogufta mond," June 13, 1989, p. 5.
Panfilova, V., "Na Zapad – vsled za Moskvoi," *Nezavisimaia Gazeta*, March 4, 2002.
Pravda Vostoka
"Declaration of Sovereignty Adopted by the Supreme Soviet of the Uzbek SSR on June 20, 1990," June 22, 1990, No. 141.
"In the Supreme Soviet of Uzbek SSR: In the Interests of the Republic and the Whole Federation," September 1, 1990, No. 199, pp. 1–2.
Reuters
"Kazakhstan President Confident," Reuters News Agency, December 11, 1991.
Reuters European Business Report, July 27, 1993 and July 21, 1994, retrieved by Nexis.

Reuters Library Report, November 25, 1993, retrieved by Nexis.
Reuters Library Report, December 6, 1992, retrieved by Nexis.
Reuters, December 3, 1993, retrieved by Nexis.
Radio Free Europe/Radio Liberty
Najibullah, F., "Tajiks buy into state power plant initiative," January 12, 2010, available at: www.rferl.org/content/Tajiks_Buy_Into_State_Power_Plant_Initiative/1927025.html.
RFE/RL Newsline: Vol. 7, No. 97, May 23, 2003; Vol. 7, No. 98, May 27, 2003; Vol. 8, No. 136, July 20, 2004; Vol. 8, No. 185, September 29, 2004; Vol. 8, No. 225, December 10, 2004; Vol. 9, No. 167, September 2, 2005; Vol. 10, No. 31, February 21, 2006; Vol. 10, No. 46, March 13, 2006; Vol. 10, No. 59, March 30, 2006; Vol. 10, No. 104, June 8, 2006; Vol. 10, No. 236, December 22, 2006; Vol. 11, No. 15, January 25, 2007; Vol. 11, No. 30, March 1, 2007; Vol. 11, No. 78, April 27, 2007; Vol. 11, No. 109, June 14, 2007; Vol. 12, No. 15, January 23, 2008; Vol. 12, No. 43, March 4, 2008.
RIA Novosti, December 19, 2004, retrieved by Nexis.
Russian Press Digest
"DPR on the nation-wide scale," July 18, 1991, retrieved by Lexis-Nexis.
Latifi, O., "Heard about the coup?," No. 35, 1991, p. 22, retrieved by Lexis-Nexis.
August 9, 1996, retrieved by Nexis.
October 5, 1996, retrieved by Nexis.
Sattorov, A., "Dardhoi miyonshikan," *Omuzgor*, October 3, 1989, p. 4.
Zainutdinov, S., "What the president was silent on," No. 35, August 30, 1991, p. 22.
"Soobshchenie komissiii prezidiuma Verkhovnogo Soveta Tadzhikskoi SSR po proverke sobytii 12–14 Fevralia 1990 g. v Dushanbe," *Sogdiana*, No. 3, special issue, 1990, p. 3.
Suleymenov, O., "The collapse of the Soviet Union is tragedy to us," interview, *Dagens Nyheter*, April 28, 1995.
Tajikistan Development Gateway, available at: www.tajik-gateway.org.
"Tajikistan hops on independence bandwagon," *Seattle News*, September 10, 1991.
TASS
"Message to the Soviet People from the State Committee for the State of Emergency," August 18, 1991.
"Tajik President: the Union Must Be Preserved," December 21, 1990.
"V reserve na vydvizhenie ne znachilsia," *Rossiia*, March 31–April 6, 1993, p. 4.
"Voprosy prinstipal'nogo znacheniia," *Agitator Tadzhikistana*, April 1989, No. 8, p. 3.
"Zachem poety novoi vlasti, esli oni poiut tiurmenye pesni, kotorym ikh obuchili Sangak i ego koresha," *Charoghi rūz*, 1993, 71(2), p. 2.
Tett, G., "Mourners for the Soviet empire," *Financial Times*, November 27, 1995, p. 14, retrieved by Nexis.

Tojikistoni Sovetī
Davlatov, S., "Vaqti mala ast," July 16, 1989, p. 3.
Sultonov, Sh., "Maromnomai partiya," September 5, 1989, p. 2.
Vahhobov, A., "Khomūshī be ki lozim?," June 13, 1989, p. 2.
United Nations, *Tajikistan Human Development Report*, 2000, p. 4, available at: http://hdr.undp.org/en/reports/nationalreports/europthecis/tajikistan/tajikistan_2000_en.pdf.
US Department of State, "Background Note: Tajikistan," available at: www.state.gov/r/pa/ei/bgn/5775.htm.

Books and journals

Abdelal, R., "Purpose and privation: nation and economy in post-Habsburg eastern Europe and post-Soviet Eurasia," *East European Politics and Societies*, 2003, 16, pp. 898–933.
Abrahamian, E., *Khomeinism* (London: Tauris, 1993).
Abrams, P., "Notes on the difficulty of studying the state," *Journal of Historical Sociology*, 1988, 1(1), pp. 58–89.
Adams, L. L., "Invention, institutionalization, and renewal in Uzbekistan's national culture," *European Journal of Cultural Studies*, 1999, 2(3), pp. 355–73.
Adams, L. L., "Tashkent museum allows for public discussion of recent past," *EurasiaNet*, 2002, available at: http://www.eurasianet.org/departments/culture/articles/eav110102.shtml, accessed September 15, 2010.
Adams, L. L., "Modernity, postcolonialism and theatrical form in Uzbekistan," *Slavic Review*, 2005, 64, pp. 333–54.
Adams, L. L., "Can we apply post-colonial theory to Central Eurasia?," *Central Eurasian Studies Review*, Spring 2008, 7(1), pp. 2–7.
Adams, L. L., "Globalization, universalism and cultural form," *Comparative Studies in Society and History*, 2008, 50(3), pp. 614–40.
Adams, L. L., *The Spectacular State: Culture and National Identity in Uzbekistan* (Durham, NC: Duke University Press, 2010).
Addleton, J., *Undermining the Centre: The Gulf Migration and Pakistan* (Karachi: Oxford University Press, 1992).
Adelson, R., *London and the Invention of the Middle East: Money, Power and War, 1902–1922* (New Haven, CT: Yale University Press, 2000).
Ageron, C. R., *France coloniale ou parti colonial?* (Paris: Presses universitaires de France, 1978).
Ahmad, F., "Review: war and society under the Young Turks, 1908–18," *Ottoman Empire: Nineteenth-Century Transformations*, 1988, 11, pp. 265–86.
Ahmed, F., "War and society under the Young Turks, 1908–1918," in A. Hourani, P. Khoury and M. Wilson (eds), *The Modern Middle East: A Reader* (Berkeley, CA: University of California Press, 1993), p. 131.

Ahmad, F., "Vanguard of a nascent bourgeoisie: the social and economic policy of the Young Turks 1908–1918," in F. Ahmad, *From Empire to Republic* (Istanbul: Istanbul Bilgi University Press, 2008).

Ahmad, F., *The Young Turks* (New York: Columbia University Press, 2010).

Ajami, F., "The end of pan-Arabism," *Foreign Affairs*, 1978, 57(2), pp. 355–73.

Akcali, P., "Islam as a 'common bond' in Central Asia: Islamic Renaissance Party and the Afghan mujahidin," *Central Asian Survey*, 1998, 17(2), pp. 267–84.

Akiner, S., "Conflict and post-conflict Tajikistan: a case study," in N. Tschirgi and F. Mancini (eds), *Impacts of Security and Development Policies in Achieving Sustainable Peace* (New York: International Peace Academy, 2006).

Aksakal, M., *The Ottoman Road to War in 1914: The Ottoman Empire and the First World War* (Cambridge: Cambridge University Press, 2008).

Alexandrowicz, C. H., *An Introduction to the History of the Law of Nations in the East Indies (16th, 17th, 18th Centuries)* (Oxford: Clarendon Press, 1967).

Alexandrowicz, C. H., "New and original states: the issue of reversion to sovereignty," *International Affairs*, 1969, 45, p. 465.

Alimov, R. K., Shoismatulloev, Sh. and Saidov, M., "Migratsionnye protsessy i natsional'nyi vopros," *Kommunist Tadzhikistana*, May 1990, 5, p. 13.

Alimova, D. and Golovanov, A., *Uzbekistan v 1917–1980-ie gg.: protivoborstvo idei i ideologii* (Uzbekistan during the period between 1917 and 1980s: struggle of ideas and ideologies) (Tashkent: Institute of History of the Academy of Sciences of the Republic of Uzbekistan, 2002).

Allain, J., "Orientalism and international law: the Middle East as the underclass of the international legal order," *Leiden Journal of International Law*, 2004, 17, p. 391.

Allworth, E. (ed.), *Central Asia* (Durham, NC: Duke University Press, 1994).

Ambrosio, T., "Catching the 'Shanghai Spirit': how the Shanghai Cooperation Organization promotes authoritarian norms in Central Asia," *Europe–Asia Studies*, October 2008, 60(8), pp. 1321–44.

Amin, S., *The Arab Nation* (London: Zed Press, 1978).

Anceschi, L., "Analyzing Turkmen foreign policy in the Berdymuhammedov era," *China and Eurasia Forum Quarterly*, 2008, 6(4), pp. 35–48.

Anceschi, L., *Turkmenistan's Foreign Policy: Positive Neutrality and the Consolidation of the Turkmen regime* (London: Routledge, 2009).

Anderson, B., *Imagined Communities: Reflections on the Origin and Spread of Nationalism* (London: Verso, 1991).

Anderson, D., *Histories of the Hanged. Britain's Dirty War in Kenya and the End of Empire* (London: Weidenfeld & Nicolson, 2005).

Anderson, L., *The State and Social Transformation in Tunisia and Libya, 1830–1980* (Princeton, NJ: Princeton University Press, 1986).

Anderson, L., "Lawless government and illegal opposition: reflections on the Middle East," *Journal of International Affairs*, 1987, 40(2), pp. 219–32.

Anderson, L., "The state in the Middle East and North Africa," *Comparative Politics*, October 1987, 20(1), pp. 1–18.

Andrew, C. M. and Kanya-Forstner, A. S., "The French 'Colonial Party', its composition, aims and influence, 1885–1914," *The Historical Journal*, 1971, 14(1), pp. 99–128.

Andrew, C. M. and Kanya-Forstner, A. S., *France Overseas: The Great War and the Climax of French Imperial Expansion* (London: Thames & Hudson, 1981).

Andrew, C. M. and Kanya-Forstner, A. S., "Centre and periphery in the making of the second French colonial empire, 1815–1920," *Journal of Imperial and Commonwealth History*, 1988, 16(3), pp. 9–34.

Andrews, J. A., "The concept of statehood and the acquisition of territory in the nineteenth century," *Law Quarterly Review*, 1978, 94, pp. 408–27.

Anghie, A., *Imperialism, Sovereignty and the Making of International Law* (Cambridge: Cambridge University Press, 2005).

Aron, L., "Gorbachev's Central Asian time bomb is ticking," *Heritage Foundation Reports*, September 28, 1990, p. 792.

Atkin, M., "The survival of Islam in Soviet Tajikistan," *Middle East Journal*, 1989, 43(4), pp. 605–18.

Atkin, M., "Religious, national, and other identities in Central Asia," in J. A. Gross (ed.), *Muslims in Central Asia* (Durham, NC: Duke University Press, 1992), pp. 51–9, 62.

Atkin, M., "Tajiks and the Persian world," in B. F. Manz (ed.), *Central Asia in Historical Perspective* (Boulder, CO: Westview Press, 1994), pp. 127–43.

Atkin, M., "Islam as faith, politics, and bogeyman in Tajikistan," in M. Bourdeaux (ed.), *The Politics of Religion in Russia and the New States of Eurasia* (Armonk, NY: Sharpe, 1995).

Atkin, M., "Tajikistan: a case study for conflict potential," *The Soviet and Post-Soviet Review*, 1997, 24(3), pp. 197–9.

Atkin, M., "Thwarted democratization in Tajikistan," in K. Dawisha and B. Parrott (eds), *Conflict, Cleavage, and Change in Central Asia and the Caucasus* (Cambridge: Cambridge University Press, 1997), p. 303.

Atovullo, D., "Za chto gibnut russkie solday v Tadzhikistane," *Charoghi rūz*, 1995, 83(5), p. 3.

Ayoob, M., *The Third World Security Predicament, State Making, Regional Conflict and the International System* (Boulder, CO: Lynne Rienner, 1995).

Ayoob, M. and Kosebalaban, H., *Religion and Politics in Saudi Arabia: Wahhabism and the State* (Boulder, CO: Lynne Rienner, 2008).

Ayubi, N. N., *Over-stating the Arab State: Politics and Society in the Middle East* (London: Tauris, 1996).

Badie, B., *The Imported State: The Westernization of the Political Order* (Stanford, CA: Stanford University Press, 2000).

Balci, B., "Fethullah Gülen's missionary schools in Central Asia and their role in the spreading of Turkism and Islam," *Religion, State & Society*, 2003, 31(2), pp. 151–77.

Barkey, K., "Thinking about consequences of empire," in K. Barkey and

M. von Hagen (eds), *After Empire: Multiethnic Societies and Nation-building* (Boulder, CO: Westview Press, 1997), pp. 99–114.

Barkey, K., "Changing modalities of empire: a comparative study of Ottoman and Habsburg decline," in J. W. Esherick, H. Kayali and E. van Young (eds), *Empire to Nation* (Lanham, MD: Rowman & Littlefield, 2006).

Barkey, K., *Empire of Difference: The Ottomans in Comparative Perspective* (Cambridge: Cambridge University Press, 2008).

Barkey, K. and von Hagen, M. (eds), *After Empire: Multiethnic Societies and Nation-building* (Boulder, CO: Westview Press, 1997).

Barnett, M. N., *Dialogues in Arab Politics: Negotiations in Regional Order* (New York: Columbia University Press, 1998).

Barnett, M. and Solingen, E., "Designed to fail or failure of design? The origins and legacy of the Arab League," in A. Acharya and A. I. Johnston (eds), *Crafting Cooperation: Regional International Institutions in Comparative Perspective* (Cambridge: Cambridge University Press, 2007).

Bashkin, O., *The Other Iraq: Pluralism and Culture in Hashemite Iraq* (Stanford, CA: Stanford University Press, 2009).

Baty, T., "Protectorates and Mandates," *British Year Book of International Law*, 1921–2, 109.

Bayat, A., *Making Islam Democratic: Social Movements and the Post-Islamist Turn* (Stanford, CA: Stanford University Press, 2007).

Beblawi, H., "The rentier state in the Arab world," in H. Beblawi and G. Luciani (eds), *The Rentier State: Vol. II* (London: Croom Helm, 1987).

Beblawi, H. and Luciani, G. (eds), *The Rentier State: Vol. II* (London: Croom Helm, 1987).

Behnam, D., "The Eastern perception of the West," in M. Mozaffari (ed.), *Globalization and Civilizations* (London: Routledge, 2002), pp. 178–97.

Beinin, J. and Lockman, Z., *Workers on the Nile: Nationalism, Communism, Islam, and the Egyptian Working Class, 1882–1954* (Princeton, NJ: Princeton University Press, 1987).

Beissinger, M. R., "Elites and ethnic identities in Soviet and post-Soviet politics," in A. J. Motyl (ed.), *The Post-Soviet Nations: Perspectives on the Demise of the USSR* (New York: Columbia University Press, 1992).

Beissinger, M. R., "Demise of an empire-state: identity, legitimacy, and the deconstruction of Soviet politics," in C. Young (ed.), *The Rising Tide of Cultural Pluralism: The Nation-State at Bay?* (Madison, WI: University of Wisconsin Press, 1993), pp. 93–115.

Beissinger, M. R., "The persisting ambiguity of empire," *Post-Soviet Affairs*, 1995, 11(2), pp. 149–84.

Beissinger, M. R., "Soviet empire as 'family resemblance,'" *Slavic Review*, 2006, 65, pp. 294–303.

Beissinger, M. R., "The persistence of empire in Eurasia," *Newsnet: News of the American Association for the Advancement of Slavic Studies*, 2008, 48, pp. 1–8.

Bennigsen, A., "Unrest in the world of Soviet Islam," *Third World Quarterly*, 1988, 10(2), pp. 770–86.

Bennigsen, A. and Broxup, M., *The Islamic Threat to the Soviet State* (London: Croom Helm, 1983).

Bennigsen, A. and Enders Wimbush, S., *Mystics and Commissars: Sufism in the Soviet Union* (London: Hurst, 1985).

Benton, L., "Colonial law and cultural difference: jurisdictional politics and the formation of the colonial state," *Comparative Studies in Society and History*, 1999, 41(3), pp. 563–88.

Berend, I. and Ranki, G., "Economic problems of the Danube region after the break-up of the Austro-Hungarian monarchy," *Journal of Contemporary History*, 1969, 4, pp. 169–85.

Berman, N., "Sovereignty in abeyance: self-determination and international law," *Wisconsin International Law Journal*, 1988–9, 7, p. 51.

Berman, N., "The Grotius Lecture Series," *American University International Law Review*, 1999, 14, p. 1515.

Berque, J., *French North Africa: The Maghrib Between Two World Wars*, trans. J. Stewart (London: Faber & Faber, 1967); *Le Maghreb entre deux guerres* (Paris: Le Seuil, 1962).

Betts, R., *Assimilation and Association in French Colonial Theory, 1890–1914* (New York: Columbia University Press, 1961).

Bhabha, H., *The Location of Culture* (London: Routledge, 1994).

Binder, L. (ed.), *Ethnic Conflict and International Politics in the Middle East* (Gainesville, FL: University Press of Florida, 1999).

Birdal, M., *The Political Economy of Ottoman Public Debt* (London: Tauris, 2010).

Black, A., *The History of Islamic Political Thought: From the Prophet to the Present* (Edinburgh: Edinburgh University Press, 2001).

Black, C. E. and Brown, L. C. (eds), *Modernization in the Middle East: The Ottoman Empire and its Afro-Asian Successors* (Princeton, NJ: Darwin Press, 1992).

Blaisdell, D. C., *European Financial Control in the Ottoman Empire* (New York: Columbia University Press, 1929).

Blitstein, P., "A cultural diversity and the interwar conjuncture: Soviet nationality policy in its comparative context," *Slavic Review*, 2006, 65(2), pp. 273–93.

Bohr, A., "Regionalism in Central Asia: new geopolitics, old regional order," *International Affairs*, 2004, 80(3), p. 490.

Bourricaud, F., "Modernity, 'universal reference' and the process of modernization," in S. N. Eisenstadt (ed.), *Patterns of Modernity, Vol. 1: The West* (New York: New York University Press, 1987), pp. 12–21.

Boyce, R., *The Great Interwar Crisis and the Collapse of Globalization* (London: Palgrave Macmillan, 2010).

Bozeman, A., "Statecraft and intelligence in the non-Western World," in

A. Bozeman (ed), *Strategic Intelligence & Statecraft – Selected Essays* (Washington, DC: Brassey's, 1992 [1985]), pp. 158–79.

Bozeman, A., "The international order in a multicultural world," in H. Bull and A. Watson (eds), *The Expansion of International Society* (Oxford: Clarendon Press, 1984), pp. 387–406.

Branche, R., "La commission de sauvegarde pendant la guerre d'Algérie: Chronique d'un échec annoncé," *Vingtième siècle. Revue d'histoire*, 1999, 61(1), pp. 14–29.

Brand, L. A., *Jordan's Inter-Arab Relations: The Political Economy of Alliance Making* (New York: Columbia University Press, 1995).

Brand, L. A., "Al-Muhajirin w-al-Ansar: Hashemite strategies for managing communal identity in Jordan," in L. Binder (ed.), *Ethnic Conflict and International Politics in the Middle East* (Gainesville, FL: University Press of Florida, 1999).

Bratton, M. and van de Walle, N., "Neopatrimonial regimes and political transitions in Africa," *World Politics*, 1994, 46(4), pp. 453–89.

Bratton, M. and van de Walle, N., *Democratic Experiments in Africa: Regime Transitions in Comparative Perspective* (Cambridge: Cambridge University Press, 1997).

Bremmer, I. and Taras, R. (eds), *New States, New Politics: Building the Post-Soviet Nations* (Cambridge: Cambridge University Press, 1997).

Brewer A., *Marxist Theories of Imperialism: A Critical Survey* (London: Routledge, 1990).

Bridge, F. R. and Bullen, R., *The Great Powers and the Europeans States System 1814–1914*, 2nd edn (London: Pearson/Longman, 2005).

Bridge, G., "Mapping the bonanza: geographies of mining investment in an era of neoliberal reform," *The Professional Geographer*, 2004, 56(3), pp. 406–21.

Bromley, S., *Rethinking Middle East Politics* (Oxford: Polity Press, 1994).

Browers, M., *Political Ideology in the Arab World: Accommodation and Transformation* (Cambridge: Cambridge University Press, 2009).

Brown, L. C., *International Politics and the Middle East: Old Rules, Dangerous Game* (Princeton, NJ: Princeton University Press, 1984).

Brown, L. C. (ed.), *Imperial Legacy: The Ottoman Imprint on the Balkans and the Middle East* (New York: Columbia University Press, 1996).

Brown, L. C. (ed.), *Diplomacy in the Middle East – the International Relations of Regional and Outside Powers* (London: Tauris, 2001).

Brown, N., *Constitutions in a Nonconstitutional World: Arab Basic Laws and the Prospects for Accountable Government* (New York: SUNY Press, 2002).

Brownlie, I., "Boundary problems and the formation of new states," in D. Freestone, S. Subedi and S. Davidson (eds), *Contemporary Issues in International Law* (The Hague: Kluwer, 2002), p. 191.

Brubaker, R., "Nationhood and the national question in the Soviet Union and post-Soviet Eurasia: an institutionalist account," *Theory and Society*, 1994, 23, pp. 47–78.

Brubaker, R., "Aftermaths of empire and the unmixing of peoples," in K. Barkey and M. von Hagen (eds), *After Empire: Multiethnic Societies and Nation-building* (Boulder, CO: Westview Press, 1997), pp. 155–80.

Brynen, R., "Economic crisis and post-rentier democratization in the Arab world: the case of Jordan," *Canadian Journal of Political Science*, March 1992, 25(1), pp. 69–97.

Brynen, R., "The politics of monarchical liberalization: Jordan," in B. Korany, R. Brynen and P. Noble (eds), *Political Liberalization and Democratization in the Arab World: Comparative Experiences, Vol. 2* (Boulder, CO: Lynne Rienner, 1998), pp. 71–100.

Brysk, A., Parsons, C. and Sandholtz, W., "After empire: national identity and post-colonial families of nations," *European Journal of International Relations*, 2002, 8(2), pp. 267–305.

Bukkvoll, T., "Astana's privatised independence: private and national interests in the foreign policy of Nursultan Nazarbayev," *Nationalities Papers*, 2004, 32(3), pp. 631–50.

Bull, H., "The emergence of a universal international society," in H. Bull and A. Watson (eds), *The Expansion of International Society* (Oxford: Clarendon Press, 1984).

Bull, H., *The Anarchical Society – A Study of Order in World Politics*, 2nd edn (New York: Columbia University Press, 1995 [1977]).

Bull, H. and Watson, A. (eds), *The Expansion of International Society* (Oxford: Clarendon Press, 1984).

Burgat, F., *L'islamisme au Maghreb: La voix du Sud* (Paris: Karthala, 1988).

Burgis, M., "(De)limiting the past for future gain: the relationship between sovereignty, colonialism and oil in the Qatar v Bahrain territorial dispute," *Yearbook of Islamic and Middle Eastern Law*, 2008, 12, p. 557.

Burgis, M., "A discourse of distinction? Palestinians, international law and the promise of humanitarianism," *Palestine Yearbook of International Law*, 2009, 15, p. 41.

Burgis, M., "Faith in the state? Traditions of territoriality and the emergence of modern Arab statehood," *Journal of the History of International Law*, 2009, 37, p. 11.

Burgis, M., *Boundaries of Discourse in the International Court of Justice: Mapping Arguments in Arab Territorial Disputes* (Leiden, Brill, 2009).

Burns, N., *The Tariff of Syria* (Beirut: American University Press, 1932).

Buzan, B., *People, States & Fear* (New York: Harvester Wheatsheaf, 1991).

Buzan, B., *From International to World Society? English School Theory and the Social Structure of Globalization* (Cambridge: Cambridge University Press, 2004).

Buzan, B., "Culture and international society," *International Affairs*, 2010, 86(1), pp. 1–25.

Cain, P. J. and Hopkins, A. G., *British Imperialism: Crisis and Deconstruction* (London: Longman, 1993).

Callinicos, A., *Imperialism and Global Political Economy* (Cambridge: Polity Press, 2009).

Cannadine, D., *Ornamentalism. How the British saw their Empire* (Oxford: Oxford University Press, 2001).

Carley, P. M., "The price of the plan: perceptions of cotton and health in Uzbekistan and Turkmenistan," *Central Asian Survey*, 1989, 8(4), pp. 1–38.

Cetinsaya, G., *Ottoman Administration of Iraq, 1890–1908* (London: Routledge, 2006).

Charrad, M. M., *States and Women's Rights: The Making of Postcolonial Tunisia, Algeria, and Morocco* (Berkeley, CA: University of California Press, 2001).

Chatterjee, P., *The Nation and Its Fragments: Colonial and Postcolonial Histories* (Princeton, NJ: Princeton University Press, 1994).

Chaudhry, K. A., "The Price of wealth: business and state in labour remittance and oil economies," *International Organisation*, Winter 1989, 43(1), pp. 101–45.

Chaudhry, K. A., "Economic liberalization and the lineages of the rentier state," *Comparative Politics*, October 1994, 27(1), pp. 1–25.

Chelabi, H. E. and Linz, J. (eds), *Sultanistic Regimes* (Baltimore, MD: Johns Hopkins University Press, 1998).

Ciaramella, E., "A linguistic analysis of the term mankurt in the Soviet and post-Soviet press," Unpublished paper, 2009.

Clancy-Smith, J., "Collaboration and empire in the Middle East and North Africa: introduction and response," *Comparative Studies of South Asia, Africa and the Middle East*, 2004, 24, pp. 125–9.

Clapham, C., *Africa and the International System: The Politics of State Survival* (Cambridge: Cambridge University Press, 1996).

Clark, E. C., "The Ottoman industrial revolution," *International Journal of Middle East Studies*, 1974, 5, pp. 65–76.

Clark, J., "Petro-politics in Congo," *Journal of Democracy*, 1997, 8(3), pp. 62–76.

Clawson, P., *Unaffordable Ambitions: Syria's Military Buildup and Economic Crisis* (Washington, DC: Washington Institute for Near East Policy, 1989).

Clay, C., "Labour migration and economic conditions in nineteenth-century Anatolia," *Middle Eastern Studies*, 1998, 34, pp. 1–32.

Colas, A., *Empire* (Cambridge: Polity Press, 2007).

Cole, J., *Napoleon's Egypt: Invading the Middle East* (New York: Palgrave Macmillan, 2007).

Cole, J. and Kandiyoti, D., "Nationalism and the colonial legacy in the Middle East and Central Asia: Introduction," *International Journal of Middle East Studies*, 2002, 34, pp. 189–203.

Collins, K., *Clan Politics and Regime Transition in Central Asia* (Cambridge: Cambridge University Press, 2006).

Collins, K., "Ideas, networks, and Islamist movements: evidence from Central Asia and the Caucasus," *World Politics*, 2007, 60(1), pp. 64–96.

Collins, K., "Economic and security regionalism among patrimonial authoritarian regimes: the case of Central Asia," *Europe-Asia Studies*, March 2009, 61(2), pp. 249–81.

Colomer, J., *Great Empires, Small Nations: The Uncertain Future of the Sovereign State* (London: Routledge, 2007).

Conklin, A., *A Mission to Civilize: The Republican Idea of Empire in France and West Africa, 1895–1930* (Stanford, CA, Stanford University Press, 1997).

Connor, W., *The National Question in Marxist-Leninist Theory and Strategy* (Princeton, NJ: Princeton University Press, 1984).

Cooley, A., *Logics of Hierarchy: The Organization of Empires, States and Military Occupations* (Ithaca, NY: Cornell University Press, 2005).

Cooper, F., *Decolonisation and African Society: The Labor Question in French and British Africa* (Cambridge: Cambridge University Press, 1996).

Cooper, F., *Africa since 1940: The Past of the Present* (Cambridge: Cambridge University Press, 2002).

Cooper, F., *Colonialism in Question: Theory, Knowledge, History* (Berkeley, CA: University of California Press, 2005).

Cooper, F., "Possibility and constraint. African independence in historical perspective," *Journal of African History*, 2008, 49(2), pp. 167–96.

Cooper, F. and Stoler, A. L., "Beyond metropole and colony: rethinking a research agenda," in F. Cooper and A. L. Stoler (eds), *Tensions of Empire: Colonial Cultures in a Bourgeois World* (Berkeley, CA: University of California Press, 1997).

Crawford, J., *The Creation of States in International Law*, 2nd edn (Cambridge: Cambridge University Press, 2006).

Crawshaw, S., *Goodbye to the USSR: The Collapse of the Soviet Power* (London: Bloomsbury, 1992).

Critchlow, J., "Corruption, nationalism and the native elites in Soviet Central Asia," *The Journal of Communist Studies*, 1988, 4(2), pp. 142–61.

Critchlow, J., *Nationalism in Uzbekistan: A Soviet Republic's Road to Sovereignty* (Boulder, CO: Westview Press, 1991).

Crosby, A., *Ecological Imperialism: The Biological Expansion of Europe, 900–1900* (Cambridge: Cambridge University Press, 1986).

Crossley, P. K., *A Translucent Mirror: History and Identity in Qing Imperial Ideology* (Berkeley, CA: University of California Press, 1999).

Crystal, J., *Oil and Politics in the Gulf. Rulers and Merchants in Kuwait and Qatar* (Cambridge: Cambridge University Press, 1990).

Cummings, S. N., *Kazakhstan: Center–Periphery Relations* (London: The Royal Institute of International Affairs, 2000).

Cummings, S. N., "Kazakhstan: an uneasy relationship – power and authority in the Nazarbaev regime," in S. N. Cummings (ed.), *Power and Change in Central Asia* (London: Routledge, 2002).

Cummings, S. N., "Eurasian bridge or murky waters between East and West? Ideas, identity and output in Kazakhstan's foreign policy," *Journal of Communist Studies and Transition Politics*, September 2003, 19(3).

Cummings, S. N., "Independent Kazakhstan: managing heterogeneity," in S. N. Cummings (ed.) *Oil, Transition and Security in Central Asia* (London: RoutledgeCurzon, 2003).

Cummings, S. N., *Kazakhstan: Power and the Elite* (London: Tauris, 2005).

Cummings, S. N., "Soviet rule, nation and film: the Kyrgyz 'wonder' years," *Nations & Nationalism*, 2009, 15(4), pp. 636–57.

Cummings, S. N. and Ochs, M., "Turkmenistan – Saparmurat Niyazov's inglorious isolation," in S. N. Cummings (ed.), *Power and Change in Central Asia* (London: Routledge, 2002).

Current Digest of the Post-Soviet Press, 45(21), June 23, 1993, retrieved by Nexis.

Current Digest of the Post-Soviet Press, 48(33), 1996, retrieved by Nexis, p. 13.

D'Encausse, H. C., *Decline of an Empire: the Soviet Socialist Republics in Revolt* (New York: Newsweek Books, 1979).

D'Encausse, H. C., *The End of the Soviet Empire: The Triumph of the Nations*, trans. Franklin Philip (New York: Basic Books, 1993).

Darwin, J., "An undeclared empire: the British in the Middle East, 1918–1939," *Journal of Imperial and Commonwealth History*, 1999, 27, p. 159.

Darwin, J., *The Empire Project: The Rise and Fall of the British World System 1830–1970* (Cambridge: Cambridge University Press, 2009).

Dave, B., "Entitlement through number: nationality and language categories in the first post-Soviet census of Kazakhstan," *Nations and Nationalism*, 2004, 10(4), pp. 439–59.

Dave, B., *Kazakhstan: Ethnicity, Language and Power* (London: Routledge, 2007).

David, S., "Explaining Third World alignment," *World Politics*, 1991, 43(2), pp. 233–56.

Davidson, R. H., "The advent of the principle of representation in the government of the Ottoman Empire," in W. R. Polk and R. L. Chambers (eds), *The Beginnings of Modernization* (Chicago, IL: Chicago University Press, 1968), pp. 96–108.

Davison, A., "Ziya Gökalp and provincializing Europe," *Comparative Studies of South Asia, Africa and the Middle East*, 2006, 26(3), pp. 377–90.

Dawisha, A., *Arab Nationalism in the Twentieth Century: From Triumph to Despair* (Princeton, NJ: Princeton University Press, 2003).

Dawisha, K. and Parrott, B. (eds), *The End of Empire? The Transformation of the USSR in Comparative Perspective* (Armonk, NY: Sharpe, 1997).

Dawn, E., "The rise of Arabism in Syria," *Middle East Journal*, 1962, 16(2), pp. 145–68.

Denison, M., "The art of the impossible: political symbolism, and the creation of national identity and collective memory in post-Soviet Turkmenistan," *Europe-Asia Studies*, 2009, 61(7), pp. 1167–87.

Deyermond, R., "Matrioshka hegemony? Multi-levelled hegemonic competition and security in post-Soviet Central Asia," *Review of International Studies*, 2009, 35, pp. 151–73.

Diamond, L., "Why are there no Arab democracies?," *Journal of Democracy*, 2010, 21(1), pp. 93–104.

Dimier, V., *Le gouvernement des colonies, regards croisés franco-britanniques* (Brussels: Editions de l'université de Bruxelles, 2004).

Djalili, M. R., Grare, F. and Akiner, S. (eds), *Tajikistan: The Trials of Independence* (New York: St. Martin's Press, 1997).

Djumaev, A., "Power structures, culture policy, and traditional music in Soviet Central Asia," in D. Christensen (ed.), *1993 Yearbook for Traditional Music* (New York: International Council for Traditional Music, 1993), pp. 43–9.

Dodge, T., *Inventing Iraq: The Failure of Nation Building and a History Denied* (New York: Columbia University Press, 2003).

Doumani, B., *Rediscovering Palestine: Merchants and peasants in Jabal Nablus, 1700–1900* (Berkeley, CA: University of California Press, 1995).

Doyle, M., *Empires* (Ithaca, NY: Cornell University Press, 1986).

Dudoignon, S. A. "Political parties and forces in Tajikistan, 1989–1993," in M. R. Djalili, F. Grare and S. Akiner (eds), *Tajikistan: The Trials of Independence* (New York: St. Martin's Press, 1997), pp. 57–8.

Duguid, S., "The politics of unity: Hamidian policy in Eastern Anatolia," *Middle Eastern Studies*, 1973, 9, pp. 139–55.

Dunn, S. and Fraser, T. G. (eds), *Europe and Ethnicity: The First World War and Contemporary Ethnic Conflict* (London: Routledge, 1996).

Dunning, T., "Resource dependence, economic performance, and political stability," *Journal of Conflict Resolution*, 2005, 49(4), p. 451–82.

Ebel, R., "Introduction," in R. Ebel (ed.), *Caspian Energy Resources: Implications for the Arab Gulf* (Abu Dhabi: The Emirates Center for Strategic Studies and Research, 2000).

Edgar, A., "Bolshevism, patriarchy, and the nation: the Soviet 'emancipation' of Muslim women in pan-Islamic perspective," *Slavic Review*, 2006, 65(2), pp. 252–72.

Edgar, A., *Tribal Nation: The Making of Soviet Turkmenistan* (Princeton, NJ: Princeton University Press, 2006).

Eickelman, D. F. (ed.), *Russia's Muslim Frontiers: New Directions in Cross-Cultural Analysis* (Bloomington, IN: Indiana University Press, 1993).

Eickelman, D. F. and Piscatori, J., *Muslim Politics* (Princeton, NJ: Princeton University Press, 1996).

Eisenstadt, S. N., *The Political Systems of Empires* (New York: Free Press, 1969).

Ekeh. P., "Colonialism and the two publics in Africa: a theoretical statement," *Comparative Studies in Society and History*, 1975, 17, pp. 91–112.

Eklof, B., Bushnell, J. and Zakharova, L. (eds), *Russia's Great Reforms, 1855–1881* (Bloomington, IN: Indiana University Press, 1995).

El-Fadl, R., "Divergent pasts, diverging choices: foreign policy and national building in Turkey and Egypt during the 1950s," DPhil thesis, Oxford University, 2010.

El-Saleh, M. A., "Une évaluation de la gestion mandataire de l'économie syrienne," in N. Méouchy (ed.), *The British and French Mandates in Comparative Perspectives* (Leiden: Brill, 2004).

El-Shibiny, M., *The Threat of Globalization to Arab Islamic Culture* (Pittsburgh, PA: Dorrance, 2005).

Entelis, J., "The emergence of civil society in Algeria," in A. R. Norton (ed.), *Civil Society in the Middle East: Vol. Two* (Leiden: Brill, 1996).

Ergil, D., "A reassessment: the Young Turks, their politics and anti-colonial struggle," *Balkan Studies*, 1975, 16, pp. 26–72.

Eskander, S., "Britain's policy in southern Kurdistan: the formation and the termination of the first Kurdish government, 1918–1919," *British Journal of Middle Eastern Studies*, 2000, 27, pp. 139–63.

Eskander, S., "Southern Kurdistan under Britain's Mesopotamian Mandate: from separation to incorporation, 1920–23," *Middle Eastern Studies*, 2001, 37, pp. 153–80.

Esposito, J., *Islam and Politics* (New York: Syracuse University Press, 1984).

Establet, C., *Etre caïd dans l'Algérie colonial* (Paris: Centre national de la recherche scientifique, 1991).

Exertzoglou, H., "The development of a Greek Ottoman bourgeoisie: investment patterns in the Ottoman Empire, 1850–1914," in D. Gondicas and C. Issawi (eds), *Ottoman Greeks in the Age of Nationalism* (Princeton, NJ: Darwin Press, 1999).

Faroqhi, S., *The Ottoman Empire: A Short History* (Princeton, NJ: Markus Wiener, 2009).

Fattah, H., "The politics of the grain trade in Iraq c. 1840–1917," *New Perspectives on Turkey*, 1991, 5–6, pp. 151–65.

Fattah, H., *The Politics of Regional Trade in Iraq, Arabia, and the Gulf 1745–1900* (Albany, NY: SUNY Press, 1997).

Fawcett, L., "Neither traditional nor modern: Constitutionalism in the Ottoman Empire and its successor states," *Journal of Modern European History*, 2008, 1, pp. 116–35.

Fawcett, L., "Alliances, cooperation and regionalism in the Middle East," *International Relations of the Middle East* (Oxford: Oxford University Press, 2009).

Fawcett, L., *Iran and the Cold War* (Cambridge: Cambridge University Press, 2009).

Fieldhouse, D. K., *The Colonial Empires: A Comparative Survey from the Eighteenth Century* (London: Weidenfeld & Nicolson, 1966).

Fieldhouse, D. K., *Western Imperialism in the Middle East 1914–1958* (Oxford: Oxford University Press, 2006).

Fierman, W., "'Glasnost' in practice: the Uzbek experience," *Central Asian Survey*, 1989, 8(2), pp. 4–5.

Fierman, W., "The Communist Party, 'Erk' and the changing Uzbek political environment," *Central Asian Survey*, 1991, 10(3), p. 63.

Findley, C., *The Turks in World History* (Oxford: Oxford University Press, 2005), ch. 5.

Franke, A., Gawrich, A. and Alakbarov, G., "Kazakhstan and Azerbaijan as post-Soviet rentier states: resource incomes and autocracy as a double 'curse' in post-Soviet regimes," *Europe–Asia Studies*, 2009, 61(2), pp. 109–40.

Freestone, D., Subedi, S. and Davidson, S. (eds), *Contemporary Issues in International Law* (The Hague: Kluwer, 2002).

Freudenberger, H., "State intervention as an obstacle to economic growth in the Habsburg monarchy," *The Journal of Economic History*, 1967, 27, pp. 493–509.

Fromkin, D., *A Peace to End All Peace: The Fall of the Ottoman Empire and the Creation of the Modern Middle East* (New York: Avon Books, 1989).

Frynas, J. G., "The oil boom in Equatorial Guinea," *African Affairs*, October 2004, 103(413), pp. 527–46.

Fuller, W., *Strategy and Power 1600–1914* (New York: The Free Press, 1992).

Furia, P. A. and Lucas, R. E., "Determinants of Arab public opinion on foreign relations," *International Studies Quarterly*, 2006, 50(3), pp. 585–605.

Furman, D., "The regime in Kazakhstan," in B. Rummer (ed.), *Central Asia at the End of the Transition* (New York: M. E. Sharpe, 2005).

Furtado Jr, C. F. and Chandler, A. (eds), *Perestroika in the Soviet Republics: Documents on the National Question* (Boulder, CO: Westview, 1992), pp. 517–19.

Gallagher J. and Robinson, R., "The imperialism of free trade," *Economic History Review*, 1953, 6(1), pp. 1–15.

Gammer, M., "Post-Soviet Central Asia and post-colonial francophone Africa: some associations," *Middle Eastern Studies*, 2000, 36(2), pp. 124–49.

Gause, F. G., "Sovereignty, statecraft and stability in the Middle East," *Journal of International Affairs*, 1992, 45(2), pp. 441–69.

Gelvin, J. L., *Divided Loyalties: Nationalism and Mass Politics in Syria at the Close of Empire* (Berkeley, CA: University of California Press, 1998).

Gerber, H., *The Social Origins of the Modern Middle East* (Boulder, CO: Lynne Rienner, 1987).

Gerschenkron, A., *Economic Backwardness in Historical Perspective: A Book of Essays* (Cambridge, MA: Belknap Press of Harvard University Press, 1962).

Giddens, A., *The Consequences of Modernity* (Stanford, CA: Stanford University Press, 1990).

Gingeras, R., *Sorrowful Shores: Violence, Ethnicity, and the End of the Ottoman Empire, 1912–1923* (New York: Oxford University Press, 2009).

Gleason, G., 'Fealty and loyalty: informal authority structures in Central Asia', *Soviet Studies*, 1991, 43(4), pp. 613–28.

Gleason, G., "The political economy of dependency under socialism: the Asian republics in the USSR," *Studies in Comparative Communism*, 1991, 24(4), pp. 335–53.

Gleason, G., *The Central Asian States: Discovering Independence* (Boulder, CO: Westview Press, 1997).

Gleason, G., "Foreign policy and domestic reform in Central Asia," *Central Asian Survey*, 2001, 20(2), pp. 167–82.

Gleason, G., *Markets and Politics in Central Asia. Structural Reform and Political Change* (London: Routledge, 2003).

Goldberg, E., "The historiography of crisis in the Egyptian political economy," in I. Gershoni, A. Singer and Y. Hakam Erdem (eds), *Middle East Historiographies: Narrating the Twentieth Century* (Seattle, WA: University of Washington Press, 2006), ch. 6.

Gommans, J., *Mughal Warfare: Indian Frontiers and Highroads to Empire, 1500–1700* (London: Routledge, 2002).

Gong, G., *The Standard of "Civilization" in International Society* (Oxford: Clarendon Press, 1984).

Gretsky, S., "Russia and Tajikistan," in A. Z. Rubinstein and O. M. Smolansky (eds), *Regional Power Rivalries in the New Eurasia: Russia, Turkey, and Iran* (Armonk, NY: Sharpe, 1995), p. 234.

Gretsky, S., *Russia's Policy Toward Central Asia* (Moscow: Carnegie Moscow Center, 1997).

Grewe, W. H., *The Epochs of International Law*, trans. M. Byers (New York: de Gruyter, 2000).

Gubarev, V., "Pamirskie zarisovki," *Charoghi rūz*, 1993, 710(2), p. 8.

Guboglo, M. N. and Chicherina, N. G. (eds), *Grazhdanskie dvizheniia v Tadzhikistane* (Civil/popular Movements in Tajikistan) (Moscow: Center for Research in International Relations, 1990).

Gudkov, L. D., "Attitudes toward Russians in the Union republics," *Sociological Research*, November–December 1992, p. 20.

Halimi, G. and. de Beauvoir, S., *Djamila Boupacha* (Paris: Gallimard, 1961).

Hall, C., *Civilising Subjects: Metropole and Colony in the English Imagination, 1830–1867* (Oxford: Polity, 2002).

Halliday, F., *Rethinking International Relations* (London: Macmillan, 1994).

Halliday, F., "The Middle East and conceptions of 'international society,'" in B. Buzan and A. Gonzalez-Pelaez (eds), *International Society and the Middle East – English School Theory at the Regional Level* (New York: Palgrave, 2009), pp. 1–23.

Halperin, C. J., *Russia and the Golden Horde: The Mongol Impact on Russian History* (London: Tauris, 1985).

Hammer, M., "Perestroika as seen by some Tajik Historians," in M. R. Djalili, F. Grare and S. Akiner (eds), *Tajikistan: The Trials of Independence* (London: Routledge, 1998), p. 48.

Hanioğlu, M. Ş., *The Young Turks in Opposition* (New York: Oxford University Press, 1995).

Hanioğlu, M. Ş., *Preparation for a Revolution: The Young Turks, 1902–1908* (New York: Oxford University Press, 2001).

Hanioğlu, M. Ş., "The second constitutional period, 1908–1918," in R. Kasaba (ed.), *The Cambridge History of Turkey, Vol. 4: Turkey in the Modern World* (Cambridge: Cambridge University Press, 2008), p. 97.

Hanioğlu, M. Ş., *A Brief History of the Late Ottoman Empire* (Princeton, NJ: Princeton University Press, 2008).

Harders, C. and Legrenzi, M. (eds), *Beyond Regionalism? Regional Cooperation, Regionalism and Regionalization in the Middle East* (Farnham: Ashgate, 2008).

Harik, I., "The origins of the Arab state system," in G. Luciani (ed.), *The Arab State* (London: Routledge, 1990), pp. 1–28.

Harris, C., *Control and Subversion: Gender Relations in Tajikistan* (London: Pluto Press, 2004).

Hartley, J., "Russia as a fiscal–military state, 1689–1825," in C. Storrs (ed.), *The Fiscal–Military State in Eighteenth-Century Europe* (Farnham: Ashgate, 2009).

Harvey, D., *The New Imperialism* (Oxford: Oxford University Press, 2005).

Haugen, A., *The Establishment of National Republics in Soviet Central Asia* (London: Palgrave Macmillan, 2003).

Heathershaw, J., *Post-Conflict Tajikistan: The Politics of Peacebuilding and the Emergence of Legitimate Order* (London: Routledge, 2009).

Herb, M., *All in the Family: Absolutism, Revolution, and Democratic Prospects in the Middle Eastern Monarchies* (Albany, NY: SUNY Press, 1999).

Hinnebusch, R., "Liberalization without democratization in 'post-populist' authoritarian states," in N. Butenschon, U. Davis and M. Hassassian (eds), *Citizenship and State in the Middle East* (Syracuse, NY: Syracuse University Press, 2000).

Hinnebusch, R., *Syria: Revolution from Above* (New York: Routledge, 2001).

Hinnebusch, R., "Chapter 2: The Middle East Regional System," in R. Hinnebusch and A. Ehteshami (eds), *The Foreign Policies of Middle East States* (London: Lynne Rienner, 2002), pp. 28–53.

Hinnebusch, R., "State formation and international behaviour," in R. Hinnebusch, *The International Politics of the Middle East* (Manchester: Manchester University Press, 2003), pp. 73–90.

Hinnebusch, R., *The International Politics of the Middle East* (Manchester: Manchester University Press, 2003).

Hinnebusch, R., "The politics of identity in the Middle East international relations," in L. Fawcett (ed.), *International Relations of the Middle East* (Oxford: Oxford University Press, 2005), pp. 151–71.

Hinnebusch, R. "Authoritarian persistence, democratization theory and the Middle East: an overview and critique," *Democratization*, 2006, 13(3), pp. 373–95.

Hinsley, F. H., *Sovereignty* (Cambridge: Cambridge University Press, 1986).

Hiro, D., *Inside Central Asia: A Political and Cultural History of Uzbekistan, Turkmenistan, Kazakhstan, Kyrgyzstan, Tajikistan, Turkey and Iran* (New York: Overlook, 2009).

Hirsch, F., "Toward an empire of nations: border-making and the formation of Soviet national identities," *Russian Review*, 59(2), 2000, pp. 201–26.

Hirsch, F., *Empire of Nations: Ethnographic Knowledge and the Making of the Soviet Union* (Ithaca, NY: Cornell University Press, 2005).

Hobson, J., *The State and International Relations* (Cambridge: Cambridge University Press, 2000).

Hobson, J. M. and Sharman, J. C., "The enduring place of hierarchy in world politics: tracing the social logics of hierarchy and political change," *European Journal of International Relations*, 2005, 11(1), pp. 63–98.

Hodges, T., *Western Sahara: The Roots of a Desert War* (Westport, CT: L. Hill, 1983).

Hoisington, W. A., "French rule and the Moroccan elite," *The Maghreb Review*, 1997, 22(1–2), pp. 138–45.

Horsman, S., "Themes in official discourses on terrorism in Central Asia," *Third World Quarterly*, 2005, 26(1), pp. 199–213.

Hostetler, L., *Qing Colonial Enterprise: Ethnography and Cartography in Early Modern China* (Chicago, IL: University of Chicago Press, 2001).

Hough, J., *Democratization and Revolution in the USSR 1985–1991* (Washington, DC: Brookings Institution Press, 1997).

Hounet, Y. B., "Des tribus en Algérie? À propos de la déstructuration tribale durant la période coloniale," *Cahiers de la Méditerranée*, 2007, 75, pp. 150–71.

Hourani, A., *A Vision of History: Near Eastern and Other Essays* (London: Constable, 1961).

Hourani, A., "Ottoman reform and the politics of notables," in W. R. Polk and R. L. Chambers (eds), *Beginnings of Modernization in the Middle East* (Chicago, IL: University of Chicago Press, 1968).

Hourani, A., "The Ottoman background to the modern Middle East," in K. Karpat (ed.), *The Ottoman State and its Place in World History* (Leiden: Brill, 1974), p. 1.

Hourani, A., *Arabic Thought in the Liberal Age 1798–1939* (Cambridge: Cambridge University Press, 1983).

Hourani, A., *A History of the Arab Peoples* (London: Faber & Faber, 2002 [1991]).

Hourani, A. and Wilson, M. (eds), *The Modern Middle East* (London: Tauris, 1993).

Hudson, M., *Arab Politics: The Search for Legitimacy* (New Haven, CT: Yale University Press, 1977).

Huskey, E., "Kyrgyzstan: the politics of demographic and economic frustration," in I. Bremmer and R. Taras (eds), *New States, New Politics: Building the Post-Soviet Nations* (Cambridge: Cambridge University Press, 1997), pp. 660–3.

Ibrahim, M., "The transformation of Ottoman sovereignty, 1908–1918," unpublished MA dissertation, University of London, 2009.

Ibrahim, S. E., "Liberalization and democratization in the Arab world: an overview," in R. Brynen, P. Noble and B. Korany (eds), *Political Liberalization and*

Democratization in the Arab World: Theoretical Perspectives (Boulder, CO: Lynne Reinner, 1995): pp. 29–60.

Igmen, A., "Building Soviet Central Asia, 1920–1939: Kyrgyz houses of culture and self-fashioning Kyrgyzness," PhD dissertation, University of Washington, 2004.

Ilkhamov, A., "Nation-state formation: features of social stratification in the late Soviet era," *International Journal of Middle East Studies*, May 2002, 34(2), pp. 317–35.

Ilkhamov, A., "Neopatrimonialism, interest groups and patronage networks: the impasses of the governance system in Uzbekistan," *Central Asian Survey*, March 2007, 26(1), pp. 65–84.

Institut Etnografii, Akademiia nauk SSSR, *Sotsial'no-kul'turnyi oblik sovetskikh natsii* SSR (Moscow: Nauka, 1986), pp. 87, 89.

Ipek, P., "The role of oil and gas in Kazakhstan's foreign policy: looking East or West?," *Europe–Asia Studies*, November 2007, 59(7), pp. 1179–99.

Ireland, P. W., *Iraq: A Study in Political Development* (London: Jonathan Cape, 1937).

Ishiyama, J., "Neopatrimonialism and the prospects for democratization in the Central Asian republics," in S. N. Cummings (ed.), *Power and Change in Central Asia* (London: Routledge, 2002).

Issawi, C., "Notes on the trade of Basra, 1800–1914," *Journal of Turkish Studies*, 1986, 10.

Issawi, C., *An Economic History of the Middle East and North Africa* (New York: Columbia University Press, 1982).

Jackson, R., *Quasi States: Sovereignty, International Relations and the Third World* (Cambridge: Cambridge University Press, 1993).

James, A., "The practice of statehood in contemporary international society," *Political Studies*, 1999, XLVII, pp. 457–73.

Jankowski, J. and Gershoni, I. (eds), *Rethinking Nationalism in the Arab Middle East* (New York: Columbia University Press, 1997).

Jessup, P. C., "Diversity and uniformity in the law of nations," *American Journal of International Law*, 1964, 58, p. 341.

Jones Luong, P., "The 'use and abuse' of Russia's energy resources: implications for state–society relations," in V. Sperling (ed.), *Building The Russian State: Institutional Crisis and the Quest for Democratic Governance* (Boulder, CO: Westview Press, 2000).

Jones Luong, P., *Institutional Change and Political Continuity in Post-Soviet Central Asia: Power, Perceptions, and Pacts* (Cambridge: Cambridge University Press, 2002).

Jones Luong, P. and Weinthal, E., "Prelude to the resource curse: explaining oil and gas development strategies in the Soviet successor states and beyond," *Comparative Political Studies*, 2001, 34(4), pp. 367–99.

Jones, R. A., *The Soviet Concept of "Limited Sovereignty" from Lenin to Gorbachev: The Brezhnev Doctrine* (Basingstoke: Macmillan, 1990).

Jonson, L., *Tajikistan in the New Central Asia* (London: Tauris, 2006).

Juraev, N. and Fayzullayev, T., *Istoriia Uzbekistana* (History of Uzbekistan for the 11th Form) (Tashkent: Sharq, 2002).

Jwaideh, A., "The Sanniya lands of Sultan Abdul Hamid II in Iraq," in G. Makdisi (ed.), *Arabic and Islamic Studies in Honor of Hamilton A. R. Gibb* (Leiden: Brill, 1965).

Kamp, M., "Between women and the state," in P. Jones Luong (ed.), *The Transformation of Central Asia: States and Societies from Soviet Rule to Independence* (Ithaca, NY: Cornell University Press, 2004).

Kamp, M., *The New Woman in Uzbekistan: Islam, Modernity, and Unveiling Under Communism* (Seattle, WA: University of Washington Press, 2006).

Kandiyoti, D., "Post-colonialism compared: potentials and limitations in the Middle East and Central Asia," *International Journal of Middle East Studies*, May 2002, 34(2), pp. 279–97.

Kandiyoti, R., *Pipelines: Flowing Oil and Crude Politics* (London: Tauris, 2008).

Kansu, A., *The Revolution of 1908 in Turkey* (Leiden: Brill, 1997).

Kappeler, A., *The Russian Empire: A Multi-Ethnic History* (New York: Longman, 2001).

Karagiannis, E. and McCauley, C., "Hizb ut-Tahrir al-Islami: evaluating the threat posed by a radical Islamic group that remains nonviolent," *Terrorism and Political Violence*, 2006, 18(2), pp. 315–34.

Karakisla, Y. S., "The 1908 strike wave in the Ottoman Empire," *Turkish Studies Association Bulletin*, 1992, 16, pp. 153–77.

Karasar, H. A., "The partition of Khorezm and the positions of Turkestanis on *Razmezhevanie*," *Europe–Asia Studies*, 2008, 60(7), pp. 1247–60.

Karl, T. L., "Ensuring fairness: the case for a transparent fiscal social contract," in M. Humphreys, J. D. Sachs and J. E. Stiglitz (eds), *Escaping the Resource Curse* (New York: Columbia University Press, 2007).

Karl, T. L., *The Paradox of Plenty: Oil Booms and Petro-States* (Berkeley, CA: University Of California Press, 1997).

Kasaba, R., *The Ottoman Empire and the World Economy* (Albany, NY: SUNY Press, 1988).

Kasaba, R. (ed.), *The Cambridge History of Turkey* (Cambridge: Cambridge University Press, 2008).

Katzenstein, P., *A World of Regions: Asia and Europe in the American Imperium* (Cornell, NY: Cornell University Press, 2005).

Kayalı, H., "The struggle for independence," in R. Kasaba (ed.), *The Cambridge History of Turkey, Vol. 4: Turkey in the Modern World* (Cambridge: Cambridge University Press, 2008), p. 119.

Kedourie, E., *Arabic Political Memoirs* (London: Routledge, 1974).

Kedourie, E., "The nation-state in the Middle East," *The Jerusalem Journal of International Relations*, 1987, 9(3), pp. 1–9.

Kedourie, E., *Politics in the Middle East* (Oxford: Oxford University Press, 1992).

Keller, S., *To Moscow, not Mecca: The Soviet Campaign Against Islam in Central Asia 1917–1941* (Westport, CT: Praeger, 2001).

Keller, S., "Going to school in Uzbekistan," in J. Sahadeo and R. Zanca (eds), *Everyday Life in Central Asia* (Bloomington, IN: Indiana University Press, 2007), pp. 248–65.

Keller, S., "Story, time and dependent nationhood in the Uzbek history curriculum," *Slavic Review*, 2007, 66, pp. 257–77.

Kennedy, D., "International law and the nineteenth century: history of an illusion," *Nordic Journal of International Law*, 1996, 65, p. 385.

Kennedy, D., "When renewal repeats: thinking against the box," *New York University Journal of International Law and Politics*, 1999–2000, 32, p. 335.

Kent, M., "Agent of empire? The National Bank of Turkey and British foreign policy," *Historical Journal*, 1975, 18, pp. 367–89.

Kerr, M., *The Arab Cold War – 1958–1964 – A Study of Ideology in Politics* (London: Oxford University Press, 1965).

Keyder, C., *State and Class in Turkey* (London: Verso, 1987).

Keyder, C., "The Ottoman Empire," in K. Barkey and M. von Hagen (eds), *After Empire: Multiethnic Societies and Nation-Building* (Boulder, CO: Westview 1997).

Khalid, A., *The Politics of Muslim Cultural Reform: Jadidism in Central Asia* (Berkeley, CA: University of California Press, 1998).

Khalid, A., "A secular Islam: nation, state, and religion in Uzbekistan," *International Journal of Middle East Studies*, 2003, 35(4), pp. 573–98.

Khalid, A., "Backwardness and the quest for civilization: early Soviet Central Asia in comparative perspective," *Slavic Review*, 2006, 65(2), pp. 231–51.

Khalid, A., *Islam After Communism: Religion and Politics in Central Asia* (Berkeley, CA: University of California Press, 2007).

Khalid, A., "Introduction: locating the (post-)colonial in Soviet history," *Central Asian Survey*, 2007, 26(4), pp. 465–73.

Khalid, A., "Russia, Central Asia and the Caucasus to 1917," in F. Robinson (ed.), *The New Cambridge History of Islam, Vol. 5* (Cambridge: Cambridge University Press, 2009), pp. 180–202.

Khalidi, R., "The origins of Arab nationalism: introduction," in R. Khalidi, L. Anderson, M. Muslih and R. S. Simon (eds), *The Origins of Arab Nationalism* (New York: Columbia University Press, 1991), pp. vii–xix.

Khalidi, R., *Resurrecting Empire, Western Footprints and America's Perilous Path in the Middle East* (New York: Beacon Press, 2004).

Khalidi, W., "Thinking the unthinkable: a sovereign Palestinian state," *Foreign Affairs*, 1978, 56(4), pp. 695–713.

Khodjibaev, K., "Russian troops and the conflict in Tajikistan," *Perspectives on Central Asia*, November 1997, 2, p. 8.

Kholiqzoda, A., *Ta"rikhi siyosii Tojikon* (Dushanbe: No publisher given, 1994).

Khoury, D. R., "The political economy of the province of Mosul: 1700–1850," unpublished PhD dissertation, Georgetown University, 1987.

Khoury, D. R., *State and Provincial Society in the Ottoman Empire: Mosul, 1540–1834* (Cambridge: Cambridge University Press, 1997).

Khoury, D. R., "The Ottoman centre versus provincial power-holders: an analysis of the historiography," in S. Faroqui (ed.), *The Cambridge History of Turkey, Vol. 3: The Later Ottoman Empire, 1603–1839* (Cambridge: Cambridge University Press, 2006), pp. 135–56.

Khoury, P. S., *Syria and the French Mandate: The Politics of Arab Nationalism 1920–1945* (Princeton, NJ: Princeton University Press, 1987).

Khoury, P. S., "Continuity and change in Syrian political life: the nineteenth and twentieth centuries," *American Historical Review*, 1991, 96, pp. 1374–95.

Kim, Y., *The Resources Curse in a Post-Communist Regime: Russia in Comparative Prospective* (Farnham: Ashgate, 2003).

Kiyotaki, K., "The practice of tax farming in the province of Baghdad in the 1830s," in C. Imber (ed.), *Frontiers of Ottoman Studies, Vol. 1* (London: Tauris, 2005).

Kjærnet, H., Satpaev, D. and Torjesen, S., "Big business and high-level politics in Kazakhstan: an everlasting symbiosis?," *China and Eurasia Forum Quarterly*, 2008, 6(1), pp. 95–107.

Klabbers, J. and Lefeber, R., "Africa: lost between self-determination and *uti possidetis*," in C. Brölmann, R. Lefeber and M. Zieck (eds), *Peoples and Minorities in International Law* (Dordrecht: Kluwer, 1993), pp. 37–76.

Korany, B., "Alien and besieged yet here to stay: the contradictions of the Arab territorial state," in G. Salamé (ed.), *The Foundations of the Arab State* (London: Croom Helm, 1987), pp. 47–74.

Koskenniemi, M., "International law and imperialism," in D. Freestone, S. Subedi and S. Davidson (eds), *Contemporary Issues in International Law: A Collection of the Josephine Onoh Memorial Lectures* (The Hague: Kluwer, 2002), pp. 197–218.

Koskenniemi, M., *The Gentle Civilizer of Nations: The Rise and Fall of International Law 1870–1960* (Cambridge: Cambridge University Press, 2002).

Koskenniemi, M., *From Apology to Utopia: The Structure of International Legal Argument* (Cambridge: Cambridge University Press, 2006).

Kraiem, M., *Nationalisme et syndicalisme en Tunisie, 1918–1929* (Tunis: UGTT, 1977).

Krasner, S. D., *Sovereignty: Organized Hypocrisy* (Princeton, NJ: Princeton University Press, 1999).

Krasner, S. (ed.), *Problematic Sovereignty* (New York: Columbia University Press, 2001).

Kuhn, D., *The Age of Confucian Rule: The Song Transformation of China* (Cambridge, MA: Belknap Press of Harvard University Press, 2009).

Kupatadze, A., "Organized crime before and after the Tulip Revolution: changing dynamics of upperworld–underworld networks," *Central Asian Survey*, 2008, 27(3).

Kuru, A., "The rentier state model and Central Asian studies: the Turkmen case," *Alternatives: Turkish Journal of International Relations*, Spring 2002, 1(1).

Kurzman, C., *Modernist Islam, 1840–1940: A Sourcebook* (Oxford: Oxford University Press, 2002).

Kuzio, T., "Nationalist riots in Kazakhstan," *Central Asian Survey*, 1988, 7(4), pp. 79–100.

L'affaire du différend territorial (Jamahiriya Arabe Libyenne c. Tchad) Arrêt de la Cour Internationale de Justice du 3 février 1994', *Annuaire français de droit international*, 1994, 40, p. 442.

Lake, D. A., *Hierarchy in International Relations* (Cornell, NY: Cornell University Press, 2009).

Langley, K. M., *The Industrialization of Iraq* (Cambridge, MA: Harvard University Press, 1961).

Laski, H. J., *Studies in the Problem of Sovereignty* (New Haven, CT: Yale University Press, 1917).

Lauterpacht, H., "The Mandate under international law in the Covenant of the League of Nations," *International Law: Being the Collected Papers of Hersch Lauterpacht, Vol. 3* (Cambridge: Cambridge University Press, 1977), pp. 29–84.

Lawrence, B. N., Osborn, E. L. and Roberts, R. L. (eds), *Intermediaries, Interpreters, and Clerks: African Employees in the Making of Colonial Africa* (Madison, WI: University of Wisconsin Press, 2006).

Lawson, F. H., *Constructing International Relations in the Arab World* (Stanford, CA: Stanford University Press, 2006).

Le Billon, P., "The political ecology of war: natural resources and armed conflicts," *Political Geography*, 2001, 20, pp. 561–84.

Le Vine, V., "African patrimonial regimes in comparative perspective," *The Journal of Modern African Studies*, 1980, 18(4), pp. 657–73.

Leander, A., "Bertrand Badie: cultural diversity changing international relations?," in O. Wæver and I. B. Neumann (eds), *The Future of International Relations – Masters in the Making* (London: Routledge, 1997), pp. 145–69.

Legvold, R. (ed.), *Russian Foreign Policy in the Twenty-first Century and the Shadow of the Past* (New York: Columbia University Press, 2007).

Lenin, V. I., *Imperialism: the Highest Stage of Capitalism* (London: Pluto Press, 1996).

Lerner, D., *The Passing of Traditional Society: Modernizing the Middle East* (New York: The Free Press of Glencoe, 1958).

Leveau, R., *Le fellah marocain, défenseur du trône* (Paris: Fondation nationale de science politique, 1976).

Lewis, B., "The hard questions: what went wrong?," *Atlantic Monthly*, 2002, 289(1), pp. 43–5.

Lewis, B., *What Went Wrong? The Clash Between Islam and Modernity in the Middle East* (New York: HarperCollins, 2003).

Lewis, B., "The Middle East in world affairs," in B. Lewis, *From Babel to Dragomans – Interpreting the Middle East* (London: Weidenfeld & Nicolson, 2004 [1957]), pp. 232–9.

Lewis, D., *The Temptations of Tyranny in Central Asia* (London: Hurst, 2008).

Lewis, G., *The Turkish Language Reform: A Catastrophic Success* (Oxford: Oxford University Press, 1999).

Lewis, M. E., *China's Cosmopolitan Empire: the Tang Dynasty* (Cambridge, MA: Belknap Press of Harvard University Press, 2009), pp. 48–50.

Liebowitz, R., "Soviet investment strategy: a further test of the 'equalization hypothesis," *Annals of the Association of American Geographers*, 1987, 77(3), pp. 396–407.

Lieven, D., *Russia and the Origins of the First World War* (London: Palgrave Macmillan, 1983).

Lieven, D., *Empire: The Russian Empire and its Rivals* (New Haven, CT: Yale University Press, 2000).

Lieven, D., "Empire, history and the contemporary global order," *Proceedings of the British Academy*, 2005, 131, pp. 127–56.

Lieven, D., "The elites," in D. Lieven (ed.), *The Cambridge History of Russia, Vol. 2: Imperial Russia, 1689–1825* (Cambridge: Cambridge University Press, 2006), pp. 227–44.

Lieven, D., *Russia against Napoleon: the Battle for Europe, 1807–1814* (London: Penguin, 2009).

Light, M., *The Soviet Theory of International Relations* (Brighton: Wheatsheaf, 1988).

Lincoln, W. B., *In the Vanguard of Reform: Russia's Enlightened Bureaucrats, 1825–1861* (DeKalb, IL: Northern Illinois University Press, 1982).

Loring, B. H., "Building socialism in Kyrgyzstan: nation-making, rural development, and social change, 1921–1932," PhD dissertation, Brandeis University, 2008.

Louis, W. R., "The era of the Mandates system and the non-European world," in H. Bull and A. Watson (eds), *The Expansion of International Society* (Oxford: Clarendon Press, 1984), pp. 201–13.

Lubin, N., *Labor and Nationality in Soviet Central Asia* (Princeton, NJ: Princeton University Press, 1984).

Lubin, N. and Rubin, B. R., *Calming the Ferghana Valley: Development and Dialogue in the Heart of Central Asia* (New York: Century Foundation Press, 2000).

Luciani, G., "Allocation vs. production states," in H. Beblawi and G. Luciani (eds), *The Rentier State: Vol. II* (London: Croom Helm, 1987).

Luciani, G., "Allocation vs. production states: a theoretical framework," in L. Giacomo (ed.), *The Arab State* (London: Routledge, 1990), pp. 63–82.

Lustick, I., *State-Building Failure in British Ireland and French Algeria* (Berkeley, CA: University of California Press, 1985).

Lustick, I., "The absence of Middle Eastern great powers: political 'backwardness' in historical perspective," *International Organization*, 1997, 51(4), pp. 653–83.

Lynch, D., "The Tajik civil war and peace process," *Civil Wars*, 2001, 4(4), pp. 49–72.

Lynch, M., *State Interests and Public Spheres: The International Politics of Jordan's Identity* (New York: Columbia University Press, 1999).

Lynch, M., *Voices of the New Arab Public – Iraq, al-Jazeera, and Middle East Politics Today* (New York: Columbia University Press, 2006).

Mahdavy, H., "The patterns and problems of economic development in rentier states: the case of Iran," in M. A. Cook (ed.), *Studies in The Economic History of The Middle East* (London: Oxford University Press, 1970).

Maluwa, T., "International law-making in post-colonial Africa: the role of the Organization of African Unity," *Netherlands International Law Review*, 2002, 81, pp. 94–5.

Mamdani, M., *Citizen and Subject: Contemporary Africa and the Legacy of Late Colonialism* (Princeton, NJ: Princeton University Press, 1996).

Mamdani, M., "Historicizing power and responses to power: indirect rule and its reform," *Social Research,* 1999, 66(3), pp. 859–86.

Mandaville, P., *Global Political Islam* (New York: Routledge, 2007).

Mann, G., "What was the *indigénat*? The 'empire of law' in French West Africa," *Journal of African History*, 2009, 50(3), pp. 331–53.

Mann, M., *The Sources of Social Power, Vols 1 and 2* (Cambridge: Cambridge University Press, 1986 and 1993).

Maoz, M., "Attempts at creating a political community in modern Syria," *Middle East Journal*, 1972, 26(4), pp. 389–404.

Maoz, M., *Asad: The Sphinx of Damascus* (New York: Grove Weidenfeld, 1988).

Marat, E., "The state–crime nexus in Central Asia: state weakness, organized crime, and corruption in Kyrgyzstan and Tajikistan," *Central Asia–Caucasus Institute and Silk Road Studies Program*, October 2006.

Marat, E., "Labour migration in Central Asia: implication of the global economic crisis," *Central Asia–Caucasus Institute and Silk Road Studies Program*, May 2009.

Mardin, Ş., "The Ottoman Empire," in K. Barkey and M. von Hagen (eds), *After Empire: Multiethnic Societies and Nation-building: The Soviet Union and the Russian, Ottoman, and Habsburg Empires* (Boulder, CO: Westview, 1997), p. 115.

Martin, T., "An affirmative action empire: the Soviet Union as the highest form of imperialism," in R. G. Suny and T. Martin (eds.), *A State of Nations* (Oxford: Oxford University Press, 2001), pp. 67–92.

Martin, T., *Affirmative Action Empire: Nations and Nationalism in the Soviet Union 1923–1939* (Ithaca, NY: Cornell University Press, 2001).

Massell, G. J., *The Surrogate Proletariat: Moslem Women and Revolutionary Strategies in Soviet Central Asia, 1919–1929* (Princeton, NJ: Princeton University Press, 1974).

Masters, B., "Aleppo: the Ottoman Empire's caravan city," in E. Eldem, D. Goffman and B. Masters (eds), *The Ottoman City between East and West* (Cambridge: Cambridge University Press, 1999).

Matsusaka, Y., *The Making of Japanese Manchuria, 1904–1932* (Cambridge, MA: Harvard University Asia Center, 2001).

Mazower, M., *No Enchanted Palace: The End of Empire and the Ideological Origins of the United Nations* (Princeton, NJ: Princeton University Press, 2009).

Mbembe, A., *On the Postcolony* (Berkeley, CA: University of California Press, 2001).

McCarthy, J., "Foundations of the Turkish republic: social and economic change," *Middle Eastern Studies*, 1983, 19, pp. 139–51.

McDougall, J., "Was there a French colonial policy?," paper presented to the Imperial History Seminar, Institute for Historical Research, London, 2009.

McDougall, J., "The secular state's Islamic empire: Muslim spaces and subjects of jurisdiction in Paris and Algiers, 1905–1957," *Comparative Studies in Society and History*, 2010, 52(3), pp. 553–80.

McFaul, M., "The sovereignty script: red book for Russian revolutionaries," in S. Krasner (ed.), *Problematic Sovereignty: Contested Rules and Political Possibilities* (New York: Columbia University Press, 2001), p. 202.

McFaul, M., "Political transitions: democracy and the former Soviet Union," *Harvard International Review*, 2006, 28(1), pp. 40–6.

McKinnon Wood, H., "The Treaty of Paris and Turkey's status in international law," *American Journal of International Law*, 1943, 37, p. 262.

Meijer, R. (ed.), *Global Salafism: Islam's New Religious Movement* (New York: Columbia University Press, 2009).

Mejcher, H., "The birth of the Mandate idea and its fulfillment in Iraq up to 1926," unpublished PhD dissertation, University of Oxford, 1970.

Merad, A., *Le réformisme musulman en Algérie de 1925 à 1940: essai d'histoire religieuse et sociale* (Paris: Mouton, 1967).

Merridale, C., *Night of Stone: Death and Memory in Russia Twentieth-Century Russia* (London: Penguin, 2002).

Meeker, M. E., *A Nation of Empire: the Ottoman Legacy of Turkish Modernity* (Berkeley, CA: University of California Press, 2002).

Michaels, P., *Curative Powers: Medicine and Empire in Stalin's Central Asia* (Pittsburgh, PA: University of Pittsburgh Press, 2003).

Miéville, C., *Between Equal Rights: A Marxist Theory of International Law* (London: Pluto, 2006 [2005]).

Migdal, J. S. *Strong Societies and Weak States: State–Society Relations and State Capabilities in the Third World* (Princeton, NJ: Princeton University Press, 1988).

Mill, J. S., *Philosophy of Scientific Method* (Cooper Press, 2008).

Miller, A. I., *The Romanov Empire and Nationalism* (Budapest: Central European University Press, 2008).

Miller, R., *Britain and Latin America in the Nineteenth and Twentieth Centuries* (London: Longman, 1993).

Mills, M. C., "The Mandatory system," *American Journal of International Law*, 1923, 17, p. 52.

Milton-Edwards, B. and Hinchcliffe, P., "Abdullah's Jordan: new king, old problems," *Middle East Report*, Winter 1999, pp. 28–31.

Mirsepassi, A., "Islam as a modernizing ideology: Al-e Ahmad and Shari'ati," in A. Mirsepassi, *Intellectual Discourse and the Politics of Modernization – Negotiating Modernity in Iran* (Cambridge: Cambridge University Press, 2000), pp. 96–128.

Mitchell, R. P., *The Society of the Muslim Brothers* (Oxford: Oxford University Press, 1969).

Mitchell, T., *Colonising Egypt* (Cambridge: Cambridge University Press, 1988).

Moaddel, M., "Conditions for ideological production: the origins of Islamic modernism in India, Egypt, and Iran," *Theory and Society*, 2001, 30, pp. 669–731.

Monroe, E., *Britain's Moment in the Middle East 1914–1956* (London: Chatto & Windus, 1963).

Motyl, A. J., "Thinking About empire," in K. Barkey and M. von Hagen (eds), *After Empire: Multiethnic Societies and Nation-Building* (Boulder, CO: Westview 1997), pp. 19–29.

Motyl, A. J., *Revolutions, Nations, Empires: Conceptual Limits and Theoretical Possibilities* (New York: Columbia University Press, 1999).

Motyl, A. J., *Imperial Ends: The Decay, Collapse, And Revival of Empires* (New York: Columbia University Press, 2001).

Motyl, A. and Krawchenko, B., "Ukraine: from empire to statehood," in I. Bremmer and R. Taras (eds), *New States, New Politics: Building the Post-Soviet Nations* (Cambridge: Cambridge University Press, 1997), pp. 245, 247–8, 251.

Muiznieks, N., "Latvia: restoring a state, rebuilding a nation," in I. Bremmer and R. Taras (eds), *New States, New Politics: Building the Post-Soviet Nations* (Cambridge: Cambridge University Press, 1997), pp. 382–4, 386–7, 389.

Munkler, H., *Empires: the Logic of World Domination from Ancient Rome to the United States* (Cambridge: Polity Press, 2007), pp. 1–17.

Murphy, E., "Theorizing ICTs in the Arab world: informational capitalism and the public sphere," *International Studies Quarterly*, 2009, 4, pp. 1131–53.

Murphy, E. C., *Economic and Political Change in Tunisia: From Bourguiba to Ben Ali* (New York: St. Martin's Press, 1999).

Murphy, J., "Illusory transition? Elite reconstitution in Kazakhstan, 1989–2002," *Europe–Asia Studies*, 2006, 58(4), pp. 523–54.

Murray Matley, I., "Industrialization (1865–1964)," in E. Allworth (ed.), *Central Asia* (Durham, NC: Duke University Press, 1994), p. 337.

Myers, R. and Peattie, M. (eds), *The Japanese Colonial Empire, 1895–1945* (Princeton, NJ: Princeton University Press, 1984).

Naff, T. and Owen, R., *Studies in 18th Century Islamic History* (Carbondale, IL: University of South Illinois Press, 1977.

Nakaya, S., "Aid and transition from a war economy to an oligarchy in post-war Tajikistan," *Central Asian Survey*, September 2009, 28(3), pp. 259–73.

Nasr, V., *Forces of Fortune – The Rise of the New Muslim Middle Class and What it Will Mean for Our World* (New York: Free Press, 2009).

Nazarbayev, N., "To Be or Not to Be," in *Without Right and Left*, trans. P. Garb and C. Carlile (London: Class Publishing, 1992), pp. 136, 150–1.

Nazpary, J., *Post-Soviet Chaos: Violence and Dispossession in Kazakhstan* (London: Pluto Press, 2002).

Nazriev, D. and Sattarov, I., *Respublika Tadzhikistan: istoriia nezavisimosti. God 1991–i (khronika sobitii)* (Republic of Tajikistan: History of Independence. Year 1991 (chronology of events)) (Dushanbe, 2002), p. 17.

Nesiah, V., "Placing international law: white spaces on a map," *Leiden Journal of International Law*, 2003, 16(1), p. 21.

Nissman, D., "Turkmenistan; just like old times," in I. Bremmer and R. Taras (eds), *New States, New Politics: Building the Post-Soviet Nations* (Cambridge: Cambridge University Press, 1997), p. 640.

Niva, S., "Contested sovereignties and postcolonial insecurities in the Middle East," in J. Weldes *et. al.* (eds), *The Culture of Insecurity – States, Communities, and the Production of Danger* (Minneapolis, MN: University of Minnesota Press, 1999), pp. 147–72.

Noble, P., "From Arab system to Middle Eastern system? – regional pressures and constraints," in B. Korany and A. E. H. Dessouki (eds), *The Foreign Policies of Arab States: The Challenge of Globalization* (Cairo: American University Press in Cairo, 2008), pp. 67–167.

Noreng, O., *Crude Power: Politics and the Oil Market* (London: Tauris, 2002).

Northrop, D., "Nationalizing backwardness: gender, empire, and Uzbek identity," in R. G. Suny and T. Martin (eds), *A State of Nations: Empire and Nation-Making in the Age of Lenin and Stalin* (Oxford: Oxford University Press, 2001).

Northrop, D. T., *Veiled Empire: Gender and Power in Stalinist Central Asia* (Ithaca, NY: Cornell University Press, 2004).

Nurmakov, A., "Resources nationalism in Kazakhstan's petroleum sector: curse or blessing?," in I. Overland, H. Kjaernet and A. Kendall-Taylor (eds), *Caspian Energy Politics: Azerbaijan, Kazakhstan and Turkmenistan* (New York: Routledge, 2010).

Odum, J. and Johnson, E., "The state of physical infrastructure in Central Asia: developments in transport, water, energy, and telecommunications," *NBR Analysis*, 2004, 15.5.

Okruhlik, G., "Rentier wealth, unruly law, and the rise of opposition: the political economy of oil states," *Comparative Politics*, April 1999, 31(3), pp. 295–315.

Olcott, M. B., "Soviet Islam and world revolution," *World Politics*, 1982, 34(4), pp. 487–504.

Olcott, M. B., "Central Asia's catapult to independence," *Foreign Affairs*, summer 1992, 71(3), pp. 108–30.

Olcott, M. B., "Kazakhstan: pushing for Eurasia," in I. Bremmer and R. Taras (eds), *New States, New Politics: Building the Post-Soviet Nations* (Cambridge: Cambridge University Press, 1997), pp. 551–3.

Olcott, M. B., *Kazakhstan: Unfulfilled Promises* (Washington, DC: Carnegie Endowment for International Peace, 2002).

Olcott, M. B., *Central Asia's Second Chance* (Washington, DC: Carnegie Endowment for International Peace, 2005).

Olcott, M. B., "Islam in Central Asia in a global context: re-examining past and present," commissioned paper, 2010.

Olimova, S. and Olimov, M., "Obrazovannyi klass Tadzhikistana v peripetiiakh XXv," *Vostok*, 1991, No. 5, p. 97.

Omgba, D. L., "On the duration of political power in Africa: the role of oil rents," *Comparative Political Studies*, March 2009, 42(3), pp. 416–36.

Onley, J., *The Arabian Frontier of the British Raj: Merchants, Rulers and the British in the Nineteenth Century Gulf* (Oxford: Oxford University Press, 2007).

Onuma, Y., "When was the law of international society born? – an inquiry into the history of international law from an intercivilizational perspective," *Journal of the History of International Law*, 2000, 2.

Ormrod, D., *The Rise of Commercial Empires: England and the Netherlands in the Age of Mercantilism, 1650–1770* (Cambridge: Cambridge University Press, 2003).

Orwell, George, *Animal Farm* (London: Secker & Warburg, 1945).

Osborn, E., "'Circle of iron': African colonial employees and the interpretation of colonial rule in French West Africa," *Journal of African History*, 2003, 44(1), pp. 29–50.

Osterhammel, J., *Colonialism: A Theoretical Overview* (Princeton, NJ: Markus Wiener 1997).

Ostrowski, W., *Politics and Oil in Kazakhstan* (London: Routledge, 2010).

Ostrowski, W., "The legacy of the 'coloured revolutions': the case of Kazakhstan," *Journal of Communist Studies and Transition Politics*, June–September 2009, 25(2–3), pp. 347–68.

Owen, R., "Egypt and Europe: from French expedition to British occupation," in R. Owen and R. B. Sutcliffe, *Studies in the Theory of Imperialism* (London: Longman, 1972), pp. 195–209.

Owen, R., *The Middle East in the World Economy 1800–1914* (London: Methuen, 1981).

Owen, R., *State, Power and Politics in the Making of the Modern Middle East* (London: Routledge, 2000 [1992]).

Ozornoy, G., "Some issues of regional inequality in the USSR under Gorbachev," *Regional Studies*, 1991, 25(5), pp. 381–93.

Pahuja, S., "The postcoloniality of international law," *Harvard International Law Journal*, 2005, 46, p. 459.

Pamuk, S., "Commodity production for world–markets and relations of production in Ottoman agriculture, 1840–1913," in H. Islamoglu-Inan (ed.), *The Ottoman Empire and the World Economy* (Cambridge: Cambridge University Press, 1987).

Pappé, I., *A History of Modern Palestine: One Land, Two Peoples* (Cambridge: Cambridge University Press, 2004).

Parrott, B., "Analyzing the transformation of the Soviet Union in comparative perspective," in K. Dawisha and B. Parrott (eds), *The End of Empire? The Transformation of the USSR in Comparative Perspective* (Armonk, NY: Sharpe, 1997), pp. 3–29.

Payne, M., "The forge of the Kazakh proletariat?: the Turksib, nativization, and industrialization during Stalin's first five-year plan," in R. G. Suny and T. Martin (eds), *A State of Nations: Empire and Nation-Making in the Age of Lenin and Stalin* (Oxford: Oxford University Press, 2001), pp. 223–52.

Peck, A. E., *Economic Development in Kazakhstan: The Role of Large Enterprises and Foreign Investment* (London: RoutledgeCurzon, 2004).

Pemberton, J., *Sovereignty: Interpretations* (London: Palgrave Macmillan, 2008).

Perkins, K. J., *A History of Modern Tunisia* (Cambridge: Cambridge University Press, 2004).

Perrault, G., *Notre ami le roi* (Paris: Gallimard, 1990).

Perthes, V., "America's 'Greater Middle East' and Europe: key issues for dialogue," *Middle East Policy*, 2004, 11(3), pp. 85–97.

Peter, F., "Dismemberment of empire and reconstitution of regional space: the emergence of 'national' industries in Damascus between 1918 and 1946," in N. Meouchy (ed.), *British and French Mandates in Comparative Perspectives* (Leiden: Brill, 2004).

Peters, B. G., *Institutional Theory in Political Science* (London: Continuum, 2005).

Pierce, S., "Looking like a state: colonialism and the discourse of corruption in northern Nigeria," *Comparative Studies in Society and History*, 2006, 48(4), pp. 887–914.

Pintak, L., "Border guards of the 'imagined' watan: Arab journalists and the new Arab consciousness," *Middle East Journal*, 2009, 63(2), pp. 191–212.

Pipes, R., *Struve: Liberal on the Right* (Cambridge, MA: Harvard University Press, 1980).

Piro, T., *The Political Economy of Market Reform in Jordan* (Lanham, MD: Rowman & Littlefield, 1998).

Poliakov, S., *Everyday Islam: Religion and Tradition in Rural Central Asia* (Armonk, NY: Sharpe, 1992).

Pomfret, R., "Kazakhstan's economy since independence: does the oil boom offer a second chance for sustainable development?," *Europe–Asia Studies*, 2005, 57(6), pp. 859–976.

Pomfret, R., *The Central Asian Economies since Independence* (Princeton, NJ: Princeton University Press, 2006).

Prochaska, D., *Making Algeria French: Colonialism in Bône 1870–1920* (Cambridge: Cambridge University Press, 1990).

Pulat, A., "Turkestan – on the road to integration," *Tsentral'naia Aziia*, November 1995, No. 1, pp. 11–15.

Qualin, A. J., "Searching for the self at the crossroads of Central Asian, Russian, and Soviet cultures: the question of identity in the works of Timur Pulatov and Chingiz Aitmatov," PhD dissertation, University of Washington, 1996.

Quataert, D., "Ottoman reform and agriculture in Anatolia, 1876–1908," unpublished PhD dissertation, University of California, Los Angeles, 1973.

Quataert, D., "Limited revolution: the impact of the Anatolian railway on Turkish transportation and the provisioning of Istanbul, 1890–1908," *Business History Review*, 1977, 51, pp. 139–60.

Quataert, D., "The age of reforms," in S. Faroqhi, B. McGowan, D. Quataert and S. Pamuk (eds), *An Economic and Social History of the Ottoman Empire, Vol. 2* (Cambridge: Cambridge University Press, 1994).

Raineau, T., "Des tableaux noirs à l'ombre du minbar: la réforme de l'université d'al-Azhar (1895–1913)," *Cahiers de la Méditerranée*, 2007, 75, pp. 90–104.

Rajagopal, B., *International Law from Below: Development, Social Movements and Third World Resistance* (Cambridge: Cambridge University Press, 2003).

Ram, H., "Imagining Eurasia: the poetics and ideology of Olzhas Suleimenov's Az i Ia," *Slavic Review*, 2001, 60, pp. 289–311.

Rasanayagam, J., "I'm not a Wahhabi: state power and Muslim orthodoxy in Uzbekistan," in C. Hann (ed.), *The Postsocialist Religious Question: Faith and Power in Central Asia and East-Central Europe* (Munich: Lit Verlag, 2006), pp. 99–124.

Rashid, A., *Jihad: The Rise of Militant Islam in Central Asia* (New Haven, CT: Yale University Press, 2002).

Ratner, S. R., "Drawing a better line: *uti possidetis* and the borders of new states," (1996) *American Journal of International Law*, 1996, 90, p. 590.

Raun, T., "Estonia: independence redefined," in I. Bremmer and R. Taras (eds), *New States, New Politics: Building the Post-Soviet Nations* (Cambridge: Cambridge University Press, 1997), pp. 412–14.

Ravindranathan, T. R., "The Young Turk revolution – July 1908 to April 1909: its immediate effects," unpublished MA thesis, Simon Fraser University, 1970.

Regional Cooperation for Development of Human Capacity and Human Security in the Region of Central Asia. Country Report on Tajikistan (Dushanbe: Scientific and Research Centre Sharq, 2005).

Reid, D. M., *Whose Pharaohs? Archaeology, Museums, and Egyptian National Identity from Napoleon to World War I* (Berkeley, CA: University of California Press. 2002).

Reilly, J. A., "Damascus merchants and trade in the transition to capitalism," *Canadian Journal of History*, 1992, 27, pp. 1–27.

Review of the Civil Administration of the Occupied Territories of Al'Iraq 1914–1918 (Baghdad: The Government Press, 1918).

Richards, J. P., *The Mughal Empire* (Cambridge: Cambridge University Press, 1993).

Rinnawi, K., *Instant Nationalism – McArabism, al-Jazeera and Transnational Media in the Arab World* (Lanham, MD: University Press of America, 2006).

Ro'i, Y., *Islam in the Soviet Union: From the Second World War to Gorbachev* (New York: Columbia University Press, 2000).

Roberts, R. L., *Litigants and Households: African Disputes and Colonial Courts in the French Soudan, 1895–1912* (Westport, CT: Praeger, 2005).

Robertson, R., "Glocalization: time–space and homogeneity–heterogeneity," in M. Featherstone, S. Lash and R. Robertson (eds), *Global Modernities* (London: Sage, 1995), pp. 25–44.

Robins, P., *A History of Jordan* (Cambridge: Cambridge University Press, 2004).

Robinson, R. and Gallagher, J., with A. Denny, *Africa and the Victorians: The Official Mind of Imperialism* (London: Macmillan, 1961).

Robinson, R., "Non-European foundations of European imperialism," in R. Owen and B. Sutcliffe (eds), *Studies in the Theory of Imperialism* (London: Longman, 1972).

Rodgers, A., "The location dynamics of Soviet industry," *Annals of the Association of American Geographers*, 1974, 64(2), pp. 226–40.

Rogan, E., *Frontiers of the State in the Late Ottoman Empire: Transjordan, 1851–1921* (Cambridge: Cambridge University Press, 1999).

Rogan, E., *The Arabs: A History* (London: Allen Lane, 2009).

Rosen, W., *Justinian's Flea: Plague, Empire and the Birth of Europe* (London: Cape, 2007).

Rosenberg, J., *The Empire of Civil Society: A Critique of the Realist Theory of International Relations* (London: Verso, 1994).

Ross, M., "The political economy of the resource curse," *World Politics*, January 1999, 51, pp. 297–322.

Ross, M., "Does oil hinder democracy?," *World Politics*, April 2001, 53(3), pp. 325–61.

Rotberg, R., "The failure and collapse of nation-states: breakdown, prevention, and repair," in R. Rotberg (ed.), *When States Fail: Causes and Consequences* (Princeton, NJ: Princeton University Press, 2004).

Rouland, M. R., "Music and the making of the Kazak nation, 1920–1936," PhD dissertation, Georgetown University, 2005.

Rowe, W., *China's Last Empire: The Great Qing* (Cambridge, MA: Belknap Press of Harvard University Press, 2009), pp. 11–19.

Roy, O., *The New Central Asia: Geopolitics and the Creation of Nations* (London: Tauris, 2000).

Rubin, B. R. and Snyder, J. (eds), *Post-Soviet Political Order* (London: Routledge, 1998).

Rumer, B. Z., *Soviet Central Asia: "A Tragic Experiment"* (Boston, MA: Unwin Hyman, 1989).

Rumer, E., "The U.S. interests and role in Central Asia after K2," *The Washington Quarterly*, 2006, 29(3), pp. 141–54.

Rywkin, M., *Moscow's Muslim Challenge: Soviet Central Asia* (Armonk, NY: Sharpe, 1990).

Sabola, S., "The creation of Soviet Central Asia: the 1924 national delimitation," *Central Asian Survey*, 1995, 14(2), pp. 225–41.

Said, E. W., *Orientalism* (New York: Vintage Books, 1994).

Salamé, G. (ed.), *Democracy without Democrats?: Renewal of Politics in the Muslim World* (London: Tauris, 1994).

Salamé, G., "The Middle East: elusive security, indefinable region," *Security Dialogue*, 1994, 25(1), pp. 17–35.

Saliba, N. E., "Wilayat Suriyya, 1876–1909," unpublished PhD dissertation, University of Michigan, 1971.

Salibi, K., *The Modern History of Jordan* (London: Tauris, 1998).

Salih, M., "Shortly about our movement," *Tsentral'aia Aziia*, November 1995, No. 1, pp. 16–19.

Salloukh, B., "State strength, permeability, and foreign policy behavior: Jordan in theoretical perspective," *Arab Studies Quarterly*, 1996, 18(2).

Salloukh, B., "Regime autonomy and regional foreign policy choices in the Middle East: a theoretical explanation," in B. Salloukh and R. Brynen (eds), *Persistent Permeability, Regionalism, Localism and Globalization in the Middle East* (Farnham: Ashgate, 2004), pp. 81–104.

Salzman, P. C., "The Middle East's tribal DNA," *Middle East Quarterly*, 2008, 15(1).

Sasse, G., *The Crimea Question: Identity, Transition and Conflict* (Cambridge, MA: Ukrainian Research Institute of Harvard University, 2007).

Sayf, A., "Free trade, competition and industrial decline: the case of Iran in the nineteenth century," *Middle Eastern Studies*, 2004, 40(3), pp. 55–74.

Sayyid, S., *A Fundamental Fear: Eurocentrism and the Emergence of Islamism*, revised edn (London: Zed Books, 2003).

Schad, G. D., "Colonialists, industrialists and politicians: the political economy of industrialization in Syria, 1920–1954," unpublished PhD dissertation, University of Pennsylvania, 2001.

Schatz, E., *Modern Clan Politics. The Power of "Blood" in Kazakhstan and Beyond* (Seattle, WA: University of Washington Press, 2004).

Schilcher, L., "The grain economy of late Ottoman Syria and the issue of large-scale commercialization," in C. Keyder and F. Tabak (eds), *Landholding and Commercial Agriculture in the Middle East* (Albany, NY: SUNY Press, 1991).

Schilcher, L., *Families in Politics: Damascene Factions and Estates of the 18th and 19th Centuries* (Stuttgart: Peter Lang, 1985).

Schlumberger, O., *Debating Arab Authoritarianism* (Stanford, CA: Stanford University Press, 2008).

Schneider, L., "Colonial legacies and postcolonial authoritarianism in Tanzania: connects and disconnects," *African Studies Review*, 2006, 49(1), pp. 93–118.

Schoenberg, P. E., "The evolution of transport in Turkey under Ottoman rule, 1856–1918," *Middle Eastern Studies*, 1977, 13, pp. 359–72.

Schwedler, J., *Faith in Moderation: Islamist Parties in Jordan and Yemen* (Cambridge: Cambridge University Press, 2006).

Seale, P., *Asad: The Struggle for the Middle East* (Berkeley, CA: University of California Press, 1988).

Seale, P., *The Struggle for Syria* (London: RIIA & Oxford University Press, 1965).

Segalla, S. D., *The Moroccan Soul: French Education, Colonial Ethnology, and Muslim Resistance, 1912–1956* (Lincoln, NE: University of Nebraska Press, 2009).

Senn, A., "Lithuania: rights and responsibilities of independence," in I. Bremmer and R. Taras (eds), *New States, New Politics: Building the Post-Soviet Nations* (Cambridge: Cambridge University Press, 1997), pp. 355–6, 359.

Shambayati, H., "The rentier state, interest groups, and the paradox of autonomy: state and business in Turkey and Iran," *Comparative Politics*, April 1994, 26(3), pp. 307–31.

Shaw, M. N., *Title to Territory in Africa: International Legal Issues* (Oxford: Clarendon Press, 1986).

Shaw, M. N., "Peoples, territories and boundaries," *European Journal of International Law*, 1997, 8, p. 478.

Shaw, M. N., "The heritage of states: the principle of *uti possidetis juris* today," *British Yearbook of International Law*, 1997, 67, p. 75.

Shaw, S. J., *The Ottoman Empire in World War I, Vol. 1* (Ankara: Turk Tarih Kurumu, 2006).

Shaxson, N., *Poisoned Wells: The Dirty Politics of African Oil* (London: Palgrave, 2007).

Shields, S. D., "An economic history of nineteenth-century Mosul," unpublished PhD dissertation, University of Chicago, 1986.

Shields, S. D., "Mosul and the free trade treaties: the non–effects of the commercial convention on an inland province," *New Perspectives on Turkey*, 1991, 7, pp. 113–23.

Shields, S. D., "Regional trade and 19th-century Mosul: revising the role of Europe in the Middle East economy," *International Journal of Middle East Studies*, 1991, 23, pp. 19–37.

Shields, S. D., "Take-off into self-sustained peripheralization," *Turkish Studies Association Bulletin*, 1991, 17, pp. 1–23.

Shields, S. D., *Mosul Before Iraq* (Albany, NY: SUNY Press, 2000).

Shyrock, A., "Dynastic modernism and its contradictions: testing the limits of pluralism, tribalism and King Hussein's example in Hashemite Jordan," *Arab Studies Quarterly*, summer 2000, 22(3), pp. 60–1.

Simon, G., *Nationalism and Policy Toward the Nationalities in the Soviet Union*, trans. K. Forster and O. Forster (Boulder, CO: Westview Press, 1991).

Simon, R. S., "The imposition of nationalism on a non-nation state: the case of

Iraq during the interwar period, 1921–1941," in J. Jankowski and I. Gershoni (eds), *Rethinking Nationalism in the Arab Middle East* (New York: Columbia University Press, 1997), ch. 5.

Singel, W., "Cultural sovereignty and transplanted law: tensions in indigenous self-rule," *Kansas Journal of Law & Public Policy*, 2006, 15, pp. 357–68.

Sinnott, P., "Population politics in Kazakhstan," *Journal of International Affairs*, 2003, 56(2), pp. 103–15.

Skocpol, T., "Rentier state and Shiᶜa Islam in the Iranian revolution," *Theory and Society*, May 11, 1982, pp. 293–300.

Skouteris, T., *The Notion of Progress in International Law Discourse* (The Hague: Asser, 2010).

Skovgaard-Petersen, J., *Al-Azhar 1922–2006* (Copenhagen: Carsten Niebuhrs Bibliotek/Vandkunsten, 2007).

Slezkine, Y., "Imperialism as the highest stage of socialism," *The Russian Review*, 2000, 59, pp. 227–34.

Sluglett, P., *Britain in Iraq 1914–1932* (London: Ithaca Press, 1976).

Sluglett, P., "Formal and informal empire in the Middle East," R. W. Winks (ed), *The Oxford History of the British Empire, Vol. V* (Oxford: Oxford University Press, 1999), pp. 416–36.

Sluglett, P., "Aspects of economy and society in the Syrian provinces: Aleppo in transition, 1880–1925, 2 in L. T. Fawaz and C. A. Bayly (eds), *Modernity and Culture* (New York: Columbia University Press, 2002).

Sluglett, P., "Les Mandates/The Mandates: some reflections on the nature of the British Presence in Iraq (1914–1932) and the French presence in Syria (1918–1946)," in N. Meouchy (ed.), *British and French Mandates in Comparative Perspective* (Leiden: Brill, 2004).

Smith, B., "Oil wealth and regime survival in the developing world, 1960–1999," *American Journal of Political Science*, April 2004, 48(2), pp. 232–46.

Smith, G. et al., *Nation-building in the Post-Soviet Borderlands: the Politics of National Identities* (Cambridge: Cambridge University Press, 1998).

Sneider, D., "Change comes slowly to Kirghizia," *Christian Science Monitor*, January 10, 1991, p. 4.

Soane, E. B., *Report on the Sulaimania District of Kurdistan* (Calcutta: Superintendent of Government Printing, 1918).

Soares de Oliveira, R., *Oil and Politics in the Gulf of Guinea* (New York: Columbia University Press, 2007).

Sørensen, G., *Changes in Statehood: The Transformation of International Relations* (Basingstoke: Palgrave, 2001).

Spear, T., "Neo-traditionalism and the limits of invention in British colonial Africa," *Journal of African History*, 2003, 44(1), pp. 3–27.

Spechler, M., *The Political Economy of Reform in Central Asia* (London: Routledge, 2008).

Spechler, D. and Spechler, M., "Uzbekistan among the great powers," *Communist and Post-Communist Studies*, 2009, 42, pp. 353–73.

Spoor, M., "Transition to market economies in former Soviet Central Asia: dependency, cotton and water', *Working Paper Series*, The Hague: International Institute of Social Studies, September 1993, No. 160.

Spruyt, H., *Ending Empire* (Ithaca, NY: Cornell University Press, 2005).

Staples, J., "Soviet uses of corruption purges as a control mechanism," *Past Imperfect*, 1993, 2, pp. 29–48.

Starrett, G., *Putting Islam to Work: Education, Politics, and Religious Transformation in Egypt* (Berkeley, CA: University of California Press, 1998).

Stevens, P., "Oil wars: resource nationalism and the Middle East," in P. Andrews-Speed (ed.), *International Competition for Resources: The Role of Law, the State and of Markets* (Dundee: Dundee University Press, 2008).

Stoler, A. L., "On degrees of imperial sovereignty," *Public Culture*, 2006, 18(1), pp. 125–46.

Stourzh, G., *Von Reich zur Republik. Studien zur Osterreichsbewusstein im 20 Jahrhundert* (Vienna: Editions Atelier, 1990).

Stronski, P., *Tashkent: Forging a Soviet City, 1930–1966* (Pittsburgh, PA: University of Pittsburgh Press, 2010).

Suny, R. G., "The empire strikes out: imperial Russia, 'national' identity, and theories of empire," in R. G. Suny and T. Martin (eds), *A State of Nations: Empire and Nation-Making in the Age of Lenin and Stalin* (Oxford: Oxford University Press, 2001), pp. 23–66.

Suny, R. G., *The Revenge of the Past* (Stanford, CA: Stanford University Press, 1993).

Suny, R., "Ambiguous categories: states, empires, and nations," *Post-Soviet Affairs* (1995), 11(2), pp. 185–96.

Suny, R. G. and Martin, T. (eds), *A State of Nations: Empire and Nation-Making in the Age of Lenin and Stalin* (Oxford: Oxford University Press, 2001).

Tabak, F., "Local merchants in peripheral areas of the empire: the fertile crescent during the long nineteenth century," *Review, a Journal of the Fernand Braudel Center* (1988), 11, pp. 179–214.

Tadjbakhsh, S., "The a-Soviet woman of the Muslim East and nativization in Tajikistan, 1989–1992," PhD dissertation, Columbia University, 1994, p. 159.

Takim, A. and Yilmaz, E., "Economic policy during Ataturk's era in Turkey (1923–1938)," *African Journal of Business Management*, 2010, 4, pp. 549–54.

Telhami, S., "Power, legitimacy and peace-making in Arab coalitions – the new Arabism," in L. Binder (ed.), *Ethnic Conflict and International Politics in the Middle East* (Gainesville, FL: University of Florida Press, 1999), pp. 43–60.

Telhami, S. and Barnett, M., "Ch. 1: introduction: identity and foreign policy in the Middle East," in S. Telhami and M. Barnett (eds), *Identity and Foreign Policy in the Middle East* (Ithaca, NY: Cornell University Press, 2002), pp. 1–25, at p. 9.

"The Events in Kazakhstan – An Eyewitness Report," from the *Arkhiv Samizdata*, AC 5913, April 10, 1987, *Central Asian Survey*, 6(3), pp. 73–5.

Thompson, E., *Colonial Citizens: Republican Rights, Paternal Privilege, and Gender in French Syria and Lebanon* (New York: Columbia University Press, 2000).

Tibi, B., *Arab Nationalism – Between Islam and the Nation-State*, 3rd edn, (London: Macmillan, 1997), pp. 88–90.

Tignor, R., *Modernization and British Colonial Rule in Egypt, 1882–1914* (Princeton, NJ: Princeton University Press, 1966).

Tilly, C., *Coercion, Capital and European States: AD 990–1992* (Cambridge, MA and Oxford: Blackwell, 1994).

Tilly, C., "How empires end," in K. Barkey and M. von Hagen (eds), *After Empire: Multiethnic Societies and Nation Building* (Boulder, CO: Westview Press, 1997), pp. 1–11.

Tomoff, K., "Uzbek music's separate path: interpreting 'anticosmopolitanism' in Stalinist Central Asia 1949–52," *The Russian Review*, 2004, 63, pp. 212–40.

Toprak, Z., "Nationalism and economics in the Young Turk era (1908–1918)," in J. Thobie and S. Kancal (eds), *Industrialisation, Communication et Rapports Sociaux en Turquie et en Mediterranee Orientale* (Paris: L'Harmattan, 1994).

Torrey, G., *Syrian Politics and the Military, 1945–1958* (Columbus, OH: Ohio State University, 1964).

Toyoda, T., "L'aspect univeraliste du droit international européen du 19ème siècle et le statut juridique de la Turquie avant 1856," *Journal of the History of International Law*, 2006, 8, p. 19.

Tripp, C., *Iraq*, 3rd edn (Cambridge: Cambridge University Press, 2007).

Tsygankov, A. P., "Defining state interests after empire: national identity, domestic structure and foreign trade policies of Latvia and Belarius," *Review of International Political Economy*, 2000, 7(1), pp. 100–37.

Tumarkin, N., *The Living and the Dead: the Rise and Fall of the Cult of World War II in Russia* (New York: Basic Books, 1995).

Tuminez, A. S., "Nationalism, ethnic pressures, and the breakup of the Soviet Union," *Journal of Cold War Studies*, 2003, 5(4), pp. 128–30.

Tuncer-Kilavuz, I., "Political and social networks in Tajikistan and Uzbekistan: 'clan', region and beyond," *Central Asian Survey*, 2009, 28(3), pp. 323–34.

Umarov, Kh. and Matqulov, N., "Protsesshoi kūchidani aholī," *Darsi kheshtanshinosī, Vol. 2* (Dushanbe: Irfon, 1991), pp. 147, 148.

Vaksberg, A., *The Soviet Mafia* (New York: St. Martin's Press, 1991).

Valbjørn, M., "Culture blind and culture blinded: images of Middle Eastern conflicts in international relations," in D. Jung (ed.), *The Middle East and Palestine: Global Politics and Regional Conflicts* (New York: Palgrave, 2004), pp. 39–78.

Valbjørn, M., "Toward a 'Mesopotamian turn': disciplinarity and the study of the international relations of the Middle East," *Journal of Mediterranean Studies*, 2004, 14(1–2), pp. 47–75.

Valbjørn, M., *A "Baedeker" to IR's Cultural Journey Before, During and After the Cultural Turn – Explorations into the (Ir)Relevance of Cultural Diversity, the IR/Area Studies Nexus and Politics in an (Un)Exceptional Middle East* (Aarhus: Politica, 2008).

Valbjørn, M., "There are clearly cultural issues at play: a note on grasping conceptual slipperiness: the idea(s) of culture and its turn(s)," Working Paper, Department of Political Science, University of Aarhus, 2008.

Valbjørn, M., "Arab nationalism(s) in transformation – from Arab interstate societies to an Arab-Islamic world society," in B. Buzan and A. Gonzalez-Pelaez (eds), *International Society and the Middle East – English School Theory at the Regional Level* (New York: Palgrave, 2009), pp. 140–69.

Valbjørn, M. and Bank, A., "Disentangling the new Arab cold war: the past as future regional order – lessons from the Summer War 2006 and the Gaza War 2008/09 on a(other) 'new Middle East,' " paper presented at the annual meeting of the International Studies Association, February 15–18, 2009, New York City.

Vandewalle, D., *A History of Modern Libya* (Cambridge: Cambridge University Press, 2006).

Vatikiotis, P. J., *Islam and the State* (London: Routledge, 1987).

Vatikiotis, P. J., *The History of Modern Egypt: from Muhammad Ali to Mubarak*, 4th edn (London: Weidenfeld & Nicolson, 1991).

Vermeren, P., "Une si difficile réforme: la réforme de l'université Qarawiyyin de Fès sous le Protectorat français au Maroc, 1912–1956," *Cahiers de la Méditerranée*, 2007, 75, pp. 119–32.

Viorst, M., *Storm over the East – The Struggle between the Arab World and the Christian West* (New York: Random House Modern Library, 2006).

Visser, R. and Stansfield, G. R. V., *An Iraq of its Regions: Cornerstones of a Federal Democracy* (New York: Columbia University Press, 2008).

Visser, R., Basra, *The Failed Gulf State* (Munster: LIT Verlag, 2005).

Vitalis, R., *America's Kingdom: Mythmaking on the Saudi Frontier* (Stanford, CA: Stanford University Press, 2007).

Volpi, F., *Political Islam Observed: Disciplinary Perspectives* (New York: Columbia University Press, 2010).

von Sivers, P., "Insurrection and accommodation: indigenous leadership in eastern Algeria, 1840–1900," *International Journal of Middle East Studies*, 1975, 6, pp. 259–75.

von Sivers, P., "Algerian landownership and rural leadership, 1860–1940: a quantitative approach," *The Maghreb Review*, 1979, 4(2), pp. 58–62.

von Sivers, P., "Les Plaisirs du collectionneur: capitalisme fiscal et chefs indigènes en Algérie (1840–1860)," *Annales: Economies, Sociétés, Civilisations*, 1980, 35(3–4), pp. 679–99.

von Sivers, P., "Indigenous administrators in Algeria, 1846–1914: manipulation and manipulators," *The Maghreb Review*, 1982, 7(5–6), pp. 116–21.

Walker, E. W., *Dissolution: Sovereignty and the Breakup of the Soviet Union* (Lanham, MD: Rowman & Littlefield, 2003).

Wallerstein, I., *The Capitalist World Economy* (Cambridge: Cambridge University Press, 1979).

Walzer, M., *On Toleration* (New Haven, CT: Yale University Press, 1997).

Walzer, M., *Just and Unjust Wars: A Moral Argument with Historical Illustrations* (New York: Basic Books, 1977), pp. 87–90, as cited in Pemberton, J., *Sovereignty: Interpretations* (Basingstoke: Palgrave Macmillan, 2009), p. 9.

Watenpaugh, K. D., *Being Modern in the Middle East* (Princeton, NJ: Princeton University Press, 2006).

Weber, M., *The Theory of Social and Economic Organization* (New York: Oxford University Press, 1947).

White, B. T., "The Kurds of Damascus in the 1930s: development of a politics of ethnicity," *Middle Eastern Studies*, 2010, 46(6), pp. 901–17.

White, B. T., "The nation-state form and the emergence of 'minorities' in French mandate Syria, 1919–1939," PhD dissertation, Oxford University, 2009.

Wien, P., Bashkin, W. and McDougall, J., "Relocating Arab nationalism," *International Journal of Middle East Studies*, 2011, 42(3), forthcoming.

Wiktorowicz, Q., "Anatomy of the Salafi movement," *Studies in Conflict & Terrorism*, 2006, 29(3), pp. 207–39.

Wills, J. E., "Maritime Asia, 1500–1800: the interactive emergence of European domination," *American Historical Review*, 1993, 98(1), pp. 83–105.

Wilson, J. E., *The Domination of Strangers, Modern Governance in Eastern India, 1780–1835* (Basingstoke: Palgrave Macmillan, 2008).

Winegar, J., "Cultural sovereignty in a global art economy: Egyptian cultural policy and the new Western interest in art from the Middle East," *Cultural Anthropology*, 2006, 21, pp. 173–204.

Wolfe, P., "History and imperialism: a century of theory, from Marx to postcolonialism," *American Historical Review*, 1997, 102(2), pp. 388–420.

Wood, T., "Contours of the Putin era," *New Left Review*, March–April 2007, 44, pp. 53–71.

Wortman, R., *Scenarios of Power, Myth and Ceremony in Russian Monarchy from Peter the Great to the Abdication of Nicholas II, Vol. 1* (Princeton, NJ: Princeton University Press, 1995).

Yaniv, A., "Syria and Israel: the politics of escalation," in M. Ma'oz and A. Yaniv (eds), *Syria under Assad: Domestic Constraints and Regional Risks* (London: Croom Helm, 1986), pp. 157–78.

Yapp, M. E., *The Making of the Modern Near East 1792–1923* (London: Longman, 1987), pp. 301–51.

Yapp, M., *The Near East Since the First World War* (London, Longman: 1991).

Yates, D., *The Rentier State in Africa: Oil Rent Dependency and Neocolonialism in the Republic of Gabon* (Trenton: Africa World Press, 1996).

Yessenova, S., "Tengiz crude: a view from below," in B. Najman, R. Pomfret and G. Raballand (eds), *The Economics and Politics of Oil in the Caspian Basin: The Redistribution of Oil Revenues in Azerbaijan and Central Asia* (London: Routledge, 2007).

Young, C., *The African Colonial State in Comparative Perspective* (New Haven, CT: Yale University Press, 1994).

Young, C. and Turner, T., *The Rise and Decline of the Zairian State* (Madison, WI: University of Wisconsin Press, 1985).

Yurdusev, A. N., "From the Eastern Question to the Western Question: rethinking the contribution of Toynbee," *Critique: Critical Middle Eastern Studies*, 2005, 14(3), pp. 323–32.

Zaslavsky, V., "The Soviet Union," in K. Barkey and M. von Hagen (eds), *After Empire: Multiethnic Societies and Nation-building* (Boulder, CO: Westview Press, 1997).

Zeghal, M., *Islamism in Morocco: The Challenge to Monarchy*, trans. G. A. Holoch (Princeton, NJ: Markus Wiener, 2008).

Zubaida, S., "The nation state in the Middle East," in S. Zubaida (ed.), *Islam, the People and the State – Political Ideas and Movements in the Middle East* (London: Tauris, 1993), pp. 121–82.

Zubaida, S., "Contested nations: Iraq and the Assyrians," *Nations and Nationalism*, 2000, 6(3), pp. 363–82.

Zubaida, S., "The fragments imagine the nation: the case of Iraq," *International Journal of Middle East Studies*, 2002, 34(2), pp. 205–15.

Zubaida, S., *Law and Power in the Islamic World* (London: Tauris, 2005).

Zubok, V., *A Failed Empire: the Soviet Union in the Cold War from Stalin to Gorbachev* (Chapel Hill, NC: University of North Carolina Press, 2007).

Zürcher, E. J., *Turkey: A Modern History* (London: Tauris, 2004 [1997]).

Zürcher, E. J., *The Young Turk Legacy* (London: Tauris, 2010).

Zviagelskaya, I., "The Tajik conflict: problems of regulation," in M. R. Djalili, F. Grare and S. Akiner (eds), *Tajikistan: The Trials of Independence* (New York: St. Martin's Press, 1997), pp. 163–4.

Index

Abdullah of Jordan, 265, 267, 268, 270, 273, 274, 275–6, 279
Abdullah II of Jordan, 277
affirmative action empire, 130, 142, 202
al-Afghani, Jamal al-din, 229–30, 232
Agzybirlik movement, 134
Akayev, Askar, 133, 136, 144, 146
Alawi in Syria, 52, 58, 266, 272, 274
Algeria, 14, 18, 27, 35, 116, 244, 250, 327, 329
  and the colonial experience, 44, 47, 51, 53, 54–6, 57, 58, 59, 60, 61, 246
  and Islam, 249
all-Union referendum on preservation of the USSR, 129, 131, 141, 143
Anatolia, 27, 68, 82–3, 96, 97, 98, 99, 102, 332
  Committee of Union and Progress (CUP), 77, 78, 83, 94, 95, 99
  economic legacy of Ottoman Empire, 68–71, 72, 73, 74
  impact of the mandate era, 76–9
  Young Turk revolution, 94, 95, 99, 230, 232, 332
Andropov, Yuri, 132, 188, 190
Anghie, Antony 108, 111, 112, 114
Arab nationalism *see* Arabism
Arab-Islamic resistance (*muqawama*), 237
Arab–Israeli War of 1948, 5, 171, 269, 271
Arab–Israeli War of 1967, 250, 271, 272
Arabism, 5, 15, 48, 59, 114, 115, 165, 168, 223, 230, 231, 232, 234, 235, 236, 264, 265, 268, 269, 270–2, 274–5, 276, 278, 279, 292, 336, 343
al-Asad, Hafiz, 272, 274, 275–6
al-Asad, Bashar, 277
Atatürk, Mustafa Kemal 36, 102, 168, 227, 233, 332, 334
Austria, 36–8
  Habsburg Empire, 34, 36

Austria-Hungary, 79, 95
al-Azhar theological center, 246, 249

Baghdad Pact, 170, 270, 271, 341
bangwagoning, 144, 146, 269, 271, 276, 278, 279
Bashmachi revolt, 251
Birlik movement, 134, 135, 147
Bolsheviks, Bolshevism, 16, 129, 130, 202, 207, 217
borders *see* boundaries
boundaries, boundary disputes 4, 5, 7, 9–10, 66, 104, 106, 115, 161, 331, 343
  Bahrain and Qatar (Hawar Islands), 115–17, 118
  Central Asia, 28, 128, 130, 140, 146, 148, 180, 181, 182–3, 187, 191, 211, 293, 333, 336, 337, 342, 343
  Libya and Chad, 118
  Middle East and North Africa, 9, 15, 46, 47, 57, 61, 71, 82, 92, 109, 114, 119, 159, 162, 166, 173, 222, 224, 233, 234–5, 270, 279, 292, 328, 332, 334, 336, 338, 341, 343
  Treaty of Lausanne, 95, 98
  Versailles treaty *see* Versailles treaty
Brezhnev, Leonid, 17, 130, 188, 246
British Empire, British administration, British military in Middle East and North Africa, 13, 17, 28, 29, 30, 34, 35, 38, 44, 45, 50, 51, 55, 56, 57, 77, 79, 81–3, 94, 96, 97, 98–9, 108, 109, 111, 114, 116–18, 160, 166, 167, 175, 180, 226, 244, 245, 246, 248, 252, 264, 265–70, 279, 330, 332, 333
Brownlie, Ian, 116
Bush, George W., 277
Buzan, Barry, 224, 231, 341

391